Emerging Trends in Sustainable Supply Chain Management and Green Logistics

Muhammad Waqas
Ghazi University, Dera Ghazi Khan, Pakistan

Syed Abdul Rehman Khan
Xuzhou University of Technology, China

Abul Quasem Al-Amin
University of Waterloo, Canada

A volume in the Advances in Industrial Ecology (AIE) Book Series

IGI Global
PUBLISHER of TIMELY KNOWLEDGE

Published in the United States of America by
IGI Global
Business Science Reference (an imprint of IGI Global)
701 E. Chocolate Avenue
Hershey PA, USA 17033
Tel: 717-533-8845
Fax: 717-533-8661
E-mail: cust@igi-global.com
Web site: http://www.igi-global.com

Library of Congress Cataloging-in-Publication Data

Names: Khan, Syed Abdul Rehman, 1987- editor. | Al-Amin, Abul Quasem, 1981- editor.
Title: Emerging trends in sustainable supply chain management and green logistics / edited by Syed Abdul Rehman Khan, Abul Quasem Al-Amin.
Description: Hershey, PA : Business Science Reference, [2023] | Includes bibliographical references and index. | Summary: "The prime objective of this book is to provide relevant practical and theoretical frameworks and the latest empirical research results in sustainable supply chain management. It will be written for professionals and students of logistics and supply chain management who want to upgrade their knowledge related to the strategic role of green logistics and supply chain management, proper treatment of end-of-life products recycling, emerging trends, and improvement in supply chain management and logistics operations Post COVID-19, the importance of digital supply chain management during a pandemic outbreak. Finally, sustainable production and consumption of individuals as actors in sustainable environments"-- Provided by publisher.
Identifiers: LCCN 2022041660 (print) | LCCN 2022041661 (ebook) | ISBN 9781668466636 (hardcover) | ISBN 9781668466643 (paperback) | ISBN 9781668466650 (ebook)
Subjects: LCSH: Business logistics--Environmental aspects. | Industrial management--Environmental aspects.
Classification: LCC HD38.5 .E4744 2023 (print) | LCC HD38.5 (ebook) | DDC 658.8--dc23/eng/20221003
LC record available at https://lccn.loc.gov/2022041660
LC ebook record available at https://lccn.loc.gov/2022041661

This book is published in the IGI Global book series Advances in Industrial Ecology (AIE) (ISSN: pending; eISSN: pending)

British Cataloguing in Publication Data
A Cataloguing in Publication record for this book is available from the British Library.

For electronic access to this publication, please contact: eresources@igi-global.com.

Advances in Industrial Ecology (AIE) Book Series

ISSN:pending
EISSN:pending

Editor-in-Chief: Syed Abdul Rehman Khan, Xuzhou University of Technology, China

MISSION

The **Advances in Industrial Ecology (AIE) Book Series** encompasses empirical, analytical, theoretical, reviews, communications, and conceptual research, and comprehensive reviews of relevant research case studies of effective applications in the areas of Industrial ecology and circular economy. It provides a practical and comprehensive forum for exchanging scientific knowledge and ideas which bridge the technological advancement and sustainable practices with industrial ecological management. The goal of this series is to bring together the expertise of professionals who are working in the field of industrial ecology and sustainability across the globe.

COVERAGE

- Reverse Supply Chain
- Pollution
- Recycling
- Material Efficiency
- Material Flow Analysis (MFA)
- Logistics Engineering and Green Practices
- Sustainability
- Resource Management
- Environmental Science
- Energy

IGI Global is currently accepting manuscripts for publication within this series. To submit a proposal for a volume in this series, please contact our Acquisition Editors at Acquisitions@igi-global.com or visit: http://www.igi-global.com/publish/.

The Advances in Industrial Ecology (AIE) Book Series (ISSN pending) is published by IGI Global, 701 E. Chocolate Avenue, Hershey, PA 17033-1240, USA, www.igi-global.com. This series is composed of titles available for purchase individually; each title is edited to be contextually exclusive from any other title within the series. For pricing and ordering information please visit http://www.igi-global.com/book-series/advances-industrial-ecology/270446. Postmaster: Send all address changes to above address.

Titles in this Series

For a list of additional titles in this series, please visit:
http://www.igi-global.com/book-series/advances-industrial-ecology/270446

Cases on Circular Economy in Practice
Pietro De Giovanni (Luiss University, Italy)
Business Science Reference • © 2022 • 297pp • H/C (ISBN: 9781668450017) • US $215.00

Green Chemistry for the Development of Eco-Friendly Products
Kavita Shakya Chahal (Government College, Bichhua, India) and Twinkle Solanki (Government College, Bichhua, India)
Engineering Science Reference • © 2022 • 276pp • H/C (ISBN: 9781799898511) • US $250.00

Innovative Nanocomposites for the Remediation and Decontamination of Wastewater
Azad Kumar (M.L.K. P.G. College, India)
Engineering Science Reference • © 2022 • 377pp • H/C (ISBN: 9781668445532) • US $240.00

Handbook of Research on SDGs for Economic Development, Social Development, and Environmental Protection
Cristina Raluca Gh. Popescu (University of Bucharest, Romania & The Bucharest University of Economic Studies, Romania)
Engineering Science Reference • © 2022 • 531pp • H/C (ISBN: 9781668451137) • US $325.00

Integrating Blockchain Technology Into the Circular Economy
Syed Abdul Rehman Khan (Xuzhou University of Technology, China)
Business Science Reference • © 2022 • 307pp • H/C (ISBN: 9781799876427) • US $250.00

For an entire list of titles in this series, please visit:
http://www.igi-global.com/book-series/advances-industrial-ecology/270446

IGI Global
PUBLISHER of TIMELY KNOWLEDGE

701 East Chocolate Avenue, Hershey, PA 17033, USA
Tel: 717-533-8845 x100 • Fax: 717-533-8661
E-Mail: cust@igi-global.com • www.igi-global.com

Table of Contents

Detailed Table of Contents

In the current digital era, digital transformations take place within every industry, and they have great impact on the management of the supply chains. Sustainability drives today's digital transformation, and the digital transformation of supply chains is essential for the sustainable viability of firms in the era of Industry 4.0. Many studies have focused on technology for big data analysis and the IoT as technologies to fulfill digital supply chains. Technological innovation is essential to achieve competitive advantages in the digital supply chain. In this rapidly developing digital era, digital transformations take place within every industry, and they have effects on the management of the supply chains.

This study unwraps the detailed literature review and highlights the development in growing research on behalf of the supply chain in the era of COVID-19. Earlier research on different disasters shows that there is a lack of research on pandemics. Therefore, the present study signifies the multi-perspective literature review on behalf of the supply chain associated with COVID-19. Further, to analyze the literature of this study from a broad perspective, the science mapping approach and the quantitative analysis were conducted on the basis of bibliometric references that were extracted from the web of science.

Digital transformation has been called the most important strategic issue for businesses around the world. The recent innovation boom brings together technologies that open up new possibilities for imagining and recreating supply flows. This chapter provides a comprehensive overview of digital transformation, enabling technologies, and the impact on traditional supply chain management (SCM) processes. It starts with the introduction of the SCM, followed by the digital shift and its consequences for organizations. It continues with a more in-depth analysis of digitalization and describes the major waves of technological development and industrial and economic leaps, and relates the most recent changes in the supply chain to these waves. Further, it provides examples and use cases to motivate, excite, and emphasize progress. It describes the difficulties in defining the concept, characteristics, and challenges of current digital supply chain (DSC) management.

Environmental concerns and sustainability issues have attracted many practitioners and researchers. Still, numerous small- and medium-sized enterprises (SMEs) in emerging economies are reluctant to invest in environmentally friendly practices with a doubt that investment in such practices might lead to negative production performance outcomes. To settle this tension, this study examines the effect of green production practices on production performance and the intervening effect of lean practices between green production practices and production performance. The study employs a quantitative research method where survey-based data were collected from 227 SMEs in an emerging economy: Pakistan. Results unveil that green production practices have a significant positive impact on production performance. The interactive effect indicates a sharp rise in production performance when a firm implements lean practices in the production process. The study helps settle the current confusion among firm managers related to the investment in green and lean practices in the production system.

Over the last few years, with the rise of natural/man-made disasters, the importance of the humanitarian supply chain has also received a significant value. Humanitarian supply chain performs under special circumstances compared to commercial supply chain such as lack of communication system, electricity, and destabilized transport infrastructure after a disaster. However, disasters are unpredictable; therefore, the demand for supplies (relief items), casualties, and required transportation modes to access the affected area are also unpredictable. Thus, the integration of different modes of transportation is essential to encounter any disaster situation promptly, such as disasters in South Asia in 2001, which caused the death of thousands due to lack of transport infrastructure, inadequate disaster relief planning, and lack of transport integration.

In response to increased competition in recent years, businesses have been pushed to adopt new procedures, such as establishing updated information and communication systems and creating more streamlined production processes. The potential for supply chains to facilitate the introduction of innovative management practices is seen as crucial to the sector's future success. Three ideas, "lean," "green," and "agile," deserve serious consideration because of their potential to significantly improve supply chain efficiency. However, combining agile and lean principles to lessen environmental consequences is a relatively new issue that is not well-defined in terms of structure. Through a comprehensive analysis of the literature on lean, green, and agile paradigms, this chapter hopes to identify potential future lines of inquiry and identify knowledge gaps. This chapter is an effort to synthesize recent findings on the interconnectedness of lean, green, and agile practices in supply chain management.

The main aim of this chapter is to explore the carbon neutrality supply chain through pooling logistics strategies. Pooling logistics is one innovative supply chain management solution to improve its sustainability. The authors carried out a comparison-based simulation study of multi-pick, multi-drop, with hub and hybridization of hub and multi-drop pooling strategies effects on CO2 emissions of supply chains. Hence, the authors developed simulation models for all these strategies with ARENA software and used them in a case study. The main result is that all the pooling strategies outperform the non-pooled supply chains. Indeed, the four pooling scenarios showed much lower CO2 emissions than the non-pooled chain. In addition, the pooling hub with a multi-drop delivery strategy gives the best results.

This chapter aims to discuss the relationship between sustainable blockchain technology and circular economy. Blockchain and circular economy have brought a revolutionary change in the global economy by making the data transparent and decentralized. The circular economy focuses on recycling, including re-manufacturing, restoration, reprocessing, and reclamation. Blockchain technology plays a potential role in sharing information to overcome fraud by providing quick, fast, timely, and accurate data. Blockchain technology is used in the banking sector, but there is a need to improve it in the banking field. Moreover, it has overcome the food shortage and supply chain issues by tackling the lack of information. Sustainable blockchain technology has brought marvelous and revolutionary changes in the health sector. It has reduced the irregularities, lack of information, costs, and issues in the records of patients. Furthermore, the obstacles in finding the data regarding the land have also been addressed by blockchain technology.

Over the last several decades, as businesses have expanded globally in search of higher profits, value chains have become longer and more intricate. Indicators like inventory levels, on-time-in-full deliveries, and shorter lead times all improved for companies that effectively embraced a lean, global style of manufacturing. Complex production networks were created with the goals of efficiency, closeness to markets, and output, but not always with openness or resilience in mind. This chapter examines how businesses in the value chains of manufactured products must rebalance their operations to better manage the inherent risk in their operations. Indicators of the risk in any given industry's value chain include the industry's susceptibility to various shocks and the inherent weaknesses of companies and the overall chain. Therefore, the authors look at the characteristics in supply chains and operations that might amplify disruption and losses as well as the management of variety of shocks.

China is the world's second-largest economy after the United States with more than 60% of the value of its trade being transported by sea. Therefore, China looks for short, safe, and inexpensive trade routes (both land and maritime) to reach Europe, Africa, and the Middle East countries. In doing so, China has taken the One Belt-One-Road (OBOR) initiative intending to develop a cost-effective transportation network ensuring timely and secure delivery. The objective of the OBOR strategy is to enhance Pakistan's infrastructure through the construction of the China-Pakistan Economic Corridor (CPEC). Therefore, this chapter aims to examine the implications of CPEC trade routes in terms of cost and delivery between China and other regions (i.e., Saudi Arabia, Iraq, Angola, Oman, Kuwait, and the United Arab Emirates) via Gwadar Port, Pakistan. The results demonstrate a significant reduction in cost and delivery time via the CPEC route in comparison with traditional trade routes.

Preface

Since the environment has started paying back what humanity has done with the environment. People from all segments of life realized that living unsustainability is not an option for the human race. According to the Anthropocene theory, the concept that the Earth has moved into a novel geological epoch characterized by human domination of the planetary system. Where the actions of humans can cause irreparable changes to the environment. We, being a manufacturer demolish mountains and dig the land to extract resources from the earth. Furthermore, technological advancement has enabled us to alter the shape and climate of the entire world.

Social and economic behaviors are the main cause of anthropocentric effects. We are producing and consuming plenty of products and services that are leaving a hazardous impact on the environment. Thus, considering the environmental conditions can handle our production and consumption pattern way under the sustainable development goals (SDG 2030). In fact, if we fail to replace our consumption with sustainable consumption will require more depletions of resources. This book provides up-to-date text and sustainable supply chain management trends at a reasonable price. Continuously the scope of a sustainable supply chain is growing speedily, which is reflected in the content of this book. This book combines different aspects and trends that emerge in supply chain operations during the COVID-19 Pandemic.

ORGANIZATION OF THE BOOK

There are 10 chapters in the book. A brief description of each of the chapters follows:

Chapter 1 aims to explain the phenomenon of fast developing digital era, digital transformations take place within every industry, and they have a great impact on the management of supply chains. Sustainability drives today's digital transformation, and the digital transformation of supply chains is essential for the sustainable viability of firms in the era of Industry 4.0.

Chapter 2 discusses and unwraps the detailed literature review and highlights the development of growing research on behalf of the supply chain in the era of

COVID-19. Earlier research on different disasters shows that there is a lack of research on pandemics. Therefore, the present study signifies the multi-perspective literature review on behalf of the supply chain associated with COVID-19.

Chapter 3 discusses and explores the basics of Digital Technologies and Supply Chain Management; from Historic, Current, and Future Perspectives. This chapter provides a comprehensive overview of digital transformation, enabling technologies, and the impact on traditional Supply Chain Management (SCM) processes. It starts with the introduction of the SCM, followed by the digital shift and its consequences for organizations.

Environmental concerns and sustainability issues attracted many practitioners' and researchers' attention still numerous small- and medium-sized enterprises (SMEs) in emerging economies are reluctant to invest in environment-friendly practices with a doubt that investment in such practices might lead to negative production performance outcomes. To settle down this tension, our study examines the effect of green production practices on production performance and the intervening effect of lean practices between green production practices and production performance.

Chapter 4 describes the nexus between environmental concerns and sustainability issues and attracted many practitioners' and researchers' attention still numerous small- and medium-sized enterprises (SMEs) in emerging economies are reluctant to invest in environment-friendly practices with a doubt that investment in such practices might lead to negative production performance outcomes. To settle down this tension, our study examines the effect of green production practices on production performance and the intervening effect of lean practices between green production practices and production performance.

Chapter 5 explores how the humanitarian supply chain has received significant value from scholars and contributed to society during the crisis. A humanitarian supply chain performs under special circumstances compared to a commercial supply chain such as a lack of communication system, electricity, and destabilized transport infrastructure after a disaster. However, disasters are unpredictable; therefore, the demand for supplies (relief items), casualties, and required transportation modes to access the affected area are also unpredictable.

Chapter 6 signifies the importance of Lean, Green, and Agile Supply Chain Practices. The chapter discusses how the potential for supply chains to facilitate the introduction of innovative management practices is seen as crucial to the sector's future success. Three ideas "lean," "green," and "agile" deserve serious consideration because of their potential to significantly improve supply chain efficiency. However, combining agile and lean principles to lessen environmental consequences is a relatively new issue that is not well-defined in terms of structure.

Chapter 7 reflects the development of simulation models to explore their effects on CO2 emissions. The main aim of this chapter is to explore the carbon neutrality supply chain through pooling logistics strategies. Pooling logistics is one innovative supply chain management solution to improve its sustainability. We carried out a comparison-based simulation study of multi-pick, multi-drop, with hub and hybridization of hub and multi-drop pooling strategies effects on CO2 emissions of supply chains.

Chapter 8 discusses the involvement Banking Sector, Sustainable Blockchain Technology, Circular Economy, Food, and Health Sector. This chapter aims to discuss the relationship between sustainable blockchain technology and circular economy. Blockchain and circular economy have brought a revolutionary change in the global economy by making data transparent and decentralized. The circular economy focuses on recycling, including re-manufacturing, restoration, reprocessing, and reclamation. Blockchain technology plays a potential role in sharing information to overcome fraud by providing quick, fast, timely, and accurate data. Blockchain technology is used in the banking sector, but there is a need of the hour to improve it in the banking field.

Chapter 9 examines how businesses in the value chains of manufactured products must rebalance their operations to better manage the inherent risk in their operations. Indicators of the risk in any given industry's value chain include the industry's susceptibility to various shocks and the inherent weaknesses of companies and the overall chain.

Chapter 10 highlights the importance of sustainable Belt and Road (OBOR) Development - A Case of the China-Pakistan Economic Corridor. This book chapter aims to examine the implications of CPEC trade routes in terms of cost and delivery between China and other regions i.e., Saudi Arabia, Iraq, Angola, Oman, Kuwait, and the United Arab Emirates via Gwadar Port, Pakistan. The results demonstrate a significant reduction in cost and delivery time via the CPEC route in comparison with traditional trade routes.

Muhammad Waqas
Ghazi University, Dera Ghazi Khan, Pakistan

Syed Abdul Rehman Khan
Xuzhou University of Technology, China

Abul Quasem Al-Amin
University of Waterloo, Canada

Acknowledgment

This book is partially supported by the Guangdong Provincial Key Laboratory of Public Finance and Taxation with Big Data Application (KF202207).

Chapter 1
Digital Supply Chain Management

Nikita Shaikh
Amity University, Raipur, India

ABSTRACT

In the current digital era, digital transformations take place within every industry, and they have great impact on the management of the supply chains. Sustainability drives today's digital transformation, and the digital transformation of supply chains is essential for the sustainable viability of firms in the era of Industry 4.0. Many studies have focused on technology for big data analysis and the IoT as technologies to fulfill digital supply chains. Technological innovation is essential to achieve competitive advantages in the digital supply chain. In this rapidly developing digital era, digital transformations take place within every industry, and they have effects on the management of the supply chains.

INTRODUCTION

The definitions and concepts pertaining to a digital supply chain explained in various studies share the common factor that it is an "advancement in supply chain operations using advanced digital technology" (Pyun & Rha, 2021). Supply chains (SCs) and production logistics processes are an important part of the daily enterprises of many professional and personal activities in modern life, and they are highly significant for global development (Min et al., 2019). In the present business set up and digital world, the supply chains are constantly evolving. Technologies and the Internet of Things (IoT)-based cyber-physical system (CPS) architecture for production logistics and SC applications have led to the implementation and acceleration of

DOI: 10.4018/978-1-6684-6663-6.ch001

innovations that are required for the digitization of the industry (Tu et al., 2018a). It is obvious that the fast-developing digital economy will fundamentally affect supply chain design and processes. Ultimately, new approaches of SCM adapted to digitalization will continue to play a central role as enabler for the new business opportunities (Farahani, 2015).

The multinational firm PricewaterhouseCoopers (PwC) defines a digital supply chain as a system that focuses on the digital connection of all physical assets beyond the automation of each machine and process, as well as integration into digital ecosystems with value chain partners.

Several emerging, technological innovations have been chosen and are defined below.

Big Data is considered as high-volume, high-velocity, and high-variety information assets that demand cost-effective, innovative forms of information processing for enhanced insight and decision making (Gartner IT Glossary, 2014d).

Smart Data, in return, is data from which signals and patterns have been extracted by intelligent algorithms, as collecting large amounts of statistics and numbers brings little benefit if there is no layer of added intelligence (Lorentz, 2013).

Cloud computing is defined as a style of computing in which scalable and elastic IT-enabled capabilities are delivered as a service using Internet technologies (Gartner IT Glossary, 2014a). Social media is an online environment in which content is created, consumed, promoted, distributed, discovered or shared for purposes that are primarily related to communities and social activities, rather than functional or task-oriented objectives. "Media" in this context is an environment characterized by storage and transmission, while "social" describes the distinct way that these messages propagate in a one-to-many or many-to-many fashion (Gartner IT Glossary, 2014b).

Predictive analytics provides organizations with actionable insights based on data. It provides an estimation regarding the likelihood of a future outcome. In order to do this, a variety of techniques are used, such as machine learning, data mining, modelling, and game theory. Predictive analytics can, for example, help to identify any risks or opportunities in the future, and with prescriptive analytics not only calculating outcomes but also proposing a "best" alternative as decision support (human) or decision automation becomes reality. (van Rijmenam, 2014).

The Internet of Things (IoT) is the network of physical objects that contain embedded technology to communicate and sense or interact with their internal states or the external environment (Gartner IT Glossary, 2014c).

Robotics is the science of making and using robots. A robot is a mechanical device that sometimes resembles a human and is capable of performing a variety of often complex human tasks on command or by being programmed in advance. (TheFreeDictionary.com, 2015; Dictionary. cambridge.org, 2015).

3D printing or additive manufacturing is a process of making three dimensional solid objects from a digital file. The creation of a 3D printed object is achieved using additive processes by laying down successive layers of material until the entire object is created. Each of these layers can be seen as a thinly sliced horizontal cross-section of the eventual object (3D Printing, 2015). Mobility enables consumers and the workforce to interact with, and contribute to sources of information, knowledge, content creation, and entertainment - anywhere and anytime (Jacobson, 2011).

As opposed to the earlier method of producing goods based on production plans that depended on market demands, these efforts are made with the digitalization of processes through the sharing of real-time information based on digital connectivity, which we know as well as the concept of digital transformation (Pyun & Rha, 2021).

The application of data analytics methods are new in the field and allow, e.g. the geospatial spread of diseases to be predicted, emerging trends in consumer behaviour during natural disasters such as hurricanes to be understood, social networks and the role of social media on public behaviour to be analyzed, blockchain-based transportation control, traffic flow during catastrophic events to be managed, and the locations of relief facilities to be optimized for maximum coverage and safety (Apte et al. 2016; Araz et al. 2013; Yucel et al. 2018; Oded et al. 2007; Choi, Wallace, and Wang 2018).

With an enhancement of the existing decision-support tools by data analytics a digital SC twin– a computerized digital SC model that represents the network state for any given moment in real time, allowing for complete end -to- end Supply Chain visibility to improve resilience and test contingency plans – can be created. A digital twin represents the physical Supply Chain based on actual transportation, inventory, demand, and capacity data and can therefore be used for planning and real-time control decisions. Supply Chain risk managers would benefit from tools that incorporate data analytics by leveraging emerging real time data and surveillance systems, predicting future impact and reactions, optimizing strategic and logistical locational decisions for efficient contingency plan execution, and building firms' control towers (Battarra, Balcik, and Xu 2018; Salman and Yucel 2015).

Digitalization refers to "the increasing penetration of digital technologies in society with the associated changes in the connection of individuals and their behaviour" (Gimpel and Roglinger et al. 2015). Digitization will create great opportunities for organizations and supply chain practices. Many organizations want to become more digital because they have observed the criticality and value of digital technologies for their growth and their own businesses, and the management support is also increasing for such initiatives (Bughin et al. 2015).

Circular economy is an efficient and responsible model for running our society with the aim of eliminating waste and enhancing resource (material) utility. Through various principled actions - reusing, sharing, repairing, refurbishing, remanufacturing, repurposing, and recycling - we can operate a close-loop ecosystem and extend the life-cycle of products, equipment and infrastructure. Thus, improving the resource utility, reducing waste, and energy consumption. The energy transition, on the other hand, is a pathway towards transformation from fossil-fuel to zero-carbon-based energy sources. Circular economy and energy transition projects can immensely benefit from the use of smart technologies supporting development of relevant policy frameworks and market instruments (Sankaran, 2019). The need to ensure sustainable production and consumption patterns has also been recognized in the United Nations Sustainable Development Goals, in particular target 12.5, aiming to "substantially reduce waste generation through prevention, reduction, recycling and reuse" (United Nations, 2020). In particular, blockchain technology has been identified as a key enabler to overcome challenges towards a circular economy (Kouhizadeh et al., 2019a). Building digital networks to distribute information about materials and supply chains transparently can lead to more circular resource flows, waste reduction, and an improved data base for decision making towards a circular economy (ibid.). The need to ensure sustainable production and consumption patterns has also been recognized in the United Nations Sustainable Development Goals, in particular target 12.5, aiming to "substantially reduce waste generation through prevention, reduction, recycling and reuse" (United Nations, 2020).

The digitalization of supply chains is expected to grow and play a crucial role within the supply chain management (SCM) context. Numerous companies seek to be more 'digital' as a result of their own observations of the relevance and usefulness of digital technology for business development (Saryatmo & Sukhotu, 2021).

LITERATURE REVIEW

The literature review showed that there are four works that link a conceptual model approach to the internet and digitalization (Alcácer and Cruz-Machado, 2019; Ardito, Petruzzelli, Panniello and Garavelli, 2018; Bag et al., 2018; Büyük.zkan and Göçer, 2018; Graham and Hardaker, 2000; Hofmann and Rüsch, 2017; Muhuri et al., 2019; Tu, 2018), thus presenting an initial and incipient incorporation of constructs and elements for Industry 4.0 within the essential components of Supply Chain Management. The research work developed by Büyük.zkan and Göçer (2018), showed a literature review for Digital Supply Chains and their enablers and proposed a framework, but the suggested components of Supply Chain Management are not supported by the basic literature review and constructs of the discipline (Garay-Rondero et al., 2020).

Current Supply Chains have an accelerated life cycle and are in constant evolution; this evolution is driven by changes in the markets and emerging needs of the Fourth

Industrial Revolution era. For this reason, new terms for digitalized Supply Chains have been flourishing. This is the case for the "Digital Supply Chain" construct, referring to the evolution of how the current Supply Chains are driven in Industry 4.0 (Garay-Rondero et al., 2020). The state of the art and definitions of the Digital Supply Chain have been proposed by some authors in recent years (Calatayud et al., 2019; Klötzer and Pflaum, 2017; Oswald and Kleinemeier, 2017; Park et al., 2018; Wu et al., 2016; Xu, 2014).

According to Graham and Hardaker (2000), the virtual value chain identifies the changing nature of value creation, but, just as importantly, indicates how new products and services are emerging through the information-driven economy (del Giudice et al., 2020).

Big data play a prominent role in improving a firm's overall performance, particularly in logistics and supply chain management (Wang et al., 2016). Previous studies have noted that big data have a positive impact on supply chain and environmental, social and economic performance (Akteret al., 2016; Gupta and George, 2016; Jeble et al., 2018; Song et al., 2017; Zhao et al., 2017). According to Raffoni et al. (2018), big data, if used with appropriate care, can help firms to achieve better performance. Big data have also been recognized as a facilitator of informed and reliable decisions for the adoption of circular economy strategies and for the implementation of circular economy business practices (Gupta et al., 2019; Jabbour et al., 2019a). Firms can more effectively take advantage of new insights gained from big data when they leverage and exploit it to drive their supply chains. Firms with better big-data-driven supply chains have better capabilities to improve their circular supply chain than those that rely on decisions based on limited data sets. In fact, big data can be used to better understand how to design supply chain processes, coordinate operations and networks, allow supply chain members to cooperate and engage employees with the circular economy paradigm (Gupta et al., 2019; Wang et al., 2016).

Figure 1. Virtual Value Chain within the Digital Supply Chain Model in Industry 4.0 (Graham and Hardaker (2000)

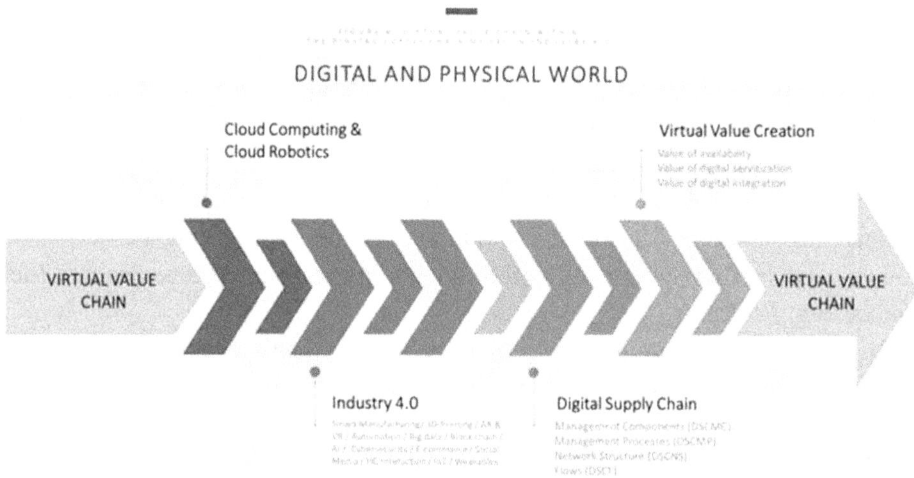

20 years after the first supply chain management (SCM) wave, a third generation of SCM is about to emerge: SCM in the digitalized economy – motivated and enabled by a tremendous technology shift and upcoming innovations. Key challenges and trends regarding current and future SCM tasks (supply chain visibility, new demand channels, new business models, supply chain complexity, etc.) across different industry groups show the need for a "Digital SCM Vision". Technologies with significant impact on current and future SCM tasks are big and smart data, Cloud computing, social media, predictive and prescriptive analytics, IoT, robotics, 3D Printing, and mobile technology. Interviews showed that investing in and implementing emerging technologies will create a sustained competitive advantage for companies through enhancing access to information, reducing costs, improving product quality, as well as responsiveness and collaboration abilities. Every industry has its own "Digital SCM Vision" based on industry-specific use cases of innovative digital technologies, and, therefore, needs a separate roadmap to improve the digital maturity of its Supply Chain Management tasks (Farahani, 2015).

Table 1. Major journals publishing digital supply chain articles (Pyun & Rha, 2021)

Source Title	Number of Articles
International Journal of Supply Chain Management	60
Sustainability	40
International Journal of Production Economics	31
Journal of Cleaner Production	30
International Journal of Production Research	29
Production Planning and Control	26
Supply Chain Management	17
International Journal of Logistics Management	11
Supply Chain Forum	11
Technological Forecasting and Social Change	11
IEEE Transactions on Engineering Management	10
Industrial Management and Data Systems	10
Benchmarking	9
International Journal of Information Management	9
Journal of Manufacturing Technology Management	9
Annals of Operations Research	8
European Journal of Operational Research	8
International Journal of Physical Distribution and Logistics Management	8

Firms willing to adopt a circular model are required to move toward technologies and business models characterized by longevity, renewability, reuse and repair in order to optimize the ways in which resources and materials already on the market are used and to reduce the consumption of raw materials and related waste (Gupta et al., 2019; Stahel, 2016). The Ellen MacArthur Foundation and McKinsey Company (2012, 2014) have emphasized the importance of progressing from sustainable supply chain management to a circular supply chain, defining it as the power of circling longer (i.e., a lengthening of the period of time during which materials are used).

A review of the literature indicates that, in order to develop a supply chain that could work in a circular economy perspective, it is necessary for a firm (a) to encourage the introduction of solutions that make the cycle of domestic production more sustainable (circular); (b) to act on a plurality of fronts to promote collaboration with external stakeholders in developing a supply chain that also has circular economy objectives; and (c) to train and manage employees so that they are aware, involved and interested in the green and sustainable objectives of the firm. Therefore, this study assumes that the circular supply chain will bring the best performance results if all elements of the firm's supply chain are aligned to support these three circular economy practices (del Giudice et al., 2020). To develop an effective circular economy supply chain, big data are certainly worthwhile; they allow rich, accurate and valuable information and insights to be extracted, and they make it possible to capture and manage knowledge for decision-making in logistics, manufacturing and order fulfillment (Gupta et al., 2019; Khan and Vorley, 2017; Liu et al., 2017; Pauleen and Wang, 2017; Renaud et al., 2019). In particular, big data should be used to emphasize stakeholder orientation (Ameri and Patil, 2012; Brettel et al., 2014; Holmstr€om;

Partanen, 2014; Pankaj et al., 2013), develop more efficient, faster and better synchronized logistics processes (Fawcett et al., 2011) and optimize the sustainable solutions that firms adopt for their supply chain management (Tseng et al., 2018).

Some recent contributions have highlighted positive returns for firms that arise from the management of big data from a sustainability perspective (Dubey et al., 2019; Jeble et al., 2018). As Hazen et al. (2016, p. 593) pointed out, "it is time to move beyond examining how big data and predictive analytics (BDPA) can be used to enhance operational – and financial based supply chain outcomes to examination of how BDPA can increase measures of supply chain sustainability that are becoming increasingly important in today's global marketplace" (del Giudice et al., 2020).

Benefits of Digital Supply Chain Management (Agrawal & Narain, 2018)

The following benefits can be attributed to the digital supply chain management:

1. Greater transparency leading to better decision making.
2. Reduced inventory levels because more just-in-time procurement will be used.
3. Clear visibility of inventory levels because of fully integrated system throughout the entire value
    1. chain.
4. More decentralized warehousing in order to reduce delivery times.
5. Reduce the delivery times since it will reduce the number of stages in the selling chain.
6. Better understanding of customer"s requirement through demand sensing and up-to-date sales
    2. information.
7. Higher sales, higher profit margin, strong bonding with customer.
8. Improved supply chain flexibility and reducing the risks and costs involved in supply chain.

9. More number of alternatives will be available in the decision-making process leading to better
    3. supply chain management decision.
10. Maintenance of competitive advantage.

As suggested by Farhani, Meier and Wilke 2017, every supply chain consist of various activities that are executed to procure raw materials, convert that material into final products, store that as finished product inventory and at the end deliver them to the ultimate customers. They have divided Supply Chain Management into seven dimensions which are suppliers, production, inventory and logistics, customers, information technology, human resources and performance measurement (see figure 3).

Figure 2. Seven dimensions of digital supply chain management.

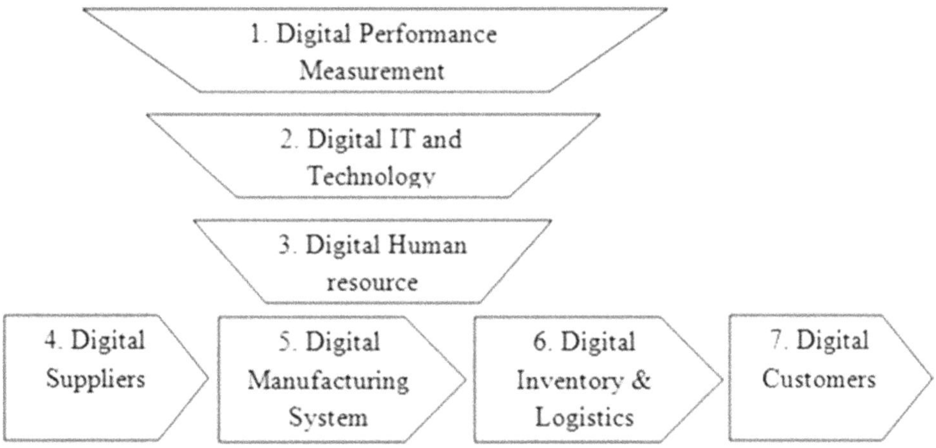

Machine vision and robotics are already in use around us, most notably in industrial applications, including the warehouse, as well as facial recognition systems used by law enforcement (Merlino & Sproge, 2017). Agile supply chain management stands for the ability to cope with unforeseen events through the use of lightning-fast decision making (Merlino & Sproge, 2017). According to Emily Rakowski (2015), research shows that companies who have embraced digital strategies are seeing real value, boosting revenue more than nine percent, market valuation more than 12%, and profitability by over 26%. Led by procurement, many of these companies will take things to the next level and enable new processes that drive more collaborative, intelligent, and transparent ways of operating (Merlino & Sproge, 2017).

Big data enables you to quickly model massive volumes of structured and unstructured data from multiple sources (Merlino & Sproge, 2017). For supply chain management, this can help increase visibility and provide deeper insights into the entire supply chain (Merlino & Sproge, 2017). Leveraging big data, your supply chain organizations can improve your response to volatile demand or supply chain risk, for example, and reduce the concerns related to the issue at hand (Merlino & Sproge, 2017). Spend matters (Spend Matters, 2016) recently published 5 Data-Driven Supply Chain Challenges to Overcome for 2016. Prioritizing the development of a big data analytics strategy can help an organization overcome many supply chain challenges (Merlino & Sproge, 2017).

BLOCKCHAIN IN 2030 AND BEYOND

The proliferation of blockchain is forcing traditional institutions to rethink their current trust facilitating models, and reinvent themselves using this technology and its underlying values. Governments should encourage innovation while protecting the interests of consumers and citizens. This requires communication and collaboration between all stakeholders, particularly with regard to regulation. Providing increased efficiency, transparency and interoperability across supply chains has been one of the most fertile areas for blockchain experimentation, and demonstrates the benefits and challenges posed by this technology. Blockchain is able to enable fairness across developing economies by providing a supply chain

framework which rewards ethical business practices. In light of the climate crisis, we should be reframing our approach to supply chain due diligence to not only consider where something came from, but also where it goes after we are no longer using it – the circular economy, and blockchain has a role to play in this, many of the benefits that can be achieved using blockchain technology already exist, and governments, international organizations and industry should be facilitating their implementation (Edward, 2019).

Limitations

This Paper supported on the market secondary data that has not been tested empirically, examined solely through secondary research. Even though we provide tables showing major journals and authors publishing digital supply chain articles, we did not analyze the co-authorship network, co-citation network, and clusters of researchers and articles on digital supply chain management. Future analysis of research trends must identify influential articles and authors by building citation networks, co-citation networks, and author networks.

Suggestions

New findings could be incorporated regarding key elements for the development and current operation of Digital Supply Chains. More research work can be undertaken with regard to the development of better roadmaps for Digital Supply Chains. These future studies could focus on the integration of emerging components and stages in the on-going implementation of Industry 4.0 in diverse Digital Supply Chains.

CONCLUSION

The topics that require further research can be identified through research trend analysis. In other words, the key function of the digital supply chain is to secure supply chain visibility by connecting the current status of operations performed by the entities in a supply chain and real-time monitoring of incidents using state-of-the-art digital technologies, and to quickly recover their correlated

functions by making immediate decisions in accordance with the response scenarios that were prepared for in advance. This study investigated the mediating effect of smart technologies on the connection between digital transformation and relationship performance. Thus, the study provides evidence to suggest that investment in smart technologies can provide firms with substantial relationship benefits. Therefore, the study contributes to research on the digital supply chain (Scuotto et al., 2017; Büyük.zkan and Göçer, 2018). As a first contribution, the findings show that digital transformation of companies alone does not have a direct effect on relationship performance. This is in line with the previous research that mentioned the importance of comprehensive procedures, strategies, and tools to experience benefits from the digital supply chain (Akter et al., 2016; Büyük.zkan and Göçer, 2018; Matt et al., 2015; Weichhart et al., 2016; Zhu et al., 2015). Second, the results support the claim that smart technologies mediate the relationship between digital transformation and relationship performance, covering both internal and external aspects (Nasiri et al., 2020). Therefore, when companies couple smart technologies with digital transformation, the impact on relationship performance will be enhanced. This is in line with previous research that mentioned building stronger collaboration in digital transformation through smart technologies (Berman, 2012; Matt et al., 2015).

Revolutionary changes will happen due to digitalization of supply chain management. Digitalization will help in improvement of supply chain visibility. Use of innovative digital technologies will allow the Modularization, simplification and standardization of product and processes. Companies should realize the importance of new business models which generate additional value to the product range and achieve new demand channels of increasingly digital customers. Hence it is necessary for the supply chain executives to find out the answers of the question that is how to use these digital technologies to extract benefits from that and how these technologies can be implemented in their current supply chain processes (Agrawal & Narain, 2018).

REFERENCES

Abugabah, A., Nizamuddin, N., & Abuqabbeh, A. (2020). A review of challenges and barriers implementing RFID technology in the Healthcare sector. *Procedia Computer Science*, *170*, 1003–1010. doi:10.1016/j.procs.2020.03.094

Agrawal, P., & Narain, R. (2018). Digital supply chain management: An Overview. *IOP Conference Series. Materials Science and Engineering*, *455*(1).

Akenroye, T. O. (2012). Factors Influencing Innovation in Healthcare: A conceptual synthesis. *The Innovation Journal*, *17*(2).

Arivazhagan, D. (2020). The Role Of Technology In Supply Chain Management. *International Journal of Scientific & Technology Research, 9*, 2. www.ijstr.org

Bashir, R., Gaur, B., & Salil, A. (2021). Logistics and IoT Based Survival Strategies to Facilitate Supply Chain Engineering during Pandemic. *Proceedings of 2nd IEEE International Conference on Computational Intelligence and Knowledge Economy, ICCIKE 2021*, 1–7. 10.1109/ICCIKE51210.2021.9410682

Blomsma, F., & Brennan, G. (2017). The Emergence of Circular Economy: A New Framing Around Prolonging Resource Productivity. *Journal of Industrial Ecology*, *21*(3), 603–614. doi:10.1111/jiec.12603

Böckel, A., Nuzum, A. K., & Weissbrod, I. (2021). Blockchain for the Circular Economy: Analysis of the Research-Practice Gap. In Sustainable Production and Consumption (Vol. 25, pp. 525–539). Elsevier B.V. doi:10.1016/j.spc.2020.12.006

del Giudice, M., Chierici, R., Mazzucchelli, A., & Fiano, F. (2020). Supply chain management in the era of circular economy: The moderating effect of big data. *International Journal of Logistics Management*, *32*(2), 337–356. doi:10.1108/IJLM-03-2020-0119

Edward, S. (2019). The Policy Environment for Blockchain Innovation and Adoption. In *2019 OECD Global Blockchain Policy Forum Summary Report*. OECD.

Farahani, P. (2015). *Digital Supply Chain Management 2020 Vision*. https://www.researchgate.net/publication/301350882

Garay-Rondero, C. L., Martinez-Flores, J. L., Smith, N. R., Caballero Morales, S. O., & Aldrette-Malacara, A. (2020). Digital supply chain model in Industry 4.0. *Journal of Manufacturing Technology Management*, *31*(5), 887–933. doi:10.1108/JMTM-08-2018-0280

Ivanov, D., & Dolgui, A. (2021). A digital supply chain twin for managing the disruption risks and resilience in the era of Industry 4.0. *Production Planning and Control*, *32*(9), 775–788. doi:10.1080/09537287.2020.1768450

Juzwishin, D. (2017). *Health System Procurement and Supply Management: Managing the Life Cycle of Technology for Maximum Value: What's New, What Stays, and What Must Go*. Academic Press.

Khan, M., Hussain, M., Gunasekaran, A., Ajmal, M. M., & Helo, P. T. (2018). Motivators of social sustainability in healthcare supply chains in the UAE—Stakeholder perspective. *Sustainable Production and Consumption*, *14*, 95–104. doi:10.1016/j.spc.2018.01.006

Marbouh, D., Abbasi, T., Maasmi, F., Omar, I. A., Debe, M. S., Salah, K., Jayaraman, R., & Ellahham, S. (2020). Blockchain for COVID-19: Review, Opportunities, and a Trusted Tracking System. *Arabian Journal for Science and Engineering*, *45*(12).

Merlino, M., & Sproge, I. (2017). The Augmented Supply Chain. *Procedia Engineering*, *178*, 308–318. doi:10.1016/j.proeng.2017.01.053

Nasiri, M., Ukko, J., Saunila, M., & Rantala, T. (2020). Managing the digital supply chain: The role of smart technologies. *Technovation*, *96-97*, 96–97. doi:10.1016/j.technovation.2020.102121

Nayak, G., & Dhaigude, A. S. (2019). A conceptual model of sustainable supply chain management in small and medium enterprises using blockchain technology. *Cogent Economics and Finance*, *7*(1), 1667184. Advance online publication. doi:10.1080/23322039.2019.1667184

Omar, I. A., Jayaraman, R., Debe, M. S., Salah, K., Yaqoob, I., & Omar, M. (2021). Automating Procurement Contracts in the Healthcare Supply Chain Using Blockchain Smart Contracts. *IEEE Access: Practical Innovations, Open Solutions*, *9*, 37397–37409. doi:10.1109/ACCESS.2021.3062471

Pyun, J., & Rha, J. S. (2021). Review of research on digital supply chain management using network text analysis. In Sustainability (Switzerland) (Vol. 13, Issue 17). MDPI. doi:10.3390u13179929

Sankaran, K. (2019). Carbon emission and plastic pollution: How circular economy, blockchain, and artificial intelligence support energy transition? *Journal of Innovation Management*, *7*(4), 7–13. doi:10.24840/2183-0606_007.004_0002

Saryatmo, M. A., & Sukhotu, V. (2021). The influence of the digital supply chain on operational performance: A study of the food and beverage industry in Indonesia. *Sustainability (Switzerland)*, *13*(9), 5109. Advance online publication. doi:10.3390u13095109

Scuotto, V., Caputo, F., Villasalero, M., & del Giudice, M. (2017). A multiple buyer–supplier relationship in the context of SMEs' digital supply chain management. *Production Planning and Control*, *28*(16), 1378–1388. doi:10.1080/09537287.2017.1375149

Yan, M. R., Chien, K. M., & Yang, T. N. (2016). Green component procurement collaboration for improving supply chain management in the high technology industries: A case study from the systems perspective. *Sustainability (Switzerland)*, *8*(2), 105. Advance online publication. doi:10.3390u8020105

Chapter 2
Evaluation of International Logistics and Supply Chain Disruption During the COVID-19 Pandemic Through Scientometric Techniques

Muzaffar Iqbal
Tianjin University, China

Muhammad Ismail
Xi'an Jiaotong University, China

Muhammad Ibrahim
Khawaja Fareed University of Engineering and Information Technology, Pakistan

Ch Hassan Khalil
Lahore Leads University, Pakistan

Ishfaq Ahmad
Northwestern Polytechnical University, China

ABSTRACT

This study unwraps the detailed literature review and highlights the development in growing research on behalf of the supply chain in the era of COVID-19. Earlier research on different disasters shows that there is a lack of research on pandemics. Therefore, the present study signifies the multi-perspective literature review on behalf of the supply chain associated with COVID-19. Further, to analyze the literature of this study from a broad perspective, the science mapping approach and the quantitative analysis were conducted on the basis of bibliometric references that were extracted from the web of science.

DOI: 10.4018/978-1-6684-6663-6.ch002

INTRODUCTION

The modern world has been facing an unprecedented outbreak with major adverse impacts on society and supply chain management operations. The supply chain operations slowed down due to pandemic situations worldwide (Aday & Aday, 2020). Recently, the supply chain has been disruptive because of the COVID-19 outbreak (Sarkis, 2020). The COVID-19 disease has been recognized as a severe contagious coronavirus with harmful impacts (Pfefferbaum & North, 2020; Van Bavel et al., 2020). COVID-19 was first discovered in China's industrial city of Wuhan, Hubei province (Sombultawee, Lenuwat, Aleenajitpong, & Boon-itt, 2022). According to the john Hopkins University research team, until May 27, 2020, total number of confirmed COVID-affected people had reached 5.69 million, and 0.357 million people were deceased (e Conhecimento, 2020). Due to the increasing number of confirmed reported cases and deaths, the World Health Organization WHO declared COVID-19 a world pandemic on March 11, 2020 (Chakraborty & Maity, 2020; Iqbal, Ahmad, Waqas, & Abrar, 2021).

The adverse impact of COVID-19 on SCs has grabbed the attention of researchers and other concerned authorities (Belhadi et al., 2021; Ivanov, 2020; Ivanov & Dolgui, 2020). Queiroz, Ivanov, Dolgui, and Wamba (2020) identified that more than 93% of organizations registered on the Fortune 1000 list were suffering from supply chain distractions because of the COVID-19 outbreak. In fact, the term supply chain is classified as "the system of firms that include a hierarchy from up streams to downstream in various operations to enhance the value of product and services acknowledged by end users." A widespread disaster of COVID-19 has reduced the efficiency and performance of supply chain operations worldwide (Chowdhury, Paul, Kaisar, & Moktadir, 2021). In the past, the supply chain encountered various disasters and outbreaks. As reported by WHO, more than 1400 epidemics happened just between 2011 to 2018 (Hudecheck, Sirén, Grichnik, & Wincent, 2020). However, the recent outbreak is matchless; it also has more severe, diversified, and adverse impacts than previous pandemics (Iqbal, Ma, Ullah, et al., 2022; Sawik, 2022; van Hoek, Gibson, & Johnson, 2020). The supply chain flow has been poorly affected worldwide e.g., demand for primary goods such as personal protective equipment, PPEs, ventilators, and COVID-19 vaccine transportation tools has increased (Ozdemir, Sharma, Dhir, & Daim, 2022).

Meanwhile, the transportation, manufacturing, and food industry capacities have been reduced due to the COVID-19 outbreak. These challenges faced by organizations are due to shutdown of borders, lockdown in regions, restrictions on public transport, presence of limited employees in the workplace, and adoption of physical distance on operations site (El Baz & Ruel, 2020). Because of the multidimensional impacts on supply chain and financial issues, it seems to be a severe long-term effect on international trade (McMaster et al., 2020; Raj, Mukherjee, de Sousa Jabbour, & Srivastava, 2022). Chowdhury et al. (2021) identified that according to the world trade organization report, global trade might reduce by up to 32% because of the unprecedented impact of COVID-19.

The harmful impact of COVID-19 on supply chains has grabbed researchers' attention towards significant research on the supply chain (Sinha, Kumar, & Chandra, 2023). As a result, thousands of research articles on the supply chain in the era of the COVID-19 situation since 2020 have been published in reputed journals. As the topic of the supply chain is getting the attention of researchers in the pandemic crisis, it is significant to identify the current literature scenario and address future research opportunities to assist the researchers in avoiding doing repetitive research in this discipline (Alkahtani et al., 2021). A comprehensive literature review could help to precise what we know, how we know it, and what could be done so that the supply chain could better perform in such types of crises (Spieske, Gebhardt, Kopyto, & Birkel, 2022; Tranfield, Denyer, & Smart, 2003).

Because of limitations in previous SC review studies in the era of various outbreaks, they have not a clear picture of state of the art from its beginning to the present. However, in this novel study, we develop the results of published articles in the pandemic era through a scientometric review of the Supply chain. A quantitative approach, science mapping, is used to identify the existing body of knowledge in the supply chain domain. This study analyzes the scope and existing supply chain knowledge body while identifying lapses and insufficiencies. This novel research can contribute to worldwide supply chain knowledge by comprehensively understanding the present supply chain situation and pinpointing where best to concentrate for future research efforts. This study can help researchers, policymakers, and other concerned authorities with a better understanding to manage the uncertain conditions of the COVID-19 pandemic.

RESEARCH METHODOLOGY

In this study, the science mapping approach is used to identify the supply chain research during the COVID-19 situation. Science mapping is used to detect the intellectual structure of a scientific domain. Science mapping is a generic domain analysis and visualization (Garcia-Buendia, Moyano-Fuentes, Maqueira-Marín, & Cobo, 2020). The science mapping approach assists in visualizing significant patterns and trends in a broader picture of literature and bibliographic data (Fahimnia, Pournader, Siemsen, Bendoly, & Wang, 2019). Science mapping research can often be adopted on a bibliometric analysis approach or scientometric analysis approach (Cobo, López-Herrera, Herrera-Viedma, & Herrera, 2011; Noruzi et al., 2022).

However, bibliometric analysis is used to focus on literature. Also scientometric technique provides a comprehensive approach that covers bibliometric tools and data to identify the significant literature and its outcomes that examine the range of patterns and trends (Feng, Zhu, & Lai, 2017). Therefore, scientometric analysis has been utilized to commence the study. Following (Okolie & Ogundeji, 2022; Udara Willhelm Abeydeera, Wadu Mesthrige, & Samarasinghalage, 2019) recommendations, the research approach was developed to wrap the following stages, adopting science mapping for tool selection, summing up the data and analysis, visualization, demonstration, elucidation, and discussion of results.

Science Mapping Tools Selection

Different science mapping tools for evaluating and visualizing structural, dynamic, and temporal patterns exist in the domain of scientific literature (Gatto, Drago, & Ruggeri, 2022; Liu, Liu, Wang, & Pan, 2019). Each tool has its function in performing the analysis. Hence, to classify any domain of study, the practical use of different tools for a different kind of study is necessary. For this novel study, VOSviewer, Gephi, and CiteSpace were selected after analyzing different science mapping tools. VOSviewer is an essential tool used to perform functions that need to develop, visualize and explore the bibliometric networks (He, Zhang, & Zeng, 2019; Pang, 2022). Gephi is an open-source software used to draw different kinds of graphs and networks to explore, interpret and visualize the data (He et al., 2019). CiteSpace, is a software that is utilized to design visual analytic tasks of science mapping (Darko, Chan, Huo, & Owusu-Manu, 2019; Lan & Hou, 2022). Further, this software tool is used to address the significant queries about the knowledge domain, including essential research areas and how these are linked with each other (Zhai, Shan, Darko, & Le, 2020). More information regarding the implementation of VOSviewer, Gephi, and CiteSpace software tools can be found in different studies (Cobo et al., 2011; Darko et al., 2020; M. Hosseini & Gordijn, 2020; Sheng, Zhou, Song, & Wang, 2022), respectively. In this novel study, different analyses through different kinds of software tools can be understood in later sections.

Data Collection

Bibliometric data was gathered from the Web of Science despite databases such as Scopus, Google Scholar, and science direct. The reason for collecting data from the Web of Science was that it possesses a broader domain of scientific publications compared with other databases (Bhatia & Gangwani, 2020). However, the Web of science has a faster indexing process, which enhances the probability of fresh publications retrieval (Darko et al., 2019). Web of Science has been widely adopted in previous review research studies (Ruiz-Rosero et al., 2017). Earlier review studies by (Bhatia & Gangwani, 2020; S. Hosseini & Ivanov, 2020; Yalcin, Shi, & Rahman, 2020), using the terms supply chain, green supply chain, and risk in the supply chain were used to regain the bibliographic data. It should be kept in mind this research does not cover all potential terms in the area because it is challenging to cover all possible times in one study (Darko & Chan, 2016). The date range limit was set in this research study, i.e., January 2020 to February 17 2021. Meanwhile, for document type, it was limited to "article." The limitation of the document type of the article was adopted for science mapping because journal articles show the most influential and reputable research (Wang, Liu, Gu, Cheng, & Li, 2019). Further, it has been categorized as certified knowledge (Ramos-Rodríguez & Ruíz-Navarro, 2004). As of February 17, 2021, 386 publications were found, and all bibliographic information was exported from the Web of Science, designing this study's dataset.

Scientometric Techniques

Su and Lee (2010) identified that the scientometric approach contains keywords co-occurrence analysis, author co-citation analysis, document co-citation analysis, etc. in this research, science mapping was utilized in two phases. The first phase includes developing a network through keywords co-occurrence analysis, citation burst analysis, outlet direct citation analysis, and co-authorship analysis, as illustrated in the next section. The second phase includes developing maps to identify the productive information from network measures, which exhibit the research field's theoretical, intellectual, or social growth, screening trends, and outliers (Cobo et al., 2011).

ANALYSIS AND RESULTS

Trends of Supply Chain Research in the Perspective of the COVID-19 Situation

The trend of supply chain research in the era of the COVID-19 situation ranges from 2020-2021 (as presented in figure 1). Compared to the last year based on average publications, recent years have more publications on the supply chain. However, it can be observed that the trend of a supply chain associated with COVID-19 publications is growing. This is notable that the journals, on the topic of supply chain associated with COVID-19 were retrieved on February 17, 2021. So, the publications appearing in WoS till this date were considered for scientometric review. Notably, the number of publications may rise in the future, and the date of extracting literature from the database was consistent with earlier studies (Laengle et al., 2021). It has been admitted that publications from 2020-2021 are pretty small because the period of the COVID-19 pandemic situation was just considered. Upcoming review studies could concentrate on retrieving additional publications related to this period which could be done through the modification in terms of literature as mentioned earlier.

Figure 1. Tendency in COVID publications

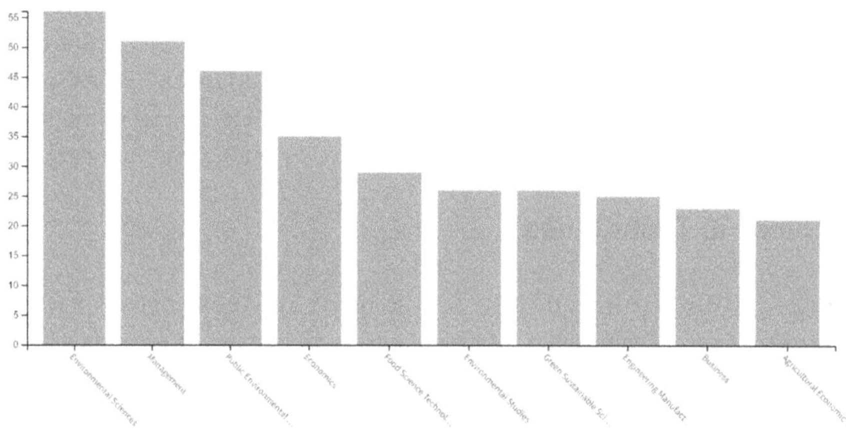

Development of a Global Body of Supply Chain-Associated Knowledge in COVID-19

Significant Research Domains via Keywords Network Analysis and Citation Burst

Analyzing the critical keywords assist in discovering the primary area of research (Laengle et al., 2021). Li, Xu, Wang, and Wang (2020) identified that keywords represent the overall picture of research publication. A keyword provides a significant image of a knowledge domain which offers insights of specific issues and how these issues are managed and intellectually related to each other (Herrera-Franco, Montalván-Burbano, Carrión-Mero, Jaya-Montalvo, & Gurumendi-Noriega, 2021). VOS viewer 1.6.8 software tool was utilized to design the network of co-occurrence of keywords. The keywords were extracted through bibliographic from the database of WoS. To attain the clear image of keywords, author keywords were acknowledged instead of other keywords. Using the fractional counting approach, 1825 keywords were achieved from the existing dataset. However, the minimum amount of occurrence to develop the standard criteria a keyword must be involved in the network, and the standard value was 8 in which threshold was 35. After retrieving the standard terms (e.g., "Covid-19", "pandemic"). After exclusion criteria, the remaining network included 26 nodes and 304 edges, as shown in (figure 1). the strength of the degree between keywords is summed up by the number of research papers in the concerned areas (Ellegaard & Wallin, 2015).

Further, the stronger node will highlight a more deep picture in the visualization network. Moreover, to examine the value of nodes in the system, the mean of the node will be calculated (Martínez-López, Merigó, Valenzuela-Fernández, & Nicolás, 2018). Also, this connection expresses the regularity of contact with each other (Davarpanah & Aslekia, 2008). To find the relation among nodes through the frequency of relationship following equation is suggested by (Zhai et al., 2020).

$$D_i = \sum_{i=1}^{n} X_{ij}$$

Where D_i Denote the primary stream value for node, i; X_{ij} Represents the assembly of all connection in symbol node i and j where n represent the total amount of nodes in the network. The system, incorporated through VOSviewer (fig2), succumbed to Gephi 0.9.2. to sum up the focal point of nodes. The findings of the analysis are shown in (the table). The significant research points were placed on the basis of focal points. The more excellent focal point represents that the research area is essential. Still, if the focal point of two research fields is the same, then the prioritization of nodes will be summed up via weighted degree value. The weighted degree is the latest version of degree focal point used to calculate the strength of links included in network nodes. The hierarchy of research directions (table) and the connection of research fields (as designated in fig) disclose different significant results, emphasizing gaps and scarcities within the supply chain research associated with COVID-19:

- Some specific research scopes have lingered unexplored and isolated. Past studies covered adverse impacts of disaster on supply chain, enhancing SC crisis, evaluation of pandemic risks in SC and financial impacts on SC in the era of outbreaks (Altay & Ramirez, 2010; Lockamy III, 2014). The research on SC associated with COVID-19 in all aspects is gaining attention to enhance the culture of best SC practices in future disasters.
- Furthermore, research areas like the crisis in the development of SC in pandemics need to be developed which could polish the process of green SC. These researchers focus on SC in an alarming environment (Anparasan & Lejeune, 2018; Huff, Beyeler, Kelley, & McNitt, 2015; Kumar & Chandra,

2010; Mohan, Viswanadham, & Trikha, 2009; Yu & Aviso, 2020) and endorse SC as an effective tool to survive for long term goals.

- Besides a lot of research on SC associated with different disasters but supply chain association with COVID-19 literature required more attention which could be possible in the following ways: (1) which type of SC research has been done in the era of COVID-19. (2) There are opportunities for future research regarding COVID-19 outbreak in the supply chain discipline.
- However, in the past, no study exists in the literature which addresses the research association of SC with COVID-19. In the present research study, terms such as influenza, logistics, supply chain resilience, supply chain disruption, model, pandemics, performance, sars-cov-2, sustainability, management, 3d printer, and personal protective equipment incorporate a significant proportion of the literature related to SC association as presented in (figure 2).
- Figure 2 represents the findings of citation burst analysis through the software of Cite space 5.3. R3. The citation burst clarifies those keywords cited in the literature in a specific time, along with fast-growing topics (Kagan, Moran-Gilad, & Fire, 2020). Also, the citation burst provides insights that grab researchers' major attention. From the data set, 1825 keywords had citation burst. Figure 2 represents the highest 27 keywords with the strongest citation burst and the top seven words with the highest strength of burst.

Figure 2. Major areas of COVID-19 (Co-occurrence network)

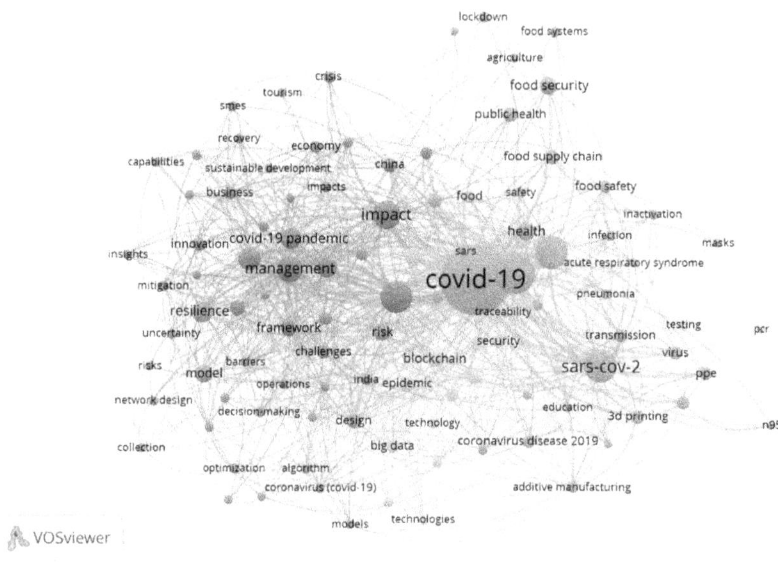

Top Research Outlets: Outlet Direct Citation Analysis

Different studies have been conducted to discover the significance of academic journals in various fields (X. Zhao, 2017). Such types of publications may be helpful for immediate readers to identify the authentic source of information that could be fruitful for publications. However, this approach also can assist journal editors

Table 1. Major supply chain research areas and their relative influence

ID	KEYWORDS	OCCURRANCES	TOTAL LINK STRENGTH
9	3D Printing	11	10
61	Agriculture	10	9
239	China	13	7
332	Coronavirus	35	21
420	Design	9	8
650	Food	9	6
671	Food security	22	15
691	Framework	11	10
773	Health	10	5
839	Impact	22	17
878	Influenza	8	5
972	Logistics	9	8
1000	Management	22	20
1067	Model	11	8
1205	Pandemics	8	5
1219	Performance	19	17
1224	Personal protective equipment	10	6
1261	Policy	8	5
1275	PPE	12	10
1359	Recovery	9	8
1378	Resilience	30	26
1411	Risk	19	15
1456	Sars-cov-2	35	19
1474	Security	8	8
1612	Supply chain disruption	10	8
1624	Supply chain resilience	13	8
1648	Sustainability	25	20

in managing research publications relevant to their journals (Haghani, Bliemer, Goerlandt, & Li, 2020). In this novel study, a direct citation analysis was utilized, which expresses the significance of research journals that broadcast SC research in the pandemic situation of COVID-19. VOSviewer software tool was adopted in which component of analysis was "sources," and the type of analysis was "citation.

Moreover, the lowest amount of publications by the journal was considered 5. Among 239 retrieved articles sources, 10 were eligible and appeared in the output network, consisting of 10 links between 40 outlets. Furthermore, the graphic visualization of different journals network was implemented through Gephi software. However, in the current study, weighted degree focal points were used internally for the measurement adjustment and coloring nodes (figure 2). The greater weighted

Figure 3. Main outlets network of supply chain literature

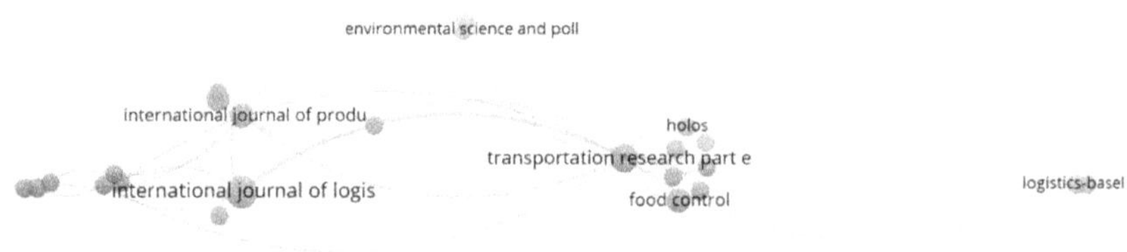

Table 2. Main 10 outlets for supply chain research

ID	Sources	Documents	Citations	Total link strength
10	Journal of agribusiness	5	0	32.33
43	Canadian Journal of agriculture economics-revenue	8	128	6
49	China agricultural economic review	6	20	12.5
87	Food security	6	26	9
108	IEEE Access	5	14	15
117	International journal of environmental research and public health	7	73	39
166	Journal of supply chain management	6	5	15.33
210	Resource conservation and recycling	6	31	32.33
215	Science of the total environment	7	84	45.03
221	sustainability	28	49	67.07

values were highlighted through more profound and broader nodes. Table 1 expresses the real outlets in figure 2,

Finally, from the study results, it has been investigated that the major journal for SC research associated with COVID-19 is sustainability, with the highest weighted degree value of 67.07. There are massive citations from sustainability to science of the total environment, resource conservation and recycling, journal of supply chain management, and agree on business and food security as expressed in figure 3. The journal of sustainability which is central in the scope of SC association in COVID-19, is reinforced by present literature and is suitable for the aim and scope of sustainability because being suitable is an essential element when picking the journal (Golinelli et al., 2020).

Collaborative Network Associated with SC Research in the COVID-19 era: Co-Authorship Analysis

To increase the efficiency and coordination of specific research availability of resources and professionals (M. R. Hosseini, Maghrebi, Akbarnezhad, Martek, & Arashpour, 2018). Retrieving knowledge from different journals and articles is significant for scholarly communication as defined by various research studies (L. Zhao, Tang, & Zou, 2019). Golan, Jernegan, and Linkov (2020) described co-authorship as a significant contribution to scientific research. Suppose the

Figure 4. Main authors in SC associated research in COVID-19

participation of researchers in the scientific coordination is less it express that there is less productivity in specific research area. Next section examines the network of co-authorship in terms of SC association with COVID-19 literature in various perspective.

Institution

In institutions, the availability of network cooperation in a sophisticated way for the association of SC in COVID disasters can assist policymakers and other concerned authorities in network creation. Further, the selection o firm as a unit symbol, VOSviewer, was utilized for co-authorship analysis with a fractional counting approach. In this process, the lowest number of documents of a firm was considered 5, and the smallest number of citations of a firm was considered 3. As a result, the total firms were 881, of which 9 met the criteria, which consisted of network output. However, GEPHI software was applied to draw the visualization, as shown in figure 5. In Gephi, hyperlink-induced topic search (HITS) is represented as hubs, authorities, and algorithms used to examine the impacts of nodes (Haghani & Bliemer, 2020). HITS algorithm develops two unrelated results: an authority score and a hub score in each node. A more excellent hub score represents the highest impact node as an essential reference source. The Authority score is the amount of fruitful information kept in a node (Sahoo & Pandey, 2020). Suppose the impact of a node is higher, then it represents the higher authority in the context of helpful information. However, comprehensive information regarding hub score and authority score could be identified from the study (Kleinberg, 1999). Before the utilization of HITS, the hub points in the system were hired to make colorful and resize the network. So, if the shadow is bright along with a big node, it will represent more excellent hub scores. e.g., institutes from different countries such as America and Canada have been enhancing research on the association of SC with COVID-19, and institutes from other countries represent limited cross-linkage institutes (figure 5, table 3)

This idea may represent less attention towards the cross-fertilization of research on SC associated with COVID-19 among institutes. Further, for the broader research activities, comprehensive examination is required in SC association with COVID-19.

Figure 5. SC literature and collaboration network of different international institutions

Table 3. Collaborative network of different global institutions in global SC research

ID	Organization	Documents	Citations	Total link strength
34	Arizona state university	6	18	41.33
46	Auburn university	5	11	6.5
69	Berlin school of economics and law	6	291	24.83
552	Rutgers state university	7	12	32
748	University of Michigan	5	9	37.17
749	University of Minnesota	5	3	47
798	University of Sydney	6	68	28
810	University of Toronto	8	18	53.33
816	University of vermont	5	8	37.17

Countries

The network system of Scientific collaboration expresses the active participation of countries in research publications (Ranganathan & Balasubramani, 2014). In the VOSviewer software tool, the network was designed to identify the most suitable countries in the scope of research contribution. In this process, countries were selected as a unit, the analysis was performed as a co-authorship, and the counting approach served as a fractional counting. However, the minimum number of documents of a country was selected as 10 and the minimum number of citations of a country was not considered. Out of 87 states, 11 states were eligible to meet the required criteria. These criteria were added to the network to perform the analysis through the software of Gephi, which could visualize a clear image of countries, as shown in figure 6.

Weighted degree values were adopted in the network to highlight the significant countries regarding publications of SC associated with COVID-19. Further, nodes were resized and colored based on weighted degree values. The nodes represent light colors, known as the minimum value of the weighted degree, and deeper colors represent the maximum value of the weighted degree. In the table, 3 significant 11 countries on behalf of more research publications concerning topics were rated on weighted degree values. The top three countries, the USA, China, and the UK are significant contributors to the more publications of SC associated with the COVID outbreak. America, China, and the UK were the major countries badly affected by COVID-19 (Chowell & Mizumoto, 2020; Singanayagam et al., 2020; Zhang et al., 2020). Experts and policymakers believe that they can improve the performance of the supply chain in the era of COVID-19 under strict protective measures. The coordination among influential countries could enhance the productivity of supply

Figure 6. GTs literature and countries based collaborative network

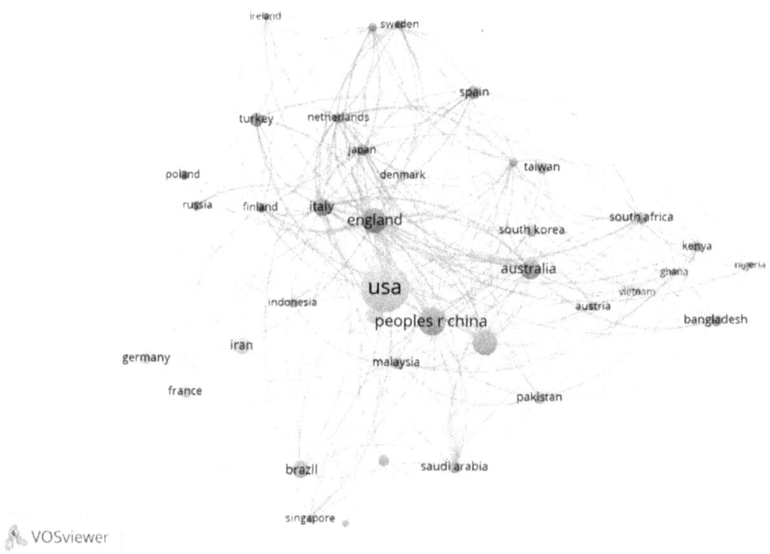

Table 4. Top 11 nations collaborating in SC research

ID	Country	Documents	Citations	Total link strength
3	Australia	26	126	909.91
10	Canada	33	210	1052.4
20	England	44	127	1830.34
24	France	16	168	688.33
25	Germany	22	330	966.16
29	India	27	53	749.14
34	Italy	18	135	706.72
50	Netherland	12	53	389.63
59	China	57	223	1785.65
68	Singapore	10	54	429.67
84	USA	148	522	2229.95

chain services and knowledge sharing in the field of SC. However, among 87 countries, there was a lack of strong association. The reason behind this deficiency was lack of cooperation among countries regarding research. Different countries such as Australia, Canada, France, India, Netherlands, and Singapore have weaker relations with the critical nodes of SC association research in the COVID-19 era. So, these countries could improve their SC practices through solid network and collaboration in draconian situations. None of the developing economies were in this network because of issues such as less interest in research and development and poor supply chain infrastructure. Therefore, the gap in research and development is a significant hindrance that must be filled.

RESULTS AND DISCUSSION

Our study identified that scientific research publications regarding COVID-19 from the SC perspective are getting more researchers' attention. In light of this, the primary purpose of the current study is to cope with the scope of such research studies that belong to SC associated with COVID-19 in the pandemic situation. To this extent, different research dimensions regarding SC in the era of COVID-19 have been identified, which could be helpful for policymakers, professionals, researchers, and other relevant authorities.

Fast and appropriate growth of knowledge and empirical studies are acute for policymakers and professionals facing disaster challenges to update their decisions via scientific evidence. This needs to be a systematic design of present knowledge to explore the flaws and overcome the scopes to enhance the institutional expertise towards improved solutions. It is believed that this research can participate in scientific applications and integrate the SC implications of such a global crisis to assist the research community. These adoptions are presented through scientometric analysis and visualization regarding the research associated with SC in the era of COVID-19. This research also covers all areas of SC, such as food, transportation, construction, manufacturing, etc. This review is the evidence of a significant part of knowledge that influences today in the contest against pandemics highlighted as a finding of a study that is presented in response to previous disasters like COVID-19 (Aviv-Reuven & Rosenfeld, 2020; Colavizza et al., 2021; Haghani et al., 2020; Patil, 2020).

Moreover, the growth of scientific research now and after the draconian disaster could help organizations and aware them for future outbreaks worldwide. So the purpose of this study is to pinpoint the supply chain dimensions that belong to the literature that somehow associate SC and COVID-19. The authors believed that such research could motivate researchers to examine the gaps in the perspective of SC dimensions, which belong to current unprecedented situations. Modeling a broad range of outstanding situational crisis-related SC research can enhance organizational and institutional learning to be aware of future outbreaks. It has been identified that outbreaks are the second-ranked disasters that could impact the supply chain of organizations and the economy (Bengtsson-Palme, 2017; Oke & Gopalakrishnan, 2009; Pendell, Leatherman, Schroeder, & Alward, 2007). Moving towards the proper management of SC activities such as food supply and transportation of personal protective tools from one place to another has so far dominated the researcher's struggles in this scenario (Iqbal, Ma, Ahmad, Ullah, & Hassan, 2022). This study tries to create an image of SC association in the COVID-19 era through scientometric visualization, which is not elaborated on in the previous literature.

CONCLUSION

The COVID-19 pandemic could severely impact the supply chain across the world. In this novel research, we presented a scientometric analysis to highlight the research associated with SC from the start of COVID-19 until now and gathered an exclusive set of research articles.

Our study found that the interplay between SC and crises such as the pandemic has conventionally focused on resource distribution issues (Huang, 2019). It has also been identified that the interaction has been conquered by influenza; however, other pandemics have also been stated in the scenario of SC. This fact highlight that COVID-19 is already upsetting the SC operations in the world. It could be observed that the exploration of pandemics on SC is novel; however, it strengthens the research perspective (Queiroz et al., 2020). This novel study highlighted the insights and influence of COVID-19 on SC which could be strong evidence for experts and scholars for future research. In this manner, our study explores the robust literature gaps and opens question opportunities for policymakers.

This novel study provides a clear picture of SC research associated with COVID-19 from the start of a pandemic to February 17, 2021. The study's findings highlighted that coordination among different countries and their research institutes is the main factor that slows down the operations of SC in the COVID-19 era. As it has also been identified in the literature, there is a weak relationship among nations regarding the SC operations in COVID-19 Moreover, coordination among different could provide fruitful results. Some recommendations that could give suitable answers to such concerns are given below.

- Business firms performing SC operations should collaborate with international firms and their research and development institutes.
- There should be strict protective measures in pandemic situations to continue the smooth operations of SC during a pandemic
- Nations should agree to fight against outbreaks that could bring an uninterrupted flow of SC operations from borders.

The limitations of this study are supposed to be as the overall investigation of the database was extracted through WoS, which have some disadvantages regarding the publication's exposure. Another drawback is to depend on insufficient keywords, and journal publications are not enough. Because of the narrow scope, it might not capture the maximum attention of literature. The future directions are that different database, software tools, their impacts on the existing situation, and the unique feature of literature could be added. The findings of this study about the association of SC with COVID-19 have been conducted through a science-mapping approach. Also, this study's result assists in apprehending the overall image of SC association with COVID-19. Two gaps are identified in this research one is that the broad scope regarding the association of SC with COVID-19 was 25, which supports such concerns are needed according to required recommendations. The concerned authorities that are experts in the field of SC could better sort out an issue that belongs to SC in COVID-19. This novel research could be helpful for researchers and policymakers to enhance the variety of SC associated with COVID-19 because a transparent research gap provides better future directions for researchers and practitioners worldwide.

REFERENCES

Aday, S., & Aday, M. S. (2020). Impact of COVID-19 on the food supply chain. *Food Quality and Safety*, *4*(4), 167–180. doi:10.1093/fqsafe/fyaa024

Alkahtani, M., Omair, M., Khalid, Q. S., Hussain, G., Ahmad, I., & Pruncu, C. (2021). A COVID-19 Supply Chain Management Strategy Based on Variable Production under Uncertain Environment Conditions. *International Journal of Environmental Research and Public Health*, *18*(4), 1662. doi:10.3390/ijerph18041662 PMID:33572380

Altay, N., & Ramirez, A. (2010). Impact of disasters on firms in different sectors: Implications for supply chains. *The Journal of Supply Chain Management*, *46*(4), 59–80. doi:10.1111/j.1745-493X.2010.03206.x

Anparasan, A. A., & Lejeune, M. A. (2018). Data laboratory for supply chain response models during epidemic outbreaks. *Annals of Operations Research*, *270*(1), 53–64. doi:10.100710479-017-2462-y

Aviv-Reuven, S., & Rosenfeld, A. (2020). *Publication Patterns' Changes due to the COVID-19 Pandemic: A longitudinal and short-term scientometric analysis.* arXiv preprint arXiv:2010.02594.

Belhadi, A., Kamble, S., Jabbour, C. J. C., Gunasekaran, A., Ndubisi, N. O., & Venkatesh, M. (2021). Manufacturing and service supply chain resilience to the COVID-19 outbreak: Lessons learned from the automobile and airline industries. *Technological Forecasting and Social Change*, *163*, 120447. doi:10.1016/j.techfore.2020.120447 PMID:33518818

Bengtsson-Palme, J. (2017). Antibiotic resistance in the food supply chain: Where can sequencing and metagenomics aid risk assessment? *Current Opinion in Food Science*, *14*, 66–71. doi:10.1016/j.cofs.2017.01.010

Bhatia, M. S., & Gangwani, K. K. (2020). Green supply chain management: Scientometric review and analysis of empirical research. *Journal of Cleaner Production*, 124722.

Chakraborty, I., & Maity, P. (2020). COVID-19 outbreak: Migration, effects on society, global environment and prevention. *The Science of the Total Environment*, *728*, 138882. doi:10.1016/j.scitotenv.2020.138882 PMID:32335410

Chowdhury, P., Paul, S. K., Kaisar, S., & Moktadir, M. A. (2021). COVID-19 pandemic related supply chain studies: A systematic review. *Transportation Research Part E, Logistics and Transportation Review*, *148*, 102271. doi:10.1016/j.tre.2021.102271 PMID:33613082

Chowell, G., & Mizumoto, K. (2020). The COVID-19 pandemic in the USA: What might we expect? *Lancet*, *395*(10230), 1093–1094. doi:10.1016/S0140-6736(20)30743-1 PMID:32247381

Cobo, M. J., López-Herrera, A. G., Herrera-Viedma, E., & Herrera, F. (2011). Science mapping software tools: Review, analysis, and cooperative study among tools. *Journal of the American Society for Information Science and Technology*, *62*(7), 1382–1402. doi:10.1002/asi.21525

Colavizza, G., Costas, R., Traag, V. A., Van Eck, N. J., Van Leeuwen, T., & Waltman, L. (2021). A scientometric overview of CORD-19. *PLoS One*, *16*(1), e0244839. doi:10.1371/journal.pone.0244839 PMID:33411846

Conhecimento, R. I. (2020). *Coronavirus COVID-19 Global Cases by the Center for Systems Science and Engineering*. CSSE.

Darko, A., & Chan, A. P. (2016). Critical analysis of green building research trend in construction journals. *Habitat International*, *57*, 53–63. doi:10.1016/j.habitatint.2016.07.001

Darko, A., Chan, A. P., Adabre, M. A., Edwards, D. J., Hosseini, M. R., & Ameyaw, E. E. (2020). Artificial intelligence in the AEC industry: Scientometric analysis and visualization of research activities. *Automation in Construction*, *112*, 103081. doi:10.1016/j.autcon.2020.103081

Darko, A., Chan, A. P., Huo, X., & Owusu-Manu, D.-G. (2019). A scientometric analysis and visualization of global green building research. *Building and Environment*, *149*, 501–511. doi:10.1016/j.buildenv.2018.12.059

Davarpanah, M., & Aslekia, S. (2008). A scientometric analysis of international LIS journals: Productivity and characteristics. *Scientometrics*, *77*(1), 21–39. doi:10.100711192-007-1803-z

El Baz, J., & Ruel, S. (2020). Can supply chain risk management practices mitigate the disruption impacts on supply chains' resilience and robustness? Evidence from an empirical survey in a COVID-19 outbreak era. *International Journal of Production Economics*, 107972.

Ellegaard, O., & Wallin, J. A. (2015). The bibliometric analysis of scholarly production: How great is the impact? *Scientometrics, 105*(3), 1809–1831.

Fahimnia, B., Pournader, M., Siemsen, E., Bendoly, E., & Wang, C. (2019). Behavioral operations and supply chain management–a review and literature mapping. *Decision Sciences, 50*(6), 1127–1183.

Feng, Y., Zhu, Q., & Lai, K.-H. (2017). Corporate social responsibility for supply chain management: A literature review and bibliometric analysis. *Journal of Cleaner Production, 158*, 296–307.

Garcia-Buendia, N., Moyano-Fuentes, J., Maqueira-Marín, J. M., & Cobo, M. (2020). 22 Years of Lean Supply Chain Management: A science mapping-based bibliometric analysis. *International Journal of Production Research*, 1–21.

Gatto, A., Drago, C., & Ruggeri, M. (2022). On the Frontline—A bibliometric Study on Sustainability, Development, Coronaviruses, and COVID-19. *Environmental Science and Pollution Research International*, 1–17.

Golan, M. S., Jernegan, L. H., & Linkov, I. (2020). Trends and applications of resilience analytics in supply chain modeling: Systematic literature review in the context of the COVID-19 pandemic. *Environment Systems & Decisions, 40*, 222–243.

Golinelli, D., Nuzzolese, A. G., Boetto, E., Rallo, F., Greco, M., Toscano, F., & Fantini, M. P. (2020). *The impact of early scientific literature in response to COVID-19: a scientometric perspective*. MedRxiv.

Haghani, M., & Bliemer, M. C. (2020). Covid-19 pandemic and the unprecedented mobilisation of scholarly efforts prompted by a health crisis: Scientometric comparisons across SARS, MERS and 2019-nCov literature. *Scientometrics, 125*(3), 2695–2726.

Haghani, M., Bliemer, M. C., Goerlandt, F., & Li, J. (2020). The scientific literature on Coronaviruses, COVID-19 and its associated safety-related research dimensions: A scientometric analysis and scoping review. *Safety Science, 129*, 104806.

He, K., Zhang, J., & Zeng, Y. (2019). Knowledge domain and emerging trends of agricultural waste management in the field of social science: A scientometric review. *The Science of the Total Environment*, *670*, 236–244.

Herrera-Franco, G., Montalván-Burbano, N., Carrión-Mero, P., Jaya-Montalvo, M., & Gurumendi-Noriega, M. (2021). Worldwide Research on Geoparks through Bibliometric Analysis. *Sustainability*, *13*(3), 1175.

Hosseini, M., & Gordijn, B. (2020). A review of the literature on ethical issues related to scientific authorship. *Accountability in Research*, *27*(5), 284–324.

Hosseini, M. R., Maghrebi, M., Akbarnezhad, A., Martek, I., & Arashpour, M. (2018). Analysis of citation networks in building information modeling research. *Journal of Construction Engineering and Management*, *144*(8), 04018064.

Hosseini, S., & Ivanov, D. (2020). Bayesian networks for supply chain risk, resilience and ripple effect analysis: A literature review. *Expert Systems with Applications*, *161*, 113649.

Huang, C.-F. (2019). Evaluation of system reliability for a stochastic delivery-flow distribution network with inventory. *Annals of Operations Research*, *277*(1), 33–45.

Hudecheck, M., Sirén, C., Grichnik, D., & Wincent, J. (2020). How companies can respond to the Coronavirus. *MIT Sloan Management Review*.

Huff, A. G., Beyeler, W. E., Kelley, N. S., & McNitt, J. A. (2015). How resilient is the United States' food system to pandemics? *Journal of Environmental Studies and Sciences*, *5*(3), 337–347.

Iqbal, M., Ahmad, N., Waqas, M., & Abrar, M. (2021). COVID-19 pandemic and construction industry: Impacts, emerging construction safety practices, and proposed crisis management. *Brazilian Journal of Operations & Production Management*, *18*(2), 1–17.

Iqbal, M., Ma, J., Ahmad, N., Ullah, Z., & Hassan, A. (2022). Energy-Efficient supply chains in construction industry: An analysis of critical success factors using ISM-MICMAC approach. *International Journal of Green Energy*, 1–19.

Iqbal, M., Ma, J., Ullah, Z., Ahmad, N., Ibrahim, M., Waqas, M., & Ahmad, M. (2022). Identifying Lockdown Relaxation Strategies and Policy Implications to Fight against COVID-19: Medical Experts Perspective from Pakistan. *Social Work in Public Health*, 1–22.

Ivanov, D. (2020). Predicting the impacts of epidemic outbreaks on global supply chains: A simulation-based analysis on the coronavirus outbreak (COVID-19/ SARS-CoV-2) case. *Transportation Research Part E, Logistics and Transportation Review*, *136*, 101922.

Ivanov, D., & Dolgui, A. (2020). Viability of intertwined supply networks: Extending the supply chain resilience angles towards survivability. A position paper motivated by COVID-19 outbreak. *International Journal of Production Research*, *58*(10), 2904–2915.

Kagan, D., Moran-Gilad, J., & Fire, M. (2020). Scientometric trends for coronaviruses and other emerging viral infections. *GigaScience, 9*(8), giaa085.

Kleinberg, J. M. (1999). Hubs, authorities, and communities. *ACM Computing Surveys*, *31*(4es), 5.

Kumar, S., & Chandra, C. (2010). Supply chain disruption by avian flu pandemic for US companies: A case study. *Transportation Journal*, *49*(4), 61–73.

Laengle, S., Lobos, V., Merigó, J. M., Herrera-Viedma, E., Cobo, M. J., & De Baets, B. (2021). Forty years of fuzzy sets and systems: A bibliometric analysis. *Fuzzy Sets and Systems*, *402*, 155–183.

Lan, W., & Hou, X. (2022). *How Physical Activity Affects The Health Of College Students During Covid-19 Pandemic-Based On Citespace Analysis.* Paper presented at the 2022 3rd Asia Sport Science Conference (ASSC).

Li, Y., Xu, Z., Wang, X., & Wang, X. (2020). A bibliometric analysis on deep learning during 2007–2019. *International Journal of Machine Learning and Cybernetics*, *11*(12), 2807–2826.

Liu, H., Liu, Y., Wang, Y., & Pan, C. (2019). Hot topics and emerging trends in tourism forecasting research: A scientometric review. *Tourism Economics*, *25*(3), 448–468.

Lockamy, A. III. (2014). Assessing disaster risks in supply chains. *Industrial Management & Data Systems.*

Martínez-López, F. J., Merigó, J. M., Valenzuela-Fernández, L., & Nicolás, C. (2018). Fifty years of the European Journal of Marketing: A bibliometric analysis. *European Journal of Marketing.*

McMaster, M., Nettleton, C., Tom, C., Xu, B., Cao, C., & Qiao, P. (2020). Risk management: Rethinking fashion supply chain management for multinational corporations in light of the COVID-19 outbreak. *Journal of Risk and Financial Management*, *13*(8), 173.

Mohan, U., Viswanadham, N., & Trikha, P. (2009). Impact of Avian Influenza in the Indian poultry industry: A supply chain risk perspective. *International Journal of Logistics Systems and Management*, *5*(1-2), 89–105.

Noruzi, A., Gholampour, B., Gholampour, S., Jafari, S., Farshid, R., Stanek, A., & Saboury, A. A. (2022). Current and Future Perspectives on the COVID-19 Vaccine: A Scientometric Review. *Journal of Clinical Medicine*, *11*(3), 750.

Oke, A., & Gopalakrishnan, M. (2009). Managing disruptions in supply chains: A case study of a retail supply chain. *International Journal of Production Economics*, *118*(1), 168–174.

Okolie, C. C., & Ogundeji, A. A. (2022). Effect of COVID-19 on agricultural production and food security: A scientometric analysis. *Humanities and Social Sciences Communications*, *9*(1), 1–13.

Ozdemir, D., Sharma, M., Dhir, A., & Daim, T. (2022). Supply chain resilience during the COVID-19 pandemic. *Technology in Society*, *68*, 101847.

Pang, X. (2022). *COVID-19 in Genomics: A Bibliometric Analysis*. Authorea Preprints.

Patil, S. (2020). *A scientometric analysis of global COVID-19 research based on dimensions database*. Available at SSRN 3631795.

Pendell, D. L., Leatherman, J. C., Schroeder, T. C., & Alward, G. S. (2007). The economic impacts of a foot-and-mouth disease outbreak: a regional analysis. *Journal of Agricultural and Applied Economics, 39*, 19-33.

Pfefferbaum, B., & North, C. S. (2020). Mental health and the Covid-19 pandemic. *The New England Journal of Medicine*, *383*(6), 510–512.

Queiroz, M. M., Ivanov, D., Dolgui, A., & Wamba, S. F. (2020). Impacts of epidemic outbreaks on supply chains: Mapping a research agenda amid the COVID-19 pandemic through a structured literature review. *Annals of Operations Research*, 1–38.

Raj, A., Mukherjee, A. A., de Sousa Jabbour, A. B. L., & Srivastava, S. K. (2022). Supply chain management during and post-COVID-19 pandemic: Mitigation strategies and practical lessons learned. *Journal of Business Research, 142*, 1125–1139.

Ramos-Rodríguez, A. R., & Ruíz-Navarro, J. (2004). Changes in the intellectual structure of strategic management research: A bibliometric study of the Strategic Management Journal, 1980–2000. *Strategic Management Journal, 25*(10), 981–1004.

Ranganathan, C., & Balasubramani, R. (2014). Scientometric profile of research activities on green energy: An Indian perspective. *International Journal of Research in Applied Natural and Social Sciences, 2*(1), 23–30.

Ruiz-Rosero, J., Ramirez-Gonzalez, G., Williams, J. M., Liu, H., Khanna, R., & Pisharody, G. (2017). Internet of things: A scientometric review. *Symmetry, 9*(12), 301.

Sahoo, S., & Pandey, S. (2020). Evaluating research performance of Coronavirus and Covid-19 pandemic using scientometric indicators. *Online Information Review*.

Sarkis, J. (2020). Supply chain sustainability: Learning from the COVID-19 pandemic. *International Journal of Operations & Production Management*.

Sawik, T. (2022). Stochastic optimization of supply chain resilience under ripple effect: A COVID-19 pandemic related study. *Omega, 109*, 102596.

Sheng, M., Zhou, J., Song, B., & Wang, E. (2022). *Knowledge Domain and Emerging Trends in Internet-based diagnosis and treatment services: A Scientometric Review Based on CiteSpace V Analysis*. Academic Press.

Singanayagam, A., Patel, M., Charlett, A., Bernal, J. L., Saliba, V., Ellis, J., ... Gopal, R. (2020). Duration of infectiousness and correlation with RT-PCR cycle threshold values in cases of COVID-19, England, January to May 2020. *Eurosurveillance, 25*(32), 2001483.

Sinha, P., Kumar, S., & Chandra, C. (2023). Strategies for ensuring required service level for COVID-19 herd immunity in Indian vaccine supply chain. *European Journal of Operational Research, 304*(1), 339–352.

Sombultawee, K., Lenuwat, P., Aleenajitpong, N., & Boon-itt, S. (2022). COVID-19 and Supply Chain Management: A Review with Bibliometric. *Sustainability, 14*(6), 3538.

Spieske, A., Gebhardt, M., Kopyto, M., & Birkel, H. (2022). Improving resilience of the healthcare supply chain in a pandemic: Evidence from Europe during the COVID-19 crisis. *Journal of Purchasing and Supply Management*, 100748.

Su, H.-N., & Lee, P.-C. (2010). Mapping knowledge structure by keyword co-occurrence: A first look at journal papers in Technology Foresight. *Scientometrics*, *85*(1), 65–79.

Tranfield, D., Denyer, D., & Smart, P. (2003). Towards a methodology for developing evidence-informed management knowledge by means of systematic review. *British Journal of Management*, *14*(3), 207–222.

Udara Willhelm Abeydeera, L. H., Wadu Mesthrige, J., & Samarasinghalage, T. I. (2019). Global research on carbon emissions: A scientometric review. *Sustainability*, *11*(14), 3972.

Van Bavel, J. J., Baicker, K., Boggio, P. S., Capraro, V., Cichocka, A., Cikara, M., ... Druckman, J. N. (2020). Using social and behavioural science to support COVID-19 pandemic response. *Nature Human Behaviour*, *4*(5), 460–471.

van Hoek, R., Gibson, B., & Johnson, M. (2020). Talent Management For a Post-COVID-19 Supply Chain—The Critical Role for Managers. *Journal of Business Logistics*.

Wang, M., Liu, P., Gu, Z., Cheng, H., & Li, X. (2019). A scientometric review of resource recycling industry. *International Journal of Environmental Research and Public Health*, *16*(23), 4654.

Yalcin, H., Shi, W., & Rahman, Z. (2020). A review and scientometric analysis of supply chain management (SCM). *Operations and Supply Chain Management: An International Journal*, *13*(2), 123–133.

Yu, K. D. S., & Aviso, K. B. (2020). Modelling the economic impact and ripple effects of disease outbreaks. *Process Integration and Optimization for Sustainability*, *4*(2), 183–186.

Zhai, Z., Shan, M., Darko, A., & Le, Y. (2020). Visualizing the Knowledge Domain of Project Governance: A Scientometric Review. *Advances in Civil Engineering*, 2020.

Zhang, S., Wang, Z., Chang, R., Wang, H., Xu, C., Yu, X., ... Cai, Y. (2020). COVID-19 containment: China provides important lessons for global response. *Frontiers of Medicine*, 1–5.

Zhao, L., Tang, Z.-y., & Zou, X. (2019). Mapping the knowledge domain of smart-city research: A bibliometric and scientometric analysis. *Sustainability*, *11*(23), 6648.

Zhao, X. (2017). A scientometric review of global BIM research: Analysis and visualization. *Automation in Construction*, *80*, 37–47.

Chapter 3
Digital Technologies and Supply Chain Management:
Historic, Current, and Future Perspectives

R. M. Ammar Zahid
https://orcid.org/0000-0002-4627-0917
School of Accounting, Yunnan Technology and Business University, China

Muzammil Khurshid
Department of Banking and Finance, University of the Punjab, Gujranwala, Pakistan

Cui Ying
School of Accounting, Yunnan Technology and Business University, China

ABSTRACT

Digital transformation has been called the most important strategic issue for businesses around the world. The recent innovation boom brings together technologies that open up new possibilities for imagining and recreating supply flows. This chapter provides a comprehensive overview of digital transformation, enabling technologies, and the impact on traditional supply chain management (SCM) processes. It starts with the introduction of the SCM, followed by the digital shift and its consequences for organizations. It continues with a more in-depth analysis of digitalization and describes the major waves of technological development and industrial and economic leaps, and relates the most recent changes in the supply chain to these waves. Further, it provides examples and use cases to motivate, excite, and emphasize progress. It describes the difficulties in defining the concept, characteristics, and challenges of current digital supply chain (DSC) management.

DOI: 10.4018/978-1-6684-6663-6.ch003

INTRODUCTION

Several aspects of global life have been impacted by the arrival of digitization in today's fast-paced, unpredictable, and intensely competitive global economy. According to statistics, over ninety percent of internet users have conducted online purchases, and forty percent of firms have used sophisticated technology for big data analytics. In addition, by 2020, 26 billion "things" will be capable of connecting to the "Internet of things" (Hung, 2017). In order to improve customer satisfaction, it would be necessary to address the problems associated with DSC installation, optimization, and development, as well as the need for new management strategies. Although these challenges have been widely addressed by practitioners and are being explored by a growing number of firms (such as DHL and DB), the phenomenon of DSC is still in its infancy in the academic world, and its potential is largely unknown (Büyüközkan & Göçer, 2018). Small enterprises and large organizations depend on supply chain management systems, which describe each stage of the manufacturing process, from the procurement of raw materials to the shipment of completed items to clients. The operations functionality should be optimized for speed and efficiency as part of a well-organized supply chain management system. Supply chain management is more than a technique to save costs or increase productivity inside an organization. Modern supply change management goes beyond these principles by combining a company's activities to improve customer service and boost revenues.

Little research has directly addressed DSC, and the information is still dispersed throughout other domains. Internet of Things (IoT), Big Data (BD), Cloud Computing (CC), and Unmanned Aerial Vehicles (UAV) are just a few of the DSC technological drivers that have been the subject of earlier research. In particular, Majeed and Rupasinghe (2017) studied how IoT may support Industry 4.0 and DSC by simplifying supply chain planning, management, and coordination. Preindl et al. (2020) investigated the impact of Industry 4.0 and digital transformation on supply chain-wide cooperation and decision-making. Moreover, Makris et al. (2019) have investigated how multinational firms in five distinct industries may profit from the transition to Supply Chain 4.0. BD and predictive analytics have increased supply chain visibility, robustness, resilience, and organizational performance. The use of cloud computing inside the supply chain is another topic that has received little theoretical or practical investigation, despite its similarity to the digital technologies outlined above. (Gunasekaran et al., 2017). Few empirical studies on this issue have been undertaken, but those that have tended to focus on the characteristics that led to the broad adoption of cloud computing (Manuel Maqueira et al., 2019; Wu et al., 2013) and the implications of cloud computing on the supply chain (Teuteberg, 2015). Cloud computing facilitates the expansion of supply networks and enhances the efficacy and flexibility of supply chain activities (Giannakis et al., 2019; Teuteberg, 2015).

The emergence of the digital age has drastically transformed the business in recent decades. These processes were difficult, sluggish, disorganized, and filled with physical labor twenty years ago. In the past, the delivery may take up to a month, but now it can be completed in a couple of hours. In the present era of automated systems and immediate communication, supply chain management is in high demand owing to the ease and efficacy it provides to the administration of a firm. This book and this chapter are particularly helpful in understanding the following questions; how is digital transformation linked to developing a company's supply chain management strategies? What impact will disruptive technologies have on the operations and activities of the supply chain? Will they resemble what we already see, or will they be drastically different? Do managers need new knowledge of SCM, or can they get by with the current one? What game-changing technologies are driving these organizational revolutions? Who is my primary adversary in the increasingly digitalized economy? What impact will the digital transformation have on the skills desired by businesses, the job, and the nature of work?

Figure 1. Containers and Ships at a busy port Source: Homeland security Digital library (hsdl.org)

Traditional Supply Chain Management (SCM)

Supply Chain Management (SCM) is a broad term that incorporates a variety of operations, such as product and service design, demand-supply planning, purchasing, supplier management, manufacturing, asset maintenance, storage, transportation, and customer replenishment. All of these projects have as their major objective and guiding principle the delivery of great customer service in the most time-and cost-efficient way possible. The seven rights that encapsulate this principle informally are: "giving the right product to the right customer at the right time, place, and price" (Bernardes, 2010).

Figure 2 depicts a simplified representation of the companies and key flows inside the supply chain. Typically, the downstream flow of commodities starts with the supplier, goes through the facility, and concludes with the customers. The product return or recycling process is characterized by upstream motion. Typically, financial resources go upstream, although data may travel in either direction. Now, let us take a deeper look at Figure 2, which illustrates a more formal and common approach to analyzing supply chain processes. Our process group began with "Plan", "Source", "Make", and "Deliver." In subsequent revisions, "Design" and "Return" were added to the beginning and end of the procedures.

Figure 2. SCM Processes and Flows (Source: Deloitte (2016)

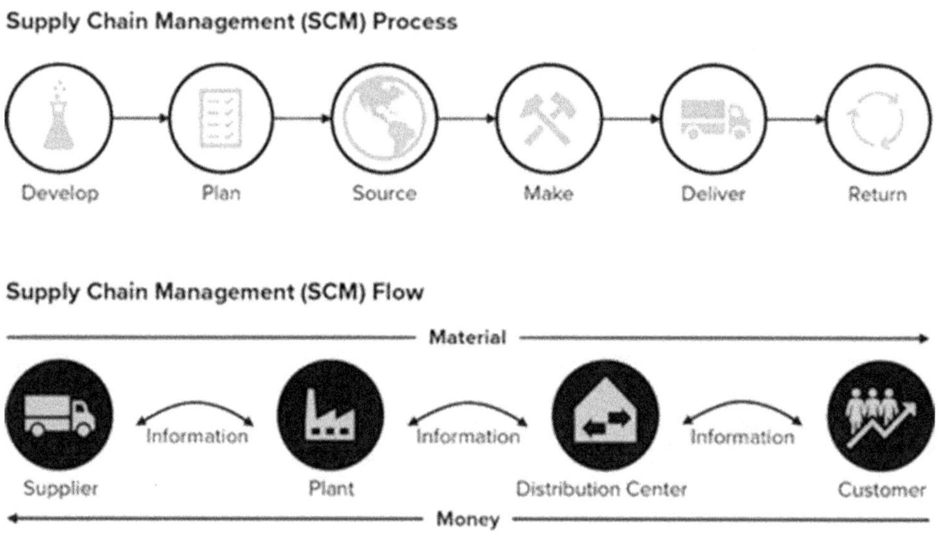

An initial demand forecast is created statistically using sales or shipping data. It is then refined by a consensus process in sales and operations planning (S&OP) with input from the sales, marketing, supply chain, and finance departments. This strategy has been useful for reducing expenses and inventories while minimizing risk. It is a multi-step process that may take some time and involves extensive planning. Consensus is formed at lower levels of detail, leading to increasing detail levels in planning and execution, including the acquisition of resources, transportation, storage, movement, processing, and fulfillment. Information flows from one node to the next, frequently in stages, triggering new decisions and actions; each of these triggers affects a different entity in the supply chain. Sampling-based market research is frequently the amount to which customers are involved in product development to gain an insight into requirements and trends. Traditional consumer communication has been notoriously slow and has concentrated on shaping demand. Before a client makes a purchase or enters a business, the goal has always been to verify stock levels.

Managing the risks associated with every link in the supply chain requires a rigorous planning and action approach. Maintaining a stock of goods is a popular corporate strategy since it helps to manage risk, eliminate shortages, and prevent income loss. A typical worldwide enterprise may have hundreds or even thousands of customers, hundreds of suppliers, and dozens of distribution locations and production sites. In addition to managing thousands of raw materials, thousands of semi-finished and finished goods, and tens of thousands of additional maintenance products, management requires tens of thousands of additional maintenance products. Modern supply chains are not just longer and more complex than ever before, but they also present new layers of uncertainty and risk for businesses and their executives.

In the current business world, a company's profitability and customer satisfaction depend on its ability to manage the movement of products and services across its various locations. How can supply chain management improve customer service, reduce operating costs, and increase a company's bottom line?

Customer Service Improvements

- Satisfied consumers' need for on-time delivery of the proper volume and range of items. If a customer buys five books from eBay, but only three arrive, one is the incorrect book, and two are missing, they are likely to be dissatisfied with the service, leave a poor review, and be deterred from making future purchases at eBay.
- Products must be available and stored in the appropriate location. If your car requires new brake pads, but the auto shop cannot immediately replace them due to a lack of stock, you will not be happy with your service.

- Rapid post-sale help is vital. There is a considerable probability of customer discontent if a heating unit offered by an appliance merchant with a warranty fails in subfreezing temperatures.

Reduce Operating Costs

- Retailers depend on supply networks to expeditiously deliver expensive commodities so that they do not have to store excessive stockpiles, which increases expenses.
- Even a day's delay in manufacturing may cost a company tens of thousands of dollars. Consequently, it is crucial to reduce production costs. This emphasizes the need for the efficient supply chain management. With consistent material delivery to assembly plants, manufacturing delays and their related expenses may be minimized.
- Effective supply chain management is vital for wholesale manufacturers and retailer suppliers to establish a network that delivers customer service goals at the lowest possible cost. The consequence is a competitive edge for businesses.

Strengthening Financial Situation

- Companies greatly appreciate supply chain managers' capacity to oversee and minimize supply chain expenses.
- Supply chain managers limit using expensive fixed assets such as factories, storage facilities, and delivery vehicles.
- Supply chain management may boost a company's cash flow by accelerating the delivery of products to customers.

SUPPLY CHAIN MANAGEMENT: ADVANCES FROM HISTORY

The present state of the art in supply chain management is the result of advancements in technology, managerial techniques, and other aspects of the supply chain. This process began in the 1960s and is characterized by the increasing integration of hitherto separate activities and responsibilities (Stock, 2013). Figure 3 depicts the development toward ever-wider arcs of integration. Before the 1950s, "logistics" was a common term in business language. It was often used for military tasks such as procurement, maintenance, and transfer of military facilities, equipment, and people (Ballou, 2006). Managing financial trade-offs and enjoying the benefits of on-time delivery of specific things were not seen as essential by most businesses. Most businesses organize the duties involved with supply chain management disorganizedly.

Figure 3. Advances in Supply Chain Management (SCM)
(Source: Ballou, 2006)

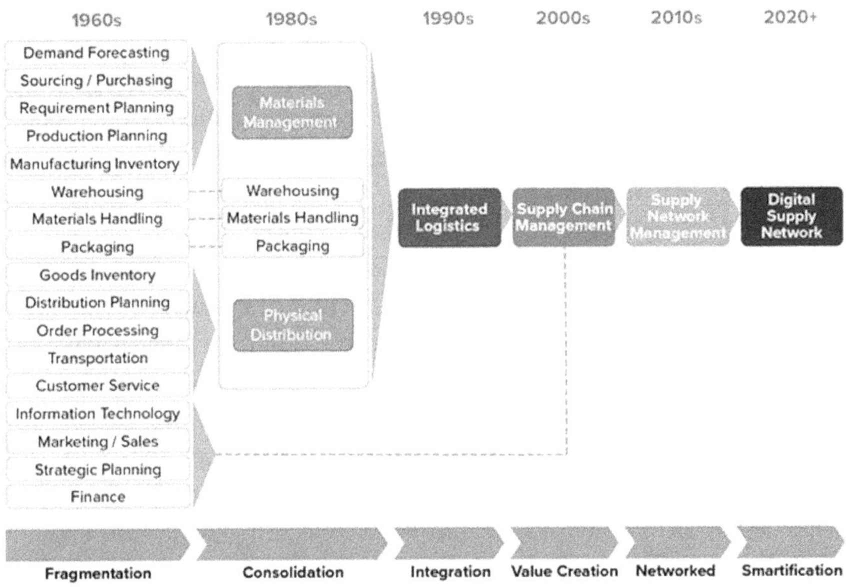

In the 1960s, the integration of historically distinct functional domains started in earnest. How senior management perceived the contribution of the physical distribution department changed significantly (La Londe et al., 1976). Thanks to the support of trade organizations, the trade press, the government, and academics, a new body of literature on management philosophy have emerged, and creative businesses have begun to adopt a more holistic approach to the sector. Near the middle of the decade, the scope was expanded to include physical supply, while it had previously solely covered the outbound conveyance of goods (Ballou, 2006). Since the railroad era, when its major focus was on buying, the purchasing profession has expanded to encompass inbound responsibilities associated with physical distribution. There was a lack of communication between the operations and production departments and the purchasing department. Operations and manufacturing incorporated logistical chores as a product function, but corporations did not pay enough attention to the whole flow. Engineers created Material Needs Planning I (MRP I) to manage the purchasing and replenish interdependent materials.

Due to the disconnected and poorly integrated nature of employment, suboptimization, inefficiency, waste, and other management concerns often develop. Initially, purchasing and business logistics professionals from opposing sides of the company's distribution process worked to accomplish functional consolidation. During the 1970s and 1980s, the distribution activity was separated into materials management (focused on the outward flow of supplies) and physical distribution as the scope and impact of a systems-based approach to the industry developed (more oriented toward the outbound movement of goods). However, management does not see material flow as a cohesive task, instead focusing on ensuring that all of its subfunctions are coordinated. MRP systems expand to include more production processes, such as demand, financial forecasts, and business planning. ERP finally replaced MRP in manufacturing (MRP II).

In the 1980s, several companies substantially reduced their inventory levels as management grew more concerned with ensuring a consistent supply of resources. However, this endeavor was mostly kept inside the four walls of the industrial organization, with the entering and outgoing material flow following a batching logic. In the 1990s, these early efforts at functional integration continued, and the focus of management switched to comprehensive internal integration. Integrated logistics is a method of conceptually grouping the activities involved in controlling the flow of products. The increasing use of enterprise resource planning (ERP) has expanded the scope of MRP to encompass administrative functions like payroll and human resources. These systems have advanced to the point where they combine numerous once distinct functions into a single, coherent system, simplifying operations and information for users inside and outside the organization. As electronic automation ended, the top management started implementing cutting-edge information and communication technologies into the material flow. The supply chain as a whole, as opposed to a single firm, has become the focus of greater efforts to control and stabilize the flow of materials. The most significant effects of these measures were improved customer service, reduced inventory, and lower operating expenditures.

At the start of the new century, the continued use of cutting-edge information and communication technologies made full integration conceivable. Supply chain management has grown in popularity. Technology development has made the integration and coordination of material, informational, and monetary flows possible. With their production and distribution techniques, businesses started to go into unknown areas, and the trend swiftly spread globally. Supply chain management has developed into a complex procedure for creating and extracting value. Supply chain or system-level optimization had become a major component of management theory at that time. Businesses have started devoting an ever-increasing amount of resources to useless efforts to anticipate and control their complicated supply networks. It is recognized that supply chain management is an essential business tool (Bernardes, 2010). The well-known Supply Chain Operations Reference (SCOR) model posits that all companies have planning, sourcing, developing, and delivering processes that link suppliers and customers to manufacturers, demonstrating the strategic importance of integration for practitioners (Frohlich & Westbrook, 2001). The dynamic and intricate structure of supply networks posed difficulties for management, rapidly realizing that changes at the tertiary supplier level (e.g., second and third tiers) are usually outside their administrative purview and control. Ahead of its time, scholars presented a conceptual model of the supply chain as a complex adaptive system, which more accurately captures the system's underlying complexity and dynamism (Choi et al., 2001). Throughout the 2010s, this strategy sparked a wealth of research with major implications for management, and the concept and insights are advancing with the arrival of new data analysis technologies.

Physical distribution and material management have been progressively mechanized since the early phases of the digital robotization wave (Figure 3). In its infancy, digitalization provided companies with tremendous value and competitive benefits. For instance, the automation of distribution center storage, material handling, and packaging has made significant gains in recent years. The conventional management paradigm largely relies on linear logic to comprehend the action as a whole. Since the plan has typified the emergence of supply chain management, the modern school of management, source, manufacture, deliver, and return model has benefitted managers and businesses.

Nonetheless, as the robotization trend advances, innovations and disruptive technologies give rise to new opportunities for rethinking the existing approaches to managing the adaptive supply chain's complexity. Progressive businesses are exploring uncharted ground and achieving amazing achievements. Digital supply networks that are intelligent, always-on, always-connected, real-time, and dynamically flexible are becoming increasingly prevalent (Mussomeli, 2019).

Digital And Technological Driven Change In Industry And Economy

The phrase "digital revolution" refers to the rethinking and redesigning whole value-creating business processes using new digital technologies. When organizations undergo a digital transformation, they are better equipped to satisfy the requirements of their customers by developing and providing innovative products and services at competitive rates. With proper optimization, productivity may reach new heights and waste can be almost eliminated.

Implementing Enterprise Resource Planning (ERP) systems, using industrial robots, digital sketching, customized planning systems, and electronic data sharing are examples of how the supply chain has been more digitized during the last two decades. The current wave of digital transformation will bring about new organizational structures, a more human-centered workplace, a more contented workforce, record-breaking value for consumers, and a better planet. At the same time, it will wreak havoc on the global order since it requires quite different skill sets, might force many people out of the workforce, and could exacerbate inequality. In addition to driving and consolidating markets and industries, it will also render conventional corporate management techniques and traditional organizations obsolete as a danger to the growing generation of digitally enabled enterprises.

Every epoch in modern history has witnessed at least one wave of revolutionary technological development, each of which has had far-reaching implications for people's daily lives, workplaces, and interpersonal relationships. Figure 4 depicts these tidal waves of technological innovation and industrial advances. It also highlights how leaders have merged technology and ideas to create new kinds of value, from "machines replacing muscles" to "machines replacing and augmenting human minds." Each tsunami ushered in dramatic changes to industrial techniques, economies, and social norms. The final result was a more equitable distribution of wealth, a change in political power reflecting economic shifts; new state policies in response to the needs of a changing society; new social trends such as urbanization and the development of labor movements; and new cultural manifestations. Due to the current wave of upheavals, new, inventive techniques for managing the supply chain and its flow of commodities are developing. Let us briefly explore some significant aspects of earlier waves and then situate the growing model in its current stage so that you can better comprehend its scope and significance.

Figure 4. Waves of Technological and Economic Progress
(Source: Sinha et al., 2021)

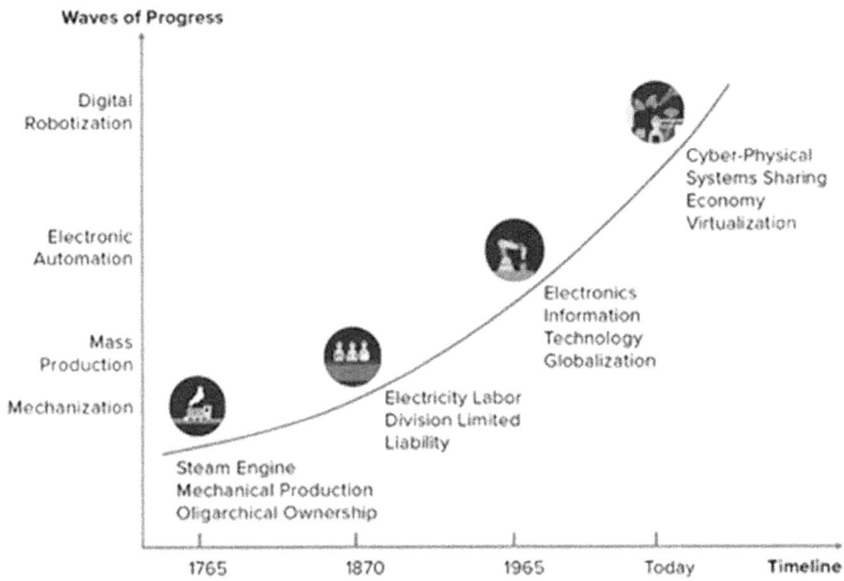

Mechanization

In the late 18th and early 19th centuries, the first swell mostly affected the United Kingdom. During this period, water and steam power enabled the automation of industry. Coal and the steam engine enabled the construction of the railroad system, forging the first industries and urban areas feasible. Due to technology, the agricultural sector of the economy is no longer the backbone of contemporary society. Cities have evolved into industrial hubs connected to other metropolitan centers, suburbs, and rural areas. The available labor force was often unskilled and cheap. The steam-powered printing press enabled universal literacy for the first time. There were enormous productivity gains for society, but many artisanal skills and tools from the old economy were lost.

Mass Production

Alternatively, mass production. In the late 19th century, new organizational structures centered on mass production evolved due to the consolidation of research and capital into vast corporate organizations. Labs were the birthplace of science, and scientific notions eventually influenced the organization of manufacturing. The widespread usage of electricity and oil during this period made the invention and development of several technologies feasible, such as the combustion engine, steel, chemical synthesis, automobile, airplane, telegraph, and the telephone. A middle class of professionals emerged during this period. Increasingly, more cities and households have access to electricity. The development of limited-liability firms reduced the risks assumed by sole proprietorships. People and institutions' purchase of common stock transformed the previous oligarchy into more widely dispersed ownership of the means of production. Due to the demands of an increasingly complex industrial society, a number of European governments socialized their economies' major industries.

Electronic Automation

Computational robotics the advent of the transistor and the microprocessor in the second half of the 20th century marked the beginning of the downsizing of electronic components. Due to a demand reduction, digital alternatives have replaced analog and mechanical technologies. Thanks to advancements in space exploration, communications, computers, and robotics, automation and simple digitalization have extended throughout many sectors. In addition to the internet, the semiconductor, the mainframe, and the personal computer were other significant advances during this period. At first glance, nuclear power seemed an excellent alternative to ancient energy-producing techniques. Companies were driven to relocate portions of their value chain to nations with lower labor costs as an alternative to automation and easier access to other manufacturing inputs (Goldsby et al., 2019). The introduction of electronics and information technology ushered in an age of enhanced industry automation and global supply networks. This phase contains the underpinnings of the recognized supply chain management paradigm.

Autonomous Computing

Since the late 20th century, a new generation of technologies has blurred the distinctions between virtual, real, and living. Technology is converging and advancing at an exponential pace, creating broad disruption across all sectors and drastically transforming the global production system and social fabric in ways that cannot be compared to previous waves, which were focused on Western Europe and its offshoots. According to the World Economic Forum, these advancements generate brand-new ways for technology to pervade society and even the human body.

This new wave of technology and industry has the same potential to improve people's lives as previous technological and industrial revolutions. With the assistance of smartphones having unrivaled processing power, storage capacity, and information access, we are on the verge of creating universal connectivity, which, paired with advances in artificial intelligence, opens the door to limitless opportunities. Internet-enabled innovations, such as crowdfunding and peer-to-peer banking, provide economic opportunity to previously disadvantaged populations as the importance of data in production rises. Computational design, additive printing, and other digital manufacturing methods are being integrated with materials engineering and synthetic biology to produce the first instances of microbial-human-product-built symbiosis (Xu et al., 2018). To the advantage of the economy's demand side, connectivity fosters more openness, greater consumer involvement, and brand-new purchasing and consumption patterns. However, the current wave of technological progress has the potential to generate vast inequalities and dramatically alter the labor market more so than in previous periods (Brynjolfsson & McAfee, 2014). Within this wider context of change, the construction of a new paradigm for controlling supply flows is considered because it has the potential to produce significant value, open up new markets, permit whole new ways of serving customers, and stimulate economic growth. Let us compare the present state of supply chain management to its origins.

Digital Supply Chain (DSC): Technology and Components

When faced with a fundamental shift, many top-level executives struggle to do more than stem the flow without initiating substantial organizational changes. Some individuals seek inventive means to get an advantage. As observed, notable companies are attempting to digitalize their supply chain procedures. Several technologies impact DSC tendencies, including sensors, cloud services, nanotechnology, and BD. Numerous significant digital technology breakthroughs offer great promise for the future of supply networks. Eight primary supporting technologies facilitate the shift to digital supply networks. As seen in Figure 5. DSC utilizes the individual strengths and capabilities of technologies and can better adapt to the ever-changing infrastructure that supports its digital core. The technologies that make this feasible will be described in depth in the next section.

Figure 5. DSC Empowering Technologies (Source: Authors complied)

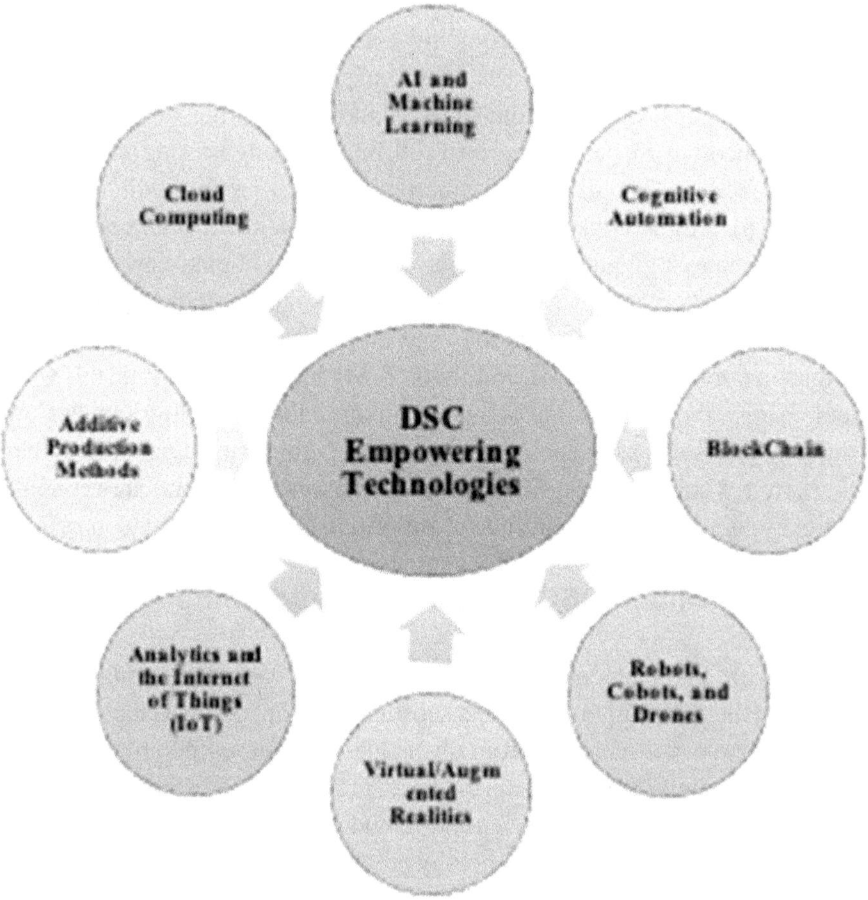

Artificial Intelligence

The purpose of artificial intelligence is to imbue machines and machines with intelligence equivalent to that of humans. The use of machine learning algorithms, which rely on pattern recognition algorithms to analyze data and translate it into real-time insights, can streamline tactical planning and automate decision-making. By examining historical and current data, machine learning can improve sourcing insights and the efficiency of the procure-to-pay process, for example. Utilize this to increase the efficiency of your operations and decrease inefficient manual work. Through the application of robotic process automation (RPA), artificial intelligence and machine learning may make slow but steady progress.

Conceptualization of Cloud Computing

The phrase "cloud computing" refers to a collection of network-based technologies that enable network access on demand to a shared pool of programmable system resources and services (Deloitte, 2016). In other words, cloud technologies utilize digital infrastructure to deliver quick and accessible data access (Ratten, 2015). With so many databases participating in a DSC, it is essential to have a method for consolidating and analyzing data. As systems become more sophisticated, systems that can simultaneously receive information from multiple nodes and store it in a centralized location become increasingly crucial. As planning becomes more dynamic, cloud computing enables rapid and accurate decision-making by providing real-time performance information. It also provides an environment for ERP applications to include the DSN seamlessly.

Additive Production Methods (3D Printing)

Additive manufacturing, often known as 3D printing, may produce physical replicas of 3D models developed digitally (Deloitte, 2016). This innovation unlocks previously unrealized value in the design, production, and distribution processes. This model-based design considerably improves production potential since digital information threads may be exchanged instantaneously and regardless of location. In addition, additive manufacturing enhances the quality of the first-time yield through virtual testing of designs before virtual prototyping, reducing the overall cost and increasing the likelihood of the prototype's success. By utilizing additive manufacturing techniques, businesses may eliminate stringent production conditions from their supply chains.

Analytics and the Internet of Things (IoT)

The Internet of Things (IoT) is a network of sensors, actuators, and other devices that collect and analyze data to disclose previously unattainable insights and alter industries such as retail and manufacturing. Three essential components of an end-to-end IoT system: sensors, a data platform, and an analytics tool. Sensors collect data in real-time and transmit it to the data platform for storage. The analytics tool mines the platform for data, which it then analyses and makes conclusions. After acquiring such information, "informed" acts are carried out in the real world. This is the digital-to-physical feedback loop of the Internet of Things in operation. Building an "always on" physical-digital-physical closed-loop supply chain demands a robust IoT platform.

Realities, Virtual and Augmented

Augmented and virtual reality (AR/VR), a combination of AR, VR, 360-degree films, and other immersive technologies, is a significant enabler in the rapidly emerging field of mixed reality (Fitzgerald, 2018). It uses data from multiple sources (sensors, cameras, etc.) to create a digital representation of the real environment. The user may then utilize a combination of gestures, voice commands, and gazes to interact with the new world (Deloitte, 2016). Even though these numerous types of virtual reality share a common thread, they differ significantly.

Robots, Cobots, and Drones

In today's industries, there are three sorts of robotic enabling technology. The first group consists of "robots," which are autonomous or semi-autonomous devices trained to perform a certain task (like the "pick and place" robots used to seal bottles on an assembly line). Cobots comprise the second classification. Cobots, or collaborative robots, are machines that work alongside people. Cobots, or collaborative robots, are machines that combine advanced robotic technology with human mobility to accomplish activities previously handled by people, such as component quality inspection on the manufacturing floor. Drones are the most recent type of robot to enter the supply chain industry. The introduction of Amazon Prime Air has helped expand awareness of their concept. These UAVs can fly with a significant degree of autonomy from human control.

Blockchain

Blockchain is a distributed, public ledger that efficiently and permanently records and verifies transactions between two parties. It encourages cooperation among competitive and unreliable supply chain participants to enhance efficiency. Smart blockchain contracts enable the establishment and automated execution of transactions on decentralized networks, giving a permanent, verifiable, and time-stamped record of all interactions (Killmeyer, 2019).

The change of the current supply chain from a linear and segmented system to a digital supply network will be driven by distributed ledger technology (Blockchain). As sensors and the Internet of Things proliferate, supply networks will become more interconnected, with blockchain functioning as the connecting tissue. Due to the importance of product movement in supply chains, blockchain is best utilized in asset management applications such as tracking, tracing, and discovery. This capability can be expanded for use in other contexts requiring real-time data visibility and data protection via secure sharing; doing so can help organizations achieve broader strategic objectives by facilitating the integration of formerly siloed areas such as supply chain, finance, human capital, and information technology.

Cognitive Automation

Cognitive automation enables the seamless integration of data from multiple sources in real-time, producing actionable insights that can be used to augment the skills of both humans and robots. Cognitive automation is, in a nutshell, the application of intelligence to jobs that significantly rely on processing information. It can comprehend issues of natural language, reasoning, and judgment (Mussomeli, 2019). Cognitive intelligence ranges from extremely simple examples of predictive intelligence, such as autofill, to complicated examples of artificial intelligence that can operate independently. The four fundamental types of cognitive automation: are artificial intelligence, intelligent automation and analytics, autonomics, and robotic process automation (Deloitte, 2016).

In conclusion, the strength of digital supply chains (DSC) depends on the digital nodes that compose and sustain them. Data must be able to seamlessly connect multiple types of networks (suppliers and distributors), stakeholders (sales and logistics), and formats (structured and unstructured) in order for DSCs to deliver valuable insights. To facilitate this connection, enabling technologies to establish interconnected systems instead of standalone apps or technology bundles.

Digitalization in Supply chain management (DSC)

The influence of digital technology on human connection with the environment has been profound. Technological breakthroughs and personal gadgets, such as mobile devices, computers, self-driving cars, drones, updated television sets, wearable devices, telephones, and smartwatches, transform societies' access to and sharing of information. Each area of the economy is affected by the emergence of new technology. Logistics and supply networks do not provide an exception to this norm. Several customer-facing operations, such as the design and delivery of goods, are undertaken separately in modern organizational structures. In conventional supply chains, facilities are deliberately positioned across an area to establish and maintain transit links between nodes. Coordination, planning, and management of products and services between suppliers and customers constitute the supply chain's backbone. Due to technological improvements, many institutional frameworks can no longer operate independently. The ubiquitous digitization that has infiltrated almost every aspect of human activity on the globe has had a dramatic effect on supply chain operations. According to market forecasts by Penthin and Dillman (2015), 76% of the world's population currently has access to the internet, with 50% actively using social media. In addition, nine out of ten internet users make purchases online, and 43 percent of businesses employ sophisticated big data analytics. By 2020, cloud storage will hold around 37% of all data. Within the same time range, there will be 26 billion online and useable "things." In addition to producing value and network effects, digitization generates sector-wide disruption. It is feasible that one day a single portable device may be sufficient to handle the logistics of a whole fleet of cars. A short electronic scan might potentially expose the contents of a cargo container. Wearable computers with sleeves are a potential future technology. With so many accessible options, organizations are concentrating on how DSC may help their operations. Due to the necessity of retaining and strengthening core competencies in today's competitive market, innovative enterprises should employ DSC techniques to conduct production and distribution with their dealers.

As the DSC is still in its infancy, the great majority of its untapped potential to generate income will never be fulfilled. Despite this, it has sparked a period of rapid transition and inventive innovation in the logistics and supply chain industries. The new digital architecture substitutes data centers for storage facilities, bits for containers, and bandwidth for transport vehicles. Conventional distribution facilities are being replaced by retailer services, which have been supplanted by broadband providers, which the internet has supplanted, and lastly, by customers themselves. DSC technologies include, but include not limited to, augmented reality, big data, cloud computing, robotics, sensor technology, omnichannel, the internet of things, autonomous cars, uncrewed aerial vehicles, nanotechnology, and 3D printing. Recent publications have highlighted the relevance of DSC, and other researchers from various sectors have studied its possible applications. Identifying the potential benefits of different DSC implementations is time-consuming since most of the value is generated from the many solutions arising from DSC implementations. This paper examines the several ways in which DSC integration might enhance supply chains and logistics. This paper examines current DSC literature and proposes a framework. Past research is compiled and examined critically to summarize the current level of knowledge on the issue. This portion of the study captures the conceptual and theoretical status of research to uncover knowledge gaps in the literature, beginning with comparing and contrasting the main digitalization components and their connection to the DSC. We have made an original contribution to the DSC literature by reviewing previously published approaches' merits, flaws, and limitations. The review's findings reflect the consequences of DSC's management and the review's emphasis on challenges and possibilities. In order to aid future researchers in organizing, conceiving, and carrying out their work on DSC, this study provides a framework by combining existing material and identifying critical biases for the field's further progress.

The rate at which the world is changing is unprecedented, and this is partly attributable to the introduction of new disruptive technologies and their convergence.

Let us use the smartphone, a product that has become omnipresent in modern society, as a simple example. These portable devices are more powerful than the mainframes that commanded the first Apollo space mission in 1969. The pace of technological advancement seems to be accelerating at an exponential rate. Due to digital technology, more has changed in the past five years than in the previous fifty years combined. In addition, market experts anticipate that this trend will continue. This has implications for many industries, civilizations, governments, and continents. The effects of the digital revolution are immediately visible on the financial markets of the globe. Digital upstarts surpass established companies, some of which have existed for more than a century. Consider the 2020 COVID-19 pandemic: firms that had initiated their digital transformation before the outbreak fared better, as did those that promptly launched digital efforts after the epidemic. Even while this change may be unpleasant, the business opportunities for digital transformation to improve existing operations, earn more revenue, start creative new initiatives, and give great value to customers, stakeholders, and society are almost limitless.

A supply chain is a network of enterprises and suppliers formed to produce and distribute a certain product. It represents the procedures required to provide a service to end consumers. Supply chain management is essential since it influences the bottom line and production cycle time. Although the traditional supply chain has its merits, it lacks many qualities necessary to suit the needs of modern enterprises. The typical supply chain comprises distinct operations that interact with one another. DSC converts traditional supply channels into a smooth, unified system by removing the bottlenecks and inefficiencies inherent to these routes. DSC refers to the management of the supply chain, whether the products or services in issue are digital or physical.

As a growing number of senior executives see the good effect digitization may have on their company's bottom line and overall competitive advantage, they are providing their support and actively engaging in digital initiatives. 31 percent of CEOs in 2013 and 23 percent in 2012 backed their firms' digital activities personally. Brown et al. (2013) performed with 850 top-level managers from various industries, locations, and sizes. Every supply chain operation faces a similar obstacle. The localized storage of supply chain data acts as a functional, organizational, and cultural center. Given the greater risk of problems arising at later stages of the supply chain and the limited reaction options, this state impedes effective and efficient collaboration across various supply chain activities (Raj & Sharma, 2014). Numerous sectors are investing significant cash in digitizing their operations and supply networks. Global logistics service providers such as DHL monitor and report on developing trends that may impact the logistics industry.

Additionally, DB Schenker, another provider of shipping services, is sponsoring a digital mobility lab. The airlines THY, Lufthansa, and Emirates have extended their paperless e-freight services to customer data cleaning. The major agricultural, Monsanto, is using ST to digitize its operations. Amazon and Alibaba, two of the world's biggest e-commerce sites, have invested in R & drone technology to enhance their supply chains and customer service.

THE IMPACT OF THE DIGITAL REVOLUTION ON ENTITIES AND SUPPLY CHAINS

The convergence of major technologies such as artificial intelligence, the cloud, robotics, the Internet of Things, additive manufacturing, and blockchain enables the automation of business activities in previously inconceivable ways. There will be a discussion of some of the most powerful enabling technologies, their consequences, and their historical background. In this book chapter, we will address the technology that enables this change, its impacts and the impetus for upending long-standing habits. In the present digital world, businesses are required to offer 24-hour customer service. Let us examine how data and technology are altering the duties of organizations as well as the method in which they interact with their clients.

Effect on Clients

Customers and the value they generate must be the focal point of a digital transformation. In today's digital environment, clients demand a relationship that is more than transactional; they must feel like an integral part of your company's success. Emotions play a significant role in deciding whether a user will become a vociferous brand evangelist, a one-time apathetic buyer, or a dissatisfied customer. By enhancing customer service, automating mundane operations, and using unstructured data (tweets, emails, etc.) connected to customer interactions, companies may leverage digital technology to transform a dissatisfied client into a loyal customer.

Several flights were recently canceled by a major airline due to severe weather. Instead of rearranging passengers on planes according to their priority status, the airline used real-time analytics to analyze passenger sentiments through social media posts. Using this information, the airline recruited agents from many time zones through virtual customer service channels to address the service emergency. It contacted affiliated airlines to identify expedited solutions for the delayed passengers. The intelligent optimization engine developed the optimal individual route plan, which also considered the company's and its partner's demands (a conventional rival). Instead of expressing complaints, hundreds of passengers' tweets expressed thanks and happiness. This resulted in several new consumers and champions for the company.

Effect on Procedure Outcome

In light of the digital revolution, an organization's design, buying, manufacturing, logistics, storage, transportation, and distribution operations have all been rethought. The ability of robots to observe, analyze, act, and improve has the potential to radically change all the parameters of traditional supply chain management. Over time, the organization may transform into a data-driven, insight-driven corporation based on a data foundation.

In the digital age, predictive strategic sourcing and automated transactional procurement are the future of sourcing. By evaluating enormous quantities of procurement data, firms may identify significant suppliers, do spending analysis, and effectively manage individual suppliers, thus enhancing the value of the network. Contracts that are intelligent and automated, made possible by blockchain technology, save indirect costs and revolutionize the contract administration process.

Components of smart manufacturing are resulting in major improvements in manufacturing efficiency, reductions in inventory costs, and quicker product flow in production operations and administration of an organization's manufacturing assets. The use of additive manufacturing methods allows higher product customization, and the application of digital twin technologies streamlines the administration and architecture of a production facility, leading to increased speed, accuracy, and security. Asset availability levels may be obtained using machine learning-based prediction algorithms.

Effects on Information and Technology

With digitization's advent, data's significance has become evident in previously unknown ways. Data-related clichés such as "data are the new oil that drives the digital economy," "data is gold," and "data is the electricity of the twenty-first century" cannot be avoided in contemporary discourse. These statements may seem overblown, yet they accurately represent the importance of data to the current digital revolution. Most digital innovations, such as self-driving automobiles, warehouse robots that carry boxes, and mathematical models that predict consumer behavior, need vast data. This data, acquired from several sources, is examined by machine learning algorithms aided by high-capacity computers to find previously unseen patterns and insights.

Numerous enabling technologies, some of which were covered in this chapter, collaborate with data to allow digital transformation. These advancements make it possible to get insights in real-time, enabling enterprises to make swift and decisive decisions, thus enabling them to adapt to the market more quickly. Technology is an integral part of digital transformation, from AI applications that use neural networks to conduct complex machine learning to physical robots that can imitate complex human activities to automate a production line fully.

Characteristics of DSC

Most of the world's leading firms have excellent supply chain operations, and some argue that commercial rivalry comes down to competition in the marketplace. For instance, Woolworths and Coles, the two largest supermarket chains in Australia, compete with their global rivals regarding high agility, superior service, and cost efficiency. Similarly, the iPad's supply chain involves three countries for manufacturing its semiconductors, two for its assembly, and a third for its monitors; nonetheless, Apple Inc. is headquartered in the United States (Xu, 2014). Recent years have seen a profound shift in supply networks. The days of traditional supply chains just transferring goods from one site to another are over. Modern supply chains include a huge and complex number of processes that must be controlled and monitored. Due to digitalization, the next generation of supply chains may evolve, allowing for more agility and efficiency. In light of the fact that digital solutions are upending traditional supply chains, each DSC has its own set of distinguishing features. Following are eleven of DSC's most critical objectives that will aid in achieving these benefits:

Speed

Companies want their inventory to be available as quickly as needed, and DSC personnel want to move more things in less time. As organizations explore novel ways to accelerate product delivery, the DSC's response to customer requirements is expected to emerge as a major point of differentiation. Amazon's Prime Air and Google's Project Wing are two drone delivery systems developed to deliver things to customers in less than 30 minutes. Even while such speeds are now considered science fiction, DSC will make them possible (Hanifan et al., 2014; Penthin & Dillman, 2015; Raj & Sharma, 2014).

Agility

The emergence of digitalization in supply chains needs the capacity to adjust rapidly and efficiently to changes in demand and supply. Not how things are carried, but how supply network problems are resolved. Natural disasters, diseases like the one in West Africa's Equatorial Zone, and political upheavals like the one in Syria are examples of events that may have a huge influence on society. However, supply chain disruptions may be minimal with planning, suitable measures, and rapid and efficient response to such situations. It is true for normal supply chains, but DSC may dramatically speed things up by using the data it gathers and models more effectively (Hanifan et al., 2014; Schrauf & Berttram, 2016).

Global Connectivity

Due to the internet's globalizing effects, the world has shrunk. Fast delivery of goods and services to clients worldwide is a major objective for many organizations. Businesses need a global supply chain to perform local delivery and responsiveness. It would be inefficient to ship a European-made product to the United States when it is needed there. A significant amount of time and money may be wasted throughout the process. As a consequence, DSC establishes a system in which global hubs may be constructed to efficiently supply items and services locally, as opposed to sending them across the world for a single request (Brown et al., 2013; Hanifan et al., 2014; Rouse, 2016; Schrauf & Berttram, 2016).

Real-Time Inventory

DSC provides the necessary capabilities to monitor real-time stock levels to maintain a constant supply to meet current demand. DSC optimizes warehouse management and constantly monitors stock levels using sensor arrays and other cutting-edge technologies. Regardless of changes in customer preferences, firms must always maintain equilibrium between supply and demand. Since consumers may place orders at any time and location, inventory levels must be monitored in real-time. This does not mean that stock levels at each distribution location should be identical. This indicates that to make wise investments, firms must anticipate customer preferences and demand for goods and services. DSC makes accessible the tools essential for complex analysis (Brown et al., 2013; Geissbauer et al., 2016; Hanifan et al., 2014; Rouse, 2016).

Intelligent

Enablers of the next generation of technology make possible the production of products with sufficient computing capability to permit self-learning and autonomous decision-making based on predefined algorithms. Transparency: In a transparent supply chain, nodes in the system comprehend the actions and desires of other connections and respond accordingly. DSC integrates this trait, facilitating improved decision-making, automated execution, and operational innovation (Hanifan et al., 2014).

Transparency

The supply chain will rapidly become anarchy if information cannot be communicated. By forecasting, modeling the network, developing what-if scenarios, and rapidly adjusting the supply chain in response to changing conditions, DSC may enable businesses to react more proactively to disruptions (Hanifan et al., 2014).

Cost-Effective

The broad use of digital technology has resulted in an overall price reduction. Initially, when deploying new technology, the related investment expenditures may be substantial, but they often diminish with time. DSC is a cost-effective strategy for enterprises because it uses technological enablers, and the supply chain management process employing DSC is cost-effective.

Scalability

Organizations confront a huge uphill fight when attempting to extend or reduce their supply networks to suit variable demand. When digitalization is integrated with conventional supply chains, scalability becomes less of a concern. This allows the replication of processes, optimization, and error detection (Bechtold et al., 2014; Schrauf & Berttram, 2016).

Innovative

DSCs are defined by their inventive nature, which is always open to new ideas and improvements. New technologies seem to be proliferating more rapidly than ever before. If DSC wants to preserve its competitive advantage and strong supply chain performance standards, it must continually seek innovative ways to incorporate these technologies into its operations. Today's cutting-edge technologies are swiftly becoming tomorrow's old antiques. Color TVs have replaced black-and-white ones, and in warehouses, paper and pencils have been replaced with smart glasses, allowing more efficient selection. Technology changes throughout time because innovation is inherent to the creative process. Information is the foundation of a company model that has not changed in a millennium. Similarly to some who claim that a stone tablet is similar to a tablet computer or that an abacus is akin to a supercomputer (Cukier & Mayer-Schoenberger, 2013), many feel that current BD is only an improvement of prior information trends. These are just a few of the countless new uses of DSC in a vast array of settings.

Proactive

DSC takes preventive actions prior to the occurrence of issues. This may be accomplished via problem-solving and prophylactic analysis of possible causes of difficulties. Coordination of these challenges requires considerable skill and preparation. DSC delivers digitally empowered consumers with an effective analytic framework and operational data, as well as proactive solutions to anticipate potential issues.

Eco-friendly

Supply chains have an impact on the environment, but they may be structured to have a positive impact on the environment. Negative publicity, environmental legislation, and public awareness are all possible business disruptors if DSC does not prioritize the environment enough. Finding a traditional supply chain that precisely complies with environmental best practices at each stage is challenging. Next-generation DSC has the potential to broaden the scope of environmentally friendly procedures.

THE BENEFITS, CHALLENGES, AND RESEARCH GAPS OF DSC

Businesses of all sizes should consider acquiring digital organization skills due to the future globalization of supply chain competition. The DSC is essential to the ongoing growth and profitability of global businesses. Consider Google, Amazon, and Apple as examples; each has diversified into several sub-sectors outside of its principal business, relying on the advantages of hardware, software, networks, and the enormous user base and the immense amount of data gathered from the enormous user base. Amazon is the most well-known example of online commerce (Xu, 2014). The biggest online retailer in the world has expanded into several allied industries, such as digital services, software services, cloud computing, mobile phones, e-readers, tablets, payments, television, media, and entertainment. Academics and corporate leaders dedicate substantial resources to these endeavors. However, much work remains in the drive for more effective supply chain organizational models and strategies. Lean supply and lean manufacturing systems, world-class manufacturing, and continuous improvement concepts (Kaizen) are among the inventions spawned by these difficulties (Hines, 2014). However, DSC may be the key to achieving and improving supply chain designs and strategies. The next section will discuss the benefits and downsides of DSC.

Implementing DSC: Obstacles and Concerns

Various problems may develop at various stages of the supply chain. According to Xu (2014), the most challenging aspects of developing DSC are gathering all the essential data from various sources and ensuring its accuracy, as well as developing software architecture and platforms that can use the data to manage and execute the supply chain. With several internal and external partners in the chain, communication will be delayed and error-prone. In addition, the logistics infrastructure may be inadequate, the quality of goods may be difficult to regulate, and the inventory levels may be insufficient to meet the demand. The following are examples of some of the challenges experienced by DSC:

- Inadequate preparation: without a thorough demand strategy or sufficient guidelines and tools
- Collaboration deficiencies: insufficient cooperation with external colleagues and inadequate input from internal functions.
- Demand forecast errors: It is typical to have an unduly optimistic perspective on demand, inventories, production, and other measures.
- Reluctance in information sharing: One of the causes of the data gap is the reluctance of firms to share information.
- The pursuit of a panacea or the conviction that everything will work out.
- Ignorance: inadequate supply chain management education and experience.
- Agility and Flexibility: Inadequate Agility and Flexibility in the Supply Chain.
- Extreme unpredictability as a result of insufficient supply chain management training.
- Over-reliance on a limited number of suppliers in certain global areas.
- Incapable of imagining how digital and analog supply chain management may function together successfully.

DSC's Long-Term Success challenges

Since the end of the automation wave and the introduction of supply chain management as a mainstream management concept, many organizations have aimed to streamline the operations involved in the physical movement inside and between enterprises. This has resulted in several successful projects to digitize diverse operations, making modern supply chains more accountable for our current way of life. Fresh, little pineapples cultivated thousands of miles away in South Africa can be purchased at a reasonable price in the morning at a grocery store in Morgantown, West Virginia, along with a bottle of Australian ginger beer produced in the United Kingdom.

Traditional supply chain management is led by a prevalent sequential and linear logic, with many activities and planning occurring in phases. This poses numerous obstacles for executives and restricts the SCM's potential despite successful integration and early digitization.

In conventional supply chain management, planning is frequently based on historical data and the underlying assumption that the past can serve as a good proxy for the future. Planned ahead of time, and when interruptions or unplanned events occur, teams must work rapidly to recover. Changes in the market necessitate extensive and occasionally painful adjustments, and collaboration occurs on a rigid, difficult-to-modify basis. In execution, scenario planning and optimization data are frequently utilized. Adjusting a plan of action requires time and resources if something unexpected occurs. Most supply chain management is devoted to responding to demand fluctuations, but even the most responsive systems fall short of the ideal. Despite the importance of speed, the supply chain's adaptability is hampered by characteristics such as the sequential pattern of activities and the number of partners with relatively weak ties. Rarely do customers have input on the creation or delivery of the services or items given to them.

Despite advancements, many supply chain operations, such as data purification and correction, extended sequential actions and exchanges across the planning and execution phases, still require significant human engagement. Regardless of the industrial sector, the design of delivery processes remains sluggish and riddled with inefficiencies. Although supplier involvement is now a cornerstone of the innovation activities of modern organizations, their potential is "still restrained and impacted by the sequential nature of operations." Since SCM was first conceptualized as a systems architecture, integration initiatives have made tremendous progress, but the absence of network-wide transparency remains a significant barrier and restriction for enterprises.

DSC's core value lies in its ability to unlock the potential for extraordinary customer satisfaction-enhancing performance. The DSC enables the production of products and services optimized for their target audience's needs, effectively manufactured, and conveniently supplied. Monitoring performance is one of the essential parts of the DSC. This measure may be examined using a range of factors, including on-time order fulfillment, delivery speed, supplier reliability, chain costs, and delays. Although there are obvious benefits to digitizing supply chains, few pioneering businesses have embraced it as routine practice. The digital revolution has not yet touched the world's oldest industry, with one significant exception. This is farming, and Monsanto is leading this transformation. Seventy-two percent of the 2,000 respondents to a recent study anticipate digitalizing their supply chains within five years (Schrauf & Berttram, 2016). The slow rate of DSC adoption may be partially attributable to the fact that neither the workforce nor its stakeholders have adequate knowledge of the advantages of digital technologies. Consequently, the achievement of the following crucial success qualities is needed for the widespread adoption of DSC:

- Real-time visibility that is dynamic, secure, and interactive throughout the supply chain enables enhanced DSC management.
- The constant harmonization of skills inside and beyond geographic boundaries improves supply chain collaboration.
- Distributor congruence: Motivating supply chain partners to increase performance and developing trust (alignment) by ensuring that all parties interests are aligned.
- Integration requires the integration of digital and non-digital supply chains to achieve a consistent and comprehensive image of inventory throughout the organization.
- The sharing features of DSC provide access to sales forecasts and production data.
- Models of operation that have experienced substantial change: The characteristics of products and services may be adjusted rapidly and easily to meet shifting market demands.
- Utilizing advanced analytics and analytical techniques Modern data analysis enhances the capacity for making accurate judgments. To increase demand knowledge and projections and solve previously undiscovered or intractable supply chain concerns. Data analytics, corporate growth, etc.
- The automation of regular jobs enables more seamless interactions between people and machines, which contributes to efficiency increases in operations.
- A fundamental advantage of digital supply chains is encouraging and enabling innovation in designs, operations, and customer interactions.
- Integration of people, processes, and Technology for optimal efficiency.
- Digital plug-and-play capabilities ease setup and reconfiguration, enabling more organizational flexibility.
- Concentrate on the consumer and customization: Through channel-centric supply networks, customized products and services may be distributed.
- Accelerating responses to the maneuvers of competitors, technological advances, and changeable demand and supply signals need improved data and sophisticated analytics.
- The use of predictive analytics inside decision support systems has the potential to enhance both adaptability and reliability.
- An interruption at the finish line: Rapid repurposing of organizational assets ensures supply is in step with fluctuating demand.

Lack of DSCM-Related Research

This section provides some observations on the feasibility of digitalization in supply chains and identifies research gaps on the potential of DSC to solve DSC's benefits and drawbacks. Despite the present rise in interest in the issue due to its great potential and disruptive nature, research on the benefits and limitations of DSC is still in its infancy. As stated in the introduction, technologies like supply chain visibility, big data analytics, the cloud, etc., enable DSC's automation characteristics and enhanced collaboration. DSC enables this digital adaptation of supply chains in response to the cutting edge of the competition. Current research is inadequate to achieve this potential in its entirety. Most research is still undertaken in segregated technology elements that enable DSCs. Although we did not focus on DSC implementation in our study, it is crucial to highlight a shortage of research investigating this process phase.

This literature review uncovers some unanswered issues in the realm of DSC research. The following is a summary of the existing gaps:

A lack of development frameworks may serve as a guide for implementing DSC in an environment with well-defined parameters and instructions. Given that supply chains may be at varying levels of DSC deployment, this would assist managers in determining which stages and locations within supply chains DSC should be implemented. In addition, development frameworks would facilitate the modification of supply chain management methods.

In a DSC context, insufficient resources are available to address supply chain challenges. Direct supplier cooperation (DSC) differs from traditional supply chains. New tools and methodologies for decision-making in a DSC environment must account for characteristics of the digitalized environment, such as the deluge of Big Data (BD) generated by ST and the Internet of Things. DSC will influence various operations, including maintenance, quality, inventory management, production planning, and procurement. There are many administrative and technological hurdles to deploying DSC. The world is experiencing a profound transformation. Businesses are in a state of upheaval and on the verge of a race to digitally transform their supply chains (CapGemini, 2016).

CONCLUSION

Experts in logistics and supply chain management have highlighted the digitalization of the supply chain as a vital research and development area. Before the DSC deployment can be deemed a complete success, there are still many technical, organizational, and strategic obstacles to overcome. Recent research on the implications of technological adoption on the supply chain has begun, but this study must be broadened. The introduction of new skills, project management methodologies, and the creation of an integrated measurement instrument for DSC performance are all crucial new avenues for DSC to explore.

Even in the supply chain, digitization has had a significant influence. It is becoming more evident that transitioning from a traditional supply chain to a Digital Supply Chain (DSC) provides a competitive advantage that may deliver long-term value to firms. A more integrated, productive, and open society is now possible thanks to digitalization. At the tail end of the previous innovation wave, the supply chain's capabilities were developed using information and communication technology; these developments significantly impacted our ability to compete and the quality of our modern lives. The Digital Supply Chain (DSC) helps organizations deliver better customer service and increase their long-term performance by enhancing the supply chain's integration and agility by developing information systems and innovative technology. In light of the expanding theory of DSC and the rising interest of managers in proposals supporting the digital transformation of the supply chain, it is essential to broaden the theoretical and empirical spectrum. Beyond innovative technology implementation research, additional strategic, organizational, and human components are necessary to create a new integrated DSC paradigm. To better understand the process of consumer or supplier integration in the digital transformation and to create a criterion framework for measuring the DSC's performance, more research is needed to develop the configuration of the DSC concerning the organization's strategy, explore new skills in the age of digitalization, propose project management approaches that support digital technologies, etc. The road to change is riddled with peril and unpredictability, but the rewards are not only valuable but necessary for survival. The DSC will focus on customers/consumers, incorporate cutting-edge technology (such as augmented reality, big data, and blockchain), reduce intra- and inter-organizational expenses while increasing business value, and incorporate cutting-edge technology (such as augmented reality, big data, and blockchain). Insecurity and uncertainty are prevalent in response to the current technological advancements. Acknowledging the rising hum of confusion and providing answers to the critical concerns that keep CEOs and supply chain managers up at night. This chapter addresses these issues by providing a comprehensive overview of digital transformation, enabling technologies, the impact on traditional SCM processes; the effect on the workforce and the nature of work; and the strategies that can assist organizations in reaching the promised land while avoiding the pitfalls.

Future research should combine qualitative and quantitative methodological and epistemological perspectives to thoroughly understand DSC-related concerns. These theoretical frameworks consist of technology acceptance models and theory, innovation adoption theory, organizational project management theory, dynamic capacity theory, and stakeholders theory, among others (Positivism, constructivism and pragmatism). Researchers have paid little attention to the digitalization of public supply chains, including public hospitals' supply chains. To help future empirical studies and activities, we have developed a shared theoretical foundation for the digital supply chain. Future research on DSC should concentrate on enhancing organizational efforts through creating conceptual models and theoretical frameworks, as well as case studies, creative practices, and projects.

REFERENCES

Ballou, R. H. (2006). *The evolution and future of logistics and supply chain management*. SciELO Brasil.

Bechtold, J., Kern, A., Lauenstein, C., & Bernhofer, L. (2014). *Industry 4.0-The Capgemini Consulting View*. Capgemnini Consulting.

Bernardes, E. S. (2010). The effect of supply management on aspects of social capital and the impact on performance: A social network perspective. *The Journal of Supply Chain Management*, *46*(1), 45–55. doi:10.1111/j.1745-493X.2009.03185.x

Brown, B., Sikes, J., & Willmott, P. (2013). Bullish on digital: McKinsey global survey results. *The McKinsey Quarterly*, *12*, 1–8.

Brynjolfsson, E., & McAfee, A. (2014). *The second machine age: Work, progress, and prosperity in a time of brilliant technologies*. WW Norton & Company.

Büyüközkan, G., & Göçer, F. (2018). Digital Supply Chain: Literature review and a proposed framework for future research. *Computers in Industry*, *97*, 157–177. doi:10.1016/j.compind.2018.02.010

CapGemini. (2016). *The current and future state of digital supply chain transformation*. GT Nexus.

Choi, T. Y., Dooley, K. J., & Rungtusanatham, M. (2001). Supply networks and complex adaptive systems: Control versus emergence. *Journal of Operations Management*, *19*(3), 351–366. doi:10.1016/S0272-6963(00)00068-1

Cukier, K., & Mayer-Schoenberger, V. (2013). The rise of big data: How it is changing the way we think about the world. *Foreign Affairs*, *92*, 28.

Deloitte. (2016). Industry 4.0 enables the digital transformation of supply chains. Deloitte University Press.

Fitzgerald, J., Cook, A., DeMarinis, T., & Smetana, K. (2018). *Utilizing virtual reality to drive supply chain innovation*. Deloitte Development LLC.

Frohlich, M. T., & Westbrook, R. (2001). Arcs of integration: An international study of supply chain strategies. *Journal of Operations Management*, *19*(2), 185–200. doi:10.1016/S0272-6963(00)00055-3

Geissbauer, R., Weissbarth, R., & Wetzstein, J. (2016). Procurement 4.0: are you ready for the digital revolution. PwC.

Giannakis, M., Spanaki, K., & Dubey, R. (2019). A cloud-based supply chain management system: Effects on supply chain responsiveness. *Journal of Enterprise Information Management*, *32*(4), 585–607. doi:10.1108/JEIM-05-2018-0106

Goldsby, T. J., Zinn, W., Closs, D. J., Daugherty, P. J., Stock, J. R., Fawcett, S. E., & Waller, M. (2019). Reflections on 40 years of the journal of business logistics: From the editors. *Journal of Business Logistics*, *40*(1), 4–29. doi:10.1111/jbl.12208

Gunasekaran, A., Papadopoulos, T., Dubey, R., Wamba, S. F., Childe, S. J., Hazen, B., & Akter, S. (2017). Big data and predictive analytics for supply chain and organizational performance. *Journal of Business Research*, *70*, 308–317. doi:10.1016/j.jbusres.2016.08.004

Hanifan, G., Sharma, A., & Newberry, C. (2014). *The digital supply network: a new paradigm for the supply chain management.* Accenture Global Management Consulting.

Hines, T. (2014). *Supply chain strategies: Demand-driven and customer-focused.* Routledge.

Hung, M. (2017). Leading the iot, Gartner insights on how to lead in a connected world. *Gartner Research*, *1*, 1–5.

Killmeyer, J., & Holdowsky, J. (2019). From siloed to distributed. Blockchain enables the digital supply network. *Deloitte Insights*. https://www2.deloitte.com/us/en/insights/topics/understandin g-blockchain-potential/digital-supply-network-blockchain-ado ption.html

La Londe, B. J., Grabner, J. R., & Robeson, J. F. (1976). Integrated Distribution Systems: a Management Perspective. In P. M. Van Buytenen, M. G. Christopher, & G. S. C. Wills (Eds.), *Business Logistics* (pp. 3–19). Springer US. doi:10.1007/978-1-4613-4379-0_1

Majeed, A. A., & Rupasinghe, T. D. (2017). Internet of things (IoT) embedded future supply chains for industry 4.0: An assessment from ERP-based fashion apparel and footwear industry. *International Journal of Supply Chain Management*, *6*(1), 25–40.

Makris, D., Hansen, Z. N. L., & Khan, O. (2019). Adapting to supply chain 4.0: An explorative study of multinational companies. *Supply Chain Forum: An International Journal*.

Manuel Maqueira, J., Moyano-Fuentes, J., & Bruque, S. (2019). Drivers and consequences of innovative technology assimilation in the supply chain: Cloud computing and supply chain integration. *International Journal of Production Research*, *57*(7), 2083–2103.

Mussomeli, A., Neier, M., Takayama, B., Sniderman, B., & Holdowsky, J. (2019). Building a cognitive digital supply network. *Deloitte Insights*. https://www2.deloitte.com/us/en/insights/focus/industry-4-0/digital-supply-networks-cognitive-automation.html

Penthin, S., & Dillman, R. (2015). *Digital SCM*. Available at: www. BearingPoint. com

Preindl, R., Nikolopoulos, K., & Litsiou, K. (2020). Transformation strategies for the supply chain: The impact of industry 4.0 and digital transformation. *Supply Chain Forum: An International Journal*.

Raj, S., & Sharma, A. (2014). Supply chain management in the cloud. *Accenture Global Management Consulting*, 1-12.

Ratten, V. (2015). Cloud computing technology innovation advances: A set of research propositions. *International Journal of Cloud Applications and Computing*, *5*(1), 69–76. doi:10.4018/ijcac.2015010106

Rouse, M. (2016). *Digital supply chain, Search manufacturing*. http://searchmanufacturingerp. TechTarget. com/definition n/digital-supply-chain? vgnextfmt= print

Schrauf, S., & Berttram, P. (2016). Industry 4.0: How digitization makes the supply chain more efficient, agile, and customer-focused. *Strateg. & Technology*, 1-32.

Sinha, A., Bernardes, E., Calderon, R., & Wuest, T. (2021). *Digital supply networks*. McGraw Hill-Ascent Audio.

Stock, J. R. (2013). Supply chain management: A look back, a look ahead. *Supply Chain Quarterly*, *2*, 22–26.

Teuteberg, A. J. F. (2015). Integrating cloud computing in supply chain processes: A comprehensive literature review. *Journal of Enterprise Information Management*, *28*(6), 872–904. doi:10.1108/JEIM-08-2014-0085

Wu, Y., Cegielski, C. G., Hazen, B. T., & Hall, D. J. (2013). Cloud computing in support of supply chain information system infrastructure: Understanding when to go to the cloud. *The Journal of Supply Chain Management*, *49*(3), 25–41. doi:10.1111/j.1745-493x.2012.03287.x

Xu, J. (2014). *Managing digital enterprise: ten essential topics*. Springer. doi:10.2991/978-94-6239-094-2

Xu, M., David, J. M., & Kim, S. H. (2018). The fourth industrial revolution: Opportunities and challenges. *International Journal of Financial Research*, *9*(2), 90–95. doi:10.5430/ijfr.v9n2p90

Chapter 4
Green-Lean Practices and Production Performance:
Evidence From SMEs of an Emerging Economy

Muhammad Junaid Ahsan
https://orcid.org/0000-0002-5754-8187
University of Pisa, Italy

Rizwan Ahmed
Riphah International University, Pakistan

ABSTRACT

Environmental concerns and sustainability issues have attracted many practitioners and researchers. Still, numerous small- and medium-sized enterprises (SMEs) in emerging economies are reluctant to invest in environmentally friendly practices with a doubt that investment in such practices might lead to negative production performance outcomes. To settle this tension, this study examines the effect of green production practices on production performance and the intervening effect of lean practices between green production practices and production performance. The study employs a quantitative research method where survey-based data were collected from 227 SMEs in an emerging economy: Pakistan. Results unveil that green production practices have a significant positive impact on production performance. The interactive effect indicates a sharp rise in production performance when a firm implements lean practices in the production process. The study helps settle the current confusion among firm managers related to the investment in green and lean practices in the production system.

DOI: 10.4018/978-1-6684-6663-6.ch004

INTRODUCTION

SMEs play an important role in the gross domestic product of many countries (Chen, Li, & Zhang, 2022), for example, 47% in the UK, 44% in the USA, 57% in Australia (Mentis, 2017), and 40% in Pakistan (SMEDA, 2018). Researchers, in manufacturing, have often focused on conventional ways like maximizing cash flow, streamlining management costs, raising the marketing bar, and making everyone a salesperson to increase the profitability of SMEs (Pangboonyanon & Kalasin, 2018). However, in recent years researchers' focus has been shifted towards the contemporary production techniques like waste reduction yet without compromising on quality and acceleration in production (Shukor, Newaz, Rahman, & Taha, 2020). Along with the increase in production performance, a very reason that compelled researchers and businesses to reduce waste is rapid environmental degradation in recent years (Ch'ng, Cheah, & Amran, 2021; Vuong et al., 2021). This reason accompanied by increasing public concentration on 'green' concerns has contributed to the rapid emergence of the environmental problem as one of the most significant study fields in the manufacturing sector (Govindan, Kannan, & Shankar, 2015). Due to the non-green process(es), there will be an increased concentration of CO^2 in the environment that harms the atmosphere as it will increase water vaporization leading to the greenhouse effect. Companies particularly in the manufacturing sector are increasing their employees' awareness of green production and enforcing employees' green behavior through green practices (Roscoe, Subramanian, Jabbour, & Chong, 2019; Yong, Yusliza, Jabbour, & Ahmad, 2019). A synergetic process with green practices constitutes lean practices aiming at the systemic and consistent removal of the waste from the system (Bergmiller & McCright, 2009),. Manufacturing concerns, particularly in SMEs, need to adopt contemporary lean manufacturing and distribution models because these will significantly contribute to environmental protection without raising product prices (Amrina, Hidayatno, & Zagloel, 2021; King & Lenox, 2001; Narwane, Raut, Gardas, Narkhede, & Awasthi, 2022). Lean is an idea of time compression – which means lower emissions – that reveals hidden quality issues and their resolution, thereby leading to cost-effective business processes(Primo, DuBois, de Oliveira, Amaro, & Moser, 2021). In short, a leaner process is often greener in terms of emissions yet maintains profitability which is a win-win for SMEs and stakeholders. Several western countries have significantly achieved a level of green manufacturing that transformed their numerous industrial systems where SMEs have achieved economies of scale by implementing environmentally sustainable activities (Bıçakcıoğlu-Peynirci & Tanyeri, 2020). However, there is much need to study green manufacturing in developing or emerging economies due to less energy efficiency and high carbon emission (Yadav et al., 2020).

For instance, most economies in the South Asian region (Pakistan, India, Bangladesh, Afghanistan, Sri Lanka, Nepal, and Bhutan) are in transition and center of global attention for climate vulnerability due to high dependence on oil and gas imports to meet their energy demands (Hou et al., 2019). In rural regions, SMEs play a critical role in alleviating poverty, inequality, and job development (Manzoor, Wei, Nurunnabi, & Abdul Subhan, 2019). There are significant source of employment, especially for women, low-skilled employees, and young people. SMEs also play a critical part in Pakistan's economy which is source of entrepreneurship skills, innovation, and new job creation. SME's have a one-of-a-kind ability to use, adapt, and spread new technologies. Therefore, this study undertakes a case of an emerging economy where SMEs account for nearly 90% of all firms and contribute around 40% to the GDP (SMEDA, 2018). In emerging economies, major challenges faced by SMEs are shortage of working capital, rigorous competition from larger companies, poor infrastructure to manage waste, and financial problems (Belhadi, Sha'ri, Touriki, & El Fezazi, 2018; Hwang & Kim, 2022).

In the past, several studies have investigated factors that may impact the environment. These factors are related to human, organization and the context in which organization id operating (Kousar et al., 2017) but there are very studies which discuss the underlying mechanism in adopting the green and lean practices together. Furthermore, thee is limited research if these green-lean practices effect the production performance or not particular in the context of Pakistan (Wassan et al., 2022). Therefore, this study examines how the implementation of green practices contributes to organizational production performance and if lean practices improve the relationship between green practices and organizational production performance. The research will help to examine the execution of lean-green production practices for SMEs. In addition, it will help managers to view green practices as a competitive advantage and support the notion to implement green practices within the firm.

LITERATURE REVIEW

Green Practices

In many sectors, organizations see their eco-friendly efficiency as a path to competitive advantage along with prices, interruptions, and quality of the product (Azzone & Noci, 1998; Gürlek & Tuna, 2018; Singh, Chen, Del Giudice, & El-Kassar, 2019). Studies on SMEs have been called to investigate how to achieve production efficiency while implementing green practices. SMEs need to optimize resources for cost-saving, elevate the company's prestige, customers trust, and loyalty, and market competitiveness by taking into consideration that their business positively impacts the environment (Agan, Acar, & Borodin, 2013; Belhadi, Touriki, & El Fezazi, 2018; Caldera, Desha, & Dawes, 2019). Nonetheless, numerous surveys have suggested that, in terms of obtaining green benefits including tax credits and incentives, improved efficiency, healthier workplaces, and price savings, SMEs are too far behind in comparison to their larger counterparts (Belhadi, Touriki, et al., 2018; Wang, 2016).

Florida (1996) conducted a business assessment and discovered that SMEs are less environmentally oriented. Del Brìo and Junquera (2003) come with the same assumption, noting that SMEs companies are typically able to disregard environmental problems and at most just meet with the basic legislation that affects them. D. H. Lee (2013) pointed out that SMEs enterprises still have a short-sighted approach to future innovation, and need to take steps to address green issues. However, Agan et al. (2013); Chen et al. (2022) reported that Asian SMEs are reluctant to green practices due to relaxed regulations and/or fewer legislations. In addition, Boiral, Baron, and Gunnlaugson (2014) showed, via interviews with 64 SMEs in Canada, that SMEs' commitment to the environment is very minimal and still needs more growth. Azzone and Noci (1998) noted that Italy's small enterprises lack adequate capital to tackle environmental concerns. It is important to understand that adoption of green practices needs an initial investment in changing the process(es) accordingly and SMEs may not be willing to invest because it can increase their production cost (Agan et al., 2013).

The critical role of green success in the growth of SMEs along with fewer production of SMEs in environmental concerns has inspired researchers recently to find ways to create a win-win environmentally and economically productive scenario. In a way by which SMEs are persuaded to implement green practices in their industries (Belhadi, Touriki, et al., 2018; Caldera et al., 2019; Govindan et al., 2015; Verrier, Rose, Caillaud, & Remita, 2014).

According to Luthra, Garg, and Haleem (2014) green production consists of elements of green transportation, green product development, and green design. Green practices, procedures, and methods (reuse and recycling) taking fewer resources and waste minimization, significantly improve the 'triple bottom line' of business (economic, social, and environmental responsibility). Implementing green practices obligates organizations to use materials that are environmentally friendly and do not have carbon prints but at the same time, these practices fairly increase production in minimum time with lower cost thus increasing the product value (Roscoe et al., 2019; Sangwan, 2011) and reduce the impact on climate change (Ali & Gölgeci, 2020). In addition, customers feel satisfied because they are using environmentally friendly products thus increasing market share (Agan et al., 2013; Mohd Suki, 2017; Supriadi, Astuti, & Firdiansyah, 2017) and improving the company's image (Sezen & Cankaya, 2013).

Due to the non-green process, there will be an increased concentration of CO^2 in the environment that is harmful to the atmosphere, as it will increase water vaporization that leads to the greenhouse effect (Parvez, Hazelton, & Guthrie, 2019). To save the earth and humans this will led to a process of Green Practices (GP). Mittal and Sangwan (2014) believed that the adoption of GP produces products that are environmental-friendly and pose a better social impact by generating more jobs, preventing overuse of resources, and protecting the environment. In addition to serving to company's profitability, such actions will create a true distinction. Implementation of GP will result in a smaller carbon footprint and scale back the number of poisons free into the atmosphere. Future generations will ultimately have the benefit of improved air and water quality, fewer landfills, and many renewable energy sources.

Ramayah, Mohamad, Omar, Marimuthu, and Leen (2013) stated that there is a need to develop a correlation between organizational practices (particularly for manufacturing), and their benefits and organizations should be aware of these benefits (such as reducing manufacturing cost by reducing and recycling waste, improved brand image to attract "Green" customers, promoting healthy and safe workplace with efficient technology). In the light of the above, we can say that introducing green practices and procedures drives organizations to lead to lean practices.

Lean Practices

The term "Lean" was initially used by Krafcik (1988) in literature but can be traced back from history in late 1970, particularly for improving business performance (Emiliani (2006). Toyota Motor adopted such lean practices in their production system during Second World War and produced the right goods in the shortest time with less waste and energy (Ohno, 1988). However, the contemporary literature on lean practices has significantly evolved and provides a better understanding of how the lean system increases the business value (Marodin & Saurin, 2013). For example, lean practices in production can be understood through a five-step of the cyclical process where quality is the first number after value stream, flow, push, and pursuit for perfection (Gupta, Digalwar, Gupta, & Goyal, 2022). However, the question arises why not still a larger chunk of companies particularly SMEs across the globe adopting lean practices? Cowger (2016) uncovered a few reasons and argued that SMEs consider the challenge of adopting lean due to a lack of sense of urgency and even cynicism to contradictory interpretations of lean, too much knowledge but a shortage of human capital, and significant time required to pursue lean measures.

In short, lean practices are meant to provide services and products without any waste in them. However, one of the major challenges for small enterprises is financial viability for implementing lean practices because adopting such practices require resources (time, machines, technical competence, and experienced manpower) to reduce/reuse/recycle waste (Mathur, Mittal, & Dangayach, 2012; Panizzolo, Garengo, Sharma, & Gore, 2012).

Production Performance

Performance in an organizational context is considered an organization's real outcomes calculated against its expected outputs (or priorities and objectives) (Richard, Devinney, Yip, & Johnson, 2009). However, production performance can be evaluated through actual output and efficiency (Bellgran & Säfsten, 2009; Koengkan et al., 2022). Over the last few decades, industrial development has progressed with the idea that how to become an efficient good manufacturer. For example, the availability of production equipment(s) and how manufacturing is structured for topical issues. The primary purpose of making processes efficient (i.e., inventory rates, manufacturing costs, cycle times, quality standards, and performance of delivery) is to increase the performance (Mackelprang & Nair, 2010). Production performance is an absolute measure that indicates what is achieved and what has to be done to achieve the further goal(s). Therefore, it is a crucial concern for the manufacturing organizations because inefficient production can lower the system's capacity which ultimately delays the orders or increase customers' dissatisfaction (Qarahasanlou, Barabadi, & Ayele, 2018).

Lean Practices, Green Behavior, and Production Performance

Implementing green practices positively impacts on firm's financial performance but at the same time, such practices influence specific operational performance indicators such as cost, quality, delivery, and flexibility (Fullerton & Wempe, 2009; Santos, Lannelongue, & Gonzalez-Benito, 2019). In the context of lean practices and production performance nexus, studies indicated that single or combined lean practices produce positive results for various performance parameters (economic, environmental, social, and financial) (Yang, Hong, & Modi, 2011). Researchers believe that adopting lean practices improves the company's image as environment-friendly (Dües, Tan, and Lim (2013) and explain the mechanism between green practices and a firm's production performance (Martínez-Jurado, Moyano-Fuentes, & Gómez, 2013). Multiple studies in different context particularly with western data and measurements and mixed findings indicate that lean practices concerning production performance and green practices requires more studies (Ahmad, Abdullah, & Talib, 2020; da Silva, Marins, Dias, & Ushizima, 2021). This study argues in the light of complementarity theory that companies particularly in manufacturing implement green practices benefiting production performance.

However, implementing lean practices can strengthen the relationship between green practices and production performance. This is because adopting and implementing lean practices independently is difficult as such, practices require a specific culture where employees are willing to learn and adopt such a system (Primo et al., 2021). However, companies already implementing green practices can hold an advantage to adopt the lean system because they have the required culture as well as they are focused on the environment. Therefore, such companies can reap the benefits and increase production performance.

In the light of the above discussion, we hypothesized,

H1: *Implementation of green practices in manufacturing SMEs increases the production performance.*

H2: *Implementation of lean practices will act as a moderator between the green practices and production performance such that the higher the implementation of lean practices the better the production performance and vice versa.*

Theoretical Framework

Figure 1 shows the hypothesized model and showed the relation between the stated variable where green production has a positive relationship with production performance and lean production as a moderator strengthens this relationship.

Figure 1. Theoretical Framework

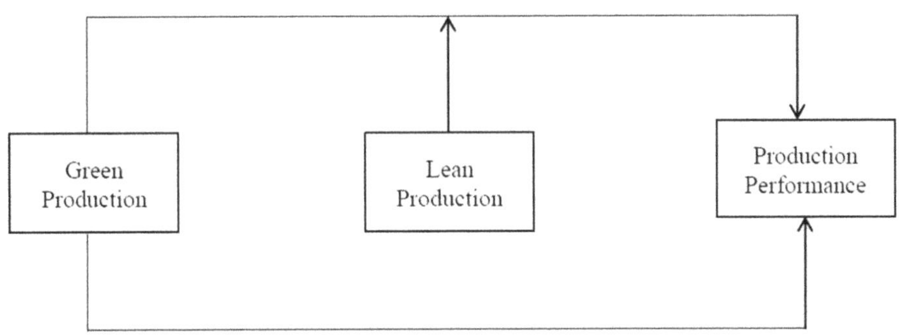

METHODOLOGY

Procedure

This study examines the performance outcomes of green production practices with moderating role of lean production practices. For this purpose, data were collected from SMEs engaged in the manufacturing business. The manufacturing industry is characterized as a highly dynamic and large business sector globally that needs to implement green and lean practices not only for making profits but for stakeholders. In addition, researchers call for the study of the nexus of green practices and production performance, particularly in the manufacturing industry (Inman & Green, 2018). The data was collected from SMEs operating in the Punjab region, the largest populated province of Pakistan with several industrial zones, through a systematic approach. A database for beverages and automotive parts manufacturing was developed with the help of the Chamber of Commerce directory. Later, a filter was applied in which we shortlisted only those businesses that are certified by International Standard Organization standards. This is because such businesses are compelled to comply with environmental regulations. A total of 400 SMEs were selected randomly and later approached to participate in this study. Surveys were distributed among all the 400 firms. While the cover letter of the survey stated the purpose of the study and the confidentiality of the response. It was explicitly mentioned that the respondent representing the firm must be from the manufacturing department with the rank of Assistant Manager, Deputy Manager, or above. A friendly reminder was sent after 12 days to those who did not respond to the survey. The questionnaire was in the English language, an official language in Pakistan. A total of 239 responses were received with a response rate of 59.75%. During the data screening, 12 responses were removed due to unengaged responses and/or missing important information led to 227 firms for the final analysis. The overall response rate was 56.75%.

Measures

Green production practices were measured through a 5-items scale developed by Kalbassi (2015) on a 3-point Likert scale, ranging from 1=Rarely) to 3=Always. A sample item is, "*Our company has outlined a policy for green production practices.*" $\alpha = 0.63$.

Lean production practices were measured through a 7-items scale developed by Kalbassi (2015) on a 3-point Likert scale, ranging from 1=Rarely to 3=Always. A sample item is, "*Our company has a program of education and training for the employees to increase employee´s skills in lean production.* $\alpha = 0.79$

Production performance was measured using a 5-items scale developed by Kalbassi (2015) on a 3-point Likert scale ranging from 1=Disagree to 3=Agree. A sample item is, "*In our company implementing Green practices led to higher production quality*". α = 0.74.

Descriptive Statistics

Table 1 shows the descriptive statistics. The sample consisted of 196 males (86.3%) and only 31 females (13.7%). In terms of work experience, 163 (71.8%) respondents had less than five years' experience, whereas the remaining 64 (28.2%) had more than five years' experience. Most of the respondents had 16 years of education (n=207) whereas the level of management consists of 17 (2.6%) senior managers, 44 (19.4%) managers, and 166 (73.1) assistant managers.

Table 1. Demographics

Variable		Frequency	Percentage
Gender	Male	196	86.3
	Female	31	13.7
Education	16 years	207	91.2
	18 years	18	7.9
	PhD	2	0.9
Experience	1 – 5 years	163	71.8
	6 – 10 years	58	25.6
	11 – 15 years	6	2.6
Level of Management	Senior Manager	17	7.5
	Manager	44	19.4
	Assistant Managers	166	73.1
Industry Type	Manufacturing	227	100

N=227

Confirmatory Factor Analysis

Reliability, convergent, and discriminant validity of the constructs were also determined in confirmatory factor analysis. Internal consistency was measured through composite reliability (CR) with a range between 0.64 and 0.79 that meets the threshold (Fornell & Larcker, 1981; Huang, Wang, Wu, & Wang, 2013). Most of the items in factor loadings were greater than 0.50 with t-values higher than 1.96 and considered significant (Liu et al., 2020).

Table 2. Items loadings, CR and the average variance extract

Construct	Item	Factor Loading	t-value	CR
Green Production	GP1	0.50	-	.640
	GP2	0.62	6.01	
	GP3	0.46	5.03	
	GP4	0.38	4.41	
	GP5	0.59	5.87	
Lean Production	LP1	0.57		
	LP2	0.43	5.38	.790
	LP3	0.59	6.89	
	LP4	0.65	7.37	
	LP5	0.52	6.31	
	LP6	0.65	7.35	
	LP7	0.71	7.79	
Production Performance	PP1	0.59	-	.723
	PP2	0.70	7.29	
	PP3	0.49	5.74	
	PP4	0.51	8.19	
	PP5	0.63	6.85	

Note: CR = Composite reliability

Measurement Model

Hypothesized 3-factor model was tested by AMOS which showed adequate fit to the data ($\chi^2/ df = 1.94$, CFI = 0.90, GFI = 0.90, IFI = 0.90, TLI = 0.88, RMSEA = .06) as compared to single-factor model ($\chi^2/ df = 2.21$; CFI = 0.87, GFI = 0.88, IFI = 0.87, TLI= 0.85; RMSEA = 0.07).

Table 3. Summary of Model Fit Indices

Model	χ2/ df	RMESA	SRMR	GFI	IFI	TLI	CFI
Three factors (GP, LP, PP)	1.94	.06	.05	.90	.90	.88	.90
Two factors (GP, PP)	2.12	.07	.09	.89	.88	.86	.88
One factor (PP)	2.21	.07	.11	.88	.87	.85	.87

Note: N=227, GP= Green Production, LP= Lean Production, PP= Production Performance

Correlation

Table 4 shows the correlations between green practices, lean practices, and production performance. Green production practices have positive and significant relationship with production performance ($r = .440$, $p < .001$). Lean production practices also have positive and significant relationship with production performance ($r = .643$, $p < .001$). A diagonal in Table 2 shows the reliabilities of scales used in this study.

Table 4. Mean, standard deviations, correlations, reliability

		Mean	SD	1	2	3
1	Green Production	2.473	0.428	***(0.63)***		
2	Lean Production	2.538	0.435	0.613**	***(0.79)***	
3	Production Performance	2.633	0.422	0.440**	0.643**	***(0.74)***

Note: N = 227; the diagonals (in bold italic) represent the Cronbach's alpha (shows the scales reliability); **p* *< 0.05; **p < 0.01.*

Hypothesis Testing

Hypotheses were tested through PROCESS Macro developed by Hayes (2013) in SPSS. The bootstrapping method was used with 5000 resamples and 95% confidence intervals, in line with the recommendations of (Hayes, 2018). The results indicate that green production practices in SMEs have a significant positive effect on production performance ($\beta = 0.133$, $t = 2.050$, $p < .05$), supporting H1. Likewise, lean production practices were found to have a significant positive effect on production performance ($\beta = 0.624$, $t = 9.933$, $p < .001$).

Table 5. Moderation Analysis

	Production Performance					
	Effect	**SE**	**T**	**P**	**LLCI**	**ULCI**
Green Production	.133	.065	2.050	.041	.005	.262
Lean Production	.624	.062	9.933	.000	.500	.748
Green Production*Lean Production	.316	.099	3.195	.001	.121	.511

Note: N=227, Bootstrap sample size = 5000; R^2 Change=.025; R^2=.442; *p < .05, **p < .01, ***p < .001.

The interaction results of green production and lean production suggest that the effect of green production practices on production performance becomes highly significantly (p-value changes from 0.05 to 0.001; beta coefficient (β) also increased from 0.133 to 0.336) when a firm uses lean production practices ($\beta = 0.316$, $p < 0.001$, $\Delta R^2 = 0.025$) thereby supporting H2. In addition to this, a slope analysis was conducted to better understand to what extent per unit change in lean practices influences the firm's production performance. Figure 2 shows a sharp rise in production performance when a firm implements an optimum level of lean practices in production.

Figure 2. Moderation Graph

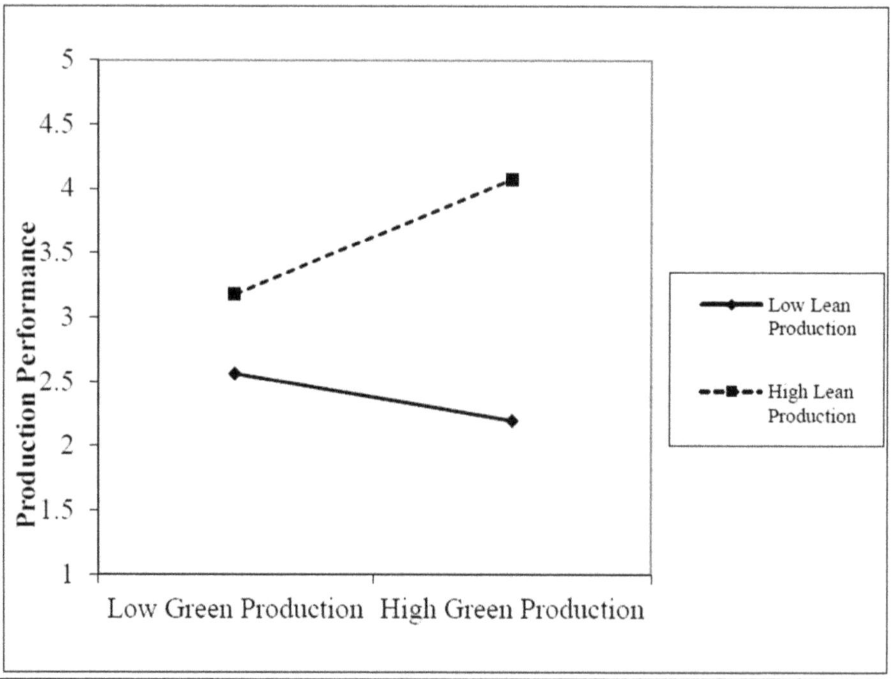

DISCUSSION

Consumption of ecological resources is one of the environmental concerns and sustainable environmental practices need to be followed particularly in manufacturing. This study was conducted in an emerging economy context where it is thought that green practices are associated with the high cost and less production performance. This study indicates that green and lean production practices help firms to increase their productivity and achieve environmental goals. Hypothesis 1 states that green practices in manufacturing SMEs improve production performance and data from ISO-certified firms supported this. This is because the implementation of green policy, ISO and green standards, recycling material, and green supply chain operation leads to higher production performance, customer satisfaction, and higher production quality (Le, Vo, & Venkatesh, 2022; Novitasari, Wijaya, Agustin, Gunardi, & Dana, 2022). These results are consistent with Tan, Zailani, Tan, and Shaharudin (2016) using a sample from the manufacturing sector in Malaysia where they also showed that green practices create a competitive advantage for a business. Another study by Choi and Hwang (2015) in the South Korean manufacturing sector showed similar findings that green practices help to improve both environmental and financial performance. Hypothesis 2 was also supported which states that implementation of lean practices strengthens the relationship between green practices and production performance in a way that higher implementation of lean practices higher the production performance. It means when a company outlines a policy for lean practices along the supply chain like waste reduction, value stream mapping, education, and training its employees to increase their skills, it increases the production performance with more pace. Few studies conducted in the past also showed that green practices may link with environmental performance but not a company's financial performance due to the cost burden to implement green practices (Baah, Opoku-Agyeman, Acquah, Issau, & Abdoulaye, 2020; Centobelli, Cerchione, & Singh, 2019). However, not directly but this study finds that implementation of lean and green practices helps to increase production which ultimately may help to increase a firm's financial performance. Similar findings were reported by two studies conducted in South Korea (K. H. Lee & Kim, 2011; S. M. Lee, Kim, & Choi, 2012). A study conducted in South Korea supported the notion that the implementation of lean practices increases the manufacturing outcomes in the form of high production performance (Wickramasinghe & Wickramasinghe, 2017).

Theoretical Implications

This work adds in several respects to current literature: First, it offers a deeper, expanded conceptualization of the relationships between green production, lean production, and production performance. The research helped to examine the execution of lean-green production practices for Pakistani SMEs. It also covers the research gap discussed by Verrier et al. (2014) about the impact of green production on production performance and the impact of lean production on production performance discussed by (Negrão, Godinho Filho, & Marodin, 2017). . The current study also examined the mediating role of lean production between green production and production performance.

Practical Implications

In the competitive market nowadays, improvement of production performance is one of the key challenges for organizations, particularly for SMEs. For enhancing the performance of organizations lean and green production practices are considered essential elements. To remain successful, SMEs enterprises (SMEs) should not only concentrate on their operating efficiency but also should incorporate the environmental goals in the business strategy through the balanced implementation of lean and green paradigms as large organizations implement. Among several implications for the manufacturing sector, the adoption of environmentally friendly practices is the most crucial that help and achieve sustainable development goals (SDGs) at a firm as well as at the national level. Manufacturing firms may coordinate and collaborate with suppliers and customers to implement green practices for production. This study showed that green production practices improve production performance; therefore, managers should devise strategies, like green training and green supply chain, to encourage their firms to implement green practices for sustainable production. Also, they can implement green production practices by considering a policy shift to green production policy, ISO, and green standards that can reduce energy consumption and increase recycling waste to ensure environmentally friendly products and services. In addition, managers should view green practices as a competitive advantage and support the notion to implement green practices within the firm because they are responsible for production performance improvement. In light of the present study's results, we argue that a combination of green and lean practices is a smart business strategy for SMEs that managers should adopt.

Limitations

This study was conducted in the manufacturing SMEs and its implications are discussed but still, a few limitations are associated with this study. Due to the limited scope of the study only green production practices were examined. Future studies may consider other types of green practices or variables like eco-design, internal environmental management system, and green distribution. Data were collected from the manufacturing SMEs sector in Pakistan though the respondents were carefully selected still results may not generalize to other industries. Therefore, a study of the service industry may bring greater insight because green practices may have different outcomes in the service industry due to the differences in operations than the manufacturing sector.

CONCLUSION

The objective of this study was to analyze if adopting green production practices allows firms to improve production performance and lean production practices further strengthen this relationship for the small manufacturing firms even those operating in an emerging economy. The results are supported by all proposed hypotheses. Though implementation of green practices has achieved enough attention in recent years still there is room to figure out the firms' capabilities needed to implement environmental and sustainable practices. The study concludes that implementation of green practices may have cost associated but these practices improve the firm's production that increases the overall revenue, and this production may be improved further upon implementing lean production practices. Given that a new study in a different context brings in new knowledge (Ali & Aboelmaged, 2021; Ali, Arslan, Khan, & Tarba, 2021).

Conflict of Interest

All the authors in this paper have no conflict of interest.

REFERENCES

Agan, Y., Acar, M. F., & Borodin, A. (2013). Drivers of environmental processes and their impact on performance: A study of Turkish SMEs. *Journal of Cleaner Production*, *51*, 23–33. doi:10.1016/j.jclepro.2012.12.043

Ahmad, S., Abdullah, A., & Talib, F. (2020). Lean-green performance management in Indian SMEs: A novel perspective using the best-worst method approach. *Benchmarking*, *28*(2), 737–765. doi:10.1108/BIJ-05-2020-0255

Ali, I., & Aboelmaged, M. G. S. (2021). Implementation of supply chain 4.0 in the food and beverage industry: Perceived drivers and barriers. *International Journal of Productivity and Performance Management*.

Ali, I., Arslan, A., Khan, Z., & Tarba, S. Y. (2021). The role of Industry 4.0 technologies in mitigating supply chain disruption: Empirical evidence from the Australian food processing industry. *IEEE Transactions on Engineering Management.*

Ali, I., & Gölgeci, I. (2020). Managing climate risks through social capital in agrifood supply chains. *Supply Chain Management.*

Amrina, U., Hidayatno, A., & Zagloel, T. Y. M. (2021). Mapping challenges in developing sustainable small and medium industries: Integrating Lean and green principles. *Journal of Industrial Engineering and Management*, *14*(2), 311–328. doi:10.3926/jiem.3401

Azzone, G., & Noci, G. (1998). Seeing ecology and "green" innovations as a source of change. *Journal of Organizational Change Management*, *11*(2), 94–111. doi:10.1108/09534819810212106

Baah, C., Opoku-Agyeman, D., Acquah, I. S. K., Issau, K., & Abdoulaye, F. A. M. (2020). Understanding the influence of environmental production practices on firm performance: A proactive versus reactive approach. *Journal of Manufacturing Technology Management*, *32*(2), 266–289. doi:10.1108/JMTM-05-2020-0195

Belhadi, A., Sha'ri, Y. B. M., Touriki, F. E., & El Fezazi, S. (2018). Lean production in SMEs: Literature review and reflection on future challenges. *Journal of Industrial and Production Engineering*, *35*(6), 368–382. doi:10.1080/21681015.2018.1508081

Belhadi, A., Touriki, F. E., & El Fezazi, S. (2018). Benefits of adopting lean production on green performance of SMEs: A case study. *Production Planning and Control*, *29*(11), 873–894. doi:10.1080/09537287.2018.1490971

Bellgran, M., & Säfsten, E. K. (2009). *Production development: design and operation of production systems* (Vol. 2). Springer Science & Business Media.

Bergmiller, G. G., & McCright, P. R. (2009). Are lean and green programs synergistic. *Proceedings of the 2009 Industrial Engineering Research Conference.*

Bıçakcıoğlu-Peynirci, N., & Tanyeri, M. (2020). Stakeholder and resource-based antecedents and performance outcomes of green export business strategy: Insights from an emerging economy. *International Journal of Emerging Markets.*

Boiral, O., Baron, C., & Gunnlaugson, O. (2014). Environmental leadership and consciousness development: A case study among Canadian SMEs. *Journal of Business Ethics*, *123*(3), 363–383. doi:10.100710551-013-1845-5

Caldera, H., Desha, C., & Dawes, L. (2019). Evaluating the enablers and barriers for successful implementation of sustainable business practice in 'lean'SMEs. *Journal of Cleaner Production*, *218*, 575–590. doi:10.1016/j.jclepro.2019.01.239

Centobelli, P., Cerchione, R., & Singh, R. (2019). The impact of leanness and innovativeness on environmental and financial performance: Insights from Indian SMEs. *International Journal of Production Economics*, *212*(3), 111–124.

Ch'ng, P.-C., Cheah, J., & Amran, A. (2021). Eco-innovation practices and sustainable business performance: The moderating effect of market turbulence in the Malaysian technology industry. *Journal of Cleaner Production*, *283*, 124556. doi:10.1016/j.jclepro.2020.124556

Chen, Y., Li, J., & Zhang, J. (2022). Digitalisation, data-driven dynamic capabilities and responsible innovation: An empirical study of SMEs in China. *Asia Pacific Journal of Management*, 1–41. doi:10.100710490-022-09845-6

Choi, D., & Hwang, T. (2015). The impact of green supply chain management practices on firm performance: The role of collaborative capability. *Operations Management Research*, *8*(3), 69–83. doi:10.100712063-015-0100-x

Cowger, G. (2016). All-out lean half measures get less than half results. *Mechanical Engineering (New York, N.Y.)*, *138*(1), 30–35. doi:10.1115/1.2016-Jan-1

da Silva, A. F., Marins, F. A. S., Dias, E. X., & Ushizima, C. A. (2021). Improving manufacturing cycle efficiency through new multiple criteria data envelopment analysis models: An application in green and lean manufacturing processes. *Production Planning and Control*, *32*(2), 104–120. doi:10.1080/09537287.2020.1713413

Del Brìo, J. A., & Junquera, B. (2003). A review of the literature on environmental innovation management in SMEs: Implications for public policies. *Technovation*, *23*(12), 939–948. doi:10.1016/S0166-4972(02)00036-6

Dües, C. M., Tan, K. H., & Lim, M. (2013). Green as the new Lean: How to use Lean practices as a catalyst to greening your supply chain. *Journal of Cleaner Production*, *V40*, 93–100. doi:10.1016/j.jclepro.2011.12.023

Emiliani, M. L. (2006). Origins of lean management in America: The role of Connecticut businesses. *Journal of Management History*, *12*(2), 167–184. doi:10.1108/13552520610654069

Florida, R. (1996). Lean and green: The move to environmentally conscious manufacturing. *California Management Review*, *39*(1), 80–105. doi:10.2307/41165877

Fornell, C., & Larcker, D. F. (1981). Evaluating structural equation models with unobservable variables and measurement error11. *JMR, Journal of Marketing Research, 18*(1), 39–50. doi:10.1177/002224378101800104

Fullerton, R. R., & Wempe, W. F. (2009). Lean manufacturing, non-financial performance measures, and financial performance. *International Journal of Operations & Production Management, 29*(3), 214–240. doi:10.1108/01443570910938970

Govindan, K., Kannan, D., & Shankar, M. (2015). Evaluation of green manufacturing practices using a hybrid MCDM model combining DANP with PROMETHEE. *International Journal of Production Research, 53*(21), 6344–6371. doi:10.1080/00207543.2014.898865

Gupta, M., Digalwar, A., Gupta, A., & Goyal, A. (2022). Integrating Theory of Constraints, Lean and Six Sigma: A framework development and its application. *Production Planning and Control*, 1–24. doi:10.1080/09537287.2022.2071351

Gürlek, M., & Tuna, M. (2018). Reinforcing competitive advantage through green organizational culture and green innovation. *Service Industries Journal, 38*(7-8), 467–491. doi:10.1080/02642069.2017.1402889

Hayes, A. F. (2013). *Introduction to mediation, moderation, and conditional process analysis: Methodology in the Social Sciences*. Academic Press.

Hayes, A. F. (2018). *Introduction to mediation, moderation, and conditional process analysis: A regression-based approach* (Vol. 2). Guilford Publications.

Hou, Y., Iqbal, W., Muhammad Shaikh, G., Iqbal, N., Ahmad Solangi, Y., & Fatima, A. (2019). Measuring energy efficiency and environmental performance: A case of South Asia. *Processes (Basel, Switzerland), 7*(6), 325. doi:10.3390/pr7060325

Huang, C.-C., Wang, Y.-M., Wu, T.-W., & Wang, P.-A. (2013). An empirical analysis of the antecedents and performance consequences of using the moodle platform. *International Journal of Information and Education Technology, 3*(2), 217–221. doi:10.7763/IJIET.2013.V3.267

Hwang, W.-S., & Kim, H.-S. (2022). Does the adoption of emerging technologies improve technical efficiency? Evidence from Korean manufacturing SMEs. *Small Business Economics, 59*(2), 627–643. doi:10.100711187-021-00554-w

Inman, R. A., & Green, K. W. (2018). Lean and green combine to impact environmental and operational performance. *International Journal of Production Research, 56*(14), 4802–4818. doi:10.1080/00207543.2018.1447705

Kalbassi, R. (2015). Lean and Green Parallel Implementation Impact on Outcomes of Supply Chain in Canadian Aerospace Industry. Concordia University.

King, A. A., & Lenox, M. J. (2001). Lean and green? An empirical examination of the relationship between lean production and environmental performance. *Production and Operations Management*, *10*(3), 244–256.

Koengkan, M., Fuinhas, J. A., Kazemzadeh, E., Osmani, F., Alavijeh, N. K., Auza, A., & Teixeira, M. (2022). Measuring the economic efficiency performance in Latin American and Caribbean countries: An empirical evidence from stochastic production frontier and data envelopment analysis. *Inter Economics*, *169*, 43–54. doi:10.1016/j.inteco.2021.11.004

Krafcik, J. F. (1988). Triumph of the lean production system. *MIT Sloan Management Review*, *30*(1), 41.

Le, T. T., Vo, X. V., & Venkatesh, V. (2022). Role of green innovation and supply chain management in driving sustainable corporate performance. *Journal of Cleaner Production*, *374*, 133875. doi:10.1016/j.jclepro.2022.133875

Lee, D. H. (2013). *The role of Triple-A in green supply chain management practices and organizational performance.* University of Nebraska - Lincoln. Retrieved from https://digitalcommons.unl.edu/dissertations/AAI3558860

Lee, K. H., & Kim, J. W. (2011). Integrating suppliers into green product innovation development: An empirical case study in the semiconductor industry. *Business Strategy and the Environment*, *20*(8), 527–538. doi:10.1002/bse.714

Lee, S. M., Kim, S. T., & Choi, D. (2012). Green supply chain management and organizational performance. *Industrial Management & Data Systems*, *112*(8), 1148–1180. doi:10.1108/02635571211264609

Luthra, S., Garg, D., & Haleem, A. (2014). Green supply chain management: Implementation and performance–a literature review and some issues. *Journal of Advances in Management Research*, *11*(1), 20–46. doi:10.1108/JAMR-07-2012-0027

Mackelprang, A. W., & Nair, A. (2010). Relationship between just-in-time manufacturing practices and performance: A meta-analytic investigation. *Journal of Operations Management*, *28*(4), 283–302. doi:10.1016/j.jom.2009.10.002

Manzoor, F., Wei, L., Nurunnabi, M., & Abdul Subhan, Q. (2019). Role of SME in poverty alleviation in SAARC region via panel data analysis. *Sustainability*, *11*(22), 6480. doi:10.3390u11226480

Marodin, G. A., & Saurin, T. A. (2013). Implementing lean production systems: Research areas and opportunities for future studies. *International Journal of Production Research*, *51*(22), 6663–6680. doi:10.1080/00207543.2013.826831

Martínez-Jurado, P. J., Moyano-Fuentes, J., & Gómez, P. J. (2013). HR management during lean production adoption. *Management Decision*, *51*(4), 742–760. doi:10.1108/00251741311326545

Mathur, A., Mittal, M., & Dangayach, G. S. (2012). Improving productivity in Indian SMEs. *Production Planning and Control*, *23*(10-11), 754–768. doi:10.1080/09537287.2011.642150

Mentis, A. (2017). *Understanding Australian small to medium businesses.* Retrieved from https://business.nab.com.au/wp-content/uploads/2017/06/J002580_MTM-Whitepaper-IPSOS-FINAL_C1-2.pdf

Mittal, V. K., & Sangwan, K. S. (2014). Prioritizing barriers to green manufacturing: Environmental, social and economic perspectives. *Procedia CIRP*, *17*, 559–564. doi:10.1016/j.procir.2014.01.075

Mohd Suki, N. (2017). Green products usage: Structural relationships on customer satisfaction and loyalty. *International Journal of Sustainable Development and World Ecology*, *24*(1), 88–95. doi:10.1080/13504509.2016.1169563

Narwane, V. S., Raut, R. D., Gardas, B. B., Narkhede, B. E., & Awasthi, A. (2022). Examining smart manufacturing challenges in the context of micro, small and medium enterprises. *International Journal of Computer Integrated Manufacturing*, 1–18. doi:10.1080/0951192X.2022.2078508

Negrão, L. L. L., Godinho Filho, M., & Marodin, G. (2017). Lean practices and their effect on performance: A literature review. *Production Planning and Control*, *28*(1), 33–56.

Novitasari, M., Wijaya, A. L., Agustin, N. M., Gunardi, A., & Dana, L. P. (2022). Corporate social responsibility and firm performance: Green supply chain management as a mediating variable. *Corporate Social Responsibility and Environmental Management*, csr.2353. doi:10.1002/csr.2353

Ohno, T. (1988). *Toyota production system: beyond large-scale production* (Vol. 3). CRC Press.

Pangboonyanon, V., & Kalasin, K. (2018). The impact of within-industry diversification on firm performance: Empirical evidence from emerging ASEAN SMEs. *International Journal of Emerging Markets.*

Panizzolo, R., Garengo, P., Sharma, M. K., & Gore, A. (2012). Lean manufacturing in developing countries: Evidence from Indian SMEs. *Production Planning and Control, 23*(10-11), 769–788. doi:10.1080/09537287.2011.642155

Parvez, M., Hazelton, J., & Guthrie, J. (2019). *Greenhouse gas emissions disclosure by cities: the expectation gap. Sustainability Accounting, Management and Policy Journal.*

Primo, M. A., DuBois, F. L., de Oliveira, M. L., Amaro, E. S. M., & Moser, D. D. (2021). Lean manufacturing implementation in time of crisis: The case of Estaleiro Atlântico Sul. *Production Planning and Control, 32*(8), 623–640. doi:10.1080/09537287.2020.1747655

Qarahasanlou, A. N., Barabadi, A., & Ayele, Y. Z. (2018). Production performance analysis during operation phase: A case study. *Proceedings of the Institution of Mechanical Engineers. Part O, Journal of Risk and Reliability, 232*(6), 559–575. doi:10.1177/1748006X17744383

Ramayah, T., Mohamad, O., Omar, A., Marimuthu, M., & Leen, J. Y. A. (2013). Green manufacturing practices and performance among SMEs: evidence from a developing nation. In *Green Technologies and Business Practices: An IT Approach* (Vol. 2, pp. 208–225). IGI Global. doi:10.4018/978-1-4666-1972-2.ch013

Richard, P. J., Devinney, T. M., Yip, G. S., & Johnson, G. (2009). Measuring organizational performance: Towards methodological best practice. *Journal of Management, 35*(3), 718–804. doi:10.1177/0149206308330560

Roscoe, S., Subramanian, N., Jabbour, C. J., & Chong, T. (2019). Green human resource management and the enablers of green organisational culture: Enhancing a firm's environmental performance for sustainable development. *Business Strategy and the Environment, 28*(5), 737–749. doi:10.1002/bse.2277

Sangwan, K. S. (2011). Quantitative and qualitative benefits of green manufacturing: an empirical study of Indian small and medium enterprises. In *Glocalized Solutions for Sustainability in Manufacturing* (Vol. 2, pp. 371–376). Springer. doi:10.1007/978-3-642-19692-8_64

Santos, H., Lannelongue, G., & Gonzalez-Benito, J. (2019). Integrating green practices into operational performance: Evidence from Brazilian manufacturers. *Sustainability, 11*(10), 2956. doi:10.3390u11102956

Shukor, A. A. A., Newaz, M. S., Rahman, M. K., & Taha, A. Z. (2020). Supply chain integration and its impact on supply chain agility and organizational flexibility in manufacturing firms. *International Journal of Emerging Markets.*

Singh, S. K., Chen, J., Del Giudice, M., & El-Kassar, A.-N. (2019). Environmental ethics, environmental performance, and competitive advantage: Role of environmental training. *Technological Forecasting and Social Change, 146*, 203–211. doi:10.1016/j.techfore.2019.05.032

SMEDA. (2018). Retrieved from https://smeda.org/

Supriadi, B., Astuti, W., & Firdiansyah, A. (2017). Green product and its impact on customer satisfaction. *IOSR Journal of Business and Management, 19*(8), 1.

Tan, C. L., Zailani, S. H. M., Tan, S. C., & Shaharudin, M. R. (2016). The impact of green supply chain management practices on firm competitiveness. *International Journal of Business Innovation and Research, 11*(4), 539–558. doi:10.1504/IJBIR.2016.079507

Verrier, B., Rose, B., Caillaud, E., & Remita, H. (2014). Combining organizational performance with sustainable development issues: The Lean and Green project benchmarking repository. *Journal of Cleaner Production, 85*, 83–93. doi:10.1016/j.jclepro.2013.12.023

Vuong, Q. H., La, V. P., Nguyen, H. K. T., Ho, M. T., Vuong, T. T., & Ho, M. T. (2021). Identifying the moral–practical gaps in corporate social responsibility missions of Vietnamese firms: An event-based analysis of sustainability feasibility. *Corporate Social Responsibility and Environmental Management, 28*(1), 30–41. doi:10.1002/csr.2029

Wang, Y. (2016). What are the biggest obstacles to growth of SMEs in developing countries?–An empirical evidence from an enterprise survey. *Borsa Istanbul Review, 16*(3), 167–176. doi:10.1016/j.bir.2016.06.001

Wickramasinghe, G., & Wickramasinghe, V. (2017). Implementation of lean production practices and manufacturing performance. *Journal of Manufacturing Technology Management, 28*(4), 531–550. doi:10.1108/JMTM-08-2016-0112

Yadav, G., Luthra, S., Huisingh, D., Mangla, S. K., Narkhede, B. E., & Liu, Y. (2020). Development of a lean manufacturing framework to enhance its adoption within manufacturing companies in developing economies. *Journal of Cleaner Production, 245*, 118726. doi:10.1016/j.jclepro.2019.118726

Yang, M. G. M., Hong, P., & Modi, S. B. (2011). Impact of lean manufacturing and environmental management on business performance: An empirical study of manufacturing firms. *International Journal of Production Economics, 129*(2), 251–261. doi:10.1016/j.ijpe.2010.10.017

Yong, J. Y., Yusliza, M.-Y., Jabbour, C. J. C., & Ahmad, N. H. (2019). Exploratory cases on the interplay between green human resource management and advanced green manufacturing in light of the Ability-Motivation-Opportunity theory. *Journal of Management Development*, *39*(1), 31–49. doi:10.1108/JMD-12-2018-0355

Chapter 5
Multimodal Transport and the Integration of Transport Modes to Support Disaster Relief Operations

Sajid Nazir
Institute of Business Management, Pakistan

Zhang Yu
School of Economics and Management, Xian, China

Khawaja Masood Raza
Institute of Business Management, Pakistan

ABSTRACT

Over the last few years, with the rise of natural/man-made disasters, the importance of the humanitarian supply chain has also received a significant value. Humanitarian supply chain performs under special circumstances compared to commercial supply chain such as lack of communication system, electricity, and destabilized transport infrastructure after a disaster. However, disasters are unpredictable; therefore, the demand for supplies (relief items), casualties, and required transportation modes to access the affected area are also unpredictable. Thus, the integration of different modes of transportation is essential to encounter any disaster situation promptly, such as disasters in South Asia in 2001, which caused the death of thousands due to lack of transport infrastructure, inadequate disaster relief planning, and lack of transport integration.

DOI: 10.4018/978-1-6684-6663-6.ch005

INTRODUCTION

Transportation plays a significant role in the movement of goods and services between two points in a commercial supply chain (Closs & Bolumole, 2015) these movements of goods and services are planned according to customer demand at the right time with the right thing at the right place (Sarjana et al., 2020). However, in the humanitarian supply chain disaster is unpredictable therefore the demand for supplies and casualties are also unpredictable (Negi, 2022). Most of the major disasters which the world has faced in recent years caused the death of thousands of people, infrastructure, and economic loss (Baidoo, 2017; Chari et al., 2020; Maghsoudi & Moshtari, 2020; Ritchie & Roser, 2020). In the past, lack of disaster pre-planning and limited capacities caused the destruction of whole civilizations such as Moen Jo Daro in Sindh, Pakistan 2500 BCE (Das, 2022) and the destruction of Pompeii city in 79 AD (Seth, 2022). However, now the increasing involvement of humanitarian organizations in disaster relief operations helps to encounter the disaster operations effectively as shown in the figure.1 (Ritchie & Roser, 2020), the number of deaths is less than 10,000, accounting for as low as 0.01 percent of all deaths.

Figure 1. Death Rates from Natural Disasters

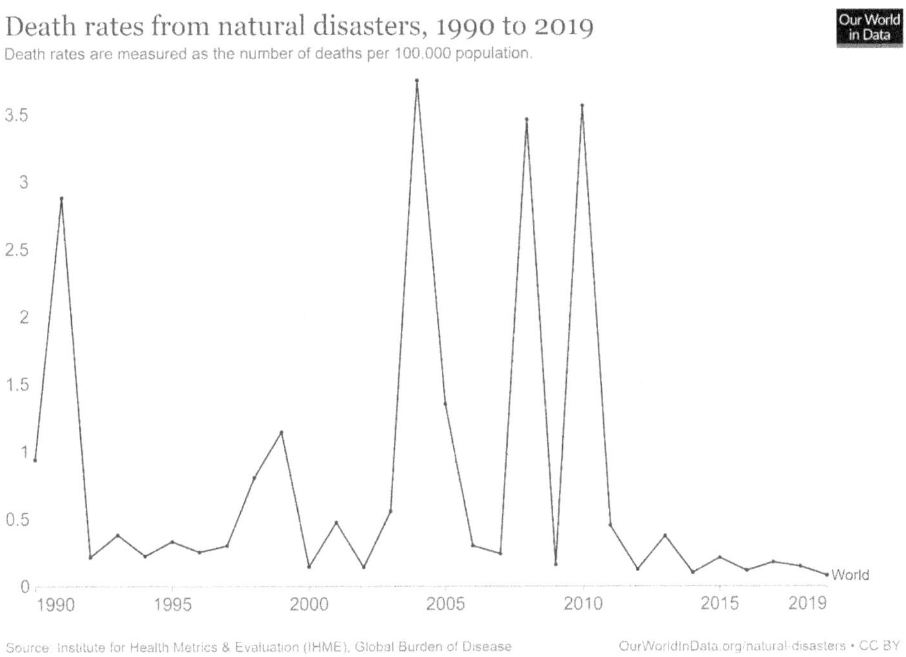

The impacts of disasters not only affect the lives of people or regions but also destroys the economy of the region as well (De Smet et al., 2015). In the figure. 2, it's showing the global economic loss from disasters (Ritchie & Roser, 2020).

Figure 2. Economic Losses due to Natural Disasters

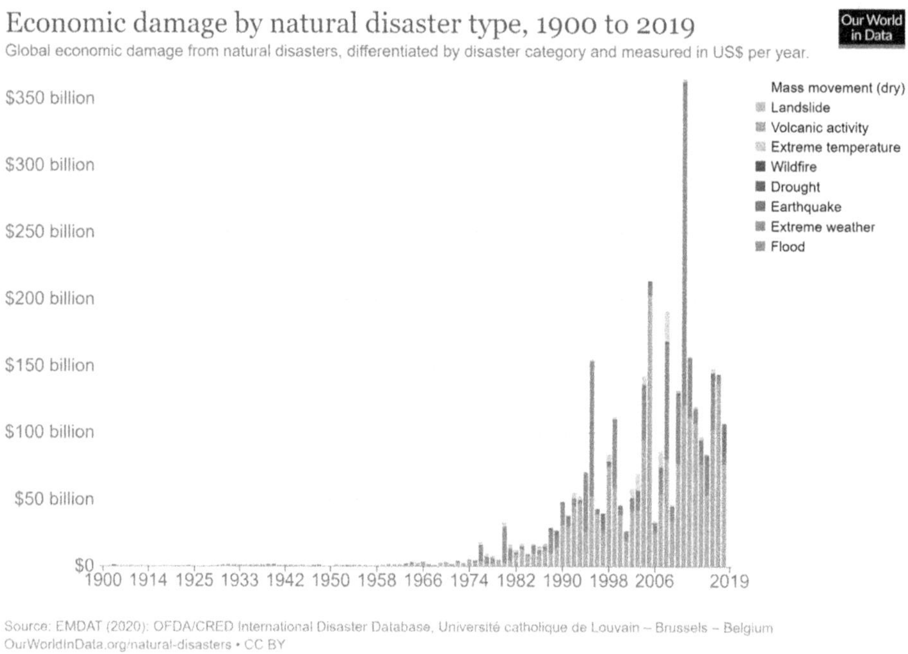

Logistics operations play an enormous role in the humanitarian supply chain as it accounts for almost eighty percent of overall disaster relief operations (Wassenhove, 2006). Consequently, a small improvement in relief activities leads to high impact on the lives of people. Therefore, researchers and institutions are searching for new alternatives to deliver speedy supplies in disaster conditions by the use of different modes of transportation efficiently and effectively (Ertem et al., 2017). The need for alternatives is critical for developing countries, such as Pakistan, due to a lack of resources and planning. Since 2001, in South Asian regions there is several natural disasters have occurred such as the 2001 earthquake & 2004 Tsunami in India, 2005 earthquake in Pakistan caused the death of 73,000 people, leaving 2.8 million people homeless, 70,000 injured and the aftermath cost US$5.2 billion (World Bank, 2005), and 2010 flood which caused the death of 1,700 individuals, affected more than 20 million people and 20% of Pakistan's land area (GoP,2011), 80% agricultural loss (WHO, 2011) and costs billions of dollar (GoP,2011).

Therefore, the use of multiple modes of transportation in disaster relief operation enhances the number of chances to access the affected region efficiently, as different disasters in different regions requires different modes of transportation (Ertem et al., 2017). For example, 2005 earthquake in Pakistan, the government has to call aviation vessels and unprecedented numbers of helicopters for the distribution of emergency supplies over 5000 sorties in affected regions due to completely cut off road access to different regions (World Bank, 2005). While in the 2010 flood in Pakistan disaster relief operations were mainly based on boats and helicopters (WHO, 2011). Since most of the disasters are unpredictable and the demand for aid supplies also varies (Kovács & Spens, 2007), thus, it is a big challenge to operate in special circumstances such as destructions of logistics infrastructure, lack of communication system, electricity, and destabilized transport routes (Christopher & Tatham, 2011).

Therefore, the main objective of this book chapter is to introduce the crucial role of humanitarian logistics in disaster relief operations, including further topics such as disaster, types of disaster, disaster management, disaster relief operations, humanitarian logistics, multimode transportation, and a case of Pakistan has been discussed. In order to achieve the aim of this book chapter, firstly the disaster, its types, and its contributions have been discussed in section 1.1. Secondly, the disaster management with each phase is given in section 1.2. After the disaster management cycle, disaster relief operations are discussed in section 1.3. Likewise, multimode transportation and integration of the components of disaster relief operations with a conceptual framework have been discussed in section 1.4. Then, in section 1.5, the significance of humanitarian logistics and the characteristics of humanitarian logistics has been discussed in section 1.6. Then, a conceptual model for efficient disaster relief operations in Pakistan has been discussed in section 2.0. Finally, section 2.1, 2.2, and 2.3, presents the disasters in Pakistan, a conceptual model for disaster relief operations in Pakistan, and lastly the conclusion of this research study and the possible directions of future research have been discussed accordingly.

What is a Disaster

The term "hazard" can be defined as "an unusual incident that has adverse impacts on human life, commodities, and the environment (De Smet et al., 2015) likewise any event that endangers or devastates human life, societies, environment and disrupts the individual's everyday life is known as a disaster (Berkoune et al., 2012). There are two types of a disaster such as natural disasters caused by Tsunamis, earthquakes, droughts, floods, extreme temperatures, etc., and man-made disasters such as nuclear war, terrorist attacks, fires, explosions, etc. In the modern era with the dramatic change in technology, the number of disasters has also increased dramatically as shown in the figure. 3, the contributions of natural catastrophes as well as man-made disasters and the deaths associated with them in the figure. 4 accordingly (Reliefweb.int, 2022).

Figure 3. Contributions of Natural & Man-made Disasters (Adapted by Author from Reliefweb. int, 2022)

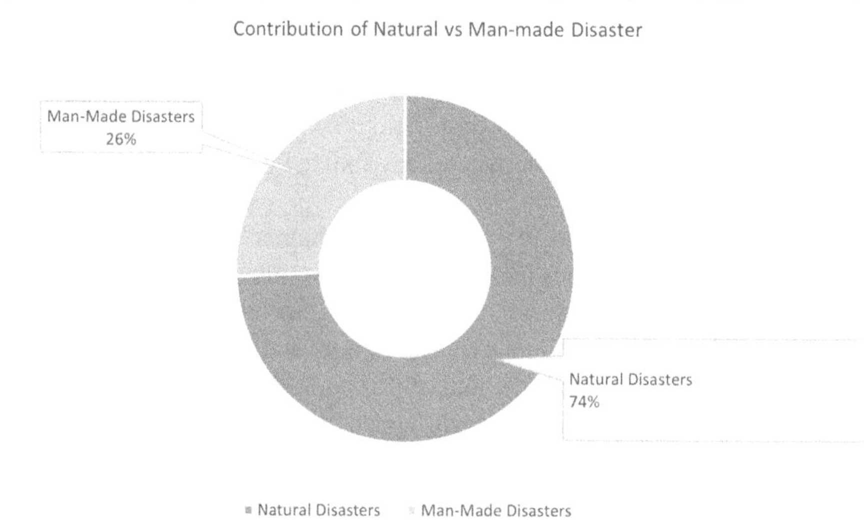

Figure 4. Disasters and associated Deaths (Adapted by Author from Reliefweb. int, 2022)

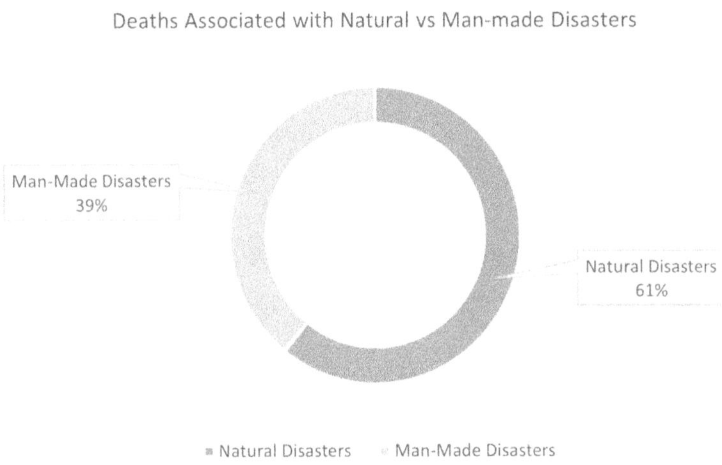

Furthermore, In the figure. 5 & figure. 6, it's demonstrating the numbers of natural disasters and death associated with them globally. The data of year (1900 to 2018) has been taken from the relief web and analyzed through Microsoft Excel eventually.

Figure 5. Natural Disaster around the Globe period (1900-2018)

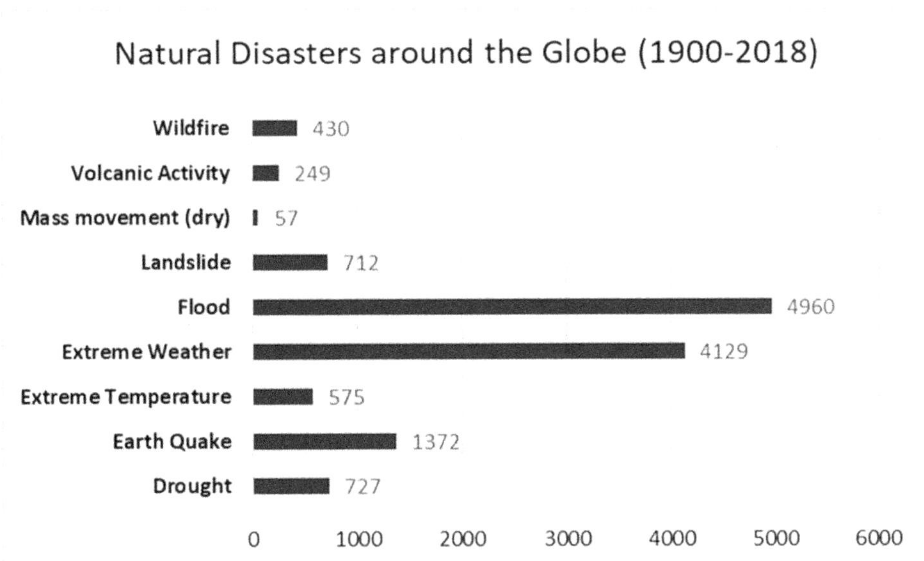

Figure 6. Global Deaths due to Natural Disaster Period (1900-2018)

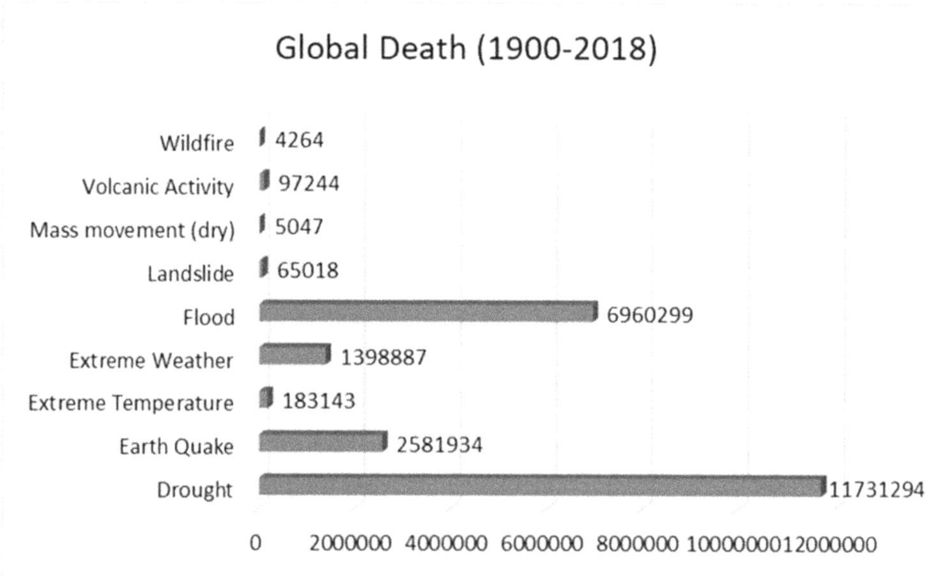

Disaster Management

Any incident that endangers or destabilizes human life, commodities, and the environment is known as a disaster (Berkoune et al., 2012; De Smet et al., 2015). However, the process of identifying, assessing, mitigating, and ultimately preventing hazards is referred to as disaster management (Haddow & Bullock, 2004). In a nutshell, disaster management is a series of measures that are designed to be carried out before, during, and after natural catastrophes in order to minimize or reduce the damages caused by them. It is widely accepted that the disaster risk management process is an effective tool for controlling or minimizing the adverse impact of disasters and their consequences (Rana et al., 2021). The disaster management cycle consists of four phases: mitigation, preparedness, response, and recovery as shown in the figure. 7 (Altay & Green, 2006; Tomasini & Wassenhove, 2009; Nikbakhsh & Farahani, 2011; Haddow et al., 2012). The further explanation of all four phases of disaster management are as follows;

Mitigation: phase helps to prevent hazards from turning into disasters as well as it also helps to minimize their destructive effects by the use of technological advancement (Scholten et al., 2014). These actions are intended to avoid or minimize the likelihood of a traumatic incident occurring and protect communities from the negative effects of a disaster after its occurrences (Carter, 2008).

Preparedness: refers to the development of a strategic plan to respond to disaster risks (He & Zhuang, 2016) and measures that allow governments, NGOs, communities, and people to respond immediately and effectively in emergency conditions. The measures of preparedness include the development of effective emergency plans, the management of supplies, and the formation of employees (Haddow et al., 2012).

Respond: refers to the measures taken in the disruptive conditions by providing emergency aid to casualties and evacuating them from affected regions (Nikbakhsh & Farahani, 2011). Furthermore, according to Carter (2008), response measures are those that are implemented both shortly before and immediately after a disaster has occurred. These kinds of steps are taken with the goals of preventing further loss of life and property as well as restoring the destruction that has already been done by the disaster. Typically, response actions should be conducted under disruptive and stressful conditions and create substantial demands for staff, types of equipment, and other resources eventually. So, the response operations aren't likely to be successful if they aren't based on prior planning, coordination, and training (De Smet et al., 2015). Furthermore, according to Ertem, et al., (2017), during emergency conditions, the purpose of all agencies is to respond quickly to the affected region with several different alternatives such as (air, road, rail, and water) could be used to deliver emergency supplies in affected regions efficiently and effectively.

Recovery: phase refers to the restoring of the destructed region into the previous state, such as the reconstruction of houses, and societies (Alexander, 2002) and it is the process through which individuals and the community as a whole are supported in restoring their normal level of activity in the aftermath of a disaster (Garnett & Moore, 2010). The process of rehabilitation can be extremely drawn out, possibly taking five to ten years, or even more in certain cases (Carter, 2008). Destruction and devastation could be severe and widespread that assessing and formulating recovery procedures is complex and time-consuming (Balamir, 2022). There are extended representations of the disaster management life cycle (Carter, 1991; Norman, 2003), but for this book chapter Nikbakhsh & Farahani's, (2011) disaster management cycle has been presented.

Figure 7. Disaster Management Cycle (Nikbakhsh & Farahani, 2011)

Disaster Relief Operations

Disaster relief activities are complicated and can substantially benefit from good planning (Nelan et al., 2018). Improved emergency preparedness can save lives, alleviate the victims, and allow communities to resume normal activities more rapidly (Escudero et al., 2018). Therefore, in order to cope with the massive disruption, it is necessary for societies/humans to plan the relief operations as well as to mitigate risk in advance (Nikbakhsh, E. & Zanjirani Farahani, R. 2011). There are a number of researches have been conducted based on disaster relief operations (Van Wassenhove, L. 2006; Balcik et al., 2008; Bradt, 2009; Pedraza et al., 2010; Who. int., 2011; Nikbakhsh & Farahani. 2011; Christopher & Tatham, 2011; Hermitte et al., 2014; He & Zhuang, 2016; Rabta et al., 2018; McIsaac et al., 2019; Maghfiroh & Hanaoka, 2020; Akbari & Shiri, 2022) with the same goal of agile relief operations. In disaster situations, various agencies such as non-governmental organizations (NGOs), regional disaster management authorities, and other special scout's teams/military come together with the same goal of saving lives by providing emergency relief to the victims such as first aid kits, water, food, medicines, and shelters (Balcik et al., 2008). In the past, there weren't enough resources to handle disaster relief activities successfully, but now the advent of new technology makes human life easier (McIsaac et al., 2019). However, even with improved technologies, communities can't handle natural or man-made disasters (such as atomic wars, explosions, transportation accidents, and other miscellaneous uncertain incidents. Therefore, in order to cope with the massive disruption, it is necessary for societies/humans to plan relief operations as well as to mitigate risk in advance (Nikbakhsh and Farahani, 2011).

According to the findings of Mohd et al. (2018), five critical factors ensure all the victims throughout the occurrence of the disaster are managed adequately. Integrated information, efficient communication, collaboration, coordination, and cooperation among several parties such as (government, NGOs, Hospitals, Fire stations, police, and army) are the five distinguishing factors that enhance the efficiency of disaster relief operations (Ab Malik et al., 2020). These factors have been further discussed in detail incorporating multimode transportation in the following sections as alone the integration of transportation system is not the solution for efficient disaster relief operations.

Multimode Transportation

The integration between two or more modes of transportation for the movement of goods from one place to its destination is known as multimodal transportation (Kengpol et al. 2014). Transportation plays an enormous role throughout the disaster management cycle as it helps to move the required materials such as shelter, medicines, food, water, etc., before the disaster, movement of victims, and emergency equipment during the disaster and post-disaster relief operations (Roy et al., 2014). However, apart from different preventive measures which have been considered in the planning phase, still, transportation faces several challenges in post-disaster relief operations (Balcik & Beamon, 2008) due to poor transport infrastructure, geographical weather conditions, and uncertainties restrict the efficiency of the logistic operation (Nikbakhsh & Farahani, 2011).

Transportation adaptability and strength can be accomplished through the use of multi-modular transportation under non-emergency situations (standard commercial operations via land, air, sea, etc.) as well as in disaster/emergency conditions (such as air ambulances, drones, military resources, and helicopters) should be accessible when other modes are inaccessible due to destabilized infrastructure. Such as a Typhoon in the Philippines (2013) and the (2008) Haiti flood, distribution supplies are the best examples of multi-modular transportation ranging from 1.4 percent to 7.9 percent (Ertem et al., 2017). Furthermore, as a result of the earthquake in the Wenchuan, region of China on May 12, 2008, a total of 19 helicopters and six cargo planes took part in relief operations within the first 24 hours. There were around 5800 military medical and rescue troops along with 150 tons of supplies that were transported to the affected area (Li & Tang, 2008).

Figure 8. Conceptual Framework (Integration of Multimode Transport to Support Disaster Relief Operations)

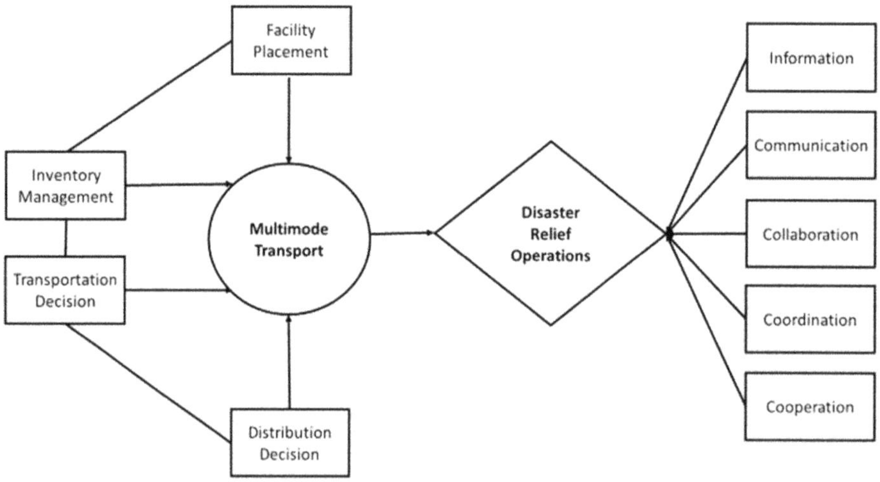

The integration of multimodal transportation with the components of disaster relief operations is necessary as alone the integration of multimode transport system is not the only solution to support disaster relief operations but the integration of information sharing, emergency communications, collaborations, coordination among several agencies, and cooperation with each other under disaster conditions could be the five distinguishing factors that increase the efficiency of emergency relief operations (Mohd et al., 2018; Ab Malik et al., 2020). Such as the first element is information, according to Lee and Zbinden (2003), an integrated information system is the essential need of humanitarian organizations in order to get more accurate, timely, and transparent information and it plays a crucial role in relief operations i.e. In a short period of time, information about the disaster may emerge from a variety of sources or from the same person and the same location. A single request from an individual may be handled by the emergency management team and non-governmental organizations at the same time (Gao et al., 2011). The second element is communication, it has significant contributions to disaster relief operations while failures in communication channels whether landlines, cell phones, or radio channels may affect the disaster relief operations as a whole. (E. Martin et al., 2016). Collaboration is the third element that plays a central role in emergency conditions i.e. majority of the emergency management team, particularly the NGOs, are unaware of how and where to communicate and retrieve catastrophe-related information with or from others (White et al., 2009). However, the integration of communication may lead to providing a platform from which they can get the necessary information timely. The fourth element is coordination i.e. the conventional methods of disaster management are generally unable to utilize their maximum capabilities because of very little or poor coordination (Rodzi et al., 2016). Likewise, lack of coordination within the disaster management team in a volatile environment, it is difficult to convey real-time information (Gao et al., 2011). Despite the chaotic nature of a disaster, still there is a need for a disaster information coordination tool. The last element is cooperation, government agencies consistently look for the cooperation of victims in emergency conditions, especially during the relocation phase (Joshi & Nishimura, 2016). Additionally, the cooperation of NGOs and non-profit organizations is required to avoid duplicating efforts, such as the rebuilding of a long-term housing program (E. Martin et al., 2016).

Humanitarian Logistics

Humanitarian logistics plays a significant role in disaster relief operations such as evacuating the victims, transporting them to a safe place, providing relief items, and supplying humanitarian aid in the affected area (Berkoune et al., 2012), no humanitarian field vehicles mean no humanitarian logistics and no humanitarian logistics mean no supply of foods, aids, and other humanitarian activities to support disaster relief operations (Wassenhove & Pedraza Martinez, 2012). The humanitarian supply chain is not like a military or commercial supply chain because of unknown demand (Wassenhove & Pedraza Martinez, 2012) in the commercial supply chain (Reza et al., 2020), there are different numbers of forecasting techniques that could be used to forecast demand based on historic data (Sharma, 2018), whereas the humanitarian supply chain operates in unseen situations (L'Hermitte et al., 2015; Charles et al., 2010) and have to face complex contextual factors resultant in high cost and lead time in delivering humanitarian aids in a timely manner (L'Hermitte et al., 2014). Humanitarian logistics plays a major role in disaster relief operations i.e. after the Asian tsunami in 2005, humanitarian logistics received significant value from logistics academicians as well as researchers' points of view (Kovács and Spens, 2007). According to Thomas (2004), speedy services in humanitarian logistics are based on post-disaster availability of aid supplies to victims and the movement of casualties by any means of transportation. An efficient humanitarian operation addresses the immediate needs of a community while reducing vulnerability in the quickest way possible with the fewest possible resources (Wassenhove, 2006). The response to a disaster could be local, national, or global scale, such as local system is typically the ones that provide an immediate response in emergency conditions. These systems consist of government institutions, and nongovernmental organizations, with local representation, (if needed the Army, the Police and Fire

Departments, and other civil agencies (Pedraza Martinez et al., 2009). Likewise, the national plan is activated when the local system is overwhelmed by disaster. Likewise, the international system is triggered if the national system is not capable to respond to catastrophes.

Structure of Humanitarian Logistics

The structure of the humanitarian logistics chain is comprised of three primary stages as shown in the figure. 9. Acquisition and purchase of supplies, pre-positioning, and storage of goods, and finally transportation (Tomasini & Wassenhove, 2009; Nikbakhsh & Farahani, 2011).

Figure 9. Structure of Humanitarian Logistics

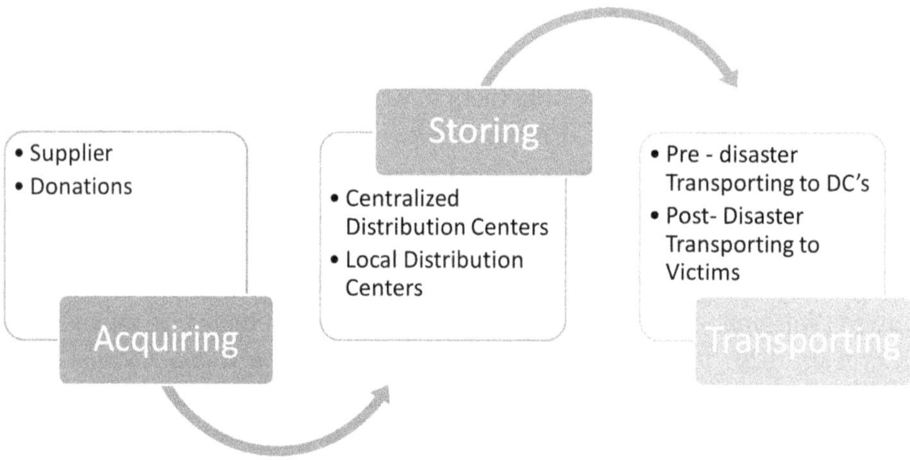

Acquisition and purchase of supplies is the initial step in any humanitarian logistics chain. It is the responsibility of every relief organization to source the necessary materials and equipment from reliable sources either (local or international) prior to the emergency situations and also strengthen the supplier relationship in order to get uninterruptable supplies from multiple sources in case of emergency. Reducing costs (especially in light of the possibility of inflation in local markets after disasters), ensuring goods are available when they're needed, minimizing lead times, and arranging in-kind donations are the primary issues at this stage (Balcik et al., 2010).

After acquiring the essential supplies and equipment before the disaster and post-disaster phases, pre-positioning and storing relief goods is the essential responsibility of relief organizations to store their goods and equipment in appropriate locations, by taking into account the proximity to potentially hazardous regions (Balcik et al.,

2010). Likewise, higher prices of building and managing permanent warehouses, costs of holding the tools and equipment, and the possibility that products could deteriorate are some of the main challenges associated with this stage. Additionally, there is a great possibility that warehouses would be destroyed during natural disasters, hence, those warehouses that are utilized for humanitarian operations must have stronger resistance against natural disasters and be positioned in an advantageous manner (Nikbakhsh & Farahani, 2011).

Finally, transportation is the final and most important stage of any humanitarian logistics network. This is the stage in which human personnel, tools, and other essential items are supplied to predefined storage locations, centralized distribution locations, and finally regions that are adversely affected by a disaster. The most challenging aspect of humanitarian logistics is transportation in the aftermath of a disaster, and this is true regardless of how many precautions and preparations have been considered (Balcik & Beamon, 2008). This is mainly due to the devastated infrastructure, geographical and climatic conditions, and high risks of uncertainties following the disaster.

HUMANITARIAN LOGISTICS - A CASE OF PAKISTAN

Considering the history of major disasters occurring in Pakistan, this bookcase aims to identify the current relief operations in Pakistan. Secondly, the reliability of this framework in a developing country like Pakistan where thousands of people lost their lives due to a lack of disaster planning, poor infrastructure, non-integrated transportation network, and information system. Data has been collected from humanitarian organizations, including the National disaster management authority of Pakistan (NDMCA, 2022).

Natural Disasters in Pakistan

Since its independence, Pakistan is facing man-made disasters due to its political issues with neighboring countries as well as natural disasters such as floods, earthquakes, droughts, rains, extreme temperatures, landslides, tropical cyclones, and depletion of glaciers. However, these natural and man-made disasters not only affect the country but also affect the economy of the country, life of thousands of people, and infrastructure. In figure. 10, it's showing the contribution of natural disasters type in Pakistan since its independence till 2016.

Figure 10. (Natural Disasters in Pakistan, 2022)

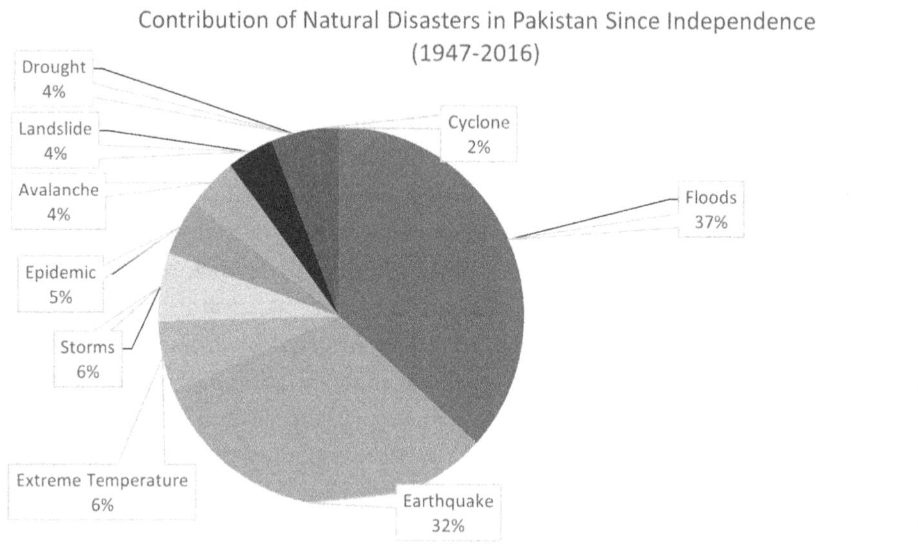

In the following figure. 11. It's showing the analysis of the past ten years of recorded disasters in Pakistan and the number of deaths associated with them.

Figure 11. Disaster Types and Deaths (NDMCA, 2022)

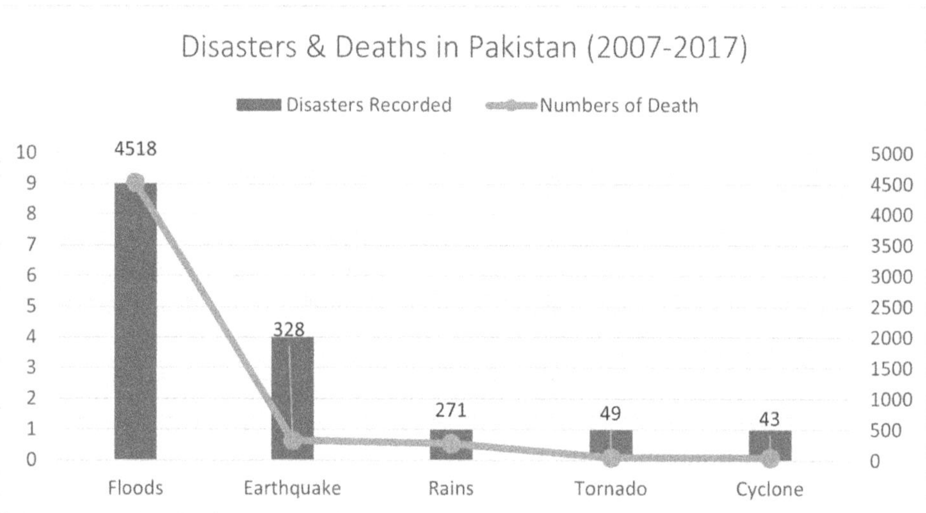

In the figure. 12, it's demonstrating the impact of natural disasters on infrastructure in Pakistan.

Figure 12. Impacts on Infrastructure (NDMCA, 2022)

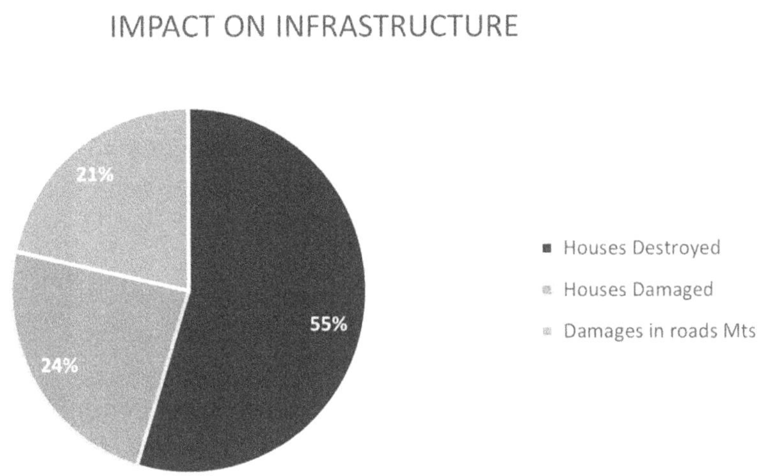

Figure 13. Conceptual Model for Efficient Disaster Relief Operations in Pakistan

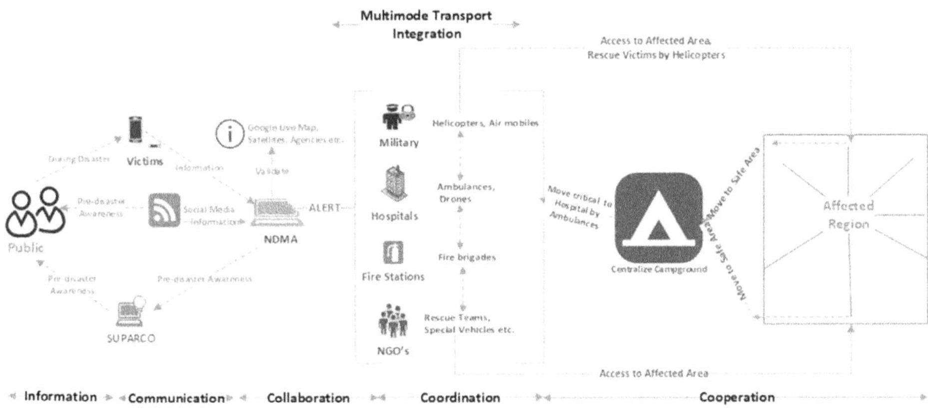

The National Disaster Management Authority (NDMA) must take initiatives to provide pre-disaster awareness to the general public through social media in cooperation with the national space agency Pakistan Space and Upper Atmosphere Research Commission (SUPARCO), with the aim to train each individual regarding action plans in emergency conditions. Such as during emergency conditions the locals give messages to NDMA via call, SMS, social media, etc. The NDMA ensures the efficacy of news or validates the information with the help of google live maps, satellites, etc., or big data analytics before sending the alerts to the participating bodies such as the army, police, fire brigades, NGOs, and hospitals, etc. based on the magnitude of the disasters. The participating bodies will make an effective disaster relief plan and act accordingly using multi modes of transport to save the life of victims via joint relief operations as shown in figure 13.

CONCLUSION

Throughout history, natural disasters have always had a tremendous impact on the lives of human beings, the economy of the country, and its infrastructure in every country whether it's developed, developing, or undeveloped. However, preventative measures to lessen the adverse effects of natural disasters are an essential step toward the achievement of better living conditions for all human beings. Despite advancements in infrastructure, disasters still continue to kill a significant number of people. Therefore, in these circumstances, the successful execution of relief efforts is the greatest concern of all participating agencies. Humanitarian logistics systems are an essential component of disaster management systems that helps to design, implement, control, and effectively manage the flow of emergency equipment to victims during devastating conditions. This chapter outlines the fundamentals of disaster management including the phases of disaster management, disaster relief operations, and the five distinguished factors that enhance the efficiency of disaster relief operations along with multimode transportation, humanitarian logistics systems, and its characteristics. Furthermore, a conceptual model for efficient disaster relief operations in Pakistan has been defined in this chapter. In the end, it appears that a number of different facets of humanitarian logistics require additional study from academics and practitioners such as the development of a more advanced integrated multi-modular transportation model with other factors of disaster relief operations for dealing with the complexities and unpredictability of catastrophes.

REFERENCES

Ab Malik, M., Omar, E., & Maon, S. (2020). Humanitarian Logistics: A Disaster Relief Operations Framework During Pandemic Covid-19 in Achieving Healthy Communities. *Advances in Business Research International Journal*, *6*(2), 101. doi:10.24191/abrij.v6i2.11114

Akbari, V., & Shiri, D. (2022). An online optimization approach for post-disaster relief distribution with online blocked edges. *Computers & Operations Research*, *137*, 105533. doi:10.1016/j.cor.2021.105533

Alexander, D. (2002). *Principles of emergency planning and management.* Terra Publishing.

Altay, N., & Green, W. III. (2006). OR/MS research in disaster operations management. *European Journal of Operational Research*, *175*(1), 475–493. doi:10.1016/j.ejor.2005.05.016

Baidoo, J. (2017). Humanitarian Logistics - An Exposition of the Challenges to Rapid Response in Disaster Relief Operations in Ghana. *Texila International Journal of Management*, *3*(2), 252–259. doi:10.21522/TIJMG.2015.03.02.Art024

Balamir, M. (2022). The "disaster cycle" (DC) and actors in disaster management. *International Journal of Disaster Resilience in the Built Environment.* Advance online publication. doi:10.1108/IJDRBE-01-2022-0008

Balcik, B., Beamon, B., Krejci, C., Muramatsu, K., & Ramirez, M. (2010). Coordination in humanitarian relief chains: Practices, challenges and opportunities. *International Journal of Production Economics*, *126*(1), 22–34. doi:10.1016/j.ijpe.2009.09.008

Balcik, B., Beamon, B. M., & Smilowitz, K. (2008). Last mile distribution in humanitarian relief. *Journal of Intelligent Transport Systems*, *12*(2), 51–63. doi:10.1080/15472450802023329

Berkoune, D., Renaud, J., Rekik, M., & Ruiz, A. (2012). Transportation in disaster response operations. *Socio-Economic Planning Sciences*, *46*(1), 23–32. doi:10.1016/j.seps.2011.05.002

Bradt, D. (2009). Evidence-Based Decision-Making (Part II): Applications in Disaster Relief Operations. *Prehospital and Disaster Medicine*, *24*(6), 479–492. doi:10.1017/S1049023X0000738X PMID:20301064

Carter, N. (2008). *Disaster Management A Disaster Manager's Handbook* (2nd ed.). Asian Development Bank.

Chari, F., Ngcamu, B., & Novukela, C. (2020). Supply chain risks in humanitarian relief operations: A case of Cyclone Idai relief efforts in Zimbabwe. *Journal Of Humanitarian Logistics And Supply Chain Management*, *11*(1), 29–45. doi:10.1108/JHLSCM-12-2019-0080

Charles, A., Lauras, M., & Van Wassenhove, L. (2010). A model to define and assess the agility of supply chains: Building on humanitarian experience. *International Journal of Physical Distribution & Logistics Management*, *40*(8/9), 722–741. doi:10.1108/09600031011079355

Chopra, S. (2013). *Supply chain management* (5th ed.). Pearson.

Christopher, M., & Tatham, P. (2011). *Humanitarian logistics* (1st ed.). Kogan.

Das, B. (2022). *A prolonged drought destroyed Indus Valley Civilisation, new study says*. nature.com. doi:10.1038/nindia.2018.61

De Smet, H., Schreurs, B., & Leysen, J. (2015). The Response Phase of the Disaster Management Life Cycle Revisited Within the Context of "Disasters Out of the Box". *Journal of Homeland Security and Emergency Management*, *12*(2). Advance online publication. doi:10.1515/jhsem-2015-0005

Emdat.be. (2022). *emdat_db*. Available at: https://www.emdat.be/emdat_db/

Ertem, M., İşbilir, M., & Şahin Arslan, A. (2017). Review of intermodal freight transportation in humanitarian logistics. *European Transport Research Review*, *9*(1), 10. doi:10.100712544-017-0226-z

Escudero, L., Garín, M., Monge, J., & Unzueta, A. (2018). On preparedness resource allocation planning for natural disaster relief under endogenous uncertainty with time-consistent risk-averse management. *Computers & Operations Research*, *98*, 84–102. doi:10.1016/j.cor.2018.05.010

Garnett, J., & Moore, M. (2010). Enhancing Disaster Recovery: Lessons from Exemplary International Disaster Management Practices. *Journal of Homeland Security and Emergency Management*, *7*(1). Advance online publication. doi:10.2202/1547-7355.1711

Gavidia, J. (2017). A model for enterprise resource planning in emergency humanitarian logistics. *Journal of Humanitarian Logistics and Supply Chain Management*, *7*(3), 246–265. doi:10.1108/JHLSCM-02-2017-0004

Government of Pakistan (GoP). (2011). *Pakistan: Flood Impact Assessment*. Available at: http://www.finance.gov.pk/survey/chapter_11/Special%20Section_2.pdf

Haddow, G. D., Bullock, J. A., & Coppola, D. P. (2008). Introduction to emergency management. In *Butterworth-Heinemann homeland security series*. Elsevier Inc.

Haddow, J. A. B. (2004). *Introduction to Emergency Management*. ButterworthHeinemann.

He, F., & Zhuang, J. (2016). Balancing pre-disaster preparedness and post-disaster relief. *European Journal of Operational Research*, *252*(1), 246–256. doi:10.1016/j.ejor.2015.12.048

Kengpol, A., Tuammee, S., & Tuominen, M. (2014). The development of a framework for route selection in multimodal transportation. *International Journal of Logistics Management*, *25*(3), 581–610. doi:10.1108/IJLM-05-2013-0064

Kovács, G., & Spens, K. (2007). Humanitarian logistics in disaster relief operations. *International Journal of Physical Distribution & Logistics Management*, *37*(2), 99–114. doi:10.1108/09600030710734820

L'Hermitte, C., Bowles, M., Tatham, P., & Brooks, B. (2015). An integrated approach to agility in humanitarian logistics. *Journal of Humanitarian Logistics and Supply Chain Management*, *5*(2), 209–233. doi:10.1108/JHLSCM-04-2014-0016

L'Hermitte, C., Tatham, P., & Bowles, M. (2014). Classifying logistics-relevant disasters: Conceptual model and empirical illustration. *Journal of Humanitarian Logistics and Supply Chain Management*, *4*(2), 155–178. doi:10.1108/JHLSCM-07-2013-0025

Lee, H. W., & Zbinden, M. (2003). *Marrying logistics and technology for effective relief*. Forced.

Li, L., & Tang, S. (2008). An Artificial Emergency-Logistics-Planning System for Severe Disasters. *IEEE Intelligent Systems*, *23*(4), 86–88. doi:10.1109/MIS.2008.56

Maghfiroh, M., & Hanaoka, S. (2020). Multi-modal relief distribution model for disaster response operations. *Progress In Disaster Science*, *6*, 100095. doi:10.1016/j.pdisas.2020.100095

Maghsoudi, A., & Moshtari, M. (2020). Challenges in disaster relief operations: Evidence from the 2017 Kermanshah earthquake. *Journal Of Humanitarian Logistics And Supply Chain Management*, *11*(1), 107–134. doi:10.1108/JHLSCM-08-2019-0054

McIsaac, J., Brulle, J., Burg, J., Tarnacki, G., Sullivan, C., & Wassel, R. (2019). Blockchain Technology for Disaster and Refugee Relief Operations. *Prehospital and Disaster Medicine*, *34*(s1), s106–s106. doi:10.1017/S1049023X1900222X

Mohd, S., Fathi, M., Harun, A., & Omar Chong, N. (2018). Key issues in the management of the humanitarian aid distribution process during and post-disaster in Malaysia. *Planning Malaysia Journal*, *16*(5). Advance online publication. doi:10.21837/pmjournal.v16.i5.425

Negi, S. (2022). Humanitarian logistics challenges in disaster relief operations: A humanitarian organisations' perspective. *Journal of Transport and Supply Chain Management*, *16*. Advance online publication. doi:10.4102/jtscm.v16i0.691

Nelan, M., Wachtendorf, T., & Penta, S. (2018). Agility in Disaster Relief: A Social Construction Approach. *Risk, Hazards &Amp. Crisis In Public Policy*, *9*(2), 132–150. doi:10.1002/rhc3.12135

Nikbakhsh, E., & Zanjirani Farahani, R. (2011). *Humanitarian Logistics Planning in Disaster Relief Operations*. Logistics Operations and Management. doi:10.1016/B978-0-12-385202-1.00015-3

Pedraza Martinez, A., Stapleton, O., & Van Wassenhove, L. (2010). Field Vehicle Fleet Management in Humanitarian Operations: A Case-Based Approach. SSRN *Electronic Journal*. doi:10.2139/ssrn.1437544

Peterman, R. (2017). *What Is Project Management?* https://project-management.com/what-is-project-management/

Rabta, B., Wankmüller, C., & Reiner, G. (2018). A drone fleet model for last-mile distribution in disaster relief operations. *International Journal of Disaster Risk Reduction*, *28*, 107–112. doi:10.1016/j.ijdrr.2018.02.020

Rana, I., Asim, M., Aslam, A., & Jamshed, A. (2021). Disaster management cycle and its application for flood risk reduction in urban areas of Pakistan. *Urban Climate*, *38*, 100893. doi:10.1016/j.uclim.2021.100893

ReliefWeb. (2005). *The Kashmir earthquake of October 8, 2005: Impacts in Pakistan - Pakistan*. Available at: https://reliefweb.int/report/pakistan/kashmir-earthquake-october-8-2005-impacts-pakistan

Reliefweb.int. (2018). *Natural catastrophes and man-made disasters in 2017: a year of record- breaking losses*. Available at: https://reliefweb.int/sites/reliefweb.int/files/resources/sigma1_2018_en.pdf

Reza, S., Mubarik, M., Naghavi, N., & Rub Nawaz, R. (2020). Relationship marketing and third-party logistics: Evidence from hotel industry. *Journal Of Hospitality And Tourism Insights*, *3*(3), 371–393. doi:10.1108/JHTI-07-2019-0095

Ritchie, H., & Roser, M. (2022). *Natural Disasters Empirical View*. Our World in Data. Available at: https://ourworldindata.org/natural-disasters

Roy, P., Albores, P., & Brewster, C. (2014). *Logistical framework for last mile relief distribution in humanitarian supply chains: Considerations from the field*. Scholar Bank. Available at: http://dr.lib.sjp.ac.lk/bitstream/handle/123456789/1598/Applicability%20of%20Last%20Mile%20Humanitarian%20Logistics%20Optimization%20for%20Natural%20Flood%20Disasters%20A%20Systematic%20Review.pdf?sequence=1&isAllowed=y

Sarjana, S., Khayati, N., Warini, L., & Wiyati, P. (2020). The Importance of Transportation Management in Optimizing Supply Chain Management at Industrial Estate. *Jurnal Transportasi Multimoda*, *18*(1). Advance online publication. doi:10.25104/mtm.v18i1.1643

Scholten, K., Sharkey Scott, P., & Fynes, B. (2014). Mitigation processes – antecedents for building supply chain resilience. *Supply Chain Management*, *19*(2), 211–228. doi:10.1108/SCM-06-2013-0191

Seth, I. (2022). *An overview of Destruction in Pompeii*. RTF. Retrieved 9 August 2022, from https://www.re-thinkingthefuture.com/city-and-architecture/a4900-an-overview-of-destruction-in-pompeii/

Sharma, V. (2018). Demand-Driven Forecasting in the Supply Chain. *The Cloud-Based Demand-Driven Supply Chain*, 1-41.

Thomas, A. (2004). *International Aid and Trade Review: Evaluating Humanitarian Logistics*. Available at: https://fritzinstitute.org/PDFs/InTheNews/2004/AidandTrade_0104.pdf

Tomasini, R., & Van Wassenhove, L. N. (2009). *Humanitarian Logistics*. Palgrave Macmillan. doi:10.1057/9780230233485

Van Wassenhove, L. (2006). Humanitarian aid logistics: Supply chain management in high gear. *The Journal of the Operational Research Society*, *57*(5), 475–489. doi:10.1057/palgrave.jors.2602125

Van Wassenhove, L., & Pedraza Martinez, A. (2010). Using OR to adapt supply chain management best practices to humanitarian logistics. *International Transactions in Operational Research*, *19*(1-2), 307–322. doi:10.1111/j.1475-3995.2010.00792.x

Who.int. (2011). *Pakistan floods 2010 Early recovery plan for the health sector.* Available at: https://www.who.int/hac/crises/pak/pakistan_early_recovery_plan_12february2011.pdf

World Bank. (2005). *Pakistan 2005 Earthquake Preliminary Damage and Needs Assessment.* Available at: http://siteresources.worldbank.org/PAKISTANEXTN/Resources/Publications-and-Reports/Damage-Assessment-Main.pdf

Chapter 6
Lean, Green, and Agile Supply Chain Practices

Ayesha Saeed
Southwest Jiaotong University, Chengdu, China

Rizwan Shoukat
Southwest Jiaotong University, Chengdu, China

ABSTRACT

In response to increased competition in recent years, businesses have been pushed to adopt new procedures, such as establishing updated information and communication systems and creating more streamlined production processes. The potential for supply chains to facilitate the introduction of innovative management practices is seen as crucial to the sector's future success. Three ideas, "lean," "green," and "agile," deserve serious consideration because of their potential to significantly improve supply chain efficiency. However, combining agile and lean principles to lessen environmental consequences is a relatively new issue that is not well-defined in terms of structure. Through a comprehensive analysis of the literature on lean, green, and agile paradigms, this chapter hopes to identify potential future lines of inquiry and identify knowledge gaps. This chapter is an effort to synthesize recent findings on the interconnectedness of lean, green, and agile practices in supply chain management.

DOI: 10.4018/978-1-6684-6663-6.ch006

INTRODUCTION

Customers now hold more sway than ever, thanks to the rise of globalization, instantaneous information gathering via the Internet and search engines like Google, and a plethora of options available to them. They look for products that are cutting edge in terms of functionality, speed, variety, dependability, quality, and price. In addition, the most discerning customers of today want their needs met nearly immediately. The typical forecast-driven lengthy supply chain is no longer viable for consumer goods due to the inherent risk. Here, we'll talk about how you rise to the issue by implementing a more streamlined and adaptable supply chain. Some people seem to have different ideas about what is meant by the terms "leanness" and "agility" in the workplace, much like the meaning of the ever-popular "quality" in business.

There are three main types of supply chain models, and these are the classic, lean, and agile approaches. It is crucial to understand the differences and the applications of each model and application, whether pure or hybrid, because many supply chains will be a combination of models. While the conventional approach to supply chain management is discussed, the focus here is on leaner, more flexible methods of operation.

This chapter is broken into two sections. A look back to lean's past, what lean supply chains (LSC) are, how they work, what characteristics they share with agile supply chains, and how they may be put into practice are the topics of this chapter.

BACKGROUND

Lean enterprises, like other tenets of the quality movement, have their roots in the industrial sector. The origins of the Lean enterprise philosophy, which is more of a philosophy than a methodology, may be traced back to the 1960s Japanese automobile industry and the book 'The Machine That Changed the World' by James P. Womack et al. (1990). The story of the Toyota production method for automobiles is told in The Machine That Changed the World. Since Henry Ford adopted the conveyor belt for producing cars in 1913, very little had changed in the production of automobiles until that point. It wasn't until Henry Ford invented the assembly line that mass production of the automobile became possible. Ford's conveyor belt (a.k.a. assembly line) method entailed having workers perform small, specialized tasks as the belt moved along. According to Ford, "the stupidest man could become an expert in two days" if the process of manufacturing were simplified to the point where even the most incompetent worker could pick up the necessary skills in that time. Using this moving conveyor belt method, Ford was able to manufacture 250,000 automobiles annually, with each car selling for $500. The car went from being something only the wealthy could buy to being a common household item.

Constraints included a high volume of routine work with little room for error, a rushed work schedule, and a constantly moving conveyer belt. The workers stopped thinking about the big vision and started treating the vehicle-building process like a series of useless tasks, like adjusting the tightness of bolts on a piece of metal that is in motion. Working on an assembly line is a horrible way to make a living, and I speak from experience when I say that. Use up a barrel containing ten thousand bolts while you stand next to it, and you'll know the meaning of disappointment. The next step is to take another 10,000 bolts and set them exactly where the original 10,000 were Walker (1952). After Ford's Model T was a smashing success, competitors immediately adopted the assembly line technology. In contrast to Ford's model exclusivity, competitors like GM and Chrysler began offering a wider variety of vehicles beginning in the 1920s. Ford stopped production for seven months as the company rushed out new models to meet the demands of the market.

Alterations to older models necessitate new tooling and dies, therefore mass production through assembly line is still in use. The job at each stage of production was still broken down to the lowest feasible level, workers were not encouraged to think critically, and inspection and testing were still relied on to assure a consistent end product. It is widely acknowledged that Toyota's Ohno Taiichi was the catalyst for the industry's next technological breakthrough. Ohno Taiichi spent time in the 1960s at American auto manufacturers, and it was there that he was inspired to create lean manufacturing once he returned to Japan. Lean Manufacturing (also known as Toyotaism or the Toyota Production System) emphasizes eliminating all excess inventory at every level of production, from raw materials and components to intermediate and final products.

Materials from specialized suppliers must be delivered to the factory floor at the precise point in production at which they are needed, followed by prompt packaging and transportation to the customer, as required by the "just-in-time" (JIT) technique. There is no wiggle room because there are no spare supplies on hand. Accurate planning of activities and resources, open communication with suppliers, reliable suppliers, and timetables are required to ensure that materials arrive on time and meet the specification, machines are kept in working order with no downtime, operators make no mistakes, and the finished product is delivered to customers on time. Cards or Kanban are frequently used to facilitate this exchange between a workstation and the downstream buffer.

Any action at the workstation is blocked until a card is inserted. The input buffer is accessed to retrieve the required elements, the operation is executed, the card is attached to the completed result, and the output buffer is accessed to save the completed result. A downstream workstation is notified that it should start the next cycle upon receiving the card, which is then delivered back upstream. Depending on how many cards are out there, a certain amount of space must be allocated for them in the buffer. A Kanban system ensures that a product is only manufactured when it is actually needed. When using the "just-in-time" method, mass production is usually not an option, hence things are frequently made in "batches" of one. Because of this, "single minute exchange of dies" (SMED) has become the norm, requiring operators to be as flexible as the system itself. Reduced numbers of managers and quality auditors are commonplace in lean operations. By learning about, and being given the authority to implement, the essential production standards, the operators effectively become their own set of inspectors and supervisors.

When the Five Ss (Sort, Set in place, Shine, Standardize, and Sustain) of Total Productive Maintenance (TPM) are put into practice, equipment reliability improves and the operator feels more "ownership" over the unit. A key component of Toyota's plan entailed maximizing output throughout all manufacturing stages. Each "Work Cell" on a moving assembly line handles a specific task, such as mounting the transmission, the seating, etc. Within the limitations of a timeframe (the allocated time on the continuous line for manufacturing to pass from one stage to the next) and the limitations of the defined requirements, every group is accountable for its section of the assembly and might be able to make minor adjustments to procedures.

By employing Quality at Source or Zero Quality Control before to production, and Poka Yoke (error proofing) throughout production, we can ensure that standards are upheld at all times. One of the most striking things a tourist to a Lean factory will notice is the complete absence of a storage area, inventories of supplies between workstations, and stocks of finished goods. Lean may seem like it's about stock control, but that's not what it really is. Lean, however, requires more than just a more efficient inventory management system; it also entails eliminating unnecessary steps, or "muda." Waste, or muda in Japanese, is the utilization of resources without the generation of any benefit to society. In this approach, eliminating waste is central to the Lean mind-set. Anything that doesn't improve the final product in some manner should be discarded, and measures should be put in place to prevent a repeat.

Everything must be named and then accounted for before it can be removed. Toyota uses a system of seven categories called 'mudas' to identify sources of waste. There are seven fundamental tenets of Buddhism known as mudas.

The following are examples of non-essential processes:

- Overproduction
- Waiting
- Unnecessary transportation
- Unnecessary motion
- Unnecessary waiting

- Stocks
- Flaws

The plan is to detect inefficiencies, investigate their root causes, eradicate them, then improve upon and standardize the remaining processes (until further improvements are found).

LSC TOOLS

Eight tools and strategies made up the original Toyota model of Lean Manufacturing, from which several hybrids emerged.

1. TPM
2. 5s
3. JIT
4. SMED
5. Jidoka
6. Functioning Production Units (Cells)
7. The Seventh Kanban
8. Poka Yoke since Toyota's Lean Manufacturing model was developed, lean thinking and the LSC have progressed and incorporated new methods, tools, and techniques. As a result, we added the following two:
9. Value-added-process-mapping value-stream diagram
10. Lean Sigma and FIT SIGMA

THE CHARACTERISTICS OF LSC

To some extent, an LSC can be understood in relation to Toyota Production Systems (TPS) and Lean Sigma. The five tenets of Lean were developed by Womack et al. (1990) and are based on TPS. Value, value stream, flow, pull, and excellence are these guiding principles. However, as time and experience have passed, things have evolved and businesses across all sectors, from manufacturing to services, have adopted Lean principles. In the past, supply chains were generally considered from the perspectives of demand planning, upstream supplier communication, and resource management.

Figure 1. Characteristics of LSC management

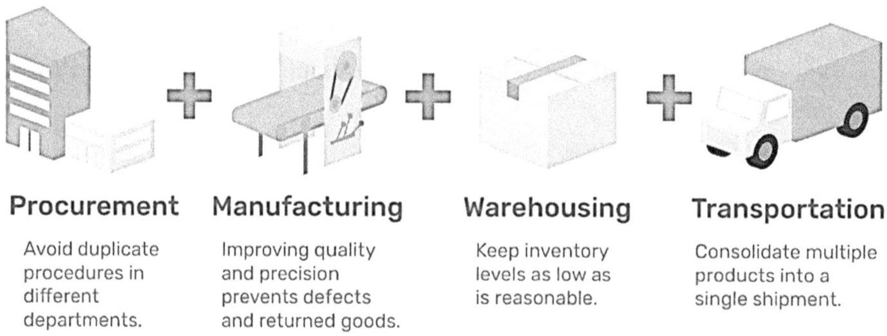

Perhaps there is a greater focus on providing for clients at the lowest possible cost. Lean is primarily driven by a desire to reduce costs, but it also places a premium on speed of production and product quality. Instead of competing with one another, supply chains compete with consumers for market share. Therefore, a supply chain must be effective, and it must have four interconnected features or aims.

1. Zero waste
2. Continuity of operations
3. Quite effective.
4. Quality control

ZERO WASTE

Waste elimination is at the heart of the lean approach as outlined by Womack et al. (1990), with the first two principles (i.e., value and value stream) focused on doing just that. Their slogan has been "eradicate inefficiency and generate wealth for your company." The first step is to map the value-adding operations in an organization, known as the "value stream," and then use that information to map the wasteful processes. Because of the importance placed on minimizing waste, the term "lean" is sometimes used interchangeably with "waste-free." Since reducing waste typically requires negligible financial outlay, it is an excellent place to begin when attempting to establish a more efficient supply chain. Surplus stock is a common source of unnecessary expenditure.

Many businesses eventually began to evaluate their "leanness" only by how efficiently they managed their inventories. There has been some success in reducing stock on hand through inventory reduction initiatives including enterprise resource planning (ERP), just-in-time (JIT), and other cutting-edge techniques to supply chain management; nevertheless, these initiatives can be further refined. The truth is that 75% of all manufacturers keep 25% extra stock than they need. Leanness Studies tends to advocate for a strategy centred on inventory (Schonberger, 2003). Using a formula of "annual cost of goods divided by value of inventory," Schonberger rated and graded businesses based on their inventory performance over the previous year. While this method is indicative of a company's inventory policy, it is not necessarily indicative of the company's actual financial performance. A company that manufactures pharmaceuticals will have a different inventory policy than one that manufactures fast-moving consumer goods (FMCGs).

Among the seven 'mudas,' inventory is just one. Decreases in cycle or lead times are another area of focus in the war on waste. The length of time it takes to complete a single cycle of a process is known as its cycle time. A customer's order processing cycle may begin with a phone call and end with the shipment of their purchase. Order entry, assembly, inspection, packaging, and shipping are only a few of the numerous individual steps that make up the larger process. Lessening the duration of the entire process, or "cycle time," can be achieved by exploring and adopting alternate methods of doing the work. Eliminating or drastically decreasing non-value-added activities is necessary to decrease cycle time. Defective repairs, machine setup and inspection times, approval wait times, testing times, and schedule delays are all examples of non-value-adding activities that can be cut out of the cycle time. Supply chain that is both lean and agile 205 For example, QRM (Suri, 1998) and SMED (Standard Method for the Effective Development and Management of Cycle Times) are two well-known and formally documented approaches of reducing production cycles (Shingo, 1985).

QRM is based on two main concepts. It's realistic to expect initial utilization rates of 80 or even 70 percent for key resources. Second, prioritize progress toward shorter lead times. These concepts are supported by material requirements planning (MRP) methodologies for production-oriented cells and continuous training. Production changeover durations can be shortened utilizing the SMED technique by first doing a thorough work analysis of the changeover process, then distinguishing between "in process" and "out of process" tasks, and finally optimizing the changeover process's planning, tooling, and operations. Shingo prefers to come up with simple solutions on his own rather than relying on elaborate methods. Although the SMED strategy has proven fruitful, it is essential to remember that its foundations are a reworking of ideas from conventional industrial engineering and work studies.

Outside of QRM and SMED, the lowering of cycle time has emerged as a central tenet of lean thinking. There has been a lot of use of value analysis centered on process mapping charts in service industries like contact centers. Reduced cycle times are achieved by the use of even flow manufacturing (Ballard, 2001) during the assembly of many identical houses. The method consists of three parts:

(1) Overlapping activities within their respective phases of work.
(2) Shortening activity durations using cycle time studies.
(3) Decreasing WIP by training workers to perform several tasks at once.

CONTINUITY OF OPERATIONS

Earlier, we said that the just-in-time (JIT) methodology is a major force behind Lean Supply Chain and that following this methodology necessitates a "like water" flow of materials and finished goods from the supplier through the manufacturing facility to the client. Eliminating the bottlenecks in capacity, synchronizing the processing times of the workstations, and maintaining minimal buffer inventories between processes are all hallmarks of lean manufacturing. The application of suitable methods is essential for efficient operation. Several methods can be used, but the three most common are:

- Constraints theory
- Kanban system
- Cell manufacturing

Traditional batch production areas are converted into flow line layouts in the cellular manufacturing concept, to have a single item go through the line at a time. In actual practice, the batch size is determined by identifying the most important work centres and the most expensive items in inventory. Work centres and processes with the greatest influence on output, customer happiness, operational costs, and inventory carrying charges are prioritized for enhancement. As part of sound management, you should stay away from a wide range of items. When demand is predictable, product diversity is limited, and production volume is high, the cellular manufacturing idea shines.

Toyota Motor Corporation of Japan developed the Kanban system in the 1980s. Both Taiichi Ohno (1988) and Shingo (1989) advocated for the use of Kanban as one of the major instruments of JIT principles as part of the Lean Manufacturing movement. Supermarkets in the United States, in particular, were motivated to implement this practice after observing how it decreased the need for storage space and the volume of goods by simply restocking shelves when they ran out. Kanban has been used to keep the flow of commodities, materials, and information in check outside of Japan with varying degrees of success.

Kanban is Japanese word "card" or "ticket." Identification cards are printed cards with quantity and component number information that are protected by a clear plastic case. It allows components and finished goods to be pushed through the production or distribution chain on demand. As a result, the term "pull system" has come to be used to describe it. The Kanban method has many variations, some of which use alternative indicators like lights, electronics, voice commands, or even hand signs to notify when work is ready. Kanban, which originated in Japan, is now widely recognized as a means of maximizing continuous flow and efficiency while simultaneously lowering costs and stockpile sizes.

As a management theory, Goldratt's Theory of Constraints (TOC) is well regarded (1992). It helps the people in charge of a system get closer to the result they wanted. Neither the idea nor the goal is novel. However, TOC may prove especially helpful in service operations, where determining the exact size of the capacity limitation can be tricky. The time of one or a small number of essential employees is often the limiting factor for businesses that rely on skilled laborer's and many service providers. Implementation Although TOC is easy to understand in theory, implementing it can be challenging since it may necessitate a radical shift in how a business is run. For instance, TOC necessitates switching from making decisions based on costs to making them based on constant enhancement. Lean Sigma is an approach to business that uses statistical techniques like Statistical Process Control to improve the efficiency with which raw materials and finished goods move through a facility.

HIGH LEVEL OF EFFICIENCY

The more prominent notions of lean operations tend to be the concepts of muda, flow and pull system. However, a preliminary review of all these approaches reveals that they all rely on the presence of sufficient machine availability, as we have described earlier. We have found that this is not the case for the vast majority of businesses that have attempted a lean transformation. Maximizing machine uptime by eradicating the sources of downtime is essential for increasing machine availability.

A company's success can be gauged by looking at how long it has been in operation in comparison to how long it was expected to last. Therefore, a high level of efficiency in the activities must be met as a prerequisite for lean principles to be effective. Traditional methods of gauging labor productivity have been supplanted by ones that focus on the control or bottleneck workstation's efficiency (such as the ratio of standard hours to hours worked). In order to maximize productivity in a LSC, one might employ a number of methods and resources. One such method (TPM) and two such tools will be discussed in this article (including OEE and the Five Ss). Japanese Total Preventative Maintenance (TPM) has been shown to maximize OEE and utilization by paying close attention to every stage of production.

TPM promotes self-determination by having operators perform certain maintenance themselves. The title misleads readers since it contains the term "maintenance." TPM is not limited to just maintenance; rather, it encompasses the entire production process. TPM's main objectives are to foster a people- and machine-centric culture of continuous improvement and to create optimal working conditions for the plant. Every worker in the factory is required to participate. Successful implementation takes time and demands dedication from upper management. The Japan Institute of Plant Maintenance is actively spreading the principles of TPM around the world (JIPM). There are five pillars upon which TPM, the manufacturing arm of TQM, is built.

1. One, the reduction of six major losses contributed to a marked increase in production productivity.
2. Establishing a framework whereby operators working in teams of three or fewer may perform maintenance without outside assistance.
3. A reliable system of planned maintenance implemented by skilled engineers.
4. A programme designed to help all full-time workers learn new skills and expand their existing horizons.
5. A preventative maintenance method in which engineers collaborate with manufacturers to minimise the servicing of equipment.

Through TPM, the manufacturing team can maximize the use of their assets and save their production costs by identifying and eliminating the biggest sources of waste in their processes. Total Productive Maintenance (TPM) identifies the following causes of these events: I breakdown, (ii) setup and adjustment, (iii) minor stoppages, (IV) decreased speed, (v) quality faults, and (VI) start-up and shut-down. The purpose of autonomous maintenance is to encourage users to perform routine maintenance tasks such as checking, cleaning, lubricating, adjusting, sizing, small repairs, and spotting abnormalities before they become major problems.

It's a methodical process that returns the machinery to as close to factory fresh as possible. That "with TPM, you do not require experienced craftsmen or engineers and all maintenance is done by operators" is a common misconception, held by certain managers. It's not like that at all. Planned maintenance relies heavily on the establishment of a maintenance policy supported by adequate facilities. TPM's cornerstone is planned maintenance. With the right training, however, operators can carry out a sizable amount of planned maintenance tasks if their skill and education levels are sufficiently high. The bare minimum expected of machine operators is the capacity to clean, lubricate, and make minor changes, as well as the foresight to see when a machine is malfunctioning.

Successful TPM implementation necessitates a systematic training program that runs in tandem with TPM's phases. One-off classes can also be utilized to address a knowledge gap. A chart is used to convey information about a particular piece of equipment and how to configure it or fix it in the workplace. Autonomous maintenance and planned maintenance can do a lot to cut down on breakdowns, but in order to get to "zero breakdowns," you need to specify parts and equipment that are created to deliver full functioning and not to fail.

Only via real-time collaboration between the user company's engineers and designers and the equipment manufacturers can a system of preventative maintenance be realized. The establishment of TPM work groups or committees ensures that all employees are actively engaged in the process. Employees may contribute to TPM in a variety of ways, but some may place a greater priority on certain areas than others (for example, "six big losses" for middle management, "autonomous maintenance" for operators, "planned maintenance" for middle management, and "maintenance prevention" for senior management). To observe a working example of a TPM system in action.

To recap, Total Productive Maintenance (TPM) is a factory-wide continuous improvement program with a focus on modifying the mentality and abilities of workers on the shop floor. Higher equipment reliability, less waste, and better safety statistics are all apparent signs of TPM success, as are the stages of autonomous maintenance that have been completed.

QUALITY CONTROL

Perfection, as proposed by Womack Jones and Roos (1990), is the fifth Lean principle, and it states that a lean manufacturer aims for perfection via an iterative (Kaizen) improvement strategy. The goal of Total Quality Management (TQM) is to eliminate all potential sources of waste in all stages of production to ensure that both the company and its outputs are always improving. An organization that is "going for lean" will have this mentality of constant improvement.

TQM is reached by building upon earlier quality control and quality assurance processes. With the help of root-cause analysis, process improvements may be maintained through standard operating procedure documentation and ongoing training, which is where quality assurance comes in. TQM, or Total Quality Management, refers to a system of continuous improvement that involves everyone in a business, from upper management to entry-level workers. Therefore, quality assurance is the primary motivator for improvement. More rigorous training deployment (e.g.

Black Belts and Green Belts), the Define, Measure, Analyze, Improve, and Control (DMAIC) approach, and measurement are all part of the Six Sigma movement, which grew out of the Total Quality Management (TQM) movement (both variances and savings). Six Sigma has evolved into Lean Sigma and FIT SIGMA, and its ideas are deeply ingrained in the road to perfection in a lean supply chain. Business processes can be made better, faster, and cheaper by combining the predictability of Six Sigma with the speed and agility of Lean, as explained by Basu and Wright (2003). Maximum value flow, shorter cycle times, and fewer defects are the results of a systematic approach to identifying and eliminating non-value-added processes. Additional features are required to maintain the impressive financial outcomes and massive training deployment of Six Sigma and Lean Sigma over the long term.

THE CHARACTERISTICS OF GREEN SUPPLY CHAIN

Environmental concerns have developed and spread faster than a forest fire during the past few of decades, from country to region to globe area, contributing significantly to climate change and global warming. Ischemic heart disease, lung cancer, COPD, stroke, dracunculiasis, cholera, hepatitis, typhoid fever, and norovirus are just few of the human diseases linked to loss of natural resources and air and water pollution. However, the green supply chain concept is put into action to reduce air, water, and waste pollution by using environmentally sound business methods (Khan et al., 2018). While the primary goal of the green concept is, undoubtedly, to promote environmental sustainability, companies often use it in order to "kill two birds with one stone." Green supply chains are gaining popularity because of the many benefits they offer, including lower pollution and production costs, increased economic growth, a competitive edge in the form of happier customers, improved brand image and reputation, and increased access to export markets in environmentally conscious nations. Corporate social responsibility, green manufacturing, waste reduction, recycling and remanufacturing, sustainable/environmentally friendly supply chain, green supply chain, etc. all serve to recognize the green concept as it evolves to encompass new innovations and techniques for protecting environmental sustainability (Cherrafi et al., 2018).

Green supply chain is a relatively new concept that is gaining popularity in order to improve environmental performance along the entire supply chain. We have identified the six crucial success indicators listed below for implementing green supply chain management to achieve greater environmental sustainability.

- Ethical leadership and internal administration
- Customer management

- Supplier management
- Competitiveness

Ethical Leadership and Internal Administration

Leadership support and encouragement are integral parts of any effective internal environment management plan. For firms to successfully adopt eco-friendly practices, internal management is essential. Management is encouraged and inspired to do their part for environmental conservation by the pressure from below. Meanwhile, people's awareness of ecological risks may have a constructive effect on their participation in environmentally friendly practices (Islam et al., 2021).

Customer Management

When it comes to sustainable production, customers may make a huge difference. Indeed, there is a lot of pressure on companies in developing countries to adopt eco-friendly supply chain practices in order to maintain their competitiveness in the modern global economy. Customers' participation is essential for green supply chain management to succeed (Zhang and Yusuf, 2021).

Supplier Management

Customers and vendors must work together to implement green supply chain strategies. Increased incentive schemes, together with increased acceptance and development of novel eco-friendly solutions, are all the result of close collaboration between manufacturers and suppliers. Businesses may be able to improve their operational and environmental performance through the use of technologies, green collaboration agreements, and the transparent application of innovative green practices (Sugandini et al., 2020).

Competitiveness

Several studies found that competence and relevant elements could contribute to the implementation of green practices in the supply chain. Organizations are putting in place green policies less out of a desire to safeguard the environment and more out of a desire to remain competitive. Additional voluntary for competitive aspects may also be attributed to the use of environmentally friendly corporate practices (Pal et al., 2023).

THE CHARACTERISTICS OF AGILE SUPPLY CHAIN

Christopher (2000) describes agility as achieving a speedy response on a worldwide scale to continually changing markets. Both volume and variety in demand variations must be accommodated by the quick response. Lead times, or the time it takes to restock items in order to meet demand, are a third factor to consider. By delaying the implementation of standard platforms until after the demand for quantity and diversity has been determined, agility can be accomplished.

Standardized parts and modules allow for minimal finished-goods inventory, whereas late assembly paves the way for rapid mass customization. As demand fluctuates, it's necessary to keep a buffer of available resources on hand. The above specified agile setup necessitates the participation of the whole global supply chain. Components can be sub assembled into modules in an inexpensive setting, whereas final assembly is typically performed near the point of consumption to localize the product.

Figure 2. Characteristics of agile supply chain

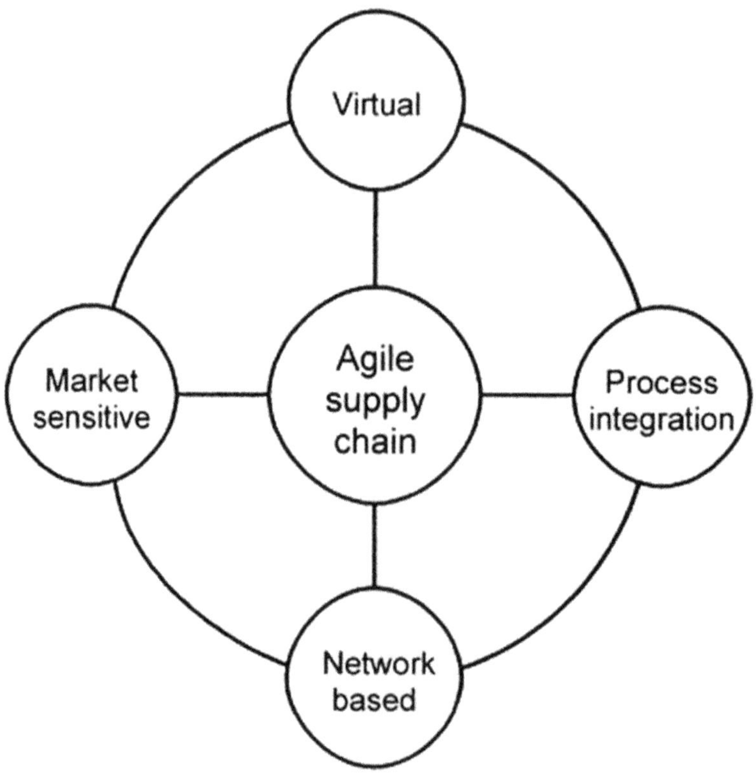

Christopher identifies four characteristics of an agile supply chain: (1) market sensitivity, or the ability to read and respond to actual demand; (2) virtual or built on a foundation of information rather than inventory; (3) process integration, or the guarantee of cooperative work between purchasers and vendors; and (4) network commitment to closer and more responsive relationships with customers. Fisher (1997) offers a similar point of view on the adaptable and reactive supply chain, categorizing it according to the degree to which demand is predictable vs unpredictable and the degree to which products are functional versus innovative. Products that serve a practical need, such as those found at grocery stores and service stations, tend to have a high volume of repeat customers and a low profit margin. The demand for novel products, such state-of-the-art MP4 players or fashionable clothing, is more erratic but also shorter. Product cycles for innovative products can be as short as three months and as long as a year, while those for practical products are typically more than two years.

Forecasting errors for practical items tend to hover around 10%, whereas those for novel ones range from 40% to 100%. Innovative products require a flexible supply chain because of their short product cycles, fluctuating demand, and difficult forecasting. Buffering and stockpiling provide for a more responsive supply chain. Fischer argues further that matching demand and supply through a flexible supply chain is essential for the successful distribution of high-margin, cutting-edge innovations. a supply network that is both lean and flexible 223 Greater profit and fewer things to sell will more than make up for the extra expense of capacity and inventory buffers.

In order to successfully establish an agile supply chain, according to Fischer, the following four guidelines must be observed: It is important to:

(1) Recognise that uncertainty is inherent in innovative products;
(2) Lessen uncertainty by uncovering data that can support better forecasting;
(3) Reduce risk by making it easier to create on demand or to relocate production to where it is needed, which will minimise lead times. ;
(4) Use buffer stock and spare capacity as a hedge against the unknown.

As stated by Yusuf et al. (2003), agile manufacturing serves four essential purposes in an agile supply chain. Adapting one's usual frameworks to deal with change and uncertainty; 2) using IT to harness the power of employees across all of an organization's departments; 3) attaining mass customization at the expense of mass production; 4) learning to adapt to new circumstances.

A more responsive supply chain is just one of the many benefits of an agile supply chain, as this list demonstrates. Consistent with our findings, we conclude that the following features of an agile supply chain are essential for delivering the kind of responsiveness needed to support the kinds of innovative products that consumer's value.

1. Flexibility
2. Market sensitivity
3. A virtual network
4. Postponement
5. Selected LSC principles

One of the hallmarks of a responsive supply chain is its ability to adapt quickly to changing conditions. When it comes to manufacturing, flexibility is being able to adapt swiftly to changes in demand, product mix, and other aspects of the supply chain. Launching new products, seasonal demand, product substitution, and sales all contribute to the volume swings. An growth in the number of stock-keeping units (SKUs) due to new items, distributors' own brands (DOB), etc., is mostly responsible for the shift in availability. Supplier and customer lead times, service level improvements, order size shifts, and other factors all contribute to supply chain fluctuations.

Companies that sought flexibility in the 1980s by investing in complex flexible manufacturing systems (FMS) occasionally met with failure. Organizational flexibility (e.g., cultural and skills integration between craftspeople and operators) was given all the focus, with mixed results. An increasing amount of focus in the service industry has shifted to understanding the interconnectedness of agile processes and learning how to use the advantages of these methods to better meet the needs of their customers. Supply chain adaptability can be improved through standardization of processes, multi-skilling of employees, and fluidity of work procedures, as well as through simplification of product requirements to allow for the greatest possible degree of mass customization.

The ability of the supply chain to adjust to actual market demand is what we mean by "market sensitivity." This necessitates a shift in focus from the annual prediction used for demand planning to actual consumer needs. Instead of planning ahead based on a guess, activities will be scheduled backwards according to client demand. Information technology, efficient consumer response (ECR) and customer relationship management (CRM) systems should be used to collect data immediately from point of sale (POS) and consumer buying habits, in addition to real customer order.

Growth of 'loyalty cards' and 'store cards' provides additional source of customer data to better control market sensitivity. Customers, vendors, planners, manufacturers, and distributors can now all be connected in a real-time, virtual network thanks to the Internet and IT. Key resources for meeting the needs of consumers around the world can be found in the use of demand visibility and collaborative planning, forecasting, and restocking (CPFR) systems. The idea of gaining a strategic edge by virtue of having exceptional plants on their own has given way to that of a unified, high-performing system.

One of the most important aspects of a flexible supply chain is the ability for its members to be connected in a digital network and to exchange real-time information. Postponement is founded on the idea that the final assembly or modification of semi-finished products and components is delayed until the needs of the client or market are known. Any flexible supply chain must adhere to the postponement principle. Key workstations' buffer capacities also contribute to the speed with which they respond to customers' individual requests.

Semi-finished goods are stored at a "de-coupling point," which is a term for the location in the supply chain where the production and distribution of goods are separated. This stage of the process needs to be located as close to the final consumer market as possible. As well as allowing businesses to quickly meet the needs of individual customers, postponement has a number of other benefits in the realms of operations, finances, and promotion. Keeping stock at a general level reduces the number of stock-keeping units (SKUs), which facilitates forecasting and leads to fewer physical goods being stored. A lower value can be expected for the stock because it is held at a less developed stage of production than for finished goods.

Mass customization allows for more options to be provided at a reduced price, and it also allows for marketing to emphasize a sense of exclusivity to consumers. Some of the same ideas or traits that define a LSC are also present in an agile supply chain. The essential features of a LSC are high levels of efficiency, quality assurance, and smooth operation flow; however, an agile supply chain also features increased responsiveness. While both the lean process and an agile supply chain aim to minimize unnecessary steps, an agile supply chain takes a different approach to buffer space and delayed inventory needs. A pure lean strategy can be used up until the de-coupling point, after which an agile approach can be taken. Up until the decoupling point, economies of scale based on volume should be attainable. This is analogous to how service operations (like banks) handle repetitive tasks in the back office using lean principles, freeing up front-line staff to focus on providing excellent, timely service to customers.

FINDINGS AND CONCLUSION

Based on our analysis, we've concluded that a pure agile supply chain works best for innovative products that have an irregular demand pattern, a high profit margin, a wide variety of items, require numerous revisions, and have a short lead time.

However, low-margin, high-volume functional products that only require small tweaks benefit most from an LSC. For the sake of efficiency, a longer lead time may be taken in exchange for a lower price in an LSC. LSC techniques, which involve long-term engagement with suppliers and consumers, were employed by a much larger percentage of manufacturers than agile supply chain methods were (Yusuf et al., 2003).

According to Christopher (2000), "there will be instances when a pure agile or a lean might be acceptable for a supply chain." Hybrid tactics, which incorporate parts of both, will be effective in a range of contexts. Naylor et al. (1999) coined the term "Leagile" to describe how agile and lean can be combined in a single supply chain. Companies that provide a wide range of products and services are becoming more frequent. Short-term or seasonal demand of novelty products is undoubtedly also observed by many high-volume manufacturers or service providers (e.g. chocolate eggs at Easter and T-shirts for Olympics) (e.g. chocolate eggs at Easter and T-shirts for the Olympics). Items with high numbers and stable, predictable demand will be the norm, but products with lesser volumes and more irregular demand will require nimbler responses. Because of this, neither lean nor agile supply chain strategies are needed. A supply chain can be lean at times, agile at other times, and both lean and agile (hybrid) at other times, hence this distinction is not absolute.

Summary Due to changing consumer and technical demands, volatile markets, and global sourcing, the traditional forecast-driven longer, and slower logistic pipelines are becoming uncompetitive and unsustainable. We've discussed some of the mechanisms through which a responsive and effective supply chain might tackle this problem in the next chapter. We've developed an "LSC," which is differentiated by its focus on streamlining, quality assurance, and getting rid of wasteful practices. Adaptability, market reactivity, virtually, the capacity to postpone some activities, and adherence to specific principles of LSC management are all hallmarks of an agile supply chain. We have also provided advice on how to put lean and agile supply chain principles into action.

Table 1. Agile and lean characteristics

	Agile	Lean	Green
Objectives	Buffer capacity with fast responsiveness and stock development	High utilization with lower cost and minimum level of stock maintenance	Economic and Ecological
Characteristics of the processes	Market sense Flexible Selection of lean supply principles Virtually controlled networking	Waste elimination Smooth process flow Quality control and assurance High effectiveness High efficiency	Design, Raw material seleciton and purchases, green distribution, green retailing, environmental monitoring
Characteristics of the products	Higher variety and margins with innovation in products	Low margin with lower variety in the products. Bringing innovation	Reducing air pollution, water pollution, and waste

Changing consumer and technical demands, uncertain markets, and global sourcing have introduced new difficulties to supply chain management, and old forecast-driven longer and slower logistic pipelines are becoming non-competitive and thus unsustainable. In this chapter, we've looked at how to implement a nimble and efficient supply chain to meet this challenge head-on. To ensure quality and efficiency, we have perfected the fundamentals of an LSC by doing away with unnecessary steps and processes and streamlining the flow of work. We have identified adaptability, responsiveness to the market, a virtual network, deferral, and a few key concepts of LSC management as the distinguishing features of an agile supply chain. We have also provided instructions on how to put lean and agile supply chain techniques to work.

REFERENCES

Ballard, G. (2001). Cycle time reduction in home building. *Proceedings of the 9th Annual Conference of the International Group for Lean Construction, 6*(8).

Basu, R., & Wright, J. N. (2012). *Quality beyond six sigma*. Routledge. doi:10.4324/9780080515502

Cherrafi, A., Garza-Reyes, J. A., Kumar, V., Mishra, N., Ghobadian, A., & Elfezazi, S. (2018). Lean, green practices and process innovation: A model for green supply chain performance. *International Journal of Production Economics, 206*, 79–92. doi:10.1016/j.ijpe.2018.09.031

Christopher, M. (2000). The agile supply chain: Competing in volatile markets. *Industrial Marketing Management, 29*(1), 37–44. doi:10.1016/S0019-8501(99)00110-8

Dettmer, H. W. (1992). *Goldratt's theory of constraints*. ASQ Quality Press.

Fisher, M. L. (1997). What is the right supply chain for your product? *Harvard Business Review, 75*, 105–117.

Islam, M. S., Karia, N., Taib, F. M., Ara, H., & Moeinzadeh, S. (2021). Ethico-religious green supply chain management (GSCM): Embedding Islamic ethics' codes for improving environmental concerns. *Journal of Islamic Accounting and Business Research.*

Khan, S. A. R., Zhang, Y., Anees, M., Golpîra, H., Lahmar, A., & Qianli, D. (2018). Green supply chain management, economic growth and environment: A GMM based evidence. *Journal of Cleaner Production, 185*, 588–599. doi:10.1016/j.jclepro.2018.02.226

Naylor, J. B., Naim, M. M., & Berry, D. (1999). Leagility: Integrating the lean and agile manufacturing paradigms in the total supply chain. *International Journal of Production Economics, 62*(1-2), 107–118. doi:10.1016/S0925-5273(98)00223-0

Ohno, T., & Bodek, N. (2019). *Toyota production system: beyond large-scale production*. Productivity Press. doi:10.4324/9780429273018

Pal, B., Sarkar, A., & Sarkar, B. (2023). Optimal decisions in a dual-channel competitive green supply chain management under promotional effort. *Expert Systems with Applications, 211*, 118315.

Schonberger, R. J. (2008). *World class manufacturing*. Simon and Schuster.

Shingo, S., & Dillon, A. P. (1989). *A study of the Toyota production system: From an Industrial Engineering Viewpoint*. CRC Press.

Shingo, S., & Dillon, A. P. (2019). *A revolution in manufacturing: the SMED system*. Routledge. doi:10.4324/9781315136479

Sugandini, D., Susilowati, C., Siswanti, Y., & Syafri, W. (2020). Green supply management and green marketing strategy on green purchase intention: SMEs cases. *Journal of Industrial Engineering and Management, 13*(1), 79–92. doi:10.3926/jiem.2795

Suri, R., & Burke, J. (2020). *Quick response manufacturing: A companywide approach to reducing lead times*. Productivity Press.

Walker, C. R., & Guest, R. H. (1952). *The man on the assembly line*. Academic Press.

Womack, J. P., Jones, D. T., & Roos, D. (1990). *The machine that changed the world*. Rawson Associates.

Womack, J. P., Jones, D. T., & Roos, D. (2007). *The machine that changed the world: The story of lean production—Toyota's secret weapon in the global car wars that is now revolutionizing world industry*. Simon and Schuster.

Yusuf, Y. Y., Gunasekaran, A., Adeleye, E. O., & Sivayoganathan, K. (2004). Agile supply chain capabilities: Determinants of competitive objectives. *European Journal of Operational Research, 159*(2), 379–392. doi:10.1016/j.ejor.2003.08.022

Zhang, X., & Yousaf, H. A. U. (2020). Green supply chain coordination considering government intervention, green investment, and customer green preferences in the petroleum industry. *Journal of Cleaner Production, 246*, 118984. doi:10.1016/j.jclepro.2019.118984

KEY TERMS AND DEFINITIONS

5s: Sort, Straighten, Shine, Standardize, and Sustain are the five steps in the 5S process for building a more organized and productive workplace. The 5S methodology lays the groundwork for introducing subsequent levels of lean production equipment and techniques.

Agile: Agile is an iterative methodology for managing projects and creating technology, which allows groups to provide more value to consumers in less time and with fewer problems. Agile teams avoid risky "big bang" launches in favor of more frequent, smaller, and more manageable product releases.

Green: Green manufacturing is one that reduces its environmental impact as much as possible.

Integrated Supply Chain: Customers and vendors establish an integrated supply chain when they join forces to improve product development, distribution, and after-sales service through the application of management strategies.

Lean: A methodology for reducing operational inefficiencies. A set of guidelines for running a business efficiently that aims to boost productivity and minimize losses.

Non-Integrated Supply Chain: A supply chain that is not integrated is one that operates in separate compartments. This could be the case for a company like one that uses a combination of truckload and less-than-truckload (LTL) shipments with their own dedicated milkrun route.

Supply Chain: The supply chain of a product includes every entity (individuals, organizations, materials, procedures, and equipment) involved in producing and distributing that product. The supply chain encompasses the entire process from the initial shipment of raw materials to the manufacturer to the final shipment of the finished product to the customer.

Total Productive Maintenance: It's an idea that establishes a coordinated network of people working together to increase the dependability of plants and machines through proactive measures as well as those used to avert potential problems before they occur.

Total Quality Management: Total quality management describes a methodical approach to managing a company or other group. Improving the efficacy and efficiency of a company's internal processes in order to raise product quality is the goal of this strategy.

Chapter 7
Pooling Strategies in Supply Chains:
Development of Simulation Models to Explore Their Effects on CO2 Emissions

Abdessalem Jerbi
https://orcid.org/0000-0001-5039-7278
University of Sfax, Tunisia

Haifa Jribi
Tunis Higher Institute of Management, Tunisia

ABSTRACT

The main aim of this chapter is to explore the carbon neutrality supply chain through pooling logistics strategies. Pooling logistics is one innovative supply chain management solution to improve its sustainability. The authors carried out a comparison-based simulation study of multi-pick, multi-drop, with hub and hybridization of hub and multi-drop pooling strategies effects on CO_2 emissions of supply chains. Hence, the authors developed simulation models for all these strategies with ARENA software and used them in a case study. The main result is that all the pooling strategies outperform the non-pooled supply chains. Indeed, the four pooling scenarios showed much lower CO_2 emissions than the non-pooled chain. In addition, the pooling hub with a multi-drop delivery strategy gives the best results.

DOI: 10.4018/978-1-6684-6663-6.ch007

INTRODUCTION

Greenhouse gas (GHG) emissions are one of the main causes of the global climate change we are currently witnessing. Almost all economic activities produce GHG, albeit to various degrees and sizes. In the area of supply chain, burning fossil fuels for logistical purposes produces CO2, one of the most prevalent GHGs (Yudi and Wei Lin, 2017, Montzka et al., 2011). This pollutant causes global warming. Indeed, the average world temperature has significantly increased because of CO2 emissions. The thermal expansion of water is one of the principal effects of this temperature rise. Growing temperatures cause sea levels to rise, posing a severe risk to civilization and the economy as melting glaciers add water to the ocean (Sulaiman and Abdul-Rahim 2018; Mohsin et al. 2019). Also, CO2 emissions have a big impact on health. Because of smog and air pollution, they lead to respiratory illnesses. Extreme weather, a disruption in the food supply, and an increase in forest fires are some additional repercussions of climate change brought on by CO2 emissions.

Many academics have looked into various strategies to reduce CO2 emissions in the supply chain. One of the key strategies to lower their CO2 emissions is a cooperation between supply chains (Duong and Chong, 2020; Ho et al., 2019). Pooling logistics resources is one of the creative supply chain collaboration strategies. This approach is mainly built on a partnership agreement to share infrastructure, vehicles, etc. It goes beyond the straightforward notion of pooling vehicles. The purpose of this sharing is to create a supply chain that is more effective and efficient. This sharing attempts to either decrease CO2 emissions specifically or boost the efficiency of supply networks (Taieb et al. 2014). Implementing pooling began with strictly economic considerations. However, supply chain managers were forced to think about pooling logistics resources for environmental goals including decreasing CO2 emissions because of new rigorous regulatory rules on eco-efficiency that were imposed at the administrative level (Ülkü 2012; Wang et al. 2011).

The study and advancement of the concepts of logistics pooling involve numerous research projects. Most scholars have studied and quantified the effects of supply chain pooling on CO2 emissions using mathematical modeling in this paradigm. Pan et al. (2013) examined how supply chain pooling affected CO2 emissions from both road and rail transportation. To assess and improve the CO2 emissions of supply chains through pooling, they created a piecewise linear optimization model. They put this approach to the test using a 12-week database of a distribution network made up of the supply chains of two French retailers. According to the findings, CO2 emissions have significantly decreased. In addition, the combined use of roads and railroads has a greater impact on this reduction. Ouhader and El kyal (2017) attempted to estimate the potential economic and environmental advantages of horizontal transport cooperation. They used a method based on bi-objective mathematical modeling to investigate the connection between CO2 emissions and transport costs. Then they attempted to combine the facility site and distribution route selections in urban freight to reduce the overall cost and environmental effects of transportation. The comparison's findings revealed a decrease in CO2 emissions, transportation expenses, and kilometers traveled as well as an improvement in vehicle load rate. Montoya-Torres et al. (2016) undertook a case study using information from three businesses in Bogota, Colombia. Each of these businesses operates a store. The authors' study was based on mathematical modeling estimating travel distance to compare a collaborative scenario to a non-collaborative one. Each company uses its stores to distribute its products in the non-collaborative scenario. In the collaborative model, distribution to clients is handled through a shared store managed by one of the three organizations, which also functions as a central hub. Based on the travel distances, the authors calculated the resulting CO2 emissions. The outcomes showed the numerical gains made possible by the collaboration of logistics activities.

A potent tool for modeling and analyzing system performance is discrete event simulation (DES). DES models enable the user to understand how shared supply chains function, forecast their behavior, and diagnose problems. In this regard, some researchers have used DES as the foundation for their studies to examine the environmental implications of logistical pooling. To lower the cost of procurement and CO2 emissions, Leitner et al. (2011) attempted to create the best possible pooled supply chain for automotive suppliers in Spain and Romania. The simulation models' findings showed that the designed pooled chain significantly decreased the number of trips, fuel consumption, and CO2 emissions. Moutaoukil et al. (2013) presented a pooled logistics simulation model of the agricultural and food supplies chain. They integrated economic, environmental, and societal dimensions into this model. The exploration using simulation of different scenarios then resulted in the choice of a particular one that minimizes the total transportation cost, the CO2 emissions of the system, and the risk of accidents per million kilometers traveled by the carriers. Mrabti et al. (2018) developed a discrete event simulation model of pooled supply chains to evaluate logistics cost, vehicle fill rates, and CO2 emissions. The authors then discussed a case study to show how the pooling strategy reduces logistics costs, improves vehicle fill rate, and reduces CO2 emissions. El Bouazzaoui et al. (2020) discussed the concepts of pooled transport and storage in the hydrocarbon supply chain in Morocco. They studied the environmental impact of pooling resources by grouping transport trucks and storage tanks on the CO2 emissions of two companies. Based on actual seven-year petroleum product flow data from two importers before and after resource pooling, simulation models were developed to determine the rate of change in CO2 emissions. The simulation results showed a reduction of approximately 46% in CO2 emissions.

These simulation-based researches looked at how various logistics pooling strategies affected the efficiency of respective supply chains. But none of them described the simulation models that were used or how they were developed. The authors of these researches concentrated on the exploration's findings while omitting any details on the simulation models. However, these models, and particularly their method of development, are crucial and can affect the outcomes of the investigation of the pooling strategies effects. The authors of these researches may have assisted supply chain managers in applying this exploration to their chains by providing simulation models. These shortcomings served as the inspiration for our work. In this study, we show how to develop stochastic simulation models of various pooling logistics techniques using the ARENA 14.0 simulation tool. Then we apply these models to investigate how these pooling logistics options affect supply chain CO2 emissions.

We structure this chapter as follows: the second section presents the supply chain pooling strategies considered by the literature. The next section details the simulation models of pooled and non-pooled supply chains. The fourth section explores, through a case study, the effects of pooling strategies on CO2 emissions in a supply chain. The last section summarizes the paper and discusses future work.

SUPPLY CHAINS POOLING STRATEGIES

We can use many pooling strategies in the transport and logistics field. These strategies can take different organizational forms depending on the parties, the means, and the products or services.

Multi-Pick Pooling Strategy

This variant of pooling strategies involves several companies and merges supplies from several suppliers to a single delivery point for grouped deliveries to a single recipient (Figure 1). Here, the goods destined for the same delivery point are collected from the different companies through a collection round by one or more vehicles. For better efficiency of this pooling strategy, the companies must be as close as possible. Multi-pick maximizes the capacity utilization of vehicles but remains a complex process to coordinate and requires a good understanding of the different actors to organize the loads in a coordinated and functional way (Abbad, 2014, Pan et al. 2014).

Figure 1. Supply chains with multi-pick pooling strategy

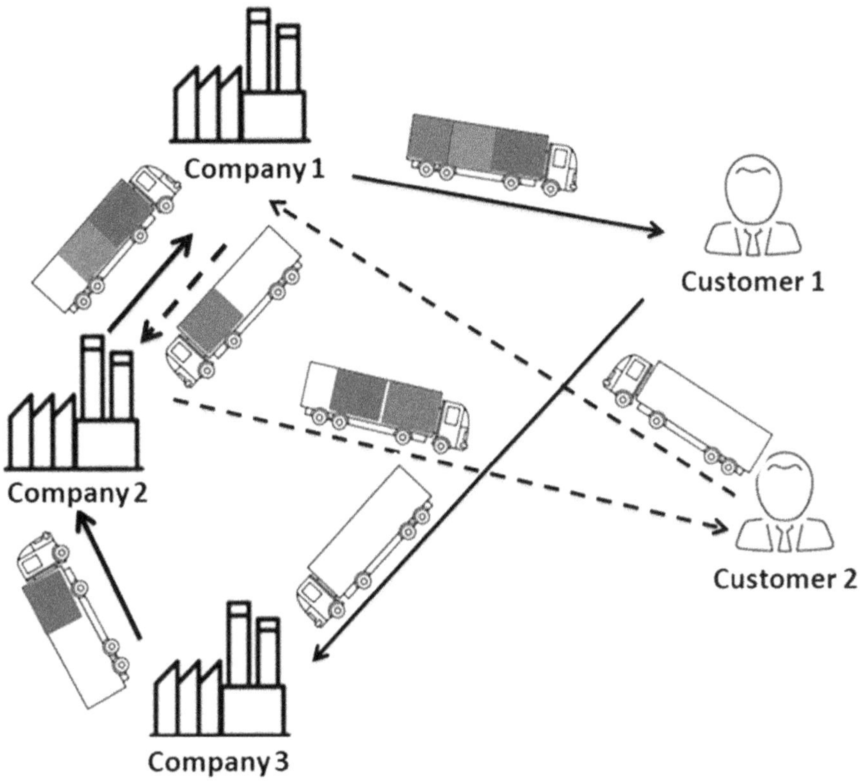

Multi-Drop Pooling Strategy

This pooling strategy pools resources among several manufacturers with a shared customer. Here, goods leave a single shipping location and go to several delivery sites (Figure 2). One or more vehicles leave the same supplier to transport different orders and deliver them successively to several customers through a distribution round. Multi-drop optimizes truck filling and increases the delivery frequency. However, to be beneficial, this mode of operation requires geographic proximity of delivery points (Pan et al. 2014, Bruzzone and Longo, 2014).

Figure 2. Supply chains with multi-drop pooling strategy

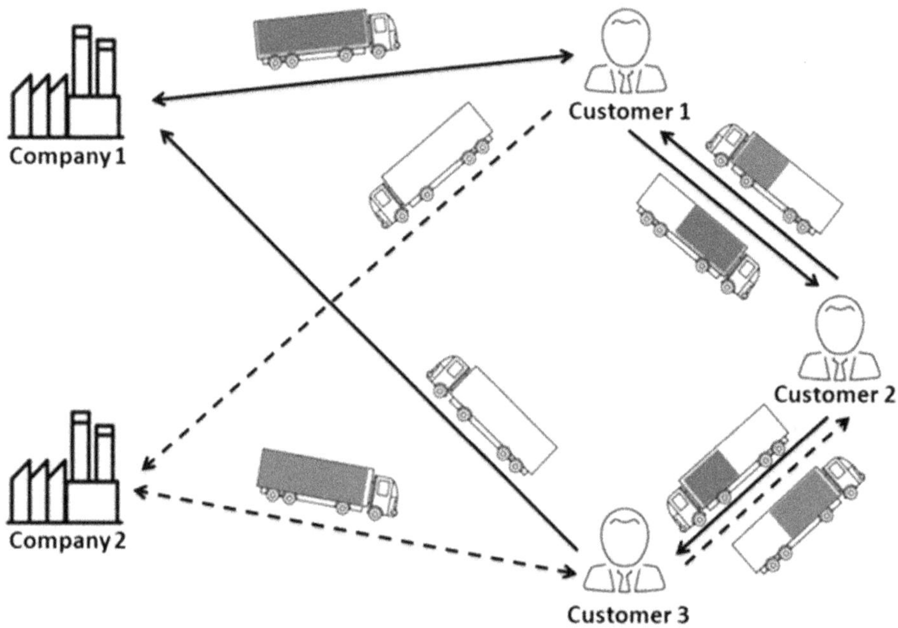

Supply Chains with Pooling Hub Strategy

In this supply management process, goods are delivered to a consolidation/deconsolidation warehouse and then shipped to the final point of sale (Figure 3). This strategy allows the distributor to reduce its inventory by increasing the frequency of delivery to the customers and improving the filling rate of the trucks by shipping potentially heterogeneous products. Deliveries are more regular and in smaller quantities without putting more trucks on the road. This pooling strategy, therefore, makes it possible to maintain or even reduce transport costs (Jun 2015).

Figure 3. Supply chains with pooling hub strategy

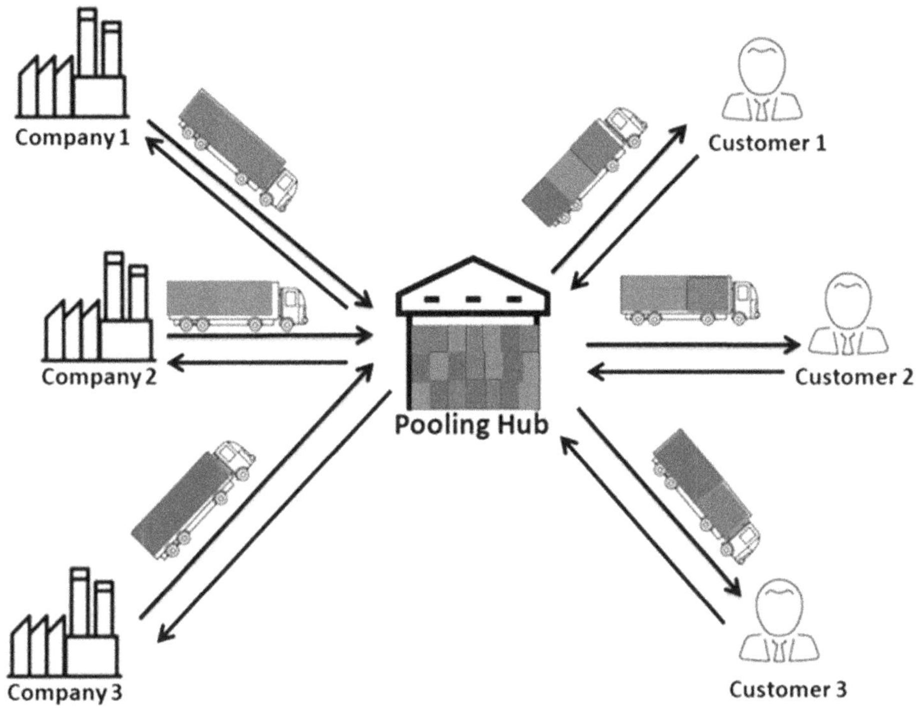

Supply Chains with Pooling Hub and Multi-Drop Delivery Strategy

This strategy is a combination of the two previous pooling strategies. The products are delivered to a consolidation/deconsolidation warehouse and then shipped to the customers using the multi-drop technique (Figure 4). Distribution rounds, therefore, made these deliveries between the pooling warehouse and the customers. This hybridization aims to improve the truck fill rate to reduce transportation costs while increasing the frequency of delivery to customers (Jun 2015; Bruzzone and Longo 2014).

Figure 4. Supply chains with pooling hub and multi-drop strategy

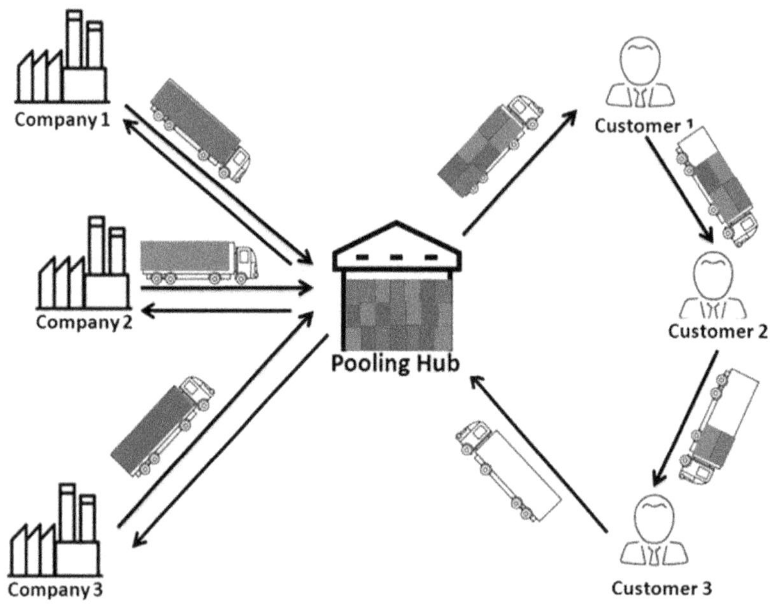

Figure 5. Distances and speeds in the pooled supplies chains

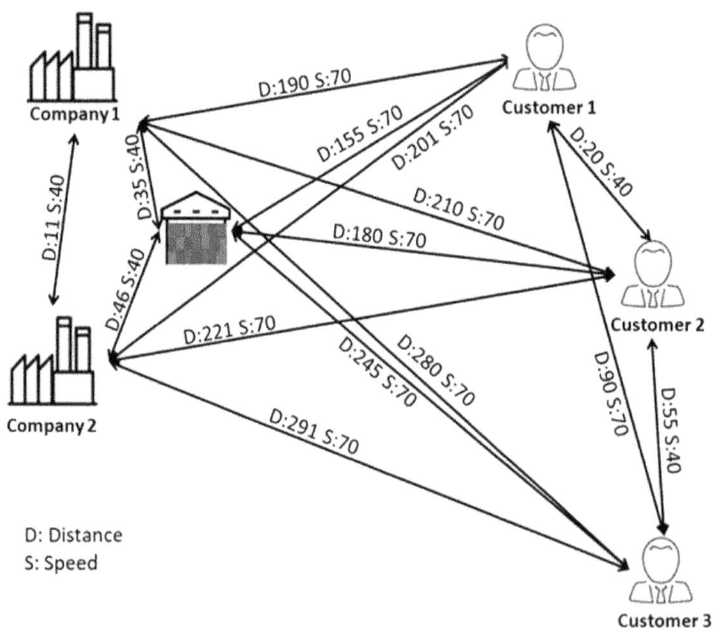

SIMULATION MODELS

We developed the simulation models of the different pooling strategies with the commercial simulation software Arena 14.0. This tool integrates all the functions necessary for discrete event simulation as animation and analysis of input and output data. We start by describing the basic model of non-discrete event logistics chains. Simulation models of the supply chains with pooling strategies are described thereafter.

Non-Pooled Supply Chains Model

The model of the non-pooled supply chains includes companies' and customers' parts. The company part contains two sub-models, each corresponding to a company, while the customer part contains three sub-models, each corresponding to a customer (Figure 6).

Figure 6. Overview of non-pooled supply chain simulation model

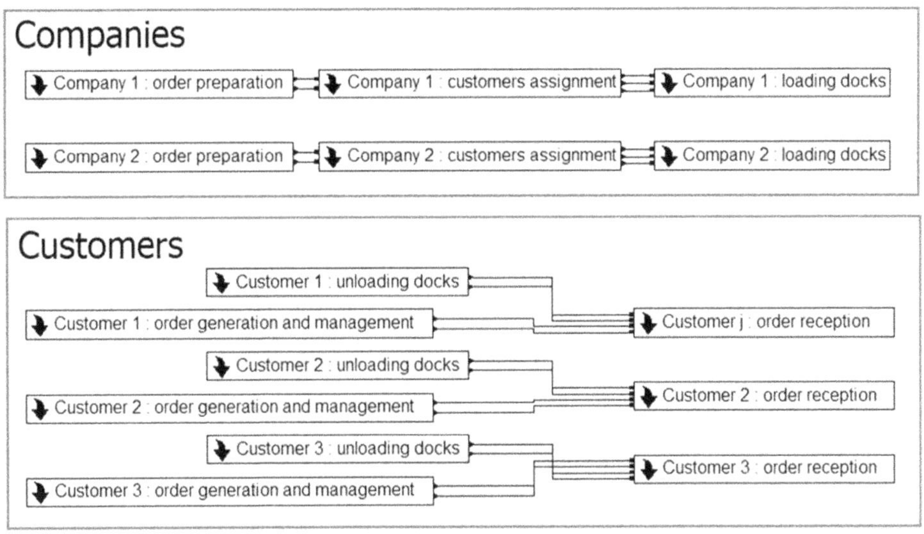

Company Sub-Model

The "Company" sub-model includes the three sections "Company i: order picking", "Company i: customer assignment" and "Company i: loading docks" (Figure 7).

Figure 7. Company i section for the non-pooled supply chain simulation model.

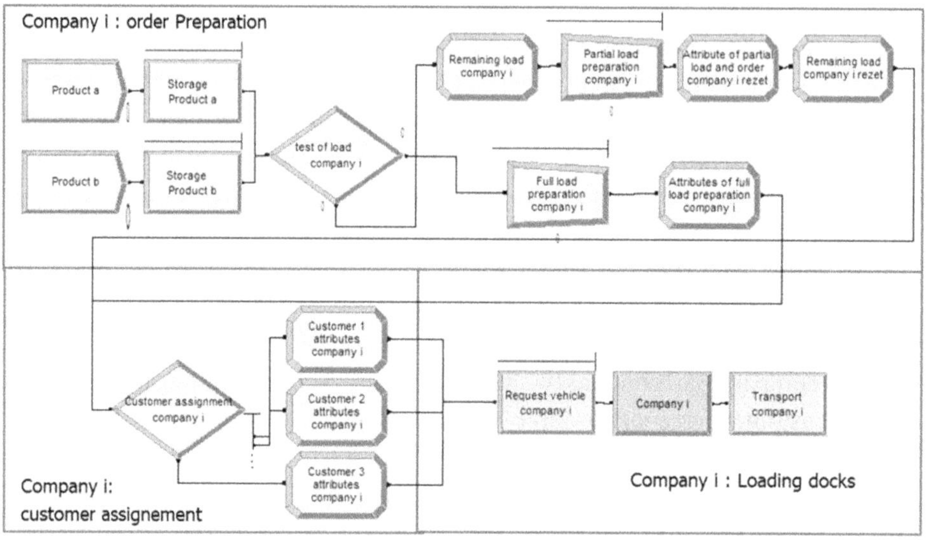

The section named "Company i: order preparation" models the production part of the company generating the product pallets. This section also manages the preparation of orders by grouping the corresponding quantities of pallets. The creation of product pallets is modeled by the "Create" modules. Once created, each product pallet is put on hold in a "Hold" module that models the company's storage area. Once a customer places an order, a signal is sent to the appropriate "Hold" module to release the necessary quantity of pallets from the storage area. The released pallets go through a test modeled by a "Decide" module to check if their number corresponds to the loading capacity of the transport vehicles:

- If the quantity of pallets is greater than or equal to this capacity, the "Batch" module "Full load preparation company i" gathers the number of pallets corresponding to this capacity. This load receives several attributes and variables related to the load and order sizes by a module "Assign". The order size variable is then reduced by the number of pallets already grouped.
- If the quantity of pallets is less than this capacity, all pallets go to the "Batch" module "Partial load preparation company i". However, a variable representing the remaining part of the order is previously incremented by the module "Assign" "Remaining load company i". This partial load goes through other "Assign" modules to increment the new value of the load size attribute and reset all the other variables.

The second section named "Company i: customer assignment" manages the assignment of each delivery to its corresponding customer by a "Decide" module linked to three "Assign" modules corresponding to one customer. These modules assign delivery attributes such as order number, number of pallets, and delivery sequence. The delivery sequences consist of steps materialized by stations defined in the "Sequence" modules.

In the third section named "Company i: Loading docks", the prepared partial and complete orders wait in a "Request" module. This module calls the nearest free vehicle to take the delivery to the corresponding company. Every loaded vehicle passes through the "Transport" module to increment the speed of the journey.

Customer Sub-Model

Each Customer "j" sub-model includes the three sections "Customer j: order generation and management", "Customer j: unloading dock" and "Customer j: order reception" (Figure8).

The "Create" module of the "Customer j: order generation and management" section generates the purchase orders. A "Separate" module named "Duplicate order customer j" will duplicate this order according to the number of companies. Each copy of the order form is sent to the corresponding company through an "Assign" module that increments the order number and assigns the value of the number of pallets ordered by product type. Each purchase order then passes through a "Decide" module named "Storage Company i Customer j" to check the availability of the pallet. If all the pallets are available, the order is validated and passes through a "Signal" module that signals the company to release the number of pallets requested. If not, the order will be canceled and classified in a "Dispose" module.

A "Release" module will release each entering vehicle to the "Customer j: unloading docks". The released loads are transmitted to different "Record" modules, the first of which stores the total number of pallets delivered, while the second calculates and stores the CO2 emissions of the order.

A "Separate" module in the "Customer j: order receipt" section will divide each delivered load into individual pallets. They are then sent to a "Batch" module to group all the pallets of each order. Then, a "Match" module matches the grouped pallets of an order to the corresponding purchase order. A final "Batch" module will group the matched informational (purchase order), and physical (pallets) flows to remove them from the model via a "Dispose" module.

Figure 8. Simulation model of a Customer j section for the non-pooled supply chain.

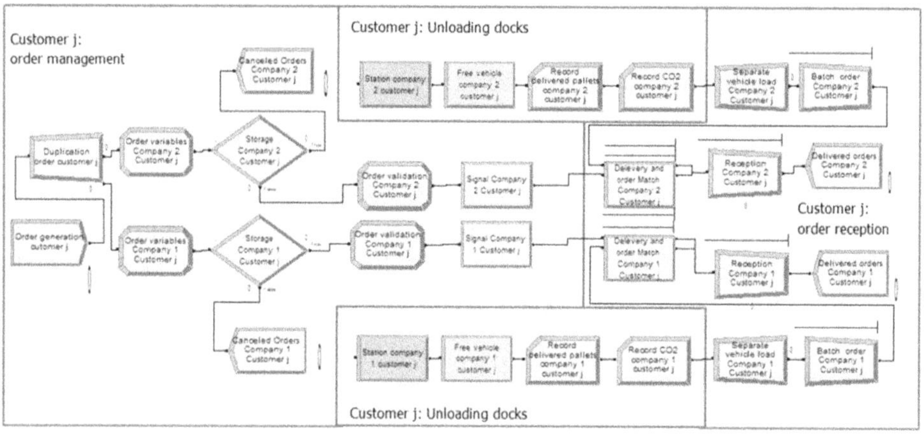

Pooled Supply Chains with Multi-Pick Model

This simulation model is based on the same structure as the non-pooled model, except for the company sub-models. A new section appears in these sub-models to handle the flow of multi-pick deliveries. In addition, each company sub-model has a different structure to manage, depending on the case, the reception of pallets in the pickup round (Figure 9).

Figure 9. Overview of pooled supply chain simulation model with multi-pick

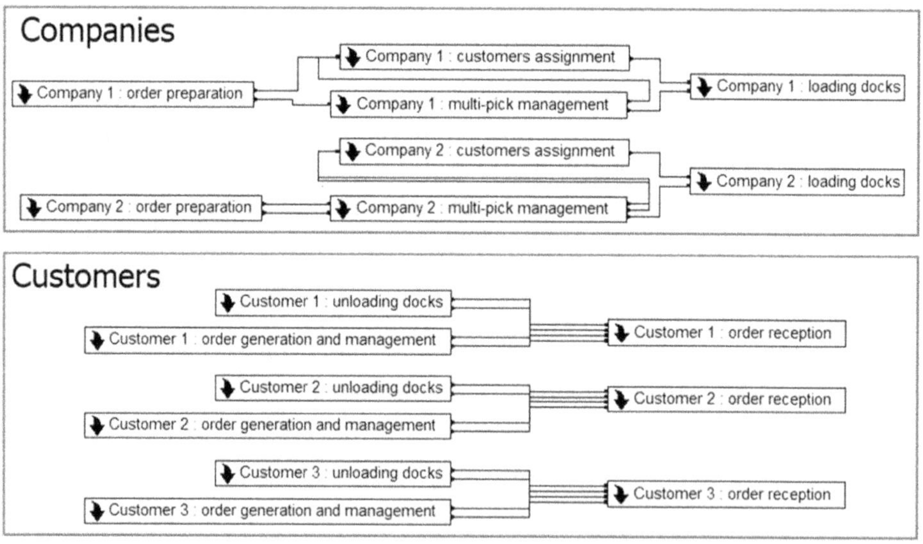

Company 1 Sub-Model

Company 1 sub-model has four sections. The three sections "Company 1: order preparation", "Company 1: customer assignment" and "Company 1: loading docks" have the same functionality and structure as the corresponding sections in the company sub-model of the non-pooled supply chain model. The fourth section, named "Company 1: multi-pick management" is used to manage the flow of multi-pick deliveries (Figure 10).

Figure 10. Simulation model of Company 1 multi-pick management sections

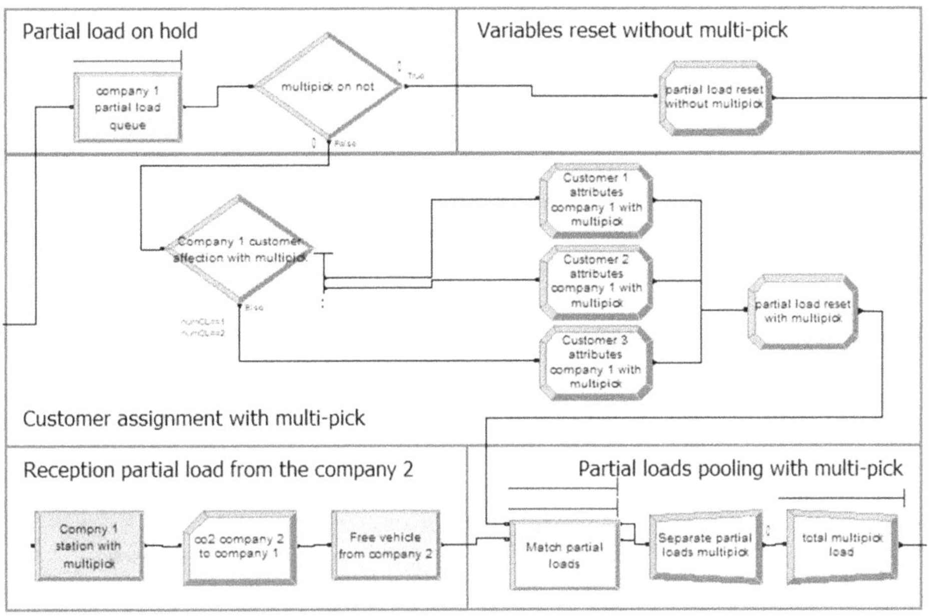

Once full loads are delivered to the customers, the remaining partial load is directed to the "Company 1: multi-pick management" section. This load must wait in the "company 1 partial load queue" "Hold" module for a signal from company 2 or from the same customer. This signal shows whether multi-pick applies. Once released, this partial load passes through a "Decide" module to be directed to one sub-section according to the applicability of multi-pick. If this applicability condition is not verified, the multi-pick procedure is canceled and the remaining load passes through an "Assign" module in the "Variables reset without multi-pick" sub-section to reset all the corresponding variables. In contrast, if multi-pick applies, this load is sent to the sub-section "Customer assignment with multi-pick". In this sub-section, the corresponding customer and the required transfer attributes are assigned to this load. Then, it passes to another "Assign" module to reset all the other variables. It is then made on hold in one queue of the "Match" module, named "Match partial loads", in the sub-section "Partial loads pooling with multi-pick". The main function of this module is to match partial loads from both companies according to the corresponding customer. These loads are ungrouped into individual pallets to be regrouped into a single load by the next "Batch" module. The second queue of the "Match" module is supplied with partial loads from the sub-section "Reception partial loads from Company 2". This sub-section receives partial loads sent from company 2 when the multi-pick policy applies. In addition, it calculates and stores the CO2 emissions of load transfers between the two companies.

Company 2 Sub-Model

As for the company1 sub-model, the company2 sub-model includes four sections. All these sections have the same structure and functionality as the corresponding ones in the other company sub-model except for the "Multi-pick management" section (Figure 11).

Figure 11. Simulation model of Company 2 multi-pick management sections

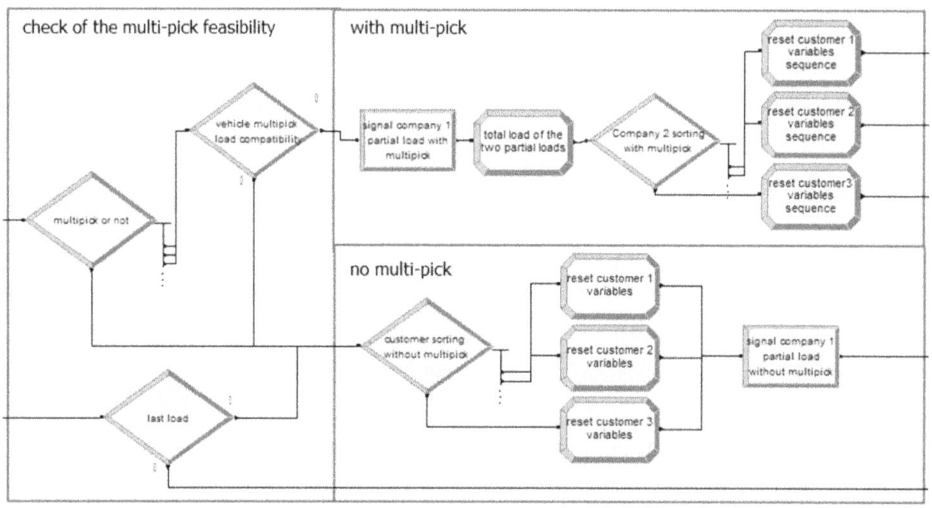

In this section, every complete load goes through the sub-section "Check of the multi-pick feasibility" where the "Decide" module, named "Last load", checks whether this load is the last one programmed in the order delivery. Here, it passes to the "no multi-pick" sub-section to reset the variables relating to the entire order. Then it passes through a "Signal" module to signal company1 that the multi-pick is not applicable. Otherwise, the complete load will be sent directly to the "Company 2: customers assignment" section. When a partial load arrives in the sub-section "Check of the multi-pick feasibility" it passes through a "Decide" module, named "Multipick or not". This module checks the possibility of the application of the multi-pick searching for another waiting partial load in company1 to be sent to the same customer. Here, a second test, named "Vehicle and multipick load compatibility" checks the compatibility between the vehicle load capacity and the quantity of all the pallets of the two partial loads to be sent to this customer. If the load compatibility condition is not verified, the partial load is sent to the "No multi-pick" sub-section. Otherwise, the compatibility is validated and the partial load passes to the "Signal" module, which signals company1 to release the partial load waiting in the "Company 1 multi-pick management" section. Then, this load passes through the "Assign" module to increment different variables and attributes. Finally, it is sent to a "Decide" module and a set of "Assign" modules to be assigned to the corresponding customer.

Pooled Supply Chains with Multi-Drop Model

Each company manages the delivery of several partial loads to different customers. A new section called "company i: multidrop management" appears in each company sub-model. Besides managing the reception of their corresponding loads, customers must deal with the sending of other part-loads to their customers through sections called "Customer j: multidrop management". These sections differ from client 1 to the other clients because this one is the closest to the companies and must manage the reception and sending of a substantial number of partial loads (Figure 12).

Figure 12. Overview of the pooled supply chain simulation model with multi-drop

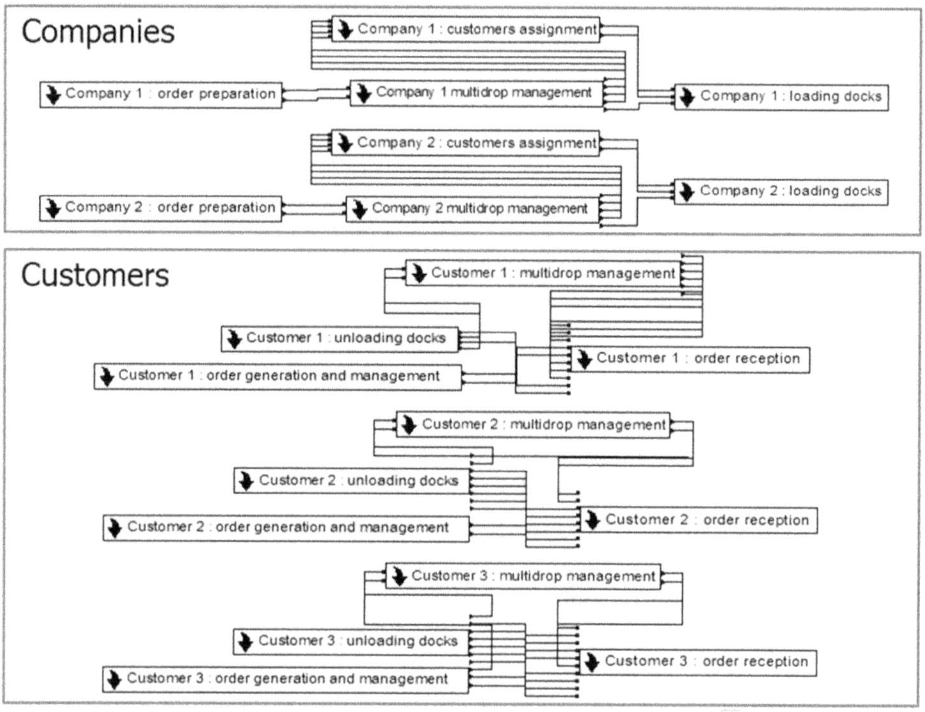

Company Sub-Model

Each sub-model includes four sections. The three sections "Company j: order preparation", "Company j: customers assignment" and "Company j: loading docks" have the same structures as the corresponding sections in the simulation model without pooling. In the "Company j: multidrop management" section, all loads are held in the queue of the "Hold" module named "Load queue". This module holds them until the load waiting in the "Request truck company j" module of the "Company j: loading docks" section is assigned to a free vehicle. Here, the released load from the queue passes through two successive loops named "Partial load search" in order to gather the waiting partial loads and improve the fill rate of the vehicle for any multi-drop delivery (Figure 13).

In the first loop, a "Search" module searches for a first waiting partial load. Once found, a "Remove" module named "Remove first partial load" will remove this load from the "Hold" queue. While the original load is sent to the "Company j: customer assignment" section. The removed partial load will be sent to an "Assign" module where different variables related to the customer and the load are incremented. This first partial load passes through a second “Search” module, in the second loop, to search the “Hold” queue for another partial load. The total number of pallets of these grouped two partial loads must not exceed the vehicle’s capacity. If such a load is not found, multi-drop delivery is not applicable and the first partial load is sent to the “Company j: customer assignment” section. Otherwise, this second partial load is removed from the “Hold” queue by the “Remove” module, named “Remove the second partial load”, and transferred to the “Assign” module to increment again the customer and load variables. Next, both partial loads are sent to the “First customer assignment” sub-section to be assigned to the corresponding customer and grouped together. Another search cycle for a third partial load will be performed to increase the fullness of the delivery vehicle. All the grouped partial loads will be sent to the “Company j: load docks” section.

Figure 13. Simulation model of Company j multi-drop management section

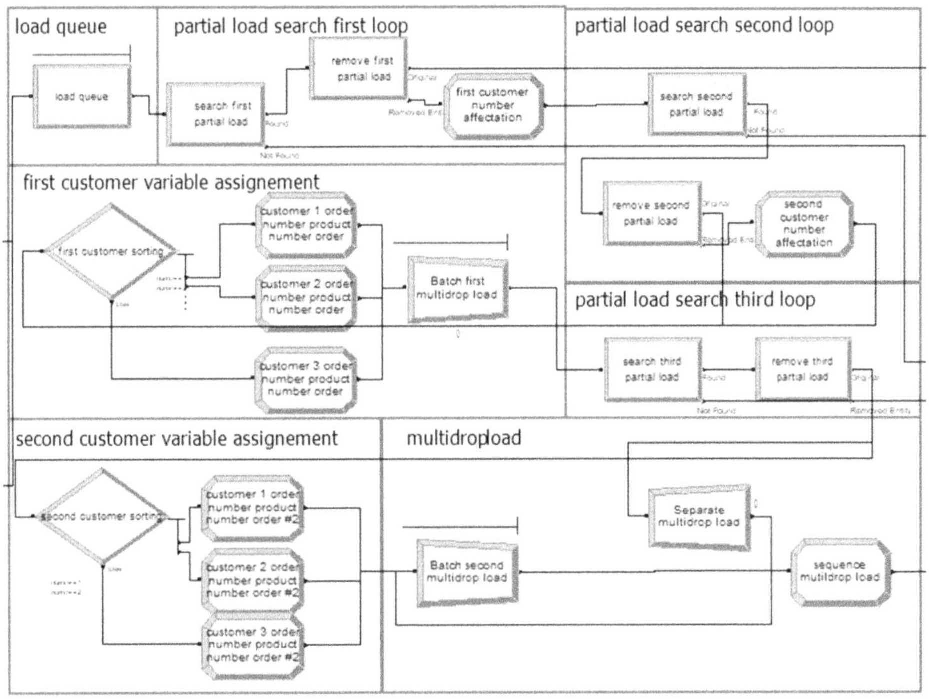

Customer Sub-Model

In the “Customer 1: multidrop management” section, the grouped partial loads are sorted by a “Decide” module according to their direction. They are separated by a “Separate” module and sorted again by a “Decide” module to extract the partial load directed to customer 1. This load is sent to the “Customer 1: order reception” section and the remaining load must be resent to another customer. It passes through an “Assign” module, where the required attributes for the following delivery are assigned. If the remaining load must be sent to two different customers, the multi-drop load will have to be recalculated in the “Assign” module named “Direction customer 3 customer 2”. This load will be batched again and sent to another “Assign” module where the new transfer sequence and other attributes will be assigned and the multi-drop variables will be reset in a subsequent “Assign” module. Finally, the load is directed to the “Station multidrop to customer 3” to be sent to customer 3 (Figure 14).

In the “Customer 2: multidrop management” and “Customer 3: multidrop management” sections the grouped partial loads are separated by a “Separate” module. Then, they are sorted by a “Decide” module to extract the partial load directed to the corresponding customer. This load is sent to the corresponding “Customer j: order reception” section and the remaining load passes through an “Assign” module where the multi-drop variable will be reset. Next, it passes into “Station multidrop customer j”, “Request multidrop customer j” and “Transport customer j” to be sent to the final customer in the multi-drop delivery (Figure 14).

Figure 14. Simulation model of Customer multi-drop management sections

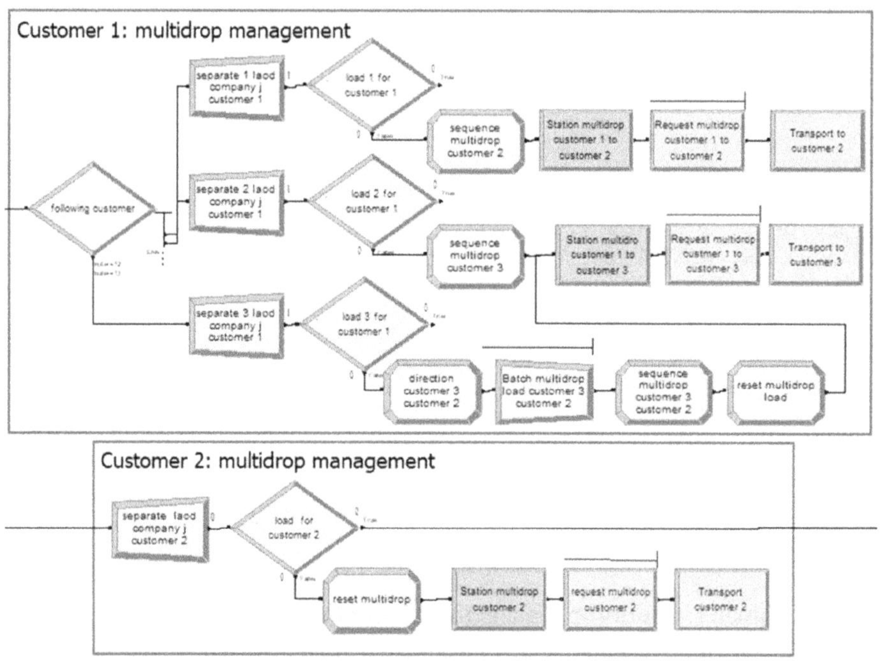

Pooled Supply Chains with Hub Model

This model includes three sub-models: the companies sub-model includes two sections corresponding to the two companies, the customers sub-model consists of three client sections, and the pooling hub sub-model. The companies made intermediate deliveries to the pooling hub. This hub is responsible for supplying the customers (Figure 15).

Figure 15. Overview of pooled supply chain simulation model with hub

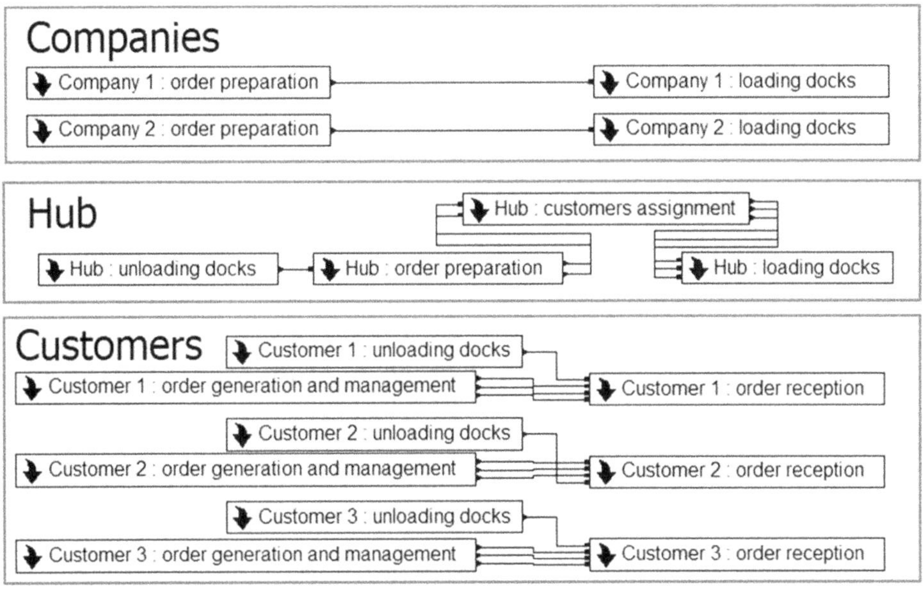

Company Sub-Model

The sub-models of the companies are similar to those modeled in the non-pooled supply chain model. Nevertheless, since the companies have no longer a direct connection to any customers, the "Company i: Customer assignment" sub-section has been eliminated. In addition, in the sub-section "Company i: order preparation" the retaining condition of the pallets in storage is changed. Indeed, each "Hold" module seizes the pallets until the pooling hub notifies it that its corresponding number of pallets has reached a minimum level. In addition, in the "Company i: load preparation" sub-section there are no longer full or partial loads. In fact, each time the pooling hub sends a product request to any company it will send a full load to the hub. The structure of this sub-section is, therefore, limited to two "Batch" modules that group the number of pallets corresponding to the vehicle capacity into a single load. In addition, an "Assign" module attributes to each load the source of its shipment (Figure 16).

Figure 16. Simulation model of company i order preparation section in the pooled supply chain simulation model with hub

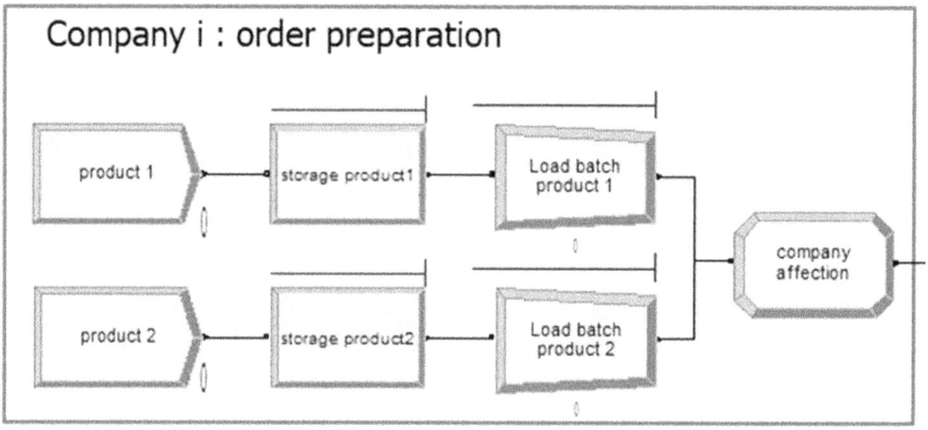

Hub Sub-Model

This sub-model includes the "Hub: unloading docks", "Hub: order preparation", "Hub: customers assignment", and "Hub: loading docks" sections. The first and last two sections are structurally similar to those used in the company sub-model of the non-pooled simulation model. All the difference appears in the "Hub: order preparation" section. In this section, a "Decide" module splits each load into individual pallets to sort them according to their types. Then, each pallet type is stored in the queue of a "Hold" module. These modules release the products according to the signals sent by the customers. Once released, the pallets are sorted according to the load type. If the load is full type, the pallets are sent to the "Batch" module, named "Full load preparation hub", to be grouped and sent to the corresponding customer. Otherwise, the pallets are sent to the "Batch" module named "Partial load preparation hub" to be grouped into a partial load and sent to the corresponding customer (Figure 17).

Figure 17. Simulation model of Hub order preparation section in the pooled supply chain simulation model with hub

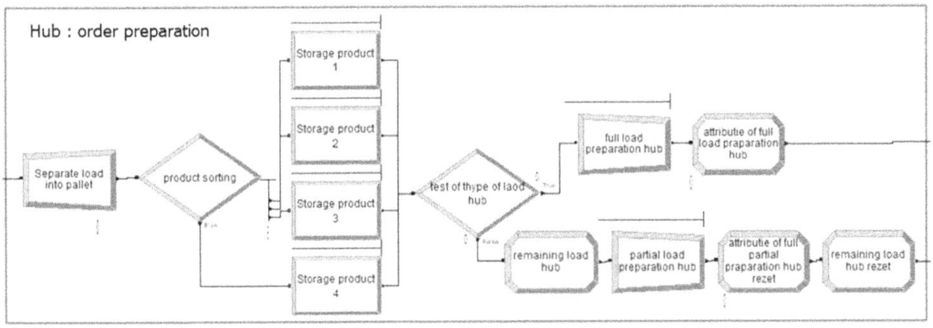

Customer Sub-Model

This sub-model is composed of three sections "Customer j: order generation and management" section, the "Customer j: unloading docks" section, and the "Customer j: order reception" section. The two last present the same structures used in the model without pooling. The differences appear in the first section. In this section, the order form is no longer divided into two. In addition, every order form goes through a stock check stage at the pooling hub. In this step, several conditions can be checked depending on the availability of the pallet types. A first condition verifies the availability of all pallets. If one of the required pallet types is missing, the verification condition falls back on the other pallet types from the second company. Finally, the order is canceled if all pallet types are missing. Once sorted, the order form passes through different "Signal" modules that send the necessary signals to the "Hold" modules of the "Hub: order preparation" section making them release the requested pallets of products (Figure 18).

Figure 18. Simulation model of Customer j order generation and management section in the pooled supply chain simulation model with hub

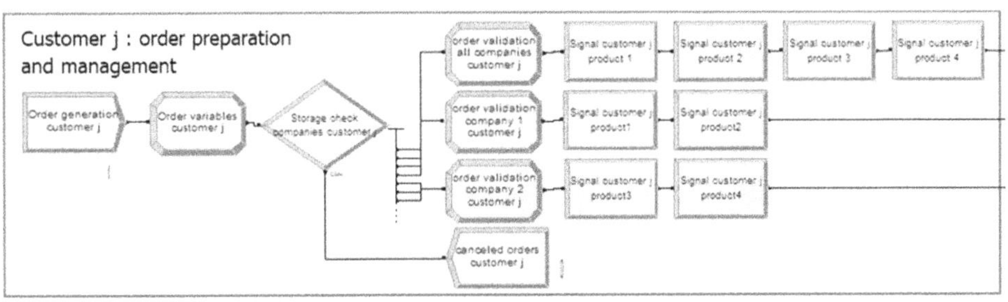

Pooled Supply Chains With Hub And Multi-Drop Model

Several modifications are necessary for the hybridization of the multi-drop delivery and the pooling hub policies. These modifications are mainly in the hub sub-models. This section incorporates the new sub-section named "Hub: multidrop management". This sub-section works as the "Enterprise j: multidrop management" subsection in the pooled supply chain with multidrop simulation model (Figure 19).

Figure 19. Overview of the pooled supply chain simulation model with hub and multi-drop

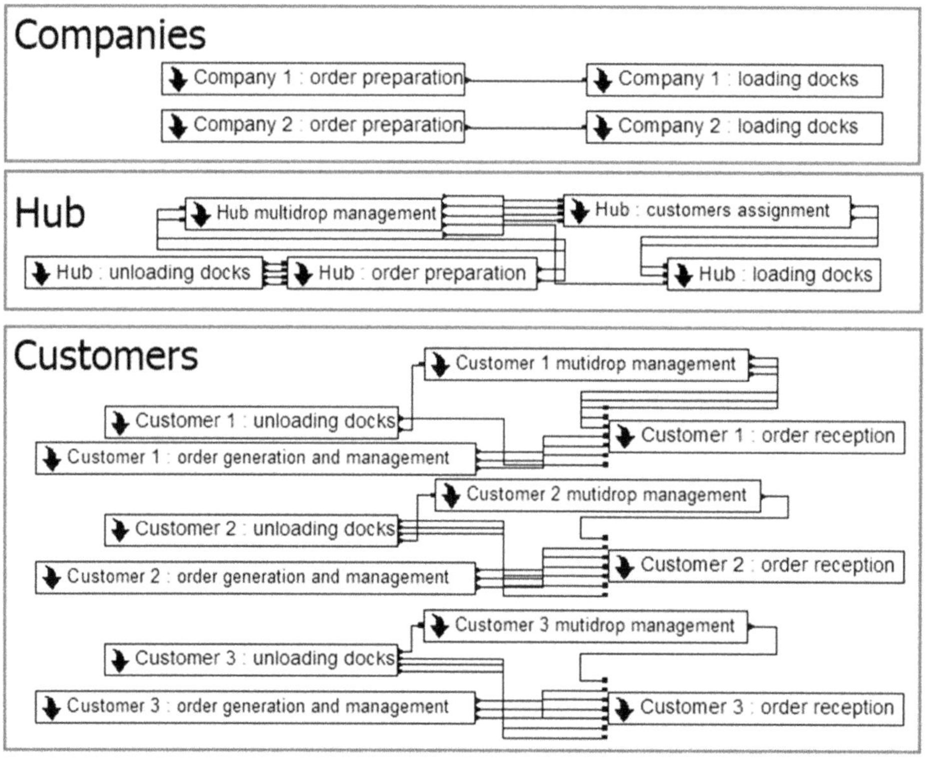

STUDY CASE

This study adopts a supply chain of two companies and three customers. The supply of products by the firms in the supply chain follows statistical distributions (Table 1). The customers submit orders to the two firms whose lead times and corresponding pallet quantities follow discrete distributions (Table 2). The average speeds of the delivery vehicles depend on the distance between the shipping and destination locations. This average speed is set at 80 kilometers per hour for long distances. For short and medium distances the speed has been reduced to 40 kilometers per hour. The distances between the supply chain components defined in kilometers and the corresponding speeds are shown in Figure 5.

Table 1. Time and quantity of pallet feeding in supply chains

Company	Product	Inter-Arrival Time	Palettes quantity
Company 1	P1	N (4, 0.5)	2
	P2	N (3, 0.5)	2
Company 2	P3	N (3.5, 0.5)	2
	P4	N (3.5, 0.5)	2

Table 2. Time between orders and quantity of pallets per order

Customer	Time between order	Quantity of pallets per order	
Customer 1	24 h	Company 1	P 1: DISC (0.6, 4, 1.0, 5), P 2: DISC (0.3, 5, 1.0, 7)
		Company 2	P 3: DISC (0.8, 6, 1.0, 7), P4: DISC (0.7, 4, 1.0, 6)
Customer 2	24 h	Com1	P1: DISC (0.4, 4, 1.0, 5); P2: DISC (0.6, 5, 1.0, 7)
		Company 2	P 3: DISC (0.5, 3, 1.0, 5); P4: DISC (0.8, 4, 1.0, 6)
Customer 3	36 h	Company 1	P 1: DISC (0.5, 3, 1.0, 6); P2: DISC (0.5, 4, 1.0, 8)
		Company 2	P 3: DISC (0.3, 3, 1.0, 6); P4 DISC (0.3, 6, 1.0, 8)

According to Mrabti et al. (2019, 2022), the formulation of the CO2 emissions indicator depends on the weight of the load transported, the capacity of the vehicle, and the distance traveled. In our case study, the following formulas for estimating CO2 emissions for delivery are adopted:

- $E_{loaded} = D_{ij} \times [E_{empty} + (E_{full} - E_{empty}) \times X]$ (1)
- $E_{unloded} = D_{ij} \times E_{empty}$ (2)

With

- E_{loaded}: The total CO2 emissions of a loaded vehicle, in KgCO2, between nodes i and j.
- $E_{unloaded}$: The total CO2 emissions of an unloaded vehicle, in KgCO2, between nodes i and j.
- D_{ij}: The distance, in kilometers, between nodes i and j.
- E_{empty}: The CO2 emissions rate, in KgCO2/Km, of an empty vehicle.
- E_{full}: The CO2 emissions rate, in KgCO2/Km, of a full loaded vehicle.
- X: The ratio between weight of the load of merchandise and the maximum payload of the vehicle.

The CO2 emissions rates of empty and fully loaded vehicles, E_{empty} and E_{full}, are related to the vehicle speed as follow (Mrabti et al. 2022):

- $E_{empty} = K + a \times v + b \times v2 + c \times v3 + d/v + e/v2 + f/v3$ (3)
- $E_{full} = E_{empty} \times C_{load}(v)$ (4)
- $C_{load}(v) = k + r \times v + s \times v2 + t \times v3 + u/v$ (5)

With

- v: The vehicle speed
- K and k: Constants determined according to the Gross Vehicle Weight Rating (GVWR).
- a, b, c, d, e, f, r, s, t, u: Coefficients determined according to the vehicle GVWR.
- C_{load}: The load correction factor

The choice of vehicles' load was based on ADEME (2014). We used trucks of 12-tonnes GVWR. The maximum loading capacity was limited to 6 tons due to pallet's volume constraints. Each company has two trucks in its fleet. These trucks were distributed between companies and the pooling hub in the case of the pooled supply chains with hub models. Hence, in these models, the companies operate one truck in common to deliver their pallets to the pooling hub. The other three trucks are assigned to the pooling hub for deliveries to customers. According to the GVWR of the trucks used and equations (3) and (4), the values of the empty and full emission rates are Eempty=0.48 KgCO2/Km and Efull=0.58 KgCO2/Km for the speed of 40 Km/hour and Eempty=0.51 KgCO2/Km and Efull=0.58 KgCO2/Km for the speed of 80 Km/hour (Mrabti et al. 2022, Hickman et al. 1999). An average load capacity of 9.79 tons was adopted for each truck (ADEME 2007).

The simulation of each model was replicated 30 times. Each replication lasted a full year of operation. The CO2 emissions mean per delivered pallet for each simulation model have been compiled (Table 3). These results were then analyzed using Minitab 18 software. Figure 20 illustrates all the values and confidence intervals of mean emissions per delivered pallet. It shows that the average CO2 emissions of the non-pooled supply chain value is the highest. This value exceeds 50.777 KgCO2/pallet, while it does not exceed 45.476 KgCO2/pallet for the different pooling strategies studied. The CO2 emissions of the different pooling strategies are close. A pair-wise comparison of the simulation results of all the transport strategies was carried out using Games-Howell's two-by-two comparison procedure. This procedure does not require the assumption of equality between the variances of the compared groups of values (Shingala et al. 2015). Figure 21 shows the results of the Games-Howell procedure. It shows that only the confidence interval for the differences between the CO2 emission averages of the hub and multi-drop pooling strategies include the value zero. Hence, the average CO2 emissions of these two pooling strategies are equivalent. The results of the other simulation models are statistically different (Figure 21). We ranked the results of all simulation scenarios in decreasing order based on the CO2 emissions (Table 4). According to the synthesis table, all pooling strategies significantly reduce the emissions of CO2 compared to the non-pooled supply chain. Indeed, the reductions vary from 10.439% to 13.58%. The substantial reduction corresponds to the Hub and multi-drop strategy.

Table 3. Simulation results CO2 emissions / palette

Rep	No pooling	Multi-pick	Multi-drop	Hub	Hub & Multi-drop
1	50.521	44.469	45.186	43.735	43.664
2	50.858	44.869	45.536	44.060	43.792
3	51.042	44.903	45.723	43.957	43.986
4	50.617	44.761	45.620	43.882	43.880
5	50.549	44.744	45.435	43.886	44.198
6	50.560	44.828	45.505	43.814	43.831
7	50.788	44.699	45.270	43.903	44.019
8	50.784	44.812	45.853	43.835	43.983
9	50.550	44.737	45.282	44.141	43.847
10	50.947	44.966	45.491	44.061	43.918
11	50.516	44.873	45.579	43.916	43.708
12	50.890	44.266	44.924	44.052	43.610
13	50.907	44.770	45.646	43.965	43.858
14	50.642	44.855	45.360	43.994	43.774
15	50.947	45.102	45.948	43.685	44.109
16	50.568	44.887	45.248	43.990	43.936
17	50.876	44.679	45.857	44.211	43.702
18	50.847	44.739	45.470	44.024	44.033
19	50.906	44.941	45.943	44.121	43.876
20	50.808	44.615	45.266	43.879	43.853
21	50.833	44.830	45.575	43.911	44.053
22	50.984	44.762	45.271	44.081	43.752
23	50.899	44.769	45.422	43.704	43.750
24	50.903	44.626	45.076	43.774	43.983
25	50.851	45.022	45.558	43.998	43.863
26	50.609	44.697	45.361	44.033	43.692
27	50.928	44.779	45.790	43.808	43.939
28	50.595	44.768	45.428	44.138	44.175
29	50.648	44.732	45.215	44.077	43.832
30	50.930	44.772	45.448	43.984	43.828

Figure 20. Average values and confidence intervals of CO2 emissions

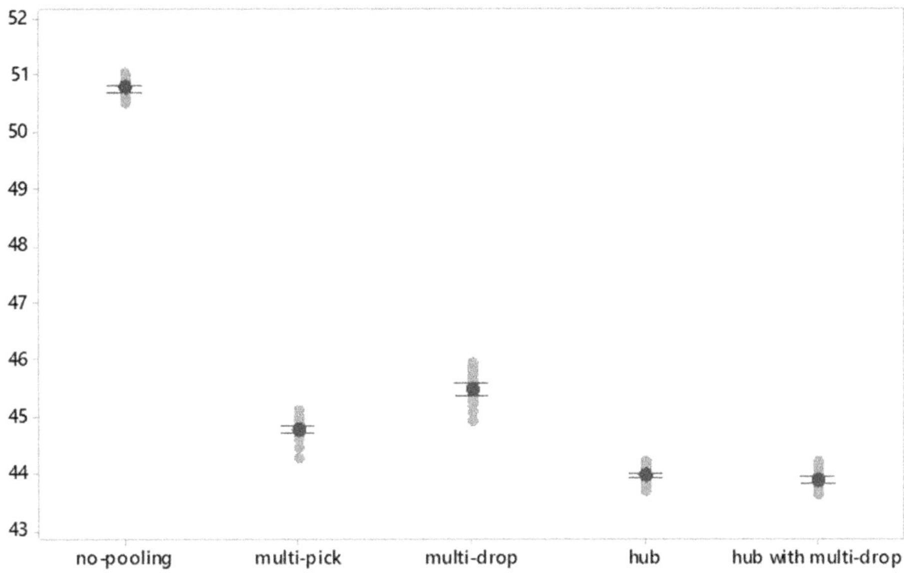

Figure 21. Games-Howell simultaneous Confidence Intervals of CO2 emissions

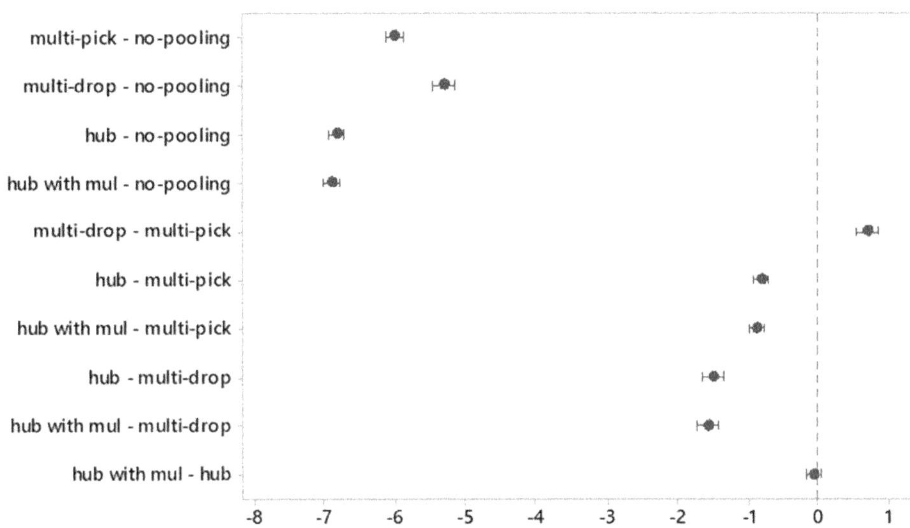

Table 4. Summary of CO2 emissions results

Pooling strategy	Non- pooled	Hub & Multi-drop	Hub	Multi-pick	Multi-drop
CO_2 emission (Kg_{CO2}/pallet)	50.777	43.881	43.954	44.776	45.476
Variation of CO_2 rate emission	Reference	-13.580%	-13.437%	-11.818%	-10.439%

CONCLUSIONS AND FUTURE WORK

One of the many factors contributing to the greenhouse effect is the CO2 emissions from supply chain activities. The challenge of lowering these emissions has been addressed in several studies. Pooling supply chains is one of the efficient solutions to this problem. The goal of the current work is to explain how to create simulation models of pooled supply chains. Using the ARENA simulation software, we provide simulation models of four logistics pooling schemes and their development modes. Multi-pick, multi-drop, pooling hub, and a mix of multi-drop and pooling hub are these four strategies. We also use the developed simulation models to investigate the effects of these supply chain pooling strategies on CO2 emissions to show their interest in meeting the objective of reducing transport-related CO2 emissions. A case study shows the effects of these supply chain pooling strategies on their CO2 emissions. The key finding shows that every supply chain pooling strategy outperforms a supply chain without a pooling. In addition, the hub pooling approach with upstream multi-drop had the best performance. In conclusion, all supply chain pooling strategies significantly reduce CO2 emissions.

This study supports several perspectives that are currently under development. We plan to extend this exploration to other pooling strategies in the first perspective. In the second perspective, we intend to explore the effects of pooling strategies on other supply chain performance. A multi-objective optimization of supply chain pooling strategies, considering other performance indicators such as order fulfillment rates, will be examined.

REFERENCES

Abbad, H. (2014). La gestion mutualisée des approvisionnements: Mythe ou réalités? *Logistique & Management*, *22*(2), 41–50. doi:10.1080/12507970.2014.11517051

ADEME. (2007). *Calcul des facteurs d'émissions et sources bibliographiques utilisées, Méthode bilan carbone*. Agence de l'Environnement, Mission Interministérielle et de la Maîtrise de l'Energie.

ADEME. (2014). *Documentation des facteurs d'émissions de la base carbone.* Agence de l'Environnement, Mission Interministérielle et de la Maîtrise de l'Energie.

Bruzzone, A., & Longo, F. (2014). An application methodology for logistics and transportation scenarios analysis and comparison within the retail supply chain. *European Journal of Industrial Engineering*, *8*(1), 112–142. doi:10.1504/EJIE.2014.059352

Duong, L. N. K., & Chong, J. (2020). Supply chain collaboration in the presence of disruptions: A literature review. *International Journal of Production Research*, *58*(11), 3488–3507. doi:10.1080/00207543.2020.1712491

El Bouazzaoui, Y., Abou Elala, M., Kébé, S., & Mimouni, F. (2020). Environmental impact assessment in the case of pooling Moroccan hydrocarbon supply chain resources. *Computer Science 2020 5th International Conference on Logistics Operations Management (GOL).*

Hickman, J., Hassel, D., Joumard, R., Samaras, Z., & Sorenson, S. (1999). *Methodology for Calculating Transport Emissions and Energy Consumption (Report for the Project MEET).* Transport Research Laboratory.

Ho, D., Kumar, A., & Shiwakoti, N. (2019). A literature review of supply chain collaboration mechanisms and their impact on performance. *Engineering Management Journal*, *31*(1), 47–68. doi:10.1080/10429247.2019.1565625

Jun, Z. (2015). Collaboration evaluation of supply logistics based on supply-hub. *2015 Seventh International Conference on Measuring Technology and Mechatronics Automation*, 279-284. 10.1109/ICMTMA.2015.74

Leitner, R., Meizer, F., Prochazka, M., & Sihn, V. (2011). Structural concepts for horizontal cooperation to increase efficiency in logistics. *CIRP Journal of Manufacturing Science and Technology*, *4*(3), 332–337. doi:10.1016/j.cirpj.2011.01.009

Mohsin, M., Abbas, Q., Zhang, J., Ikram, M., & Iqbal, N. (2019). Integrated effect of energy consumption, economic development, and population growth on CO2 based environmental degradation: A case of transport sector. *Environmental Science and Pollution Research International*, *26*(32), 32824–32835. doi:10.100711356-019-06372-8 PMID:31502046

Montoya-Torres, J. R., Muñoz-Villamizar, A., & Vega-Mejía, C. A. (2016). On the impact of collaborative strategies for goods delivery in city logistics. *Production Planning and Control*, *27*(6), 443–455. doi:10.1080/09537287.2016.1147092

Montzka, S., Dlugokencky, E., & Butler, J. (2011). Non-CO2 greenhouse gases and climate change. *Nature*, *476*(7358), 43–50. doi:10.1038/nature10322 PMID:21814274

Moutaoukil, A., Derrouiche, R., & Neubert, G. (2013). *Modélisation d'une stratégie de mutualisation logistique en intégrant les objectifs de Développement Durable pour des PME agroalimentaires*. In 13e Congrès International de Génie Industriel (CIGI'13), la rochelle, France.

Mrabti, N., Hamani, N., & Delahoche, L. (2018). Mutualisation logistique, approche par simulation. In 12ème Conférence Internationale de Modélisation, Optimisation et SIMulation, MOSIM 2018, Toulouse, France.

Mrabti, N., Hamani, N., & Delahoche, L. (2019). Vers un modèle de simulation de la mutualisation logistique 4.0. *Logistique & Management*, 1-15.

Mrabti, N., Hamani, N., & Delahoche, L. (2022). A sustainable collaborative approach to the distribution network design problem with CO2 emissions allocation. *International Journal of Shipping and Transport Logistics*, *14*(1-2), 114–140. doi:10.1504/IJSTL.2022.120676

Ouhader, H., & El Kyal, M. (2017). The impact of horizontal collaboration on CO2 emissions due to road transportation. *Proceedings of the International Conference on Industrial Engineering and Operations Management*, 11-13.

Pan, S., Ballot, E., & Fontane, F. (2013). The reduction of greenhouse gas emissions from freight transport by pooling supply chains. *International Journal of Production Economics*, *143*(1), 86–94. doi:10.1016/j.ijpe.2010.10.023

Pan, S., Ballot, E., Fontane, F., & Hakimi, D. (2014). Environmental and economic issues arising from the pooling of SMEs' supply chains: Case study of the food industry in western France. *Flexible Services and Manufacturing Journal*, *26*(1-2), 92–118. doi:10.100710696-012-9162-3

Shingala, M. C., & Rajyaguru, A. (2015). Comparison of post hoc tests for unequal variance. *International Journal of New Technologies in Science and Engineering*, *2*, 22–33.

Sulaiman, C., & Abdul-Rahim, A. S. (2018). Population growth and CO2 emission in Nigeria: A recursive ARDL approach. *SAGE Open*, *8*(2). doi:10.1177/2158244018765916

Taieb, N. H., Mellouli, R., & Affes, H. (2014). Impact of means and resources pooling on supply-chain management: Case of large distribution. *2014 International Conference on Advanced Logistics and Transport (ICALT)*, 160-166. 10.1109/ICAdLT.2014.6864111

Ülkü, M. A. (2012). Dare to care: Shipment consolidation reduces not only costs, but also environmental damage. *International Journal of Production Economics*, *139*(2), 438–446. doi:10.1016/j.ijpe.2011.09.015

Wang, F., Lai, X., & Shi, N. (2011). A multi-objective optimization for green supply chain network design. *Decision Support Systems*, *51*(2), 262–269. doi:10.1016/j.dss.2010.11.020

Yudi, F., & Wei Lin, H. (2017). Impacts of energy management practices on energy efficiency and carbon emissions reduction: A survey of malaysian manufacturing firms. *Resources, Conservation and Recycling*, *126*, 62–73. doi:10.1016/j.resconrec.2017.07.023

KEY TERMS AND DEFINITIONS

CO_2 Emissions: Are the total release of carbon dioxide into the atmosphere. CO_2 emissions caused by human pollution are constantly increasing. They contribute to global warming.

Discrete Event Simulation: A discrete event simulation models the operation of a system as a succession of events. Each event occurs at a particular point in time and marks a change of state in the system.

Multi-Drop: This pooling strategy pools the resources of multiple manufacturers to merge deliveries to a customer in common.

Multi-Pick: It is a pooling strategy that gathers supplies from several suppliers at a single delivery point for grouped deliveries to a single recipient.

Pooling Hub: Refers to the process of reorganizing and grouping products in a warehouse to unify storage and transport management.

Pooling Strategies: Are logistic collaborations between companies to increase the competitiveness of their logistic networks, optimizing the use of their transport means.

Supply Chain Management: Includes all the processes of managing the flow of goods that involve actively streamlining a company's supply activities to customers to gain a competitive advantage in the marketplace.

Sustainability: It is a mode of development that meets the needs of the present without compromising the ability of future generations to meet their own needs.

Chapter 8
Sustainable Blockchain Technologies in the Circular Economy

Muzammil Khurshid
Department of Banking and Finance, University of the Punjab, Gujranwala, Pakistan

R. M. Ammar Zahid
https://orcid.org/0000-0002-4627-0917
School of Accounting, Yunnan Technology and Business University, China

Wasim ul Rehman
Department of Banking and Finance, University of the Punjab, Gujranwala, Pakistan

ABSTRACT

This chapter aims to discuss the relationship between sustainable blockchain technology and circular economy. Blockchain and circular economy have brought a revolutionary change in the global economy by making the data transparent and decentralized. The circular economy focuses on recycling, including re-manufacturing, restoration, reprocessing, and reclamation. Blockchain technology plays a potential role in sharing information to overcome fraud by providing quick, fast, timely, and accurate data. Blockchain technology is used in the banking sector, but there is a need to improve it in the banking field. Moreover, it has overcome the food shortage and supply chain issues by tackling the lack of information. Sustainable blockchain technology has brought marvelous and revolutionary changes in the health sector. It has reduced the irregularities, lack of information, costs, and issues in the records of patients. Furthermore, the obstacles in finding the data regarding the land have also been addressed by blockchain technology.

DOI: 10.4018/978-1-6684-6663-6.ch008

INTRODUCTION

In the present world, prompt information sharing has become the need of the hour in the field of the supply chain (De Sousa, Jabbour, Godinho and Roubaud, 2018; Saberi, Kouhizadeh, Sarkis and Shen, 2018). Prompt information sharing can reduce fraud, falsification and risks involved in the smooth transmission of supply chains. However, unfortunately, it has become a serious challenge to trace the exact information through different supply chain networks. A few decades ago, researchers and futurists revealed that technology would be invented to send and receive data safely and securely. They knew that the future ruler of this global village is information technology, however, it was also deemed that the businesses, companies, corporations and industries will use computer-based software and technologies for their operations and will also compete with their competitors based on these technologies (Berg, Davidson & Potts, 2019). However, unfortunately, in the current era, businesses use these technologies. However, their data on these technologies is never considered safe and secure. It was also seen that the data was formatted due to some unknown problems in the technological systems. To overcome this type of problem computer scientists and software engineers were trying to build an immutable technology.

Civilizational history, religious history, economical history, etc., are just a few instances of history. These pasts have either been settled permanently or remained constant while recounting. Nevertheless, documenting its past is a daunting task considering the rate at which technology advances. Additionally, people from various locations have had vastly different technical past experiences. While some governments are manufacturing spaceships, others are focusing on infrastructure enhancements such as the installation of new water pipelines and power plants. Recently, the world has experienced a future breakthrough in maintaining the supply chains by adopting sustainable blockchain technologies (Polvora, Nascimento, Lourenço and Scapolo, 2020). Blockchain technology manages the data electronically to make it transparent. Blockchain is a decentralized and public ledger system. The blockchain network's regulations are well-known and understood by many users. Using mathematical and cryptographic techniques, blockchain technology allows each member to independently validate the book's history and content. This is the same as enhancing accountability and progressively lowering trust risk, and it guarantees that the transaction history is accurate and has not been tampered with.

The concept of Blockchain technology has been introduced recently which is used to transmit data pear-to-pear safely, timely and accurately. It is a newly invented technology that is considered very helpful nowadays, which is transparent, open, independent from any kind of influence by its members and decentralized. The evolution of blockchain technology happened with the development of Bitcoin after the global crisis in 2008 when Nakamoto developed the first cryptocurrency, and after that, blockchain technology evolved (Kelly, 2019). Blockchain technology emerged to facilitate financial transactions through bitcoin and cryptocurrency, the most popular blockchain technologies (Crosby, Nachiappan, Pattanayak, Verma and Kalyanaraman, 2016). In this regard, blockchain technology is used to share information with all the concerned stakeholders. It is a technology in which the user can only create and update a record but cannot delete any record (Ito, Narula, and Ali, 2017; Iansiti and Lakhani, 2017). Blockchain technology is an "Open, distributed ledger that can record transactions between two parties efficiently and in a verifiable and permanent way" (Friedman and Ormiston, 2022).

Blockchain technology's open-source nature paves the way for cooperation amongst teams of programmers, academics, and businesses to share knowledge, improve processes, and find workable solutions to issues more streamlined and securely. As a result, blockchain technology is now seen as one of the foundational technologies required to underpin the next generation of worldwide credit certification and value Internet. There is no denying blockchain technology's significance for China's industrial upgrading. Blockchain technology has been introduced as a sustainability-oriented innovation that addresses the issues and challenges related to sustainable supply chains (Adams, Jeanrenaud, Bessant, Denyer and Overy, 2016; Aste, Tasca and Matteo, 2017).

A blockchain is essentially a distributed database of records or decentralized ledger of all transactions or digital events that have been executed and shared among participating parties. It keeps the record of every saved transaction, which can never be removed. It is working safely for both financial and non-financial world applications. It has put us at ease as we can completely rely on it in dealing with our digital matters without the fear of being hacked, manipulated, or compromised. For example, we can trustfully send money through online transactions without getting any scams. Nobody can alter the transactions recorded in the blocks, and the users in the network can easily detect any change. One can easily post his daily life matters on social media apps and communicate with them without being hacked. Bitcoin is the most popular example, which helps control the ownership of money. In this way, it has wide applications, including smart property, financial and non-financial institutions and the existing market.

Figure 1. How Blockchain Works (Source: IP Specialist (How Blockchain Technology Works. Problem Statement: | by IP Specialist | Medium)

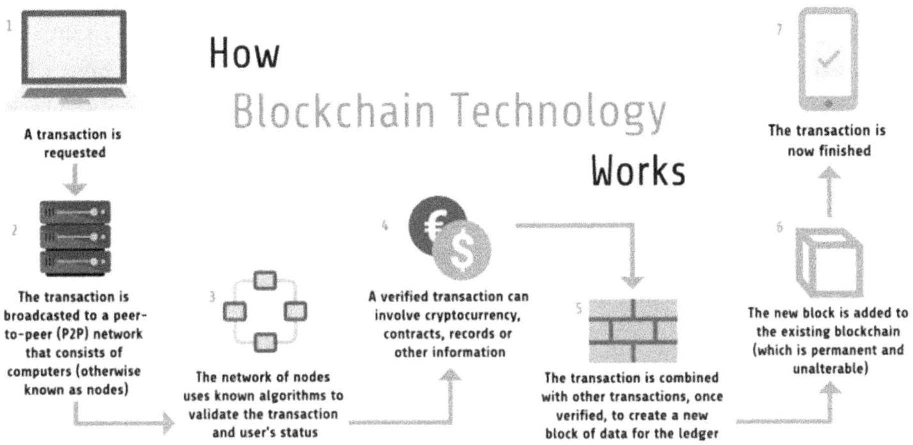

It is important to remember that the blockchain is still in its infancy, and the following suggestions might be kept in mind while putting blockchain technology to use:

(1) The correct application field must be chosen by a group of people, yet there is such a thing as having too many people involved. To address the major advantages of friction, which must be weighed against the primary risks accepted by all parties, the parties work together to establish smart contracts.
(2) Ensuring the mathematical and cryptographic methods are comprehensive, secure, and reliable while preventing the introduction of new hazards is essential for the technology's success.
(3) Considering the trade-offs between free innovation and rules and regulations.
(4) Considering the needs and schedules of all parties involved in the blockchain's implementation and marketing.

KEY DRIVERS AND ATTRIBUTES OF BLOCKCHAIN TECHNOLOGY

Turning out the key drivers and attributes of Blockchain Technology, transparency and decentralization are considered the major key drivers involved in validating the transactions and requests chronologically, which is a critical process due to the creation of ownership. The transactions and rules among the nodes to interact with one another are not governed by a single authority due to the absence of a central authority. In this regard, a set of nodes approves the exact order to make the transactions transparent. Moreover, blockchain cannot be irreversible and tampered with, leading to its security. That is why, blockchain is also known as the trust machine which cannot be changed by an individual or a group of individuals (The Economist, 2015). Human interaction and involvement have been almost finished in blockchain technology through automation. The software performs all the activities automatically to execute and verify the transactions. Metadata is another vital driver of blockchain technology. Blockchain permits banks to construct new networks that can digitize their current stock to operate securely and safely.

Over time, many have started to use and understand blockchain technologies, especially its working, purpose and challenges. When fully developed, blockchain technology may fundamentally alter how businesses are run in the future. Using a distributed ledger like blockchain is essential. Significant efficiency may be gained by using blockchain technology in global supply chains. We will show that certain blockchain applications represent a disruptive innovation since they allow for the development of much more cost-effective solutions, which in turn threatens to upend established markets. There are following four main types of blockchain:

Public Blockchains

The original developers of blockchain technology envisioned a public blockchain as a distributed ledger where everyone could see and interact with the ledger, where transactions would be added only if they were legitimate, and where anyone could participate in reaching a consensus. As was previously mentioned, the consensus procedure controls which blocks are added to the chain and the overall state. Security on the public blockchain is provided not by a centralized server but by cryptographic verification backed by incentives for miners. Those transactions may be mined and published by anybody. Due to the lack of implicit confidence in the public blockchain's users, the network adheres to an algorithm that validates transactions via the use of software and hardware resources to solve a problem in a brute-force manner (i.e., by solving the cryptographic puzzle). Each new answer, together with the transactions needed to validate it, provides the foundation for solving the next issue, and the miner who gets the solution first is rewarded. Proof-of-work and proof-of-stake are the two main verification ideas.

Private Blockchains

One definition of a private blockchain is one in which only a single entity can access the ledger and may make changes. Permissions to read might be completely open, or they can be severely limited. Database administration and internal auditing are possible uses; therefore, general readability may not be required. However, in other circumstances, public audibility is desirable. Private blockchains might solve compliance brokers for laws for the banking sector. Private blockchain initiatives like the Gem Health network and the Linux Foundation's Hyperledger project are currently under development.

Distinguishing between open, consortium, and private blockchains is crucial. A distributed ledger's cryptographic audibility is available even to "old school" users who choose a centralized solution. Private blockchains provide many benefits not available on public blockchains. A blockchain's rules may be modified at any time by the blockchain's private operator. Assuming the blockchain in question is used by banks and other financial institutions, erroneous transactions may be corrected as soon as they are identified. Similarly, they will be allowed to make adjustments to accounts and reverse previous actions. To that end, there seems to be a path. Property registries, for example, may need this capability in the event of a clerical error or a malicious actor fraudulently assuming property ownership. The same thing holds if the government possesses backdoor access keys to a public blockchain, as they had under the Clinton administration.

Consortium Blockchains

A predetermined group of nodes manages the consensus process in a consortium blockchain like R3; for instance, a group of nine financial institutions maintains a node, and five (like the US Supreme Court) must sign every block for the block to be legitimate. The public may have access to the blockchain, or it may be restricted to participants only; there are also hybrid options, such as making the root hashes of the blocks publicly available alongside an API that allows the public to make a limited number of queries and receive cryptographic proofs of some parts of the blockchain state. These blockchains may be thought of as "partially decentralized" distributed ledgers.

Comparing Blockchains

Since private blockchain transactions only need to be confirmed by a small set of nodes that have access to a large amount of computing power, they are cheaper to process. As scaling technologies are developed, the price of public blockchain transactions will decrease, making them competitive with private blockchains. Due to the high reliability of the network's nodes and the ease with which problems may be resolved by human involvement, consensus methods with substantially lower block periods are feasible. Private blockchains will always be faster, and the latency difference will never disappear because, unfortunately, the speed of light does not increase by 2x every two years, like Moore's law. However, improvements in public blockchain technology, such as Ethereum's proof-of-stake, can bring public blockchains closer to the "instant confirmation" ideal. Private blockchains may increase privacy if access to the ledger is limited.

Considering everything, it may be easy to conclude that private blockchains are the superior option for institutions. However, public blockchains still offer effective use even in the institutional setting. The philosophical principles of freedom, impartiality, and openness are central to the case for public blockchains and are a major source of their value. There are two main areas for public blockchain benefits:

One method in which public blockchains safeguard app users from app developers is by defining that app developers have no control over certain matters.

Second, since public blockchains are accessible to anybody, they are used by several organizations, which results in the emergence of networking effects. A smart contract can reduce costs to almost nothing if asset-holding systems and money are both stored on the blockchain. If Party A delivers the item to trustworthy software that runs on a public blockchain, then Party B may pay for its transfer in a matter of seconds. Keep in mind that this can only be implemented effectively if two asset classes from entirely unrelated sectors share the same database.

CIRCULAR ECONOMY

Over the decades, the shortage of resources and efficient usage of these resources have been discussed in economics, where different economic theories have been presented focusing on the use of factors of production. However, unfortunately, such theories never provided any solution to reuse these resources. That is why this approach is known as the linear economy. To tackle the scarcity of resources, a circular economy was introduced in 2008 when China became the first nation in the world to approve a circular economy law (CIRAIG, 2015). The discussions about industrial development have given more consideration to the circular economy as a strategy to address environmental issues and advance sustainable development. Moreover, some new economies have emerged over a few decades, like the service economy, collaborative economy, healthy economy and circular economy.

The Circular Economy has the potential to contribute to the development of a brighter future for humanity by maximizing resource use and minimizing waste via the application of cutting-edge technology and intelligent design. Ecoboost, for instance, recycles plastics like straws, bags, and toothbrush bristles into functional booths for events. Incentivizing new behaviors like sustainable resource production and consumption, product repurposing, and recycling is essential to the success of the Circular Economy. Another step is to verify that the products consumers and businesses purchase that have been reused or recycled do not include any "virgin" components. Lacking such honesty and openness, the economy will likely return to its previous linear form.

The circular economy is concerned with the variety of characteristics that initiates the recycling of the material, including re-manufacturing, restoration, reprocessing and reclamation (Murray, Skene and Haynes, 2017). This cyclical approach is known as 3Rs, consisting of the product's production, utilization, recovery, recycling and re-manufacturing. The concept of a circular economy revolves around the ecosystem (Ghisellini, Cialani, Ulgiati, 2016; Geissdoerfer, Savaget, Bocken and Hultink, 2017). The traditional system of production and consumption was a natural system of the world before technological innovations. These technological innovations opened new horizons of excess production, promoting the idea to increase wealth maximization. These technological changes benefited the industrialists and raised the people's standard of living, according to Heyes, Sharmina, Mendoza, Schmid and Azapagic. (2018), circular economy seeks to enhance the efficient use of resources by focusing the supply chain management at every level. It reduces material use, redesigns materials to be less resource intensive and recaptures waste as a resource to manufacture raw materials and products. Products gain value as they are manufactured through the input of materials, labor and energy.

Figure 2. Circular Economy Process (Source: News European Parliament)

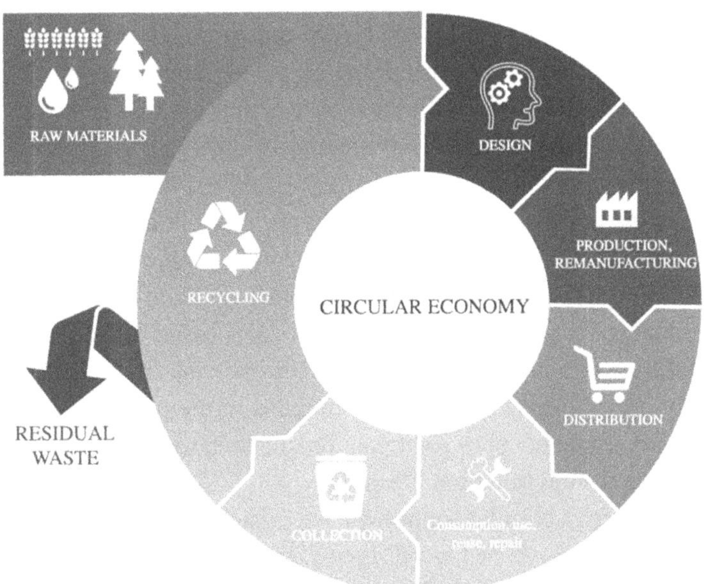

Regarding garbage, the circular economy goes beyond recycling and instead centers on a restorative industrial system that views trash as a valuable commodity. Origins of the "circular economy" notion go back quite a way. Since the late 1970s or early 1980s, the practical applications to modern economic systems and industrial processes have gained traction. Germany was the birthplace of the cradle-to-cradle idea and certification procedure. The idea is based on the principle that all materials used in production and commerce are nutrients, with (a) technological and (b) biological agents. The cradle-to-cradle paradigm prioritizes resource conservation and waste elimination across the product life cycle. Incorporating the reliable and fruitful natural processes of "biological metabolism" into the cradle-to-grave design has provided a blueprint for creating a "technological metabolism" flow of manufactured goods. Products and parts can be recovered and reused as technical and biological nutrition inside these metabolisms is needed.

It is a system that reduces human dependency in the production process. It is seen as a crucial strategy for attaining sustainable economic and environmental development, and it is accepted in policy and corporate development contexts (EMAF, 2012; Korhonen, Nuur, Feldmann and Birkie, 2018). The circular economy uses the energy of biomass and waste to produce products (Rashid et al., 2013; Mihelcic et al., 2003; Lazarevic and Valve, 2017; Naustdalslid, 2017). Circular economy and all of these other ideas have admirable intentions and great meanings; they provide conceptual difficulties for researchers. A circular Economy can be defined in terms of many aspects. It can be defined in terms of the existing knowledge base of the field, which identifies conceptual aspects as well as major channels of publication (Singh, Chakraborty and Roy, 2017). It contributes to sustainable development initiatives which were designed for the future generation to meet their own needs. "Is liable to be contested for reasons better or worse; but whatever the strength of the reasons they usually carry with them an assumption of agreement, as to the kind of use that is appropriate to the concept in question, between its user and anyone who contests his particular use of it." (Gallie, 1956). The transition from a traditional economy to a circular economy is a revolutionary change that has entirely changed the concept of production and consumption. It has also changed the required industrial infrastructure and the process of manufacturing the products. In the traditional economy, the production process is based on human activity and more material is required in production due to the one-way flow. On the other hand, a circular economy eliminates the role of humans in the production process. The circular economy is a concept of reducing, reusing and recycling material to avoid waste and to keep the environment clean.

The foundations of a circular economy have existed for quite some time. Cleaner production programs, waste to landfill levies (tax on landfill disposal), collection and recycling of household packaging and paper, metals recycling, regional waste strategies, infrastructure planning and investment, waste and recycling legislation, and other regulatory interventions under state-based environment protection acts are all examples of what has been implemented. Many unrealized economic possibilities may be realized by adopting a circular economy strategy. Sustainable economic development, reversing environmental deterioration, and halting resource depletion are all goals of a circular economic system, a key component of which is circular consumption. The reduce, recycle and reuse (3R) concept may help with circular consumption. To achieve a zero-waste society, circular consumption promotes the reuse of materials. Solid and liquid waste management, pollution reduction in water, air, and land, resource conservation, the greening of industrial sectors, and many other activities are all included in the remit of the circular economy. The goals of CE are to increase the value of materials and products, extend their useful life, and reuse or recycle them when they reach the end of their usefulness. The shift to a circular economy often necessitates a rethinking and redesigning of current company structures and practices. This shift is facilitated by digital technologies such as data collecting, analysis, and integration. In this piece, we lay out our underlying premise: blockchain is an emerging technology with the potential to underpin the CE paradigm.

Obstacles to The Circular Economy

Changing from a linear to a circular model is likely nothing short of revolutionary, requiring new urban and industrial infrastructure and procedures for each product's supply chain and new mindsets. Assuming that a circular economy can be founded on the same metaphysical (ontological and teleological) assumptions about the modern self-interested, secular, individualistic, self-determined human and the kind of society and economy that is necessary to facilitate the purpose of such a human, perhaps, unrealistic. Suppose the producer's primary goal is to maximize wealth, and the consumer's primary goal is to maintain or increase their standard of living indefinitely. In that case, such goals may conflict with establishing a circular system, typically done to preserve ecological balance in mind. Creating a sustainable ecology is in direct opposition to pursuing ever-greater material comforts and hedonic experiences. In a contemporary capitalist free market economy, where producers and consumers engage in a competitive race of continual maximum, the notion of a circular economy with top boundaries beyond which the environment starts to be damaged is in direct conflict with the concept of perpetual growth.

Therefore, in a world where governments evaluate their performance based on economic growth, where international financial institutions like the International Monetary Fund lend to governments based on their predicted economic growth, where the shareholders of every listed company seek to maximize their returns perpetually, and where the business students at every university are taught the same ideology and science of perpetual growth, the concept of a circular economy can only be seen as a work of fiction. The ideology on which political choices are formed; the philosophy on which the architecture of contemporary institutions like the public and private institutions is based, seems to be the fundamental obstacle to the circular economy, rather than technology, structure, or politics. Those same organizations, however, are credited with developing innovations that might be crucial for switching to a circular economy.

New initiatives that get private investment are evaluated based on the financial return that may be expected. A perpetual growth economic model must be in place for such yields to materialize. Projects that include the cost of caring for all stakeholders may be difficult to fund under economic models that limit surplus value generation for environmental reasons. The current worldview and mindset, which idealizes everlasting wealth expansion, may make investments in a circular economy seem like an unnecessary luxury. Barriers to circularity exist, however, due to the beliefs of investors and governmental authorities, and hence the beliefs of producers and consumers in today's secular capitalist society.

Blockchain Technologies in Circular Economy

These two emerging concepts, blockchain and circular economy, may bring a revolutionary change and advancement in the global economy (Okorie, Salonitis, Charnley, Moreno, Turner and Tiwari, 2018; Carson, Romanelli, Walsh and Zhumaev, 2018). Blockchain technology and circular economy are based on the two megatrends, sustainability and digitalization. There are several ways in which blockchain technology might hasten the shift to CE. Businesses may benefit from using blockchain technology internally if implemented in the CE. In this way, a blockchain may be useful for huge organizations with dispersed and complicated infrastructures, such as banks and utilities.

Using blockchain, organizational operations and shop floor monitoring may track anything from raw supplies to finished goods to waste to energy use. As a result, green performance assessment and management may build on the digitalization of business operations. Blockchain technology can potentially improve or even eliminate resource-intensive and waste-producing operations in the CE. For successful CE implementation, closed-loop processes, including reuse, recycling, re-manufacturing, and recovery, are especially dependent on cooperative interactions amongst supply chain stakeholders. To this end, blockchain technology improves supply chain transparency and traceability while also facilitating product recovery. Like the traceability of inputs and outputs in closed-loop supply chains, end-of-life processes benefit greatly from blockchain technology. Reducing garbage output has positive effects on the environment. It is possible to eliminate waste at every stage of the supply chain, but measuring waste in the chain's last segment, the downstream, presents a significant challenge. However, blockchain's implementation offers a platform to connect all CE stakeholders, including consumers, which helps alleviate this worry. Supply chain waste can be tracked with greater ease thanks to the technology's openness and traceability. Tokenization may incentivize consumers to adopt more sustainable practices by rewarding them for helping producers determine how much waste has to be cut. Waste management and reduction efforts benefit from and are supported by this data. Using smart contracts, blockchain can digitally record the terms and conditions of waste management schemes and launch the associated recovery operations. Businesses will be able to better control their trash with this capacity.

There is a substantial impediment to the efficient application of CE standards due to a lack of information throughout the lifespan of goods. Therefore, CE stakeholders may benefit from tracing closed-loop supply chain activities thanks to the powers of blockchain to enable trustworthy and accurate information exchange. Blockchain users may easily track past transactions, verify a product's current condition, and share relevant data. The distributed ledger technology (Blockchain) also provides a standardized and trustworthy environment in which to conduct business-related transactions and share resources. In addition, the technology offers several ways to address CE and sustainability concerns. More equitable distribution of CE resources is made possible by blockchain technology. Vendors may pool their idle assets with this technology in a trust-free peer-to-peer system. Blockchain was developed to remove intermediaries and boost confidence in business transactions, streamlining and simplifying value exchange across CE parties.

Some have suggested that blockchain might be used as a social technology or a tool for cooperation in the circular economy context. It facilitates the linking and coordination of dispersed databases, allowing for their simultaneous updating and public accessibility. Cooperation and rivalry inside the loop benefit the circular economy, which uses a decentralized value production and circulation paradigm rather than value creation and appropriation. The blockchain's key features of decentralization, distributiveness and tamper-resistance make this a powerful tool for fostering the results of a circular economy.

Supply chain management is one area where blockchain technology shows promise. Waste minimization and efficiency improvement are ongoing goals in the supply chain industry. By connecting all the nodes in the supply chain's distributed ledgers and databases with blockchain technology, we can increase productivity while cutting down on wasteful processes and unnecessary expenditures. Key data recorded on the blockchain throughout the product's path from raw material source to producer to the client makes tracking lengthy and complicated supply chains relatively simple and efficient.

Blockchain technologies are useful in different circular economy sectors like financial institutions, businesses, agriculture, the environment, etc. Blockchain technology is beneficial to avoid corruption activities and inefficiencies in every field of life. We discuss the usage of important blockchain technologies in the different sectors of the circular economy.

BLOCKCHAIN TECHNOLOGY AND FINANCIAL INSTITUTIONS

Financial institutions need to make a heavy expense on workforce, funds and resources to arrange the database of their customers. Even they have to spend handsome money to update and maintain the system. From the perspective of blockchain technology, banks and financial institutions are not reluctant to use blockchain technologies. Bitcoin, Litecoin, primecoin, cryptocurrency and smart contracts. These are virtual and digital currencies that are generally used for procurement. The banking sector, considered the most important part of the global financial system, adopted this technology to perform all the transactions safely and to keep the record safe for an indefinite period. The adoption of this technology in the banking system is estimated by a survey organized by IBM in 2016. IBM surveyed 200 banks from 16 different countries and revealed that by the year 2020, about 66% of banks worldwide would use blockchain for their safe and secure transactions and record keeping (IBM, 2016). Accenture (2016) also performed a research-based survey, revealing that 9 out of 10 banks from developed countries were using this technology. However, a proper model to smoothly adopt this technology in the banking industry is still needed. In 2014, an adaptation model was introduced for blockchain technology in the banking industry. It tells about the organizational behavior toward adopting blockchain in the banking sector. It not only judges organizational behavior but is also beneficial in overcoming the problems that hamper the smooth adaptation of blockchain in the banking industry (Gangwar, Date and Raoot, 2014).

There is a lack of proper legislation behind this technology; research is also lacking in this field. To indulge this technology in any industry, we should have proper research in this particular area and then consult the results of our research with the industry's practitioners to identify the correct model that describes the variables, which reveals to us that the model is enough good to analyze the factors affecting the blockchain technology in the industry as well as banking sector or not? Time different studies were performed in this field, and researchers observed many models, but no one is still considered accurate. Wang et al., 2017 studied the maturity measuring model of the technology, but the problem is that this study was performed in general and not specific to any industry. Further research was performed to identify the factors influencing blockchain adaptation in the banking industry. IBM also surveyed approximately 200 different banks to check their level of blockchain adaptation. Accordingly, Iansiti & Lakhani (2017) performed another research and provided a framework for adaptation of this model in the banking sector. They also compared the internet with blockchain technology. They concluded that both technologies are very significant in the banking sector. However, much research is still needed to identify the blockchain adaptation model in the banking field. This study is another step in this field to identify factors influencing the banking sector to adopt blockchain technology. This research can at least understand the main factors influencing banks to adopt this technology. It is also beneficial in the way this study is another step in determining the model for blockchain adaptation in the banking industry. Further research could be performed based on the factors identified in this study to formulate a perfect model to adopt blockchain in the banking sector.

Blockchain Technology and Food Sector

Globally, the sustainable food system is passing through a decline phase due to erratic supply chain patterns. The food system influences the economic, social and environmental aspects of society. So, it is crucial to tackling these irregular patterns that damage society's aspects (Hoekstra and Wiedmann, 2014). Recently, the food sector has experienced major technological revolutions. Blockchain technology has penetrated the medical and health industry. The key drivers of blockchain technology have eradicated the shortcomings in the field of health and medicine. Traditionally, the organizations functioned in a centralized manner where sharing of information and lack of transparency were the main shortcomings of a centralized system. Blockchain technology has minimized these deficiencies and made the system more transparent. To guarantee food security and hazard control, experts say that the underlying characteristics of Blockchain technology should be used. Customers' health is at stake when food-borne illnesses are widespread; therefore, it is crucial to track where each food item comes from in the event of an epidemic. The safety of consumers is a major concern, and the financial security of businesses that are held liable for food safety issues makes preserving the integrity of the food we sell an essential aspect of any sustainable business model.

Blockchain Technology and Health Sector

From the perspective of the health sector, blockchain technology is used for transparency in medical equipment records regarding procurement. It has also been considered a real solution to the problems and issues faced by doctors regarding data sharing (Tandon, Dhir, Islam and Mantymaki, 2020; Yue, Wang, Jin, Li and Jiang, 2016). Blockchain technology also provides the solution to reduce asymmetry costs and make the data more valuable and sustainable (Massaro, Dal Mas, Chiappetta Jabbour and Bagnoli, 2020; De Aguiar, Faiçal, Krishnamachari and Ueyama, 2020). The following factors render this method of acquiring and exchanging health data inefficient:

- It takes time since patients have to wait for copies of their medical records to be made, transported, and collected. Although providers have up to 30 days to furnish patients with their medical data, some may just need 5-10 working days to generate noncritical health documents.
- It is unsafe because patients' hard copies of their information might be lost or stolen during transit.
- A patient's medical record may be missing because the information is spread across many unconnected databases. Since there is no centralized repository for an individual's medical history, it is the patient's responsibility to keep track of the dates and locations of their healthcare visits.

Because current healthcare systems are provider-centric rather than patient-centric, people cannot exercise agency over their health records or know who has viewed or modified their information.

For patients to find them, accrediting bodies to recognize them, and payers to compensate them correctly, health care providers (both individuals and organizations) must publish accurate and up-to-date information about their location and the services they provide. Perhaps the data's accuracy and reliability might be enhanced by using a blockchain. Supply chain management is where blockchain technology has found the most widespread use. Medication, clinical supplies, blood products, and medical equipment have supply chains, and blockchains are being utilized to manage these chains. For instance, because of increasing demand, healthcare systems find it difficult to get medical equipment and supplies to fight COVID-19. The disruption of established supply networks with reliable suppliers raises serious trust concerns. Standards compliance, customs certification, timely delivery of products, and fraud are some issues customers have with new suppliers. These confidence problems are exacerbated by the fact that many providers want payment in advance. Blockchain may be the way to go if you want to verify your suppliers' legitimacy and monitor your shipments in real time. IBM Rapid Supplier Link, a blockchain-enabled network, was unveiled in April 2020 to connect governments and healthcare organizations with non-traditional equipment, devices, and supply suppliers to address COVID-19.

Blockchain Technology and Real Estate Sector

In a traditional economy, the traceability of the historical data and finding the actual owner of the land was a very complicated exercise, and a bulk amount of money was wasted to get the real owner. Moreover, the transfer of land was a hectic job because of legal complications. With the emergence of blockchain technology, accurate land record, information and transparency has become in the real estate sector worldwide. Inevitably, the housing market will undergo shifts. The title search procedure, which is required as part of title insurance, may be time-consuming and costly for homeowners purchasing or refinancing the property. One may list real estate on the blockchain to increase trust between sellers and purchasers. Title searches are now performed manually at a high cost. If title insurance is used in the United States, it might be purchased rapidly and at a reduced cost. To safeguard their investment, mortgage lenders often insist on this coverage. There are a lot of unknowns and added costs when buying or selling a property because of all the intermediaries involved. Presently, a transaction cannot be finalized without the services of a broker, a government property database, a title company, a property insurance database, an escrow company, an inspector, an appraiser, and a notary public. We are holding our breath and relying on them. We cannot access the information they have or utilize their services because we lack the requisite expertise in the current real estate transaction environment in which they operate. Public blockchains will permit swifter and cheaper transaction costs while removing most, if not all, of these obstacles.

CONCLUSION

Sustainable blockchain technology has played a crucial role in uplifting the economies of different countries. It is a revolutionary technology that keeps the data transparent and provides a way forward. Blockchain's decentralized and unalterable algorithmic structure is meant to win over stakeholders' confidence. Blockchain's ability to enhance track and trace is the basis for applications in a wide range of industries. As a result of decentralization, middlemen that charge fees to access information, such as agents, brokers, attorneys, and banks, are rendered obsolete. In addition to the moral and societal benefits, cutting out middlemen also saves time and money for the parties involved in the deal. We examine the sustainability implications of blockchain technology in the circular economy and how it is being used in various industries.

The circular economy is a process of recycling, re-manufacturing and recreating the material to make the products usable. The role of blockchain technology is transforming the data in the field of the food sector. Globally, blockchain technology has improved the health sector, and modern technology is being used to minimize the obstacles in the health sector. Our research proves that blockchain's decentralized, distributive, and highly secure qualities help to further the circular economy. Our research demonstrates that blockchain technology has the potential to improve the circular economy in a number of ways. These include lowering transaction fees, improving supply chain efficiency and communication, safeguarding human rights, protecting the privacy of healthcare records, improving patient outcomes, and lowering environmental impact.

REFERENCES

Accenture. (2016). *Blockchain Technology: How Banks are Building a Real-Time Global Payment Network*. https://www.accenture.com/_acnmedia/pdf-35/accenture-blockchain-how-banksbuilding-real-time-global-payment-network.pdf

Adams, R., Jeanrenaud, S., Bessant, J., Denyer, D., & Overy, P. (2016). Sustainability oriented innovation: A systematic review. *International Journal of Management Reviews*, *18*(2), 180–205. doi:10.1111/ijmr.12068

Aste, T., Tasca, P., & Di Matteo, T. (2017). Blockchain Technologies: The Foreseeable Impact on Society and Industry. *Computer*, *50*(9), 18–28. doi:10.1109/MC.2017.3571064

Berg, C., Davidson, S., & Potts, J. (2019). Blockchain Technology as Economic Infrastructure: Revisiting the Electronic Markets Hypothesis. *Front. Blockchain*, *2*(22), 1–6. doi:10.3389/fbloc.2019.00022

Carson, B., Romanelli, G., Walsh, P., & Zhumaev, A. (2018). *Blockchain beyond the hype: What is the strategic business value*. McKinsey Company. https://www.mckinsey.com/business-functions/mckinsey-digital/our-insights/blockchain-beyond-the-hype-what-is-the-strategic-businessvalue

CRAIG (International Reference Centre for the Life Cycle of Products Processes and Services). (2015). *Circular Economy: a Critical Literature Review of Concepts*. Author.

Crosby, M., Nachiappan, P., Verma, S., & Kalyanaraman, V. (2016). Blockchain Technology: Beyond Bitcoin. *Applied Innovation Review*, *2*, 6–19.

De Aguiar, E. J., Faiçal, B. S., Krishnamachari, B., & Ueyama, J. (2020). A survey of blockchain-based strategies for healthcare. *ACM Computing Surveys*, *53*(2), 1–27. doi:10.1145/3376915

De Sousa Jabbour, A. B. L., Jabbour, C. J. C., Godinho Filho, M., & Roubaud, D. (2018). Industry 4.0 and the circular economy: A proposed research agenda and original roadmap for sustainable operations. *Annals of Operations Research*, *270*(1-2), 273–286. doi:10.100710479-018-2772-8

EMAF (Ellen MacArthur Foundation). (2012). Towards the Circular Economy. FICF and McKinsey.

Friedman, N., & Ormiston, J. (2022). Blockchain as a sustainability-oriented innovation?: Opportunities for and resistance to Blockchain technology as a driver of sustainability in global food supply chains. *Technological Forecasting and Social Change*, *175*, 121403. doi:10.1016/j.techfore.2021.121403

Gallie, W. B. (1956). Essentially contested concepts. *Proceedings of the Aristotelian Society*, *55*(1), 167–198. doi:10.1093/aristotelian/56.1.167

Gangwar, H., Date, H., & Raoot, A. D. (2014). Review on IT Adoption: Insights from Recent Technologies. *Journal of Enterprise Information Management*, *27*(4), 488–502. doi:10.1108/JEIM-08-2012-0047

Geissdoerfer, M., Savaget, P., Bocken, M. N. P., & Hultink, E. J. (2017). The Circular Economy – a new sustainability paradigm? *Journal of Cleaner Production*, *143*, 757–768. doi:10.1016/j.jclepro.2016.12.048

Ghisellini, P., Cialani, C., & Ulgiati, S. (2016). A review on circular economy: the expected transition to a balanced interplay of environmental and economic systems. *J. Clean. Prod.*, *114*, 11–32. Available at: https://www.sciencedirect.com/science/article/pii/S0959652615012287

Heyes, G., Sharmina, M., Mendoza, J. M. F., Schmid, A. J., & Azapagic, A. (2018). Developing and Implementing Circular Economy Business Models in Service – Oriented Technology Companies. *Journal of Cleaner Production*, *177*, 621–632. doi:10.1016/j.jclepro.2017.12.168

Hoekstra, A., & Wiedmann, T. (2014). Humanity's unsustainable environmental footprint. *Science*, *344*(6188), 1114–1117. doi:10.1126cience.1248365 PMID:24904155

Iansiti, M., & Lakhani, K. R. (2017). The truth about blockchain. *Harvard Business Review*, 1–11.

IBM. (2016). *Leading the Pack in Blockchain Banking*. https://www.ibm.com/downloads/cas/PA8V4RMX

Ito, J., Narula, N., & Ali, R. (2017). *The Blockchain Will do to the Financial System what the internet did to Media*. https://hbr.org/2017/03/the-blockchain-will-do-to-banks-and-law-firms-whatthe-internet-did-to-media

Jesse, N. (2018). Organizational evolution - how digital disruption enforces organizational agility. *IFAC-PapersOnLine*, *51*(30), 486–491. doi:10.1016/j.ifacol.2018.11.310

Kelly, J. (2019). Craig Wright Has In No Way Been Officially "Recognised" As Satoshi Nakamoto. *Financial Times*. https://ftalphaville.ft.com/2019/05/22/1558547272000/Craig-W
right-has-in-noway-been-officially--recognised--as-Satoshi-N
akamoto/

Korhonen, J., Nuur, C., Feldmann, A., & Birkie, S. E. (2018). Circular Economy as an Essentially Contested Concept. *Journal of Cleaner Production*, *175*, 544–552. doi:10.1016/j.jclepro.2017.12.111

Lazarevic, D., & Valve, H. (2017). Narrating expectations for the circular economy: Towards a common and contested European transition. *Energy Research & Social Science*, *31*, 60–69. doi:10.1016/j.erss.2017.05.006

Massaro, M., Dal Mas, F., Chiappetta Jabbour, C. J., & Bagnoli, C. (2020). Crypto-economy and new sustainable business models: Reflections and projections using a case study analysis. *Corporate Social Responsibility and Environmental Management*, *27*(5), 2150–2160.

Mihelcic, J. R., Crittenden, J. C., Small, M. J., Shonnard, D. R., Hokanson, D. R., Zhang, Q., Chen, H., Sorby, S. A., James, V. U., Sutherland, J. W., & Schnoor, J. L. (2003). Sustainability science and engineering: The emergence of a new Meta Discipline. *Environmental Science & Technology*, *37*, 5314–5324.

Murray, A., Skene, K., & Haynes, K. (2017). The Circular Economy: An Interdisciplinary Exploration of the Concept and Application in a Global Context. *Journal of Business Ethics*, *140*(3), 369–380.

Naustdalslid, J., (2017). Circular economy in China e the environmental dimension of the harmonious society. *Int. J. Sustain. Dev. World Ecol.*, *21*(4), 303-313.

News European Parliament. (2022). *Circular economy: the importance of reusingreusing products and materials | News | European Parliament*. Europa. EU.

Okorie, O., Salonitis, K., Charnley, F., Moreno, M., Turner, C., & Tiwari, A. (2018). Digitisation and the Circular Economy: A Review of Current Research and Future Trends. *Energies, 11*(11), 3009.

Polvora, ´. A., Nascimento, S., Lourenço, J. S., & Scapolo, F. (2020). Blockchain for industrial transformations: A forward-looking approach with multi-stakeholder engagement for policy advice. *Technological Forecasting and Social Change, 157*, 120091.

Rashid, A., Asif, F., Krajnik, P., & Nicolescu, C. M. (2013). Resource Conservative Manufacturing: An essential change in business and technology paradigm for sustainable manufacturing. *Journal of Cleaner Production, 57*, 166–177.

Saberi, S., Kouhizadeh, M., Sarkis, J., & Shen, L. (2018). Blockchain technology and its relationships to sustainable supply chain management. *International Journal of Production Research, 57*, 2117–2135.

Singh, M. P., Chakraborty, A., & Roy, M. (2017). *Developing an Extended Theory of Planned Behavior Model to Explore Circular Economy Readiness in Manufacturing MSMEs, India. Resources, Conservation and Recycling.* Available at https://www.sciencedirect.com/science/article/pii/S0921344917301945

IP Specialist. (2022). *How Blockchain Technology Works.* Medium.

Tandon, A., Dhir, A., Islam, N., & Mantymaki, M. (2020). Blockchain in healthcare: A systematic literature review, synthesizing framework and future research agenda. *Computers in Industry*, 1–22.

The Economist Newspaper Limited. (2015). The trust machine. *The Economist.* https://www.economist.com/leaders/2015/10/31/the-trust-machine

Yue, X., Wang, H., Jin, D., Li, M., & Jiang, W. (2016). Healthcare data gateways: Found healthcare intelligence on blockchain with novel privacy risk control. *Journal of Medical Systems, 40*(10), 1–8.

Chapter 9
The Security of Global Value Chains (GVC):
Recent Trends, Challenges, and Future Risk Management

Ziyue Hong
School of Accounting, Yunnan Technology and Business University, China

R. M. Ammar Zahid
https://orcid.org/0000-0002-4627-0917
School of Accounting, Yunnan Technology and Business University, China

ABSTRACT

Over the last several decades, as businesses have expanded globally in search of higher profits, value chains have become longer and more intricate. Indicators like inventory levels, on-time-in-full deliveries, and shorter lead times all improved for companies that effectively embraced a lean, global style of manufacturing. Complex production networks were created with the goals of efficiency, closeness to markets, and output, but not always with openness or resilience in mind. This chapter examines how businesses in the value chains of manufactured products must rebalance their operations to better manage the inherent risk in their operations. Indicators of the risk in any given industry's value chain include the industry's susceptibility to various shocks and the inherent weaknesses of companies and the overall chain. Therefore, the authors look at the characteristics in supply chains and operations that might amplify disruption and losses as well as the management of variety of shocks.

DOI: 10.4018/978-1-6684-6663-6.ch009

INTRODUCTION

The last several years have been thought-provoking for globalization. Despite benefits, Global Value Chains' (GVCs') face potential dangers due to their dispersed nature and the lack of anyone controlling entity. To acquire raw materials, transform these materials into predetermined finished products, and deliver these finished products to customers, A supply chain (SC) is a network of enterprises that work together to provide a seamless flow of goods from raw materials to finished goods.

Figure 1. Global Value Chain (GVC) Source: https://www.wcore.com/apec-publishes-a-report-on-smes-integration-into-global-value-chains-in-services-industries-tourism-sector-produced-by-washington-core/

Companies have been able to establish GVCs genuinely because of advancements in communication and transportation during the last quarter of a century. Connections between raw material producers and manufacturers of intermediate and final products are stronger than ever. They were then connected to the manufacturers of the finished goods and, from there, to the distribution networks that brought those goods to customers all over the globe. These intricately coordinated value chains account for over 95% of world commerce. The value of intermediate products shipped across borders increased to more than $10 trillion per year in the two decades before the COVID-19 epidemic. However, introducing complexity into a system might invite unwanted guests. These extensive value chains are effective but vulnerable to the more frequent and severe interruptions to which they are subject. Many of these dangers are caused by the elements, such as earthquakes, tornadoes, and hurricanes, while others are artificial. Disputes over trade, cyberattacks, terrorism, industrial accidents, and infrastructure breakdowns make a list. Similar to this shock, but on a bigger scale in terms of its effects on GVCs, is the COVID-19 pandemic. The COVID-19 pandemic is predicted to cause a 9.2% fall in world merchandise trade in 2020, with a minor recovery in 2021, according to the World Trade Organization's October 2020 update (WTO, 2020). Especially, in the recent research (Awan and Ali 2022), because of the complexity of today's GVCs, they are vulnerable to a variety of risks, vulnerabilities, and disruptions. Pakistan has been a terrorism-stricken state since 9/11, resulting in a loss of political and economic stability, as well as a reduction in infrastructure development and Foreign Direct Investment (FDI).

Organizations are worried about GVCs sustainability risks and vulnerabilities because they affect industry performance and profitability. Vulnerability is defined as the probability or prospect of loss. It is a significant topic that is widely explored as being crucial for the creation of mitigation strategies for mitigating the consequences of hazards at the industrial, national, and worldwide levels (Hashim et al., 2021). Businesses have been compelled to prioritize the development of supply chain and operational resilience in the wake of the epidemic, which follows on the heels of Brexit and US-China trade tensions. To be resilient, one must first know what things might go wrong and how much they can hurt. Resilience is a multidimensional notion. It indicates to a system's or an organization's capacity to prepare for, take in, endure, and adjust to shocks and disruptions. (Pettit et al., 2020). The interacting dynamics between system-level components along the entire chain must be taken into account in analyses of resilience in GVCs. A more convincing post-COVID-19 scenario for resilience entails better risk management in addition to reorganizing global supply chains to retain the operational effectiveness of global manufacturing. Among the alternatives are diversifying suppliers to reduce reliance on a small number of trading partners, investing in regional supply chains, facilitating logistical gains and deeper ties with domestic businesses, and forming strategic international alliances with nations that share similar core values, security concerns, and innovation opportunities.(Gereffi et al,. 2022).

On the other hand, not every global value chain is equally vulnerable to the same threats. As the world has recently discovered, unexpected shocks may have contrasting effects on supply and demand. Demand can plummet for many different types of items, even while providers rush to stock shelves with food, medicine, and other necessities. The leading business in a commodity chain is responsible for shaping, controlling, coordinating, and distributing value throughout the chain (Mahutga, 2012), so it's important to look at the sectors involved and the authority and power relationships that have developed within them (Azmeh and Nadvi, 2014). Thus, it has been shown that commodity chains may be either buyer-or producer-driven, with the former characterized by the leading corporation's primary position as a merchandiser and its responsibility for ensuring the smooth functioning of the whole enterprise (Gereffi and Korzeniewicz, 1994). Alternatively, other researchers have zeroed in on supply chains, studying how this notion helps businesses better understand their connections between vendors and consumers to more efficiently and cheaply distribute goods to end users (Christopher, 2005). Further, the value chain idea describes how related businesses generate value that is a source of competitive advantage (Al-Mudimigh et al., 2004; Stabell and Fjeldstad, 1998). The latter idea accounts for privileged consumers by catering to their wants and satisfying their requirements by examining the processes of value generation and capture (Cox, 1999; Di Domenico et al., 2007; Gereffi and Lee, 2012).

In addition, GVCs is created when various businesses and organizations are linked across international boundaries (De Marchi et al., 2014; Mudambi and Puck, 2016). As such, the "entire spectrum of activities that firms and individuals execute to transport a product from its conception to end consumption and beyond" is the global value chain, which happens on a global scale and may be executed by one or more companies (Gereffi and Fernandez-Stark, 2011, p. 4). Some researchers have pointed to a new system called the "global factory" (Buckley, 2011; Buckley and Ghauri, 2004) to describe this intricate arrangement of processes. The global value chain allows multinational businesses to reduce location and transaction expenses by linking all activities via international flows of intermediate commodities that the MNC controls but does not necessarily own (Buckley and Strange, 2015).

Rapid Globalization to Slowbalization

The research on globalization from the 1990s through the 2020s often divides it into two distinct eras. Thomas Friedman (2005) and Richard Baldwin (2016), among others, have discussed the first phase, a period of rapid integration from the 1990s until around 2008. Subramanian and Kessler (2013) have used the term "hyper-globalization" to describe this phenomenon. During this time, the price of ICT dropped dramatically, and global value chains (GVCs)—a system of sharing manufacturing across borders—grew rapidly.

The second stage, slowbalization, was ushered in by the global financial crisis's effect on trade, which caused a precipitous drop in global trade volumes (World Bank, 2020). The events that spurred hyper-globalization, such as the fall of the Soviet Union and the People's Republic of China's admission into the global trade system, inevitably led to a slowdown, as pointed out by Antràs (2020a). And yet, it is also true that, in recent years, a vociferous resistance to globalization has grown (Krugman 2019; Autor, Dorn, and Hanson 2013), with protectionist measures emerging on the political agendas of nations all over the globe (de Bolle and Zettelmeyer 2019). Given this, globalization might experience a reversal rather than a mere stall.

In conclusion, the slowbalization period is characterized by declining value chain lengths and flattening global value chain (GVC) participation rates. The PRC and the United States, two of the hyper-globalization era's primary drivers of GVCs, have suffered significant slowdowns in expanding their GVC commerce. However, numerous new, lesser participants from the developing world are emerging. The Philippines in business services, Vietnam in electricals, and Bangladesh in textiles and apparel are just a few examples. This suggests globalization isn't happening everywhere.

Figure 2. Global background (Source: https://pixabay.com/zh/illustrations/map-of-the-world-background-paper-2401458/)

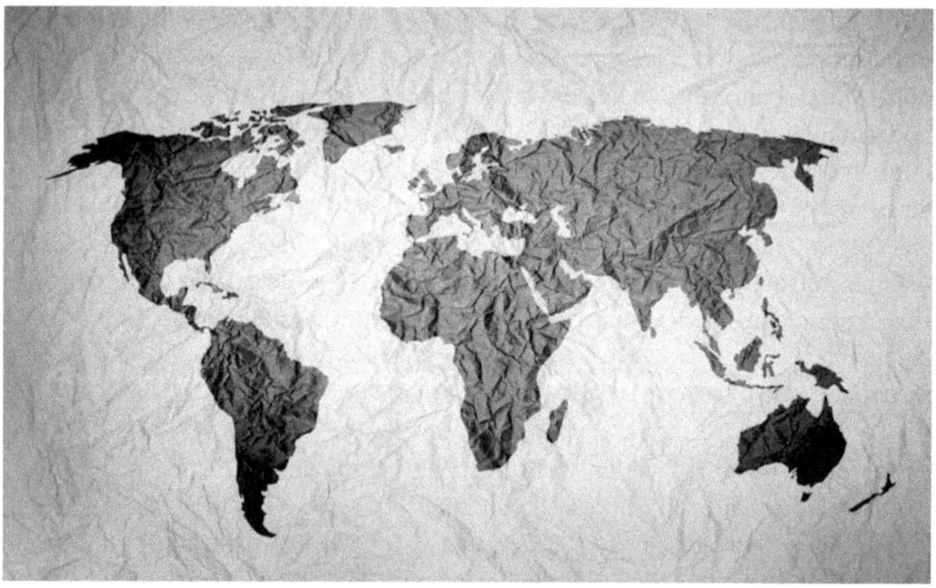

Multinational Firms Contribution

The enterprises, rather than national economies or specific industries, are responsible for fragmented production. There are three main reasons why this is an important consideration: This first brings to light the very concentrated character of corporate involvement in GVCs. Only 15% of businesses worldwide engage in international commerce regularly, yet they account for 80% of all imports and exports (a clear sign of a GVC business) (World Bank 2020). Second, Antràs (2020a) argues that GVCs are inherently relational. Production networks are formed by companies that repeatedly interact, making them "sticky" instead of a worldwide market of impersonal buyers and sellers. Thirdly, a significant portion of revenues for multinational corporations comes through local affiliates set up using FDI However, GVCs are sometimes underestimated because their operations are categorized as "domestic" in host countries.

The United States may be seen as the global demand center toward which all economies' value-added development is directed, either directly or indirectly, via their service and/or manufacturing networks, both domestic and international. Also, the People's Republic of China was the only country whose economy benefited from the United States' value addition. In 2016, there was a subtle shift in the transnational network of services businesses, with more value-added being transferred to the United States from third economies like Germany and the People's Republic of China. When compared to the results obtained from evaluating individual economic sectors, the insights gained from identifying networks' domestic and foreign ownership are striking. For instance, the supply chains of local manufacturers are more regionalized than those of multinational corporations operating in the same field. When looking at the supply side of the services industry, however, domestic service providers actually have stronger international ties than multinational conglomerates in the services industry. From the consumer's point of view, local and MNC networks vary somewhat; for instance, German MNCs play a larger role in the services industry than their domestic counterparts.

This New Regional Focus

In 2020, according to the World Trade Organization figures, there were approximately 300 RTAs in effect. The Regional Comprehensive Economic Partnership, which includes 15 economies in Asia and the Pacific, is the biggest RTA but has not yet been approved (Heijmans and Nguyen, 2020). There has been a slowdown in the number of new RTAs in recent years, but the number is still larger than before 1990 when the trend began to climb sharply.

In addition, post-Brexit uncertainty is anticipated to provide a boost to more RTAs in 2021. The United Kingdom is looking for trade agreements. The conflict between global and local concerns has always been present. Most-favored-nation treatment is a key component of globalism since it guarantees that tariff reductions and other trade concessions are applied uniformly across all participating countries. The goal of regionalism is to encourage commerce within a certain geographical area (Frankel

1997). The members of the Regional Comprehensive Economic Partnership, the European Union, and the North American Free Trade Agreement are all quite near to one another geographically. In recent years, however, participation in organizations like the Comprehensive and Progressive.

The ramifications of the home sector link to international commerce in a highly integrated global economy are substantial. According to Koopman, Wang, and Wei (2008), developing a measure of the domestic content of exports is crucial for determining the potential impact of currency appreciation on an economy and estimating the impact of trade on wages.

Banga (2014) believes that the capacity of domestic sectors to acquire value-added from these activities is crucial to maximizing profits from participation in GVCs. This may be done by redefining domestic links to domestic value-added. Policymakers must quantify the benefits of GVC operations, which can only be done by tracking the extent to which they are linked to local firms. Recent research has shown that domestic connections further complicate GVCs. Through the manufacture of intermediate items for subsequent export or the use of inputs from vertically integrated sectors, domestic operations are indirectly linked to GVC activities (Mercer-Blackman, Foronda, and Mariasingham 2017; Tang, Wang, and Wang 2020). However, existing measurements of GVC involvement do not represent the contribution of domestic sectors to global trade activities due to the small number of enterprises that participate in a trade directly (Bernard et al., 2007). That means the present measures understate the role of home industries in global value chains. The importance of home ties in the decline of international commerce is also highlighted. Slowbalization sheds information on the efforts of economies to bring back on-shore functions that have previously been outsourced (The Economist 2019, Titievskaia et al. 2020). Protectionism and trade wars were on the increase at this time. Risk management strategies like reshoring have gained prominence after the COVID-19 outbreak. The advantages of cost-based manufacturing process fragmentation may be nullified in a fully connected global economy due to supply chain vulnerabilities (Giuseppina and Michele, 2018). As a result, there are now more financial incentives to bring formerly exported jobs back to the United States. The existence of such inducements justifies the creation of a metric for tracking ties inside the country.

CHALLENGES TO GVC-GLOBAL

Risk in the value chain results from both external and internal factors. Value chain risk is the result of an external factor exposing internal flaws. The risk of any given industry is based on the different types of shocks it can be hit by and the weaknesses of any given firm or ecosystem.

There are Four Primary Exposure-Side Shock Generators

- Events of ***force majeure*** are rare yet catastrophic occurrences that cause a shutdown of normal operations. Catastrophes such as storms, floods, earthquakes, wildfires, and volcanic eruptions fall within this category. Many of these occurrences have local impacts but have global repercussions due to the bottlenecking of production and transport networks. Some, like the COVID epidemic, affect the whole planet.
- ***Financial crises***, trade disputes, unexpected regulatory adjustments, recessions, and even war and terrorism are all examples of macropolitical shocks.
- ***Cyberattacks***, theft, and fake products are just some of the ways bad actors may cause trouble.
- The impacts of ***idiosyncratic shocks*** are often localized to a single or a small number of firms, but they may have far-reaching consequences. Things like IT breakdowns, supplier bankruptcies, and labor problems in the workplace are all examples. A second typical event is a sudden increase or decrease in the cost of a vital input.

Both the industry's value chain and individual companies might contribute to a state of ***vulnerability.*** It may show up in places like supply chain management and long-term planning when things like single-source sourcing were effective before becoming bottlenecks during an emergency. If businesses rely on shoddy infrastructure, it might impact shipping and logistics. There's a chance it's hiding on the books somewhere, in the form of excessive leverage or inadequate cash reserves, that would bring the firm perilously near to insolvency in the event of even the briefest setback. Missing a brief sales window may be disastrous for a business, especially if the product is complicated and relies on specific inputs. And if a firm doesn't have an efficient supply chain management team, it may not be able to anticipate potential problems or prepare for them in a timely manner.

Impact and Duration of Shocks

Every shock to GVCs is not the same; while some are temporary, others may cripple a whole sector for weeks or months. However, the magnitude and duration of a shock's effect on production and GVCs depend on factors outside the shock's original cause. An important aspect is the length of time that businesses have to prepare for an event. However, natural disasters like earthquakes and cyberattacks don't have any warning; economic imbalances, differing standards, and geopolitical tensions may accumulate over months and even years, which is reflected in trade conflicts. The severity of an economic shock also depends on whether it just affects supply or impacts demand. The greatest damage is done by events that hit supply and demand simultaneously, such as a pandemic or a major conflict.

The worst shocks affect supply, demand, and capital access. They persist through time and space: major pandemics and military battles such as the Covid-19 pandemic or the Ukraine war are two great examples. The cost of such catastrophic incidents may easily reach billions of dollars. It's true that the damage caused by natural catastrophes is usually less severe. Their intensity and frequency are increasing, and they have historically caused hundreds of billions of dollars worth of damage between property destruction and temporary disruptions to supply systems. Milder shocks, with expenditures in the tens of billions of dollars, are more diffuse and less devastating. These factors include changes in regulations and small-scale wars. Finally, businesses often face a variety of unique shocks, including disruptions in information technology, strikes, and accidents in the workplace. They usually incur expenditures that are unique to a single company and are usually not high enough to warrant macroeconomic attention. Input price shocks, however, are a typical cause of disruption for many value chains, and not all sectors can equally pass these increased costs on to downstream clients. This is because of things like changes in commodity prices, shortages caused by natural disasters, and trade conflicts.

Don't be surprised if anything unexpected happens.

Many shocks range in intensity and predictability. Historical instances from the last several decades are presented with hypothetical scenarios.For instance, if a meteor smashed into a big city, the resulting explosion would be comparable to nuclear bombs. The frequency of such events is believed to be 2-3 times per century (Paul Rincon, 2019). In the Russian city of Chelyabinsk in 2013, a meteor the size of a six-story skyscraper exploded, hurting thousands yet causing far less damage than it might have if its speed and course had been slightly different.[1] Potentially catastrophic hypothetical events include the deployment of nuclear or biological weapons in an act of terrorism; the emergence of a virus more fatal and contagious than COVID; or the eruption of a supervolcano that covers a large region in ash. Even if the possibilities are beyond the range for which businesses can prepare fairly or economically, they have all been subjected to rigorous scientific and governmental evaluation. As the global economy undergoes fundamental changes, shocks become more frequent and severe.

Natural disasters are nothing new. However, the scope of what might occur has broadened, and these events can now affect global value chains in various ways. Shocks may now flow from one region of the globe to another quicker than ever before because of globalized industrial value chains and increased global interconnections. Any kind of global movement has the potential to spread contagion. The impacts of a bottleneck ripple outward when the flow of products or services is impeded. Given the growing reliance on global and digital financial services across all industries, financial contagion has the potential to spread rapidly and widely. Within a few weeks, the coronavirus had spread to practically every country on Earth, thanks to international visitors. There is a lot of digitization in all fields, which leaves businesses open to attacks, viruses, and network failures. According to climate scientists, extreme weather like heat waves and wildfires may worsen, happen more often, or do both as global temperatures increase. Besides the acute risks brought on by extreme weather events, climate change is also contributing to developing a new class of chronic hazards.

Viral transmission from animals to humans is facilitated by habitat loss. The mechanisms for exponential spread are made possible by modern communications and the unparalleled density of today's urban centers. Many different types of influenza have spread widely over the globe since the year 2000, including SARS, swine flu, MERS, Ebola, Zika, and avian flu. The scale of the current COVID epidemic, which is neither the first nor is it likely to be the last new infectious illness to spread across our globally linked society, has made all of these previous disasters seem quite small by comparison.

Finally, the ***potential for conflict*** rises in an unstable and ever-changing geopolitical context. This is true whether we're talking about military conflicts, terrorism, economic disputes, IP theft, or different standards for technology, privacy, or other concerns (Richard Haas, 2020). [2] Some Western countries, longtime advocates of free trade, have begun to embrace protectionism. After decades of progress toward a unified Europe, borders have again been erected, with consequences that we do not yet fully understand. Trade liberalization has been going on for decades, but there is a danger that tariffs and nontariff obstacles may continue to climb. Businesses must be flexible regarding regulatory policies, tax legislation, and tariffs.

Looking at value chain archetypes, those that rely heavily on human labor are the most vulnerable to ***natural disasters***; many of these value chains are situated in places that are particularly vulnerable to floods, which may cause a wide variety of problems, including sickness, heat fatigue (from having to labor), and economic loss.

Last but not least, ***communications equipment*** has the greatest vulnerability to all the shocks we evaluated at the value chain level. There is a high probability that trade disputes will affect this value chain because of its global nature and concentration in Asia and the Pacific, which are highly susceptible to natural disasters such as earthquakes, tsunamis, and typhoons. The importance of IP and digital assets also makes them more susceptible to hacking.

The apparel industry is the next most vulnerable industry value chain. Its labor-intensive nature and subsequent decline in customer demand make it vulnerable to shutdowns during a pandemic. And many of the nations that export clothing are prone to heat waves and floods. The petroleum products value chain is the third most vulnerable among the six shocks we examined. The dramatic decline in demand caused by a pandemic (which temporarily pushed oil futures negative during the current epidemic) makes this value chain very vulnerable, even though a pandemic does not immediately affect production in this value chain (Stephanie Kelly,2019). The value chain's heavy dependence on physical and digital capital makes it vulnerable to cyberattacks. Also, because of where it is made, its value chain is one of the top ten most likely to be affected by natural disasters, heat stress, and floods.

Hazards to GVC-Firm level

Internal Weaknesses in Businesses and Supply Networks

Weak spots occur not just inside individual organizations but also throughout wider value chains, and shocks have a way of zeroing in and exploiting them. Some are just part and parcel of doing business in a certain field. Complex supply chains are inevitable in producing high-tech goods like smartphones, computers, vehicles, and aircraft. Due to the perishable nature of many agricultural and food goods, even small delays in manufacturing and shipping may quickly lead to spoilage. Exporters may rapidly get into difficulties when other stressors are introduced, such as the potential for additional customs duties due to Brexit.

Still, deliberate actions may cause vulnerabilities. The use of tailored inputs with few replacements, for instance, or the use of lean manufacturing techniques, are all ways to increase profitability. Even while these alternatives may seem like an improvement in the short term, they may have undesirable results when a disruption occurs. These are still options for how to run the business, but they become risky when not paired with an equal focus on resilience. One problem that most major businesses have is a lack of insight into their supply chain's lower levels. Insofar as it affords businesses redundancy and maneuverability, complexity is not in and of itself a drawback. However, the scales may shift, and if a network is too complicated, it will be difficult to understand. Even a single huge multinational corporation may work with tens of thousands of suppliers across many levels of the supply chain. Companies may not be aware of their reliance on secondary suppliers located in volatile parts of the globe unless they are given complete information about those relationships. The balance sheet is another potential weak spot. Some trends, such as large fixed expenses, high levels of debt, and limited cash on hand, are similar across sectors and make it difficult to maneuver and retain solvency in a crisis. Weak points in an organization's structure may also bite it during times of crisis.

Bottlenecks of Concentrated Production

There may be bottlenecks in the production of certain goods because of their increased concentration in the value chain. When most of a network's suppliers are based in one area, a crisis caused by a natural catastrophe or regional war might disrupt operations worldwide.

Companies have been able to take advantage of economies of scale and improve their level of competence because of the clustering that has occurred at the national level in some sectors due to globalization over the last two decades. Because of this, industries like computing and cell phone manufacturing are more concentrated in a few locations. However, when unexpected events occur, this might cause delays. But the reverse has occurred in medical devices and aircraft sectors, as more nations have joined the value chain. However, some items may be manufactured in various locations but suffer catastrophic bottlenecks if production is interrupted for any reason. While numerous nations may be exporting the same commodity, most commercial activity occurs within regional groups rather than worldwide. When an importer's main exporter has a disruption, it might be difficult to immediately find a replacement. Finally, industrial diversity is not always good, especially in regions more vulnerable to shocks.

Concentration risk affects both downstream consumers (who might run out of supplies) and upstream suppliers (who could cease receiving orders). A sudden drop in demand from overseas consumers might have catastrophic results when a nation's economy is highly dependent on a single export sector. For example, most of Bangladesh's exports come from the textile and garment sectors. During the COVID epidemic, businesses canceled billions of dollars worth of orders when consumer spending dropped dramatically in the United States and Europe. This strained not only Bangladeshi suppliers but also caused severe suffering for textile workers whose earnings abruptly dried up (Elizabeth Paton,2020). Clothing manufacturers in China stopped operating at the beginning of 2020. A number of additional clothing factories, including those in Bangladesh, India, Mexico, and Pakistan, suspended production as the virus spread to other nations (Castañeda-Navarrete, Hauge, and López-Gómez, 2020).

--Case study--

Sometimes, even in more regionally dispersed value chains, there are still significant manufacturing concentrations for essential items. While the aerospace industry is regionalized, the production of engines, turboprops, and big aircraft tends to be concentrated in a single nation. China and India provide a lot of the low-value or basic components for medications.

According to UN Comtrade statistics, China and India together export 42% of the world's antibiotic-active pharmaceutical component products (by value, not volume), with China dominating the export value of some varieties, such as streptomycin (75% of the value) and penicillin (88% of the value) (52%). There is also a geographical concentration of semiconductor and consumer electronics exports. As an example, South Korea exports 50% of the world's value in semiconductor memory devices, while Taiwan exports 43% of the global value in electronic integrated circuits. Mainland Nearly three-quarters of the world's PCs and two-thirds of its telephones are shipped out of China. While food and drink are often produced in a decentralized fashion throughout the country, there may be instances of extreme concentration. Most of the crustaceans that export 85% of the value of the world's frozen lobsters live on Canada's Atlantic coast.

Figure 3. (Source: UN Comtrade)

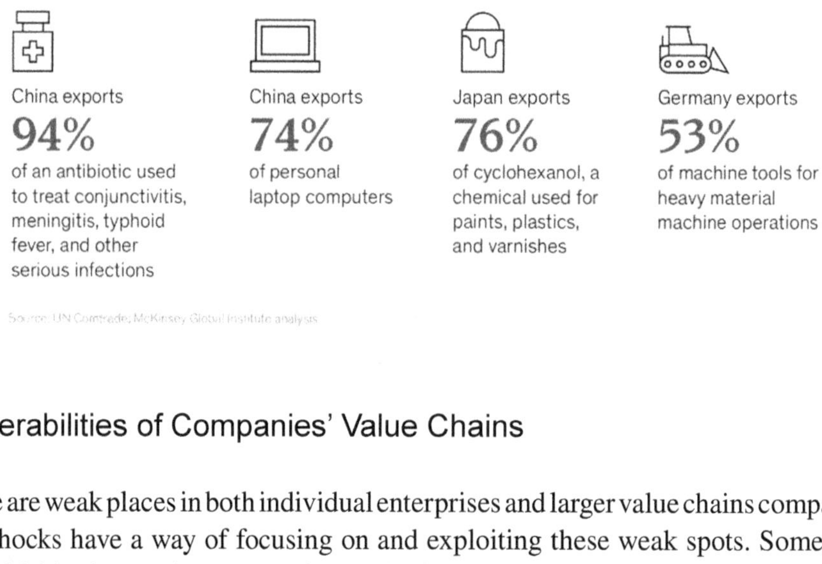

Vulnerabilities of Companies' Value Chains

There are weak places in both individual enterprises and larger value chains company, and shocks have a way of focusing on and exploiting these weak spots. Some are unavoidable due to the nature of a particular sector and are just part of the deal. Automobiles, computers, vehicles, and other high-complexity items have numerous moving parts and intricate supply systems. Delays in production and distribution can easily cause spoilage because a lot of food and agricultural products are prone to deterioration. Exporters might experience immediate difficulties if further pressure is applied, such as Brexit, which could need increased tariff restrictions.

Despite this, a portion of the sensitivity stems from deliberate actions. Adopting waste-free manufacturing techniques, minimizing stock on hand, buying only from one source, and relying heavily on unique, one-of-a-kind inputs are all ways to boost productivity and earnings. While these alternatives may seem like a good idea in the midst of turmoil, they might have undesirable side effects in the long run. These are future-oriented choices for operations that are achievable and practicable. Fragility develops when stress is given without enough resistance. A common problem for corporations of all sizes is a lack of insight into their supplier chains.

As long as it offers the company redundancy and adaptability, complexity is not always a drawback. In some cases, however, the balance can be thrown off, and overly complex networks can become opaque. A large multinational corporation may have tens of suppliers at various levels. Without complete transparency, businesses risk failing to recognize how much they rely on lower-level suppliers in vulnerable parts of the world. Balance sheets may also contain hidden vulnerabilities. High fixed costs, high debt, and insufficient funds on hand can make maintaining the ability to respond and pay in a crisis difficult. Some of these patterns are found in a variety of industries. Organizational flaws have the potential to impede businesses during times of crisis.

When weaknesses in operations and supply networks are combined with the possibility of external shocks, a value chain is at risk. Since fractures tend to appear in the same locations, businesses must thoroughly investigate these spots. We pinpoint at least five potential weak points, including ***demand planning and inventory choices, supplier network structure, transportation and logistics; financial instability; and product complexity.***

Planning for Supply and Demand and Keeping Track of Stock

Limitations in the capacity to prepare for and predict demand may be a serious weakness. When it comes to demand planning, high degrees of uncertainty, seasonality, and cyclicality may make things more difficult across different value chains. These features are not set in stone. When it came to the fashion industry, for instance, different seasons and lengthy lead periods formerly ruled. A significant chunk of the industry has shifted into fast fashion, which requires rapid production cycles to keep up with fleeting consumer trends, many of which are driven by social media influencers. Short product cycles and expenditure spikes over shorter holiday periods make demand forecasting more challenging in the electronics business.

Inventory levels are another weak spot in a supplier network. Inventories are held in a wide range of ways depending on the value chain. Industries like medical devices with low inventory-to-sales ratios are more susceptible to interruptions than those with larger stockpiles, such as fabricated metal items, computers, and electronics. Just-in-time production has been held up as the gold standard of efficiency for quite some time now. One of the primary advantages of this workflow technique is that it allows businesses to avoid the high expenses of maintaining big inventories based on the assumptions of highly responsive suppliers and fast rotations through each phase in a manufacturing system. When a new batch of components arrives, they are immediately put to use and sent to the next phase of the process. However, there is little room for mistakes at any value chain stage if lean manufacturing is perfected. Supply failures may swiftly escalate into bottlenecks that reverberate throughout the network. In a twist of fate, the tendency toward regionalization may hasten the pace at which disruptions are perceived. When inputs are just a few hours away by truck rather than a few days away by cargo ship, businesses may feel more comfortable keeping smaller stockpiles.

Organization of Supplier Networks

Identifying all the participants in a company's supply chain is not a simple operation, but it is necessary to conduct a thorough risk assessment. Most companies can see the dangers associated with their tier-one suppliers, but they have no idea what can happen with their secondary suppliers.

Inevitably, industries that produce more sophisticated goods, like autos, airplanes, computers, and electronics, have the highest average number of tier-one suppliers, as shown by our research of public disclosures of key customer-supplier connections. Some of the most complex organizations are not even hinted at by the number of tier-one suppliers made public by Airbus, GM, and Volkswagen. Regulatory filings from GM or its suppliers include more than 850 tier-one suppliers. GM, however, claims that as many as 18,000 suppliers make up its ecosystem (GM report, 2018). As more and more businesses want to reduce the number of their tier-one suppliers, their networks have an opportunity to grow exponentially beyond that level. According to our analysis of publicly available data, the number of suppliers a company works with might be seven to seventeen times higher than in tier one.

A company's supply chain may be both a weak point and a strength, depending on how it is set up, and there is no universal solution. For procurement and operations, having a large number of tier-one suppliers may be problematic unless the downstream firm intentionally forms a more coordinated and coherent core group into which all others feed. However, losing one of them might cause major disruptions across your supply chain if you have a very small number of suppliers. Each business must strike a balance between the risks it is willing to take and the resources it has at its disposal.

The number of intermediaries involved in transforming raw materials into a final product is a measure of the supply chain's "depth." Deeper supply chains with more levels may be more opaque and difficult to track, which is often the outcome of a cascade of outsourcing choices. At least a third of all supply chain interruptions arise at the intermediate and lower levels of the system, according to a recent assessment(Rachael Elliott, Catherine Thomas, and Kamal Muhammad, 2019).

The extent to which things are connected is also crucial to analyze. Suppliers who play a pivotal role in production ecosystems should be given special attention regardless of how much money those firms spend with them farther down the supply chain. Many businesses in the technology sector fit this description since they perform tasks similar to those of a public utility.

Businesses must draw a comprehensive picture of their networks, considering not just their direct rivals but also those in related fields. Take two sectors that both rely on the same resource. Suppliers may prefer their larger clients in the event of an unanticipated shortage, which leaves the smaller buyer at a disadvantage. Similarly, a sector may rely on the waste products of another. The current epidemic caused a decrease in ethanol output as fuel demand dropped. Because of this, the cost of carbon dioxide (CO_2) utilized by the beverage sector increased, putting a strain on beer producers despite rising alcohol sales (Stephanie Kelly and Lisa Baertlein, 2020). A supply chain's robustness may also be diminished by dependent suppliers or those that rely on a small number of customers for most of their business. For instance, it is common for significant suppliers to be directly linked to one of the industry's top automakers in the automobile industry. But for the large network of suppliers that depend on a single downstream company so much, the effects could be disastrous.

Insight

Analyzing a company's network might help reveal potential weak spots.

A common method used by businesses to evaluate the safety of their supply chains is to look just at the costs involved, with an emphasis on the most pricey commodities or suppliers to whom they allocate the majority of their budget. But focusing just on costs may cause you to overlook critical security flaws in the system. We depict the first- and second-tier supplier ecosystems associated with four large Fortune 500 corporations to demonstrate how network analysis may identify some hidden relationships in supply chains. Each is like its own little world, with thousands of vendors. This activity visually illustrates these networks' layered complexity and global reach while debunking the myth that supply chains are flexible and simple to rearrange. It also demonstrates that firms within the same sector might make radically diverse choices regarding the risk profile of their supplier networks.

Using publicly accessible information on their tier-one and tier-two suppliers, we examine the supply chains of four major companies: two consumer electronics manufacturers (Lenovo and Dell) and two food and beverage corporations (Nestlé and Pepsi). Complex ecosystems, including all levels down to primary components, would be much more expansive, convoluted, and difficult to track. Since Dell also competes in the cloud computing and virtualization software businesses and Lenovo manufactures mobile phones, it is difficult to compare their supply chain systems directly. [1].

There are 2,700 and 7,000 tier-one and tier-two suppliers for the four firms. It is not surprising that most of Lenovo and Dell's supply chain partners are located in Southeast Asia, given the region's prominent role in the larger industrial value chain. While Nestlé and Pepsi employees are more geographically distributed, this reflects the regionalized and less-tradable structure of the food and beverage supply chain. In the European Union, Nestlé's proportion of suppliers is the greatest, whereas Pepsi's is the largest in the United States. Raw and intermediate agricultural inputs, such as palm oil, are increasingly sourced from emerging economies (especially Indonesia and nations in central Africa). There is no change in the geographic distribution of suppliers between tiers one and two for consumer electronics manufacturers. At the same time, there is an increase in the number of Chinese and South Korean suppliers for food and beverage manufacturers. As a whole, tier two has a somewhat larger geographical concentration.

Compared to Dell and Pepsi, Lenovo and Nestlé have more organized and integrated supplier networks. The networks of the latter two businesses are more concentrated. Among the firms in the dataset, Pepsi uses the fewest (89), each of which depends on its own reasonably integrated network of linked suppliers. Clusters in the network may represent individual stages in the value chain, such as sourcing of inputs, production, distribution, and so on. Closing a single, crucial supplier at a lower tier in an interconnected supply chain may lead to widespread disruptions. It might have severe consequences if a tier-one provider goes down in a network with many relatively isolated clusters. The ability of downstream businesses to detect issues early and take corrective action before they spiral out of control is proportional to the number of links in the supply chain. It would indicate that Lenovo and Nestlé have supplier networks with more than twice as many levels as Dell and Pepsi.

Distributed procurement increases the risk of interruption. Some crucial entities are revealed by analyzing each supplier's centrality (degree of connectivity) across all four networks. If they run into problems, it's more likely that they will ripple through the system, affecting businesses with multiple suppliers or at multiple levels. According to our research, twenty of Dell's most important suppliers are also among Lenovo's top twenty, and vice versa for the two companies. Foxconn, IBM, and Microsoft are major hardware and software providers to both firms and have extensive ties across both communities. Both Dell and Lenovo's current operations and their capacity to find alternate supplies would be negatively impacted if either were to experience a disruption.

Figure 4. supply chain structures for Dell, Lenovo, and Pepsi. co, and Nestlé

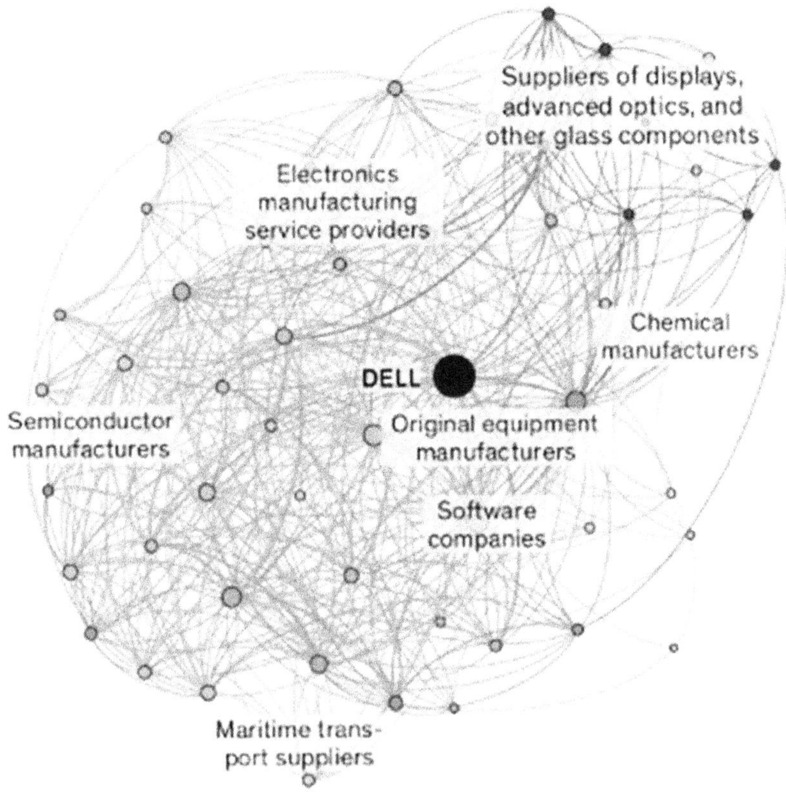

Systems for Transportation and Logistics

The supply chain can no longer afford to make any mistakes in terms of timing or accuracy as the chain's length grows and the supply network's fatness shrinks. Logistics is the backbone of complex supply chains, moving materials from one stage to the next and ultimately getting finished goods to consumers. The value of these services is reflected in the fact that in 2019, 7.6 percent of GDP was spent on logistics by US businesses. With a global market value of approximately $260 billion, the third-party contract logistics industry is a major player in the global economy.

Better transportation links reduce the time and effort needed to transport products between factories and across international boundaries. The UN Council for Trade and Development's Liner Shipping Connectivity Index reveals that, on average, nations' shipping capacity and frequency have increased by 30 percent since 2010. Contrarily, container shipping faces both economic risks (such as cargo theft, supplier insolvency, and even ship fires) and natural disasters (such as hurricanes) that may disrupt logistical operations by physically blocking infrastructure and routes. According to 15.8% of respondents in a 2019 poll of worldwide executives, transportation issues are among the top five sources of interruptions in their supply chain. (Rachael Elliott, Catherine Thomas, and Kamal Muhammad,2019).

The World Bank ranks countries' proficiency in international logistics across six metrics: customs clearance times, infrastructure quality, the simplicity with which competitively priced shipments can be arranged, the quality of logistics service providers, shipment traceability, and delivery timelines. Germany was the top performer in 2018. Despite being the world's top exporter, China rated just 26th, behind the United States (which placed 14th) (due in part to its lower customs scores).

Figure 5. Systems of logistics (Source: https://pixabay.com/zh/photos/logistics-truck-cargo-ship-group-3125131/)

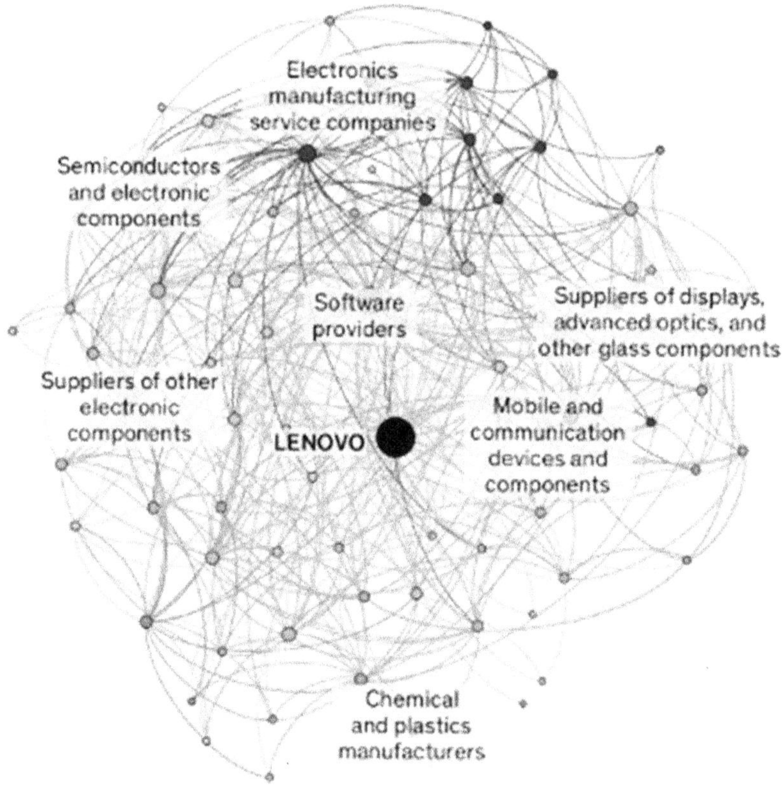

The Weakness of the Financial System

The financial health of an individual business may either increase its susceptibility to shocks or its capacity to adapt to them. In the face of shocks and shutdowns, companies with high debt burdens or little financial reserves may have few options. Throughout the value chain, there are consistent monetary patterns. Industries like mining that rely heavily on financial intermediaries are more vulnerable during market downturns. In contrast, those producing petroleum products rely less on the financial system. Both debt and liquidity levels vary significantly from sector to sector.

Having too many small-market-cap or financially unstable suppliers, particularly if they are the only source of supply, might leave a downstream firm vulnerable to interruptions, no matter how solid its financial situation is. When demand dropped during the recent pandemic, several small automobile suppliers came dangerously close to going out of business(Nick Carey and Ben Klayman, 2020) When it comes to sterilizing medical equipment, many medical device manufacturers depend on smaller suppliers; if they go out of business, that crucial last step before shipping the product to market cannot be accomplished. In times of crisis, the resilience of downstream businesses depends on the reliability of their supply chains.

Portfolio and Product Complexity

Certain aspects of a product may be inherently unsafe. For instance, the lifespan of certain goods is rather brief. As a result of restricted choices for keeping and reselling items, their manufacturers might be disproportionately impacted by interruptions that impede or delay their delivery to market. Businesses may be unable to locate suitable replacements or alternatives due to using proprietary inputs or non-modular production techniques.

The proportionate amount of resources (or skilled labor) needed to produce a product is one indicator of its complexity. This index works on the premise that products produced in fewer countries require more expertise to produce and are therefore more complex (Felipe et al, 2012). Comparing these index scores across different global value chains shows that aircraft, auto-motives, machinery & equipment, and medical devices are the most detailed product categories. Value chains in industries where plenty of people and materials are used have lower levels of complexity. supply chain complexity positively moderated on supply chain resilience enablers and supply chain resilience.

Growing product lines have opened up more avenues for profit and added layers of complexity in the last several decades. Various new channels have emerged in the retail environment, each with specific demands for product packaging and presentation. In an effort to secure shelf space and tap into rapidly increasing niche markets, consumer goods businesses have rapidly increased the number of items they provide and the length of current product lines (such as wellness products and organic foods). In spite of its potential to spur expansion, this approach places pressure on supply chain management and demand forecasting.

According to research conducted by McKinsey (2020), the complexity of product portfolios may cost the food and beverage industry up to $50 billion in gross profit annually in the United States. In North America, one multinational food producer raised its stock-keeping unit (SKU) count by 66% over three years thanks to introducing new line extensions and items tailored as retail house brands (Adams et al., 2016). The risk of spoilage and waste increases along with the number of products in a company's portfolio as more and more products are added. Even in prosperous times, operational drag from a complicated product portfolio may reduce value. However, this weakness becomes very apparent at times of stress. The recent research by Hussain et al., (2022) find supply chain complexity moderated supply chain resilience enablers and supply chain resilience significantly. Some food and drink companies have responded by working on backup recipes in case key ingredients run out and by reducing the number of products they sell in stores to save money on production and shipping costs.

Disruption of Supply is Costly

The destruction caused by the kind of events—natural catastrophes, industrial accidents, criminal acts—affects more than simply a company's bottom line. As a first and main concern, many of these catastrophes may inflict physical harm to communities and even take lives.

Naturally, businesses will be interested in how this will affect their bottom lines, but production halts have the potential to compound the damage done to society by the first shock. In the event of an emergency, shortages may occur if items are delayed in reaching the market. Loss of employment and tax income for the government increases as closure lengthens.

As was mentioned before in this study, disruptions are often sudden yet occur frequently nevertheless. Every 3.7 years, a significant business will encounter a disruption lasting at least a month. Here, we put a dollar amount on such losses so that corporate heads will know what to prepare for and may make more informed decisions about where to put their money in terms of resilience.

A protracted interruption might wipe off fifty percent or more of annual revenues, depending on the sector. In light of these findings and the likelihood of real occurrences, we conclude that, on average, businesses may anticipate interruptions to wipe out over 45 percent of annual revenues over a decade. These aren't hypothetical dangers of the far future; they've established tendencies right now. There is also the possibility of irreversible market share loss to rivals better equipped to weather the storm, bounce back quickly, or capitalize on the situation to provide novel solutions.

The bright side is that businesses may lessen their losses by adopting precautions. We estimate the impact of a shock on two fictitious businesses, one of which is willing to bear the continuing expenses associated with disaster preparedness while the other is not. The vast disparity in financial outcomes suggests that prevention may be worth the investment over the long term, despite its higher upfront cost.

Insight

Supply Chain Challenges

The example constructed hypothetical corporations' representative income statements and balance sheets by taking real data from the 25 biggest public firms in 13 different sectors. This way, it assesses how well the finances hold up under pressure. Two potential scenario outcomes:

The first scenario involves an interruption in the supply chain that forces a 100-day production halt. Companies would still be able to get their wares to consumers if distribution and logistics networks were unaffected. As soon as their buffer supply of goods is gone, they will no longer be able to generate income.

The second scenario: involves the same environmental factors as the first, but they also disrupt the supply chain. As a result, businesses will be unable to make a profit while having usable stock on hand.

Dmitry Ivanov (2020) predicated the decision to simulate an interruption lasting 100 days on a thorough analysis of past occurrences. More than two thousand locations were impacted by the top five supply chain disruptions in 2018, with manufacturers needing between 22 and 29 weeks to get back up and running. Typhoon Mangkhut, which hit southeastern China in 2018, was one such incident; it caused widespread power outages and floods in the region's industrial heartland. A large aluminum mill in Brazil had to half its capacity and decrease workers across several months that year due to excessive rains and environmental worries about water contamination, leading to shortages and price hikes. 64 Accidents in the manufacturing sector may sometimes result in significant delays. There was a worldwide scarcity of a specialized resin used in vehicle manufacture after an explosion at an Evonik factory in Germany halted output for six months in 2012 (David Simchi-Levi, Willian Schmidt, and Yehua Wei, 2014).

Through the use of a simulated 100-day shock, we can demonstrate how the two scenarios diverge due to differences in inventory holding patterns and fixed-cost structures across sectors. For shocks of shorter duration, when safety stockpiles may be quickly depleted, the profit advantage will be nullified in industries whose inventory holdings satisfy demand throughout the shock. A larger profit impact is shown for longer shocks when fixed expenses are lower. According to the simulations, most businesses would lose between 30 and 50 percent of their EBITDA for a whole year if a supply chain interruption hit production but not distribution. Some businesses may lose much more money if a disaster messes with their supply chains.

After analyzing the effects of a single catastrophic shock in the first stress test, we project future losses by factoring in the likelihood of other events over ten years. This perspective integrates data on how often and for how long value chains are disrupted with data on the resulting financial effect on businesses across all sectors.

Figure 6. (Source: S&P Capital IQ; McKinsey Global Institute analysis)

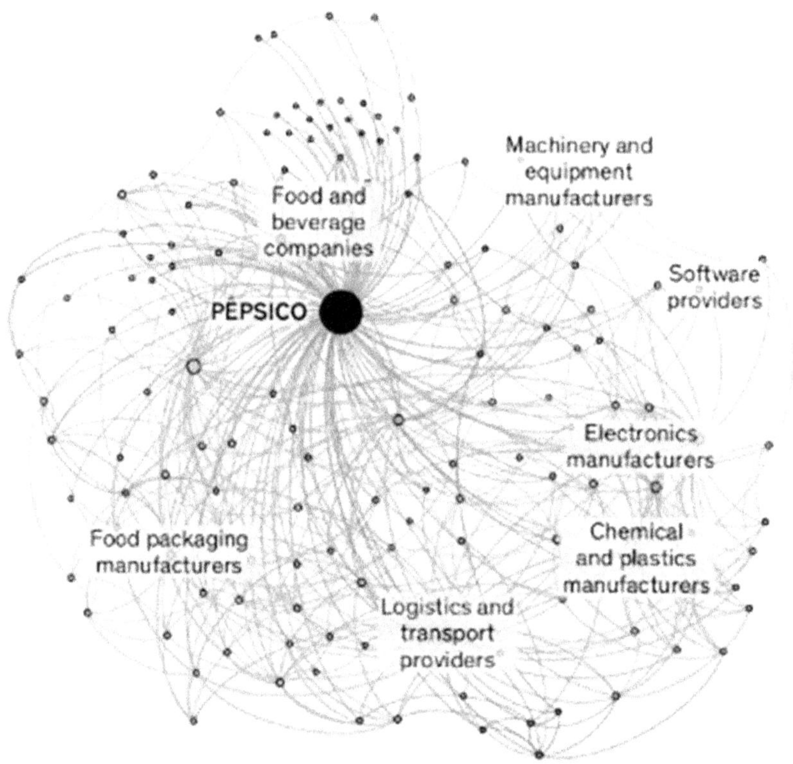

Over a decade, the research anticipates that businesses will lose about 45% of their annual revenues. This is equivalent to an annualized drop of seven percentage points in EBITDA over a ten-year timeframe. These aren't simply projections for the future, but an accurate depiction of what many businesses are really facing right now. Our simulations show that pharmaceutical and food and beverage firms suffer the least aggregate financial losses. The aerospace, automobile, and mining industries are especially vulnerable to setbacks. We do not estimate how much of the damage caused by these disturbances has already been included in market prices. The average predicted profits effect of a 50-day shock is 35% of a year's EBITDA across the sectors we selected over ten years. The average expected earnings impact of a 25-day shock is 28% during the same period.

Each company within the industries mentioned above may fare better or worse than the hypothetical enterprises depicted here, based on its particular sensitivity to shocks, the specific vulnerabilities within its operations and supply chains, and the mitigation steps it has previously implemented. These other approaches are not considered in our study. Value lost by shareholders may not be immediately apparent following a shock, and such losses are not included here. (Kevin B. Hendricks and Vinod R. Singhal. 2003)

Furthermore, certain external shocks may actually be beneficial for some businesses. The market share of a rival firm may increase, at the very least temporarily, and potentially permanently if an event affects just the operations and suppliers of the first firm but not of the second. Amid adversity, some may take the opportunity to innovate rapidly and effectively in ways that foster sustained development (for details, see Nassim Taleb, 2018)

In the short term, inventory serves as a crucial cushion, but fixed expenses come into play in the long term.

The financial impact of shocks is mitigated for businesses with greater inventories and lower fixed expenditures. A sufficient quantity of safety stock is an important buffer in a natural catastrophe affecting a provider, but distribution systems remain operational. However, after the fact, when it's time to refill drawn-down safety stock, enterprises farther down the supply chain that depend on their inventory to maintain sales during a crisis risk a financial outflow.

Although the number and proportion of inputs and components, semifinished items, and finished goods held in inventory vary from industry to industry, there are certain consistent tendencies. For instance, retailers own most of the garment industry's finished product inventory (our analysis does not capture it). It's possible for there to be large regional variances in the performance of some sectors. European automakers than their American counterparts hold more inventory because of the widespread use of factory-owned dealerships in Europe as opposed to independent dealers in the United States. A typical week's worth of stock in the IT and electronics business could only be a few days' worths of goods. However, businesses in the pharmaceutical sector often stockpile enough completed items to last many months. The complexity of production and the regularity of interruptions are reflected in these choices. Industries producing goods with shorter shelf life will, for instance, naturally carry fewer stock.

FUTURE RISK MANAGEMENT

Companies in today's developed economies understand the need for risk management and have a better grasp on implementing it. Unfortunately, the outbreak occurred as scientific advancements were speeding up. Analytics and AI, IoT, advanced robots, and digital platforms are relatively new to the realm of global manufacturing. Businesses now have cutting-edge resources for doing what-if analyses, weighing alternatives, increasing transparency, acting swiftly, and even rebalancing production economics (George, Ramaswamy, and Rassey, 2014).

Below, we've categorized several possible methods into three distinct groups. Increasing supply chain transparency and improving risk management are the focus of the first set of efforts. Shock reduction is front and center in the second. The fourth set of actions aims to increase the business's operational and financial resilience.

Figure 7. strategies for risk management (source: McKinsey Global Institute analysis)

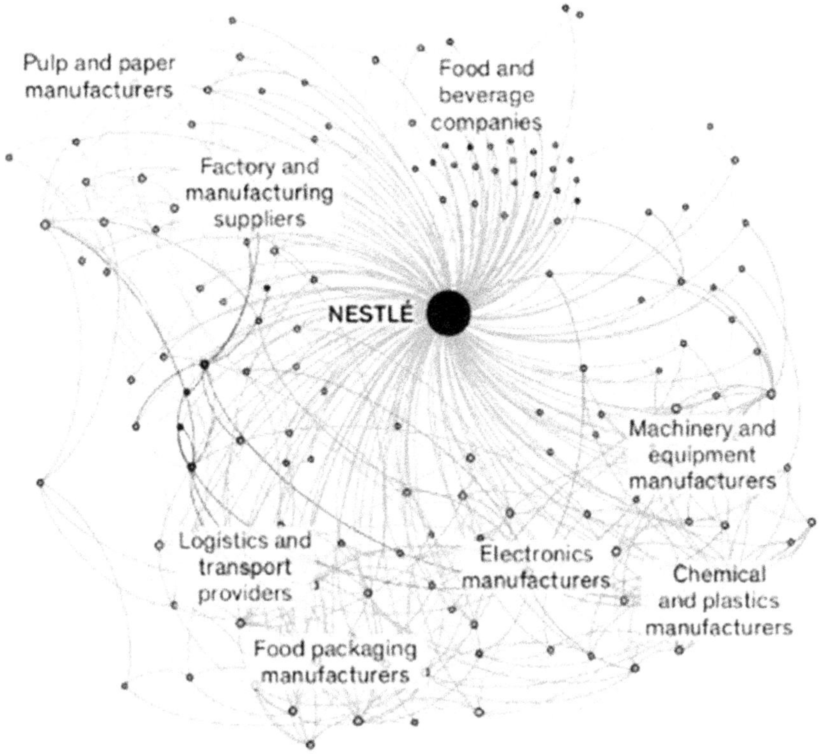

Increase Supply Chain Risk Management and Transparency

After the 2008 financial crisis, the top banks worldwide began conducting rigorous yearly stress tests of their balance sheets to see whether they would survive a severe recession. These kinds of stress tests are becoming widespread. In light of recent shocks that have hit firms throughout the world, many manufacturing and industrial companies are considering adopting similar methods to supply chain risk (Mazingo, Pepanides., Petrov, and Schröck, 2014).

Create a Detailed Map of Your Value Chain

The ability to recognize threats, anticipate interruptions, and react to them depends on having a thorough understanding of your supply chain. However, most major companies have a vague idea when it comes to their suppliers beyond tiers one and two. Many people, however, lack knowledge of the higher-tier suppliers that provide crucial components (Choi, Shao, and Shi, 2015). Even the most modern businesses still haven't achieved the golden grail of complete transparency across the whole value chain, from the manufacture of raw materials to customer service.

Going through each product's bill of materials with the operations and manufacturing teams, you may see whether any key inputs are sent in from high-risk regions and don't have close alternatives. For each component and commodity, we may calculate a risk score based on the rarity and location of their respective suppliers.

The first step in finding weak hidden linkages is creating a thorough picture of the supply chain via rigorous sub-tier mapping. Working more closely with tier-one suppliers is one-way businesses can improve their openness. Tier-one suppliers are also likely to share similar worries about their suppliers. However, not everyone is out in the open, and some may choose to keep their sources hidden. Risk management teams may need to use their best judgment by triangulating data from various sources, including commercially available databases. After tracing the origins of their products to their upstream suppliers, businesses should investigate their manufacturing footprint and the financial security of their partners in the value chain (Resilience report, 2019).

Use Technology to its Full Capacity to Monitor, Connect, and Collaborate across the Supply Chain

The industrial sector has been hearing about the potential benefits of the integration of analytics, AI, robots, networked sensors and controls, tracking technologies, and augmented reality for quite some time. These might improve the efficiency and dependability of industrial settings and, in the long term, link all the links in the value chain via a constant stream of data. In the past, hundreds of establishments throughout the globe made their own choices about disaster preparedness and response. Nowadays, a centralized control tower system provides a company-wide view of regions and goods. For its production facilities and those of its suppliers and distributors, it combines a wide variety of real-time information, including stock levels, traffic conditions, and weather predictions.

Reduce the Chance of Shocks

In a world where disruptions are becoming more regular and severe, businesses cannot afford to remain just reactive. Investment in preemptive measures to fortify weak spots may mitigate shocks and speed up recoveries. Some of them include expanding one's pool of potential suppliers, strengthening relationships with key suppliers, expanding one's range of available transportation and logistics options, designing products with modular and reusable parts, and reinforcing one's physical infrastructure and assets. Every business's unique risk profile will inform the best course of action.

Diversify Supplier Network and Geographic Footprint

The supply of some key components or raw materials is increasingly concentrated in the hands of a few businesses. They did this because, in certain cases, they found that just one vendor had the special expertise to provide what was needed. Others, on the other hand, seek to streamline the procurement process or negotiate better costs with a single supplier, regardless of the presence of others. Even if the supply is domestic, this might be a significant problem.

If a provider goes out of business, supply might dry up, making it harder to meet unexpectedly high demand. Due to the nature of specialization, even if a business uses many different suppliers, those businesses may all be located in the same area.

Businesses can diversify their network of suppliers to increase flexibility and redundancy. It is possible to reduce the likelihood that isolated natural disasters in one area may create bottlenecks in the value chain by sourcing from other or lower-risk regions. Investing in identifying, pre-qualifying, and onboarding backup suppliers can provide much-needed capacity in the case of a crisis, reducing interruptions and avoiding hasty judgments under pressure. While it's true that it takes money to screen new suppliers and deal with a large number of sources, in the end, this preparation allows firms to shift production to multiple suppliers, facilities, and countries as needed, giving them an advantage over competitors (Linton and Vakil, 2020).

Boost Crucial Vendors or In-House Produces Essential Components

Just as they must fortify their operations, big businesses must think about the preparedness of their most important suppliers. These companies must prioritize risk planning and monitoring in addition to common risk mitigation strategies like establishing multiple sources of supply, building up emergency funds, and setting aside funds for predicting future demand. Larger businesses might consider investing in expanding their suppliers' skills or working together on crucial components.

Create Alternatives in Logistics and Transportation

Important parts and finished goods may become stuck when port facilities are broken, highways are blocked, or planes are canceled. It was difficult to move items into lockdown zones during the COVID outbreak. Trucking companies could not find enough drivers, and many cargo flights were canceled. Logistics of every kind became clogged. Having the appropriate connections and backup plans in place can help you avoid this situation. Businesses can enter contracts with various logistics services and choose backup suppliers for each important route.

WHEN A SHOCK DOES STRIKE, COMPANIES NEED TO BE ABLE TO REACT QUICKLY

Increase Inventory and Safety Stock

As a result of adopting "just-in-time" and "lean manufacturing" techniques, businesses could improve their efficiency and spend less money on working capital in the past. However, they may need to find a new equilibrium between "just in time" and "just in case." Supply interruptions may have a significant effect on a company's bottom line. Therefore it's crucial to have a sufficient buffer in the form of backup and safety inventories on key components. Furthermore, this method may put businesses in a better position to handle demand spikes. The ability to continue production after a shock may be ensured by adjusting component manufacturing processes and maintaining production capacity flexibility across facilities. To do all this, organizations need advanced digital systems and analytics that let them simulate outcomes depending on many inputs. Nike utilized predictive analytics to slash prices early and cut production strategically before the epidemic struck. Nike's "direct-to-consumer" internet sales, with the help of its training APP, have also helped the company shift its product focus from brick-and-mortar locations to online marketplaces. Due to this, Nike's sales decline has been less severe than that of some of its rivals.

When a crisis hits, cash flow control is important for every business. However, those at the top of the value chain have an additional responsibility to safeguard the supplier networks upon which they depend. Some businesses have thrown critical vendors a bone in the global financial crisis by accelerating payments and guaranteeing bank loans.

Flexibility Among Vendors, Locations, and Consumer Channels

In the wake of a shock, businesses can continue operating if they have the flexibility to reroute components and transfer production between sites. The most advanced in this area is probably the automakers, who have put in place manufacturing platforms that allow parts to be shared between different product lines and manufacturing facilities (Yasuyuki Todo, Kentaro Nakajima, and Petr Matous, 2015). This kind of modular strategy minimizes the number of potential bottlenecks and gives automakers the flexibility to respond quickly to natural catastrophes or tariffs by shifting production.

Make Cash Flow and Balance-Sheet Buffers for Suppliers

Firms with solid balance sheets are better prepared to absorb shocks; heavily indebted corporations have limited wiggle space when revenue suddenly disappears. Non-financial company debt has been increasing for years, as our continuing debt and deleveraging research has shown. It reached an all-time high of $74 trillion at the start of 2020, putting many firms in jeopardy on the eve of the COVID epidemic. Some significant players have declared bankruptcy, and more are on the verge.

Companies may improve their balance sheets during good times by decreasing debt, developing reserves, and securing enough credit lines (Birshan, Gerken, SKemmer, Petrov, and Polyakov, 2020). Based on their analysis of 1,000 publicly traded companies' results during the Great Recession and its aftermath, McKinsey researchers have concluded that around 10% of these companies fared better than their peers. One of their defining characteristics is that they took steps to establish a financial buffer before the onset of the financial crisis. This allowed them to shift into acquisition mode at the first sign of recovery, using their cash to buy assets their rivals were divesting to survive.

In addition, there is the possibility of taking further steps to safeguard them against known financial dangers. Some businesses, like airlines, use hedging to prepare for unpredictable increases or decreases in the cost of fuel, while others, like farmers, protect themselves from these kinds of market swings. Regularly reviewing your insurance policies is also essential.

A wide range of methods is available to businesses for dealing with interruptions and minimizing risk. However, commitments should be made well in advance of the event. After a crisis, it is far more difficult to implement a new technology system or switch to a different supplier. It takes self-control and a focus on the future to make an investment in resilience worthwhile. Still, in an increasingly unpredictable world, preparing for various outcomes is essential.

REFERENCES

Adams. C., Alldredge. K., Mueller. C., & Whitmore. J. (2020). *Simpler is (sometimes) better: Managing complexity in consumer goods*. McKinsey.com.

Adams, C., Buck, R., Herzberg, G., Mandel, J., & Mueller, C. (2020). *We are harnessing the power of simplicity in a complex consumer-product environment*. McKinsey.com.

Al-Mudimigh, A., Zairi, M., & Ahmed, A.M.M., (2004). Extending the concept of the supply chain: the effective management of value chains. *Int. J. Prod. Econ., 87*, 309-320.

Antràs, P. (2020). *Conceptual Aspects of Global Value Chains*. Discussion Paper. No. DP14191. London: Centre for Economic Policy Research.

Awan, M.A., & Ali, Y. (2022). Risk Assessment in Supply Chain Networks of China–Pakistan Economic Corridor (CPEC). *Chin. Polit. Sci. Rev*. doi:10.1007/s41111-021-00199-w

Azmeh, S., & Nadvi, K., (2014). Asian firms and the restructuring of global value chains. *Int. Bus. Rev., 23*(4), 708-717.

Baldwin, R., & Lopez-Gonzalez, J., (2015). Supply-chain trade: a portrait of global patterns and several testable hypotheses. *World Econ., 38*(11), 1682-1721.

Banga, R. (2014). Linking into Global Value Chains Is Not Sufficient: Do You Export Domestic Value-Added Contents? *Journal of Economic Integration*, *29*(2), 267–297. doi:10.11130/jei.2014.29.2.267

Barrientos, S., Gereffifi, G., & Rossi, A., (2011). Economic and social upgrading in global production networks: a new paradigm for a changing world. *Int. Labour Rev., 150*(3-4), 319-340.

Bernard, A. B., Jensen, J. B., Redding, S. J., & Schott, P. K. (2007). Firms in International Trade. *The Journal of Economic Perspectives*, *21*(3), 105–130. doi:10.1257/jep.21.3.105

Buckley, P.J. (2011). International integration and coordination in the global factory. *Manage. Int. Rev., 51*, 269-283.

Buckley, P.J., & Ghauri, P.N. (2004). Globalisation, economic geography and the strategy of multinational enterprises. *J. Int. Bus. Stud., 35*(2), 81-98.

Buckley, P.J., & Strange, R. (2015). The governance of the global factory: Location and control of world economic activity. *Acad. Manage. Perspect., 29*(2), 237-249.

Carey, N., & Klayman, B. (n.d.). *May is crunch time for US auto suppliers amid coronavirus shutdown*. Reuters.

Castañeda-Navarrete, J., Hauge, J., & López-Gómez, C. (2020). COVID-19's impacts on global value chains, as seen in the apparel industry. *Development Policy Review*, *39*(6), 953–970. Advance online publication. doi:10.1111/dpr.12539

Choi, T. Y., Shao, B. B. M., & Shi, Z. (2015). Hidden suppliers can make or break your operations. *Harvard Business Review*.

Christopher, M. (2005). *Logistics and Supply Chain Management: Creating Value-added Networks*. Pearson Education.

Cox, A. (1999). Power, value and supply chain management. *Supply Chain Manage. Int. J., 4*(4), 167-175.

de Bolle, M., & Zettelmeyer, J. (2019). *Measuring the Rice of Economic Nationalism*. PIIE Working Paper. No. 19–15. Washington, DC: Peterson Institute for International Economics.

De Marchi, V.D., Maria, E.D., & Micelli, S. (2013). Environmental strategies, upgrading and competitive advantage in global value chains. *Bus. Strategy Environ., 22*(1), 62-72.

Di Domenico, C., Ouzrout, Y., Savinno, M. M., & Bouras, B. (2007). Supply chain management analysis: a simulation approach of the value chain operations reference model (VCOR). In Advances in Production Management Systems. Springer.

Dmitry Ivanov, D. (2020). Predicting the impacts of epidemic outbreaks on global supply chains: A simulation-based analysis on the coronavirus outbreak (COVID-19/ SARS-CoV-2) case. *Transportation Research Part E, Logistics and Transportation Review, 2020*(136).

Elliott. R., Thomas. C., & Muhammad. K. (2019). *Supply chain resilience report 2019*. Business Continuity Institute.

Explainer. (2013). *What have scientists learned from the Chelyabinsk meteor?* RadioFreeEurope/RadioLiberty. Retrieved from https:// www.rferl.org/a/explainer-meteor-russia/25161323.htm
1

Felipe. J. (2012). Product complexity and economic development. *Structural Change and Economic Dynamics, 23*(1), 36-68.

Frankel, J. A. (1997). *Regional Trading Blocs in the World Economic System*. Peterson Institute for International Economics.

General Motors. (2018). *Our management approach to supply chain*. gmsustainability. com/manage/supply.html.

George, K. G, Ramaswamy, S., & Ramsey, L. (2014). Next-shoring: A CEO's guide. *McKinsey Quarterly*.

Gereffi, G., Pananond, P., & Pedersen, T. (2022). Resilience Decoded: The Role of Firms, Global Value Chains, and the State in COVID-19 Medical Supplies. *California Management Review*, (2), 46–70. Advance online publication. doi:10.1177/00081256211069420

Gereffifi, G., & Fernandez-Stark, K. (2011). *Global Value Chain Analysis: A Primer. Center on Globalization, Governance & Competitiveness (CGGC)*. Duke University.

Giuseppina, T., & Michele, S. (2018). Re-shoring and Resilience in Italy During and After the Crisis. *American Journal of Industrial and Business Management.*, *8*(05), 1172–1196. doi:10.4236/ajibm.2018.85081

Goering, K., Kelly, R., & Mellors, N. (2018). The next horizon for industrial manufacturing: Adopting disruptive digital technologies in making and delivering. *McKinsey Quarterly*.

Hashim, M., Nazam, M., Zia-ur-Rehman, M., Abrar, M., Baig, S., Nazim, M., & Hussain, Z. (2022). Modeling Supply Chain Sustainability-Related Risks and Vulnerability: Insights from the Textile Sector of Pakistan. *AUTEX Research Journal*, *22*(1), 123–134. doi:10.2478/aut-2021-0008

Heijmans & Nguyen. (2020, Nov. 15). Asia Pacific Nations Sign Biggest Regional Trade Deal. *Bloomberg*.

Hendricks, B. K., & Singhal, R. V. (2003). *An empirical analysis of the effect of supply chain disruption on long-run stock price performance and equity risk of the firm*. Academic Press.

Hussain, G., Nazir, M. S., Rashid, M. A., & Sattar, M. A. (2022). From supply chain resilience to supply chain disruption orientation: The moderating role of supply chain complexity. *Journal of Enterprise Information Management*. Advance online publication. doi:10.1108/JEIM-12-2020-0558

Kelly, S. (2020). *Oil price crashes into negative territory for the first time in history amid pandemic*. Reuters.

Kelly, S., & Baertlein, L. (2020). *Beer may lose its fizz as CO2 supplies go flat during a pandemic*. Reuters.

Koopman, R., Wang, Z., & Wei, S. (2008). *How Much of Chinese Exports Is Really Made in China? Assessing Domestic Value-Added When Processing Trade Is Pervasive*. NBER Working Paper. No. 14109. Cambridge, MA: National Bureau of Economic Research.

Linton, T., & Vakil, B. (2020). Coronavirus is proving we need more resilient supply chains. *Harvard Business Review*.

Mahutga, M. C. (2011). When do value chains go global? A theory of the spatialization of global value chains. *Global Networks, 12*(1), 1–21. doi:10.1111/j.1471-0374.2011.00322.x

Mazingo, C., Peptides, T., Petrov, A., & Schröck, G. (2014). *Introducing a holistic approach to stress testing*. McKinsey.com.

Paton, E. (2020). Our situation is apocalyptic: Bangladesh garment workers face ruin. *New York Times*.

Pettit, T. J., Fiksel, J., & Croxton, K. L. (2010). Ensuring Supply Chain Resilience: Development of a Conceptual Framework. *Journal of Business Logistics*, *31*(1), 1–21. https://doi.org/10.1002/j.2158-1592.2010.tb00125.x

Shao, B. B. M., Shi, Z., Choi, T. Y., & Chae, S. (2018). A data-analytics approach to identifying hidden critical suppliers in supply networks: Development of nexus supplier index. *Decision Support Systems, 114*, 37–48. doi:10.1016/j.dss.2018.08.008

Sheffi, Y. (2016). The power of resilience: how the best companies manage the unexpected. *Choice Reviews Online, 53*(7). doi:10.5860/choice.195121

Simchi-Levi, D., Schmidt, W., & Wei, Y. (2014). From superstorms to factory fires: Managing unpredictable supply chain disruptions. *Harvard Business Review*.

Stabell, C.B., & Fjeldstad, Ø.D. (1998). Configuring value for competitive advantage: on chains, shops, and networks. *Strateg. Manage. J.,* 413-437.

Subramanian, A., & Kessler, M. (2013). *The Hyperglobalization of Trade and Its Future*. Working Paper Series No. 13-6. Washington, DC: Peterson Institute for International Economics.

Titievskaia, J., Kononenko, V., Navarra, C., Stamegna, C., & Zumer, K. (2020). *Slowing Down or Changing Track? Understanding the Dynamics of "Slowbalisation."* European Parliamentary Research Service.

Todo, Y., Nakajima, K., & Matous, P. (2015). How do supply chain networks affect the resilience of firms to natural disasters? Evidence from the Great East Japan Earthquake. *Journal of Regional Science*, *55*(2).

World Trade Organization. (2020). *Trade shows signs of rebound from COVID- 19, recovery still uncertain*. https://www.wto.org/engli sh/news_e/pres20_e/pr862_e.htm

ENDNOTE

1 Data from the Bloomberg Supply Chain database, based on regulatory filings and other public disclosures.

Chapter 10
Sustainable Belt and Road (OBOR) Development:
A Case of the China-Pakistan Economic Corridor

Sajid Nazir
Institute of Business Management, Pakistan

Zhang Yu
School of Economics and Management, Xian, China

ABSTRACT

China is the world's second-largest economy after the United States with more than 60% of the value of its trade being transported by sea. Therefore, China looks for short, safe, and inexpensive trade routes (both land and maritime) to reach Europe, Africa, and the Middle East countries. In doing so, China has taken the One Belt-One-Road (OBOR) initiative intending to develop a cost-effective transportation network ensuring timely and secure delivery. The objective of the OBOR strategy is to enhance Pakistan's infrastructure through the construction of the China-Pakistan Economic Corridor (CPEC). Therefore, this chapter aims to examine the implications of CPEC trade routes in terms of cost and delivery between China and other regions (i.e., Saudi Arabia, Iraq, Angola, Oman, Kuwait, and the United Arab Emirates) via Gwadar Port, Pakistan. The results demonstrate a significant reduction in cost and delivery time via the CPEC route in comparison with traditional trade routes.

DOI: 10.4018/978-1-6684-6663-6.ch010

INTRODUCTION

The concept of "Sustainability", which refers to the integration of social, environmental, and economic concerns, has gained significant value after the Paris climate summit presented a binding agreement (Coyne, 2020) that helps the nations to meet a common cause to start fruitful actions for fighting against the climate issues (Mahapatra & Ratha, 2016). The concept of sustainable transportation is essential to sustainable development because it seeks to achieve the goals of universal access (Oswald Beiler, 2012) such as improved safety and efficiency, lower environmental impacts, and increased resilience (Garceau et al., 2013; Reza et al., 2020; Mubarik et al., 2021). Consequently, it is crucial for the success of the Paris agreement on climate change and the 2030 agenda for Sustainable Development (Shah, 2016). These goals can only be attained by developing an interconnection between Sustainable Development Goals (SDGs) and sustainable transportation and their respective targets (Hong, 2016; Abdel Warith et al., 2019). Transport networks have a major impact on society, economy, and environmental sustainability (Zheng et al., 2013; Alam et al., 2020; Mubarik et al., 2021) and it is essential for fostering connectivity, economic progress, trade activities, and employment (Parton, 2013). Likewise, besides offering mobility services and infrastructure, sustainable transportation is a game-changer in many aspects (Litman, 2007) for example it has the potential to accelerate progress toward other essential goals, such as eradicating poverty in all of its forms, empowering women, decreasing inequality, and dealing with climate change effectively (Mubarik et al., 2020; Menhas et al., 2022).

The United Nations' Sustainable Development Goals (SDGs) and the Chinese 'One Belt, One Road (OBOR) initiatives are two global development frameworks that have emerged since 2013 (Shah, 2016). In China, there is a massive rise in sustainable development planning due to increasing concern about worldwide environmental issues and the nation's dependency on oil imports (Maizland, 2021) and OBOR could be the first regional effort to execute the SDGs (Shah, 2016). China plans to foster massive economic expansion in Europe, Asia, and Africa by initiating the OBOR plan (ZHANG & ZHANG, 2016) which is a vast multinational trading network with various trade corridors spanning around sixty countries (Menhas et al., 2022). The OBOR plan was firstly introduced in 2013 by President Xi Jinping, which intends to further link Europe, Asia, and Africa through the expansion of land and sea infrastructure (Anwar et al., 2017). The OBOR initiative consists of two components; One Belt, which is also known as the "Marine Silk Road" intends to link China's coastline with Africa and Europe through Southeast Asia while One Road, also known as the "Land Silk Road", aims to connect the mainland of China with Europe and Central Asia as shown in figure 1 (Hosain, & Hossain, 2019).

Figure 1. OBOR Routes (Hosain, & Hossain, 2019)

This OBOR plan aims to develop a sustainable transport network enabling safe and timely delivery, lower transportation costs, strengthening relationships among urban and rural areas, and expediting the flow of information between different regions (Shah, 2016; Menhas et al., 2022). The development of the China Pakistan-Economic- Corridor (CPEC) under the OBOR initiative will link the Chinese province of Xinjiang to the port of Gwadar, Pakistan via integrated transportation network and infrastructure development spanning around 3000 kilometers (Li et al., 2017; Iqbal, 2017). The new Silk Route is a strategic, large-scale mega project that represents China's long-term foreign policy vision (Kong, 2015) and considers the most significant foreign policy effort by President Xi's administration to connect Asia, Europe, and Africa (Hosain, & Hossain, 2019). There are several projects under the OBOR initiative and participating countries as shown in the figure below (ESCAP, 2017).

Table 1. List of Participating Countries (ESCAP, 2017)

S. No	Corridor	Participating Countries
01	The New Eurasian Land Bridge	China-Russia, Kazakhstan, Russia, Belarus, and Poland,
02	The China-Mongolia-Russia Corridor	China-Mongolia-Russia
03	The China-Central Asia-West Asia Corridor	China, Kazakhstan, Kyrgyzstan, Uzbekistan, Tajikistan, Turkmenistan, Iran and Turkey.
04	The China-Indochina Peninsula Corridor	Thailand, Myanmar, Laos, Cambodia and Vietnam Malaysia and Singapore
05	The China-Pakistan Corridor	China, Pakistan
06	The Bangladesh-China-India-Myanmar Corridor	The Bangladesh-China-India-Myanmar Corridor

Figure 2. OBOR Projects (ESCAP, 2017)

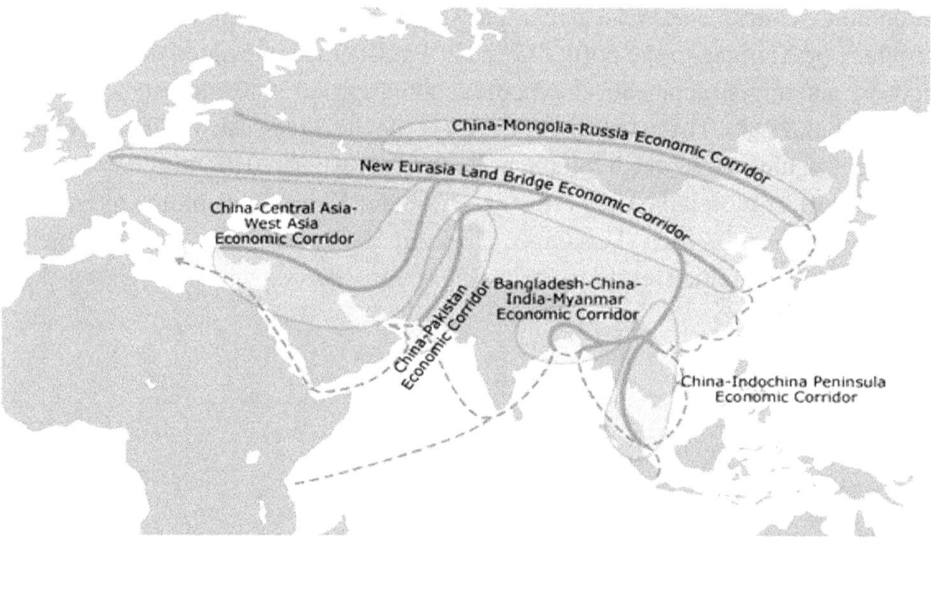

Currently, these two routes (South China Sea & Malacca Strait) account for 70 percent of China's energy trade. However, in the case of a conflict between these two states would disrupt the energy supplies and require ships to travel hundreds of kilometers along a separate transit route (Mehar, 2017). Therefore, China looks for a speedy, low-cost, and safe alternative trade route to reach South-East Asia, Europe, South Asia, and Africa (Hosain, & Hossain, 2019). However, the China-Pakistan Economic Corridor (CPEC) could provide this opportunity by enabling the closest route from China to the Middle East and Europe via South East Asia (Ahmad & Mi, 2017) through the development of road and sea routes, railway lines, and energy infrastructure as a part of CPEC to accomplish the OBOR plan (Mehar, 2017). Therefore, the primary aim of this study is to investigate how the development of infrastructure as part of the CPEC can contribute to Pakistan's long-term economic growth. Secondly, this book chapter presents the analysis of current trade routes and CPEC routes in terms of cost and delivery time. Furthermore, this chapter also presents the challenges associated with the development of this project by incorporating the Political, Economic, Social, Technological, Legal, and Environmental (PESTLE) analysis (Zalengera et al., 2014).

In accordance with the purpose of this book chapter, initially in the following section 2, presents a comprehensive introduction to the China-Pakistan Economic Corridor. Likewise, section 2.1, determines the components of CPEC, and section 2.2 presents the logistical infrastructure of CPEC. Furthermore, the Chinese import of oil from Saudi Arabia, Iraq, Angola, Oman, Kuwait, and the United Arab Emirates has been discussed in section 3. After discussing the current trade routes in section 4, the CPEC route has been presented in section 5. Likewise, section 6 demonstrates the comparison of both routes in terms of distance, transit time, and cost. Then, section 7 presents the PESTLE analysis. Finally, section 8, presents the conclusion and possible future directions of this research chapter.

CHINA PAKISTAN ECONOMIC CORRIDOR

CPEC is a huge bilateral initiative aimed to develop Pakistan's infrastructure for improved trade with China and regional integration (Shah, 2015). In the beginning, the concept of CPEC was only a rumor for several years, but in 2013, it became a reality during the visit of Chinese Premier Li Keqiang for the development of the Gwadar port (Ahmad, & Mi, 2017). The China-Pakistan Economic Corridor, or CPEC, is a series of infrastructural as well as other projects being built across Pakistan as shown in figure 3 (CPIC-Global, 2022). The project's original value was USD 46 billion (Khan & Liu, 2018; Alam et al., 2019; Khadim et al., 2021), however by 2017, its value had increased to USD 62 billion (Surahio et al., 2022).

Figure 3. Project under CPEC Development (CPIC-Global, 2022)

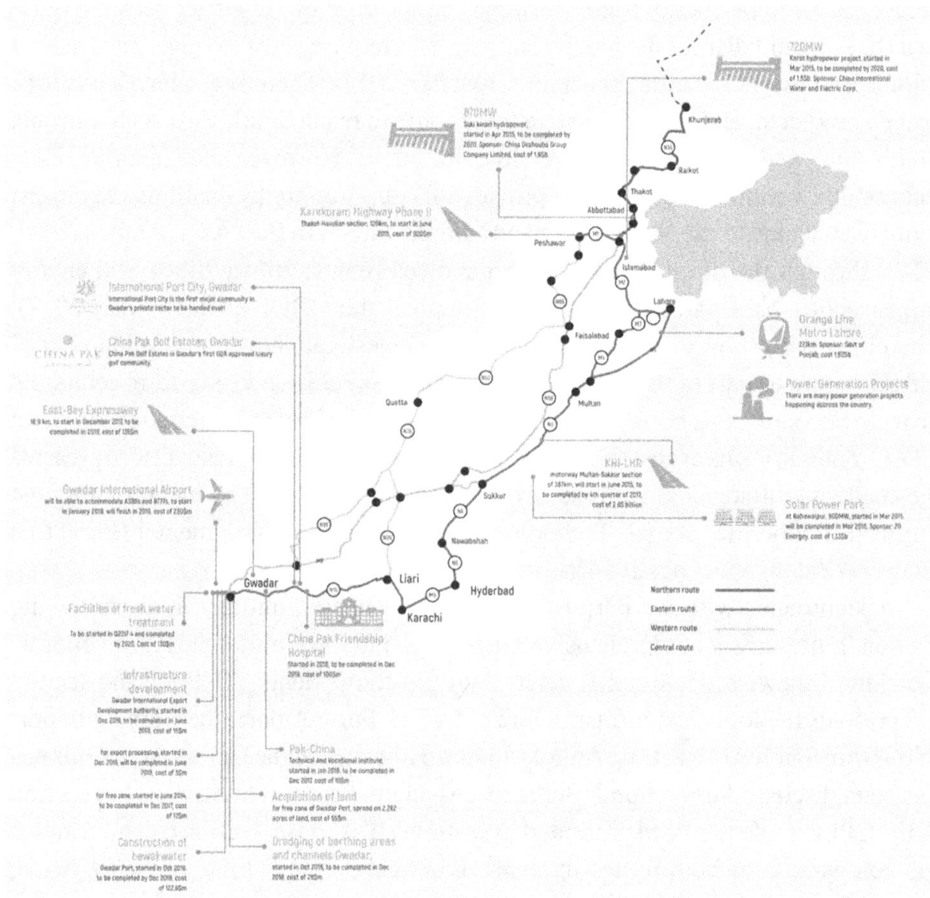

The goal of the China-Pakistan Economic Corridor (CPEC) is to transform Pakistan's economy by building an advanced sustainable transportation infrastructure (including roads, motorways, rail, and air) and maritime network to link the ocean, via the ports of Gwadar and Karachi in Pakistan, with China's Xinjiang region as well as other zones via overland routes. This will lower the shipping cost and time by avoiding the Malacca Strait and the South China Sea (Ibrahim, 2017). Presently, these two routes (including the Indian Ocean and strait of Malacca) are very long and both are responsible for more than seventy percent of China's energy trade however, in the event of any confrontation between these two nations the energy supplies would be disrupted, and require ships to travel hundreds of additional miles along a separate transit route (Alam et al., 2019). However, the development of Gwadar port will allow China to reach countries in Europe, Middle-East, and

Africa via direct trade channels (Chowdhary, 2015; Mehar, 2017). It is expected that the CPEC projects will be finished by 2030, including the construction of special economic zones, energy projects, road networks, railway tracks, fiber optics for communication, and Gwadar port (Ministry of Planning, Development, and Reform, 2017). The following section presents the components of CPEC.

Components of CPEC

The China-Pakistan Economic Corridor (CPEC) is making significant progress through the continuous development of various elements of the project. These components include the construction of transport infrastructure, optical fiber network, energy sector, social & economic developments, and various projects at Gwadar port to achieve CPEC goals (Naz & Ali, 2018). CPEC can help Pakistan overcome its energy shortage and improve its economy (Shah Afridi et al., 2016). China is the Pakistan's second-largest trade partner and investor in infrastructure, seaports, energy, and industrialization (Jamil et al., 2019). Therefore, the expansion and advancement of CPEC make Pakistan the trading hub for the second-largest economy in South Asia (Khan et al., 2019). Currently, Pakistan has had energy challenges and restricted trade issues because of disputes with the neighboring countries since independence, but the expansion of logistics infrastructure under the CPEC project will offer new trade routes to access neighboring countries located in the east and west of the country via functional trade routes (Rizvi, 2015).

Figure 4. Components of CPEC (Ministry of Planning, 2022)

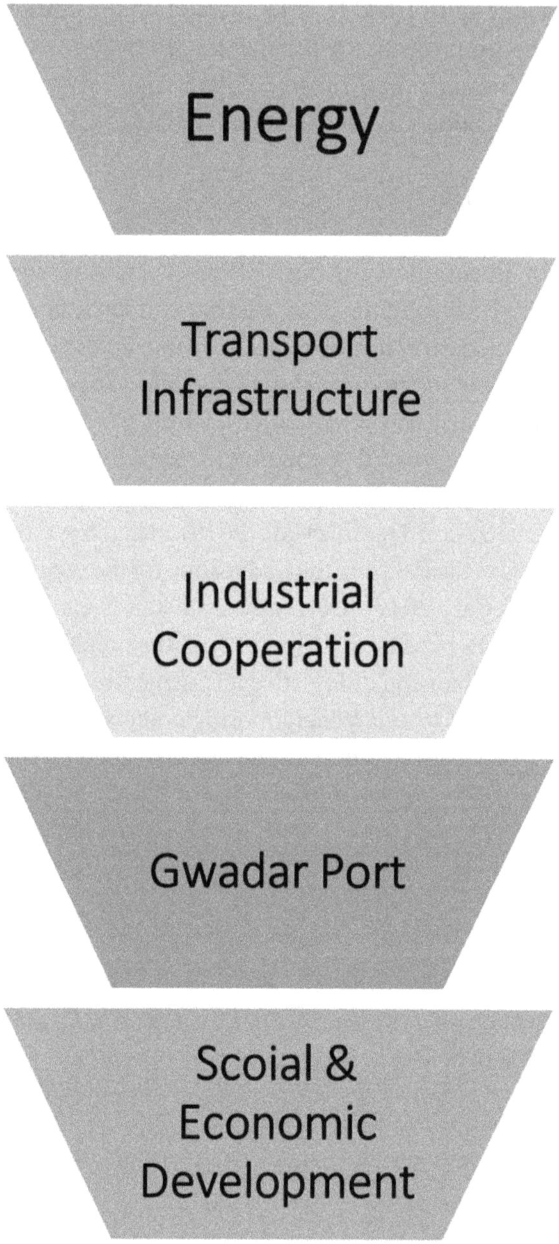

The following table presents the current progress of CPEC projects

Table 2. CPEC Projects Progress (Ministry of Planning, 2022)

S.No	Project	Completed	Under Construction	Projects In Pipeline
1	Energy	11	5	5
2	Transport Infrastructure	6	5	8
3	Gwadar Port	4	6	4
4	Industrial Cooperation	5	12	10
5	Social & Economic Development	-	-	-

Logistics Infrastructure

Due to the strategically advantageous location of Gwadar Port, the development of the mega project aims to connect Pakistan's Gwadar Port with Xinjiang, China (Shah Afridi et al., 2016) in order to improve trade between these two nations (Jamil et al., 2019) as well as to import crude petroleum from Saudi Arabia, Iraq, Angola, Oman, Kuwait, and the United Arab Emirates via safe and short transit route via Gwadar Port. These countries are the big exporter of crude petroleum to China and fulfilling more than half of China's energy requirements. The transportation infrastructure of CPEC includes the construction of roads, railway and pipeline networks, airports, and maritime routes as shown in figure 5 with an estimated cost of USD 11 billion or 23.91 percent of entire investments (Ministry of Planning, Development, and Reform, 2022). The construction of the 1100-kilometer-long, Karachi-Lahore motorway and the extension of the Karakorum Highway (KKH) will boost internal connectivity and economic growth (Menhas et al., 2022).

Figure 5. Logistics Infrastructure (Ministry of Planning, Development, and Reform, 2022)

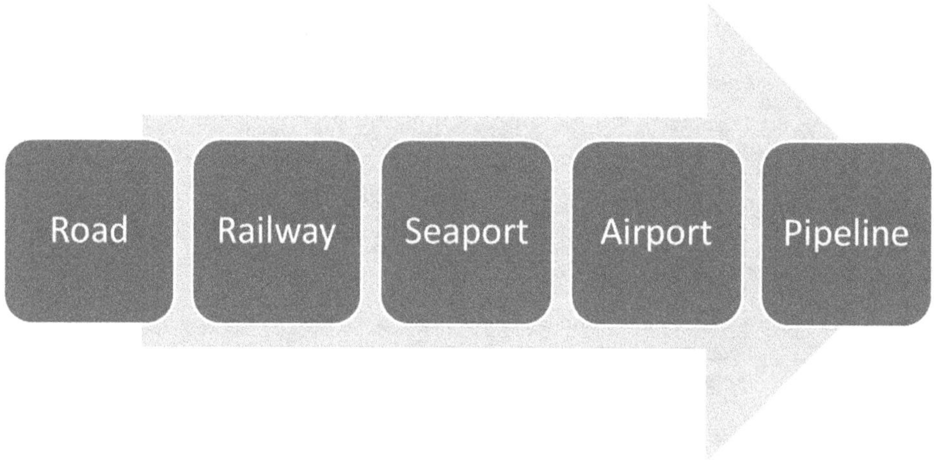

Pakistan's capacity to transfer goods and services within the territories of the Economic Cooperation Organization (ECO) depends on a well-developed and reliable logistics system. However, the development of CPEC will assist this collaboration in achieving the ECO's prime goal. ECO was founded in 1985 by the close collaboration of 3 nations (Pakistan, Iran, & Turkey) to foster cultural, economic, and technical cooperation. After the formation of the ECO, seven more nations also joined this collaboration: Afghanistan, Azerbaijan, Kazakhstan, Kyrgyzstan, Tajikistan, Turkmenistan, and Uzbekistan are the newest members of the ECO (Joshi, 2017). The components of logistics infrastructure under CPEC constructions are discussed in detail in the following section.

Roads

The construction of road and motorways network will modernize the infrastructure of Pakistan. In doing so, the country would be able to export more of its manufactured goods to other countries at a lower cost via safe and fast transit routes (Ahmad & Mi, 2017). It is essential to choose the right mode of shipping mode to deliver goods by a short and safe route at the lowest possible price to maximize profits (Shahin & Jaferi, 2015). As shown in figure (6) the development of road infrastructure under CPEC.

Figure 6. CPEC-Road Infrastructure (Ministry of Planning, Development, and Reform, 2022)

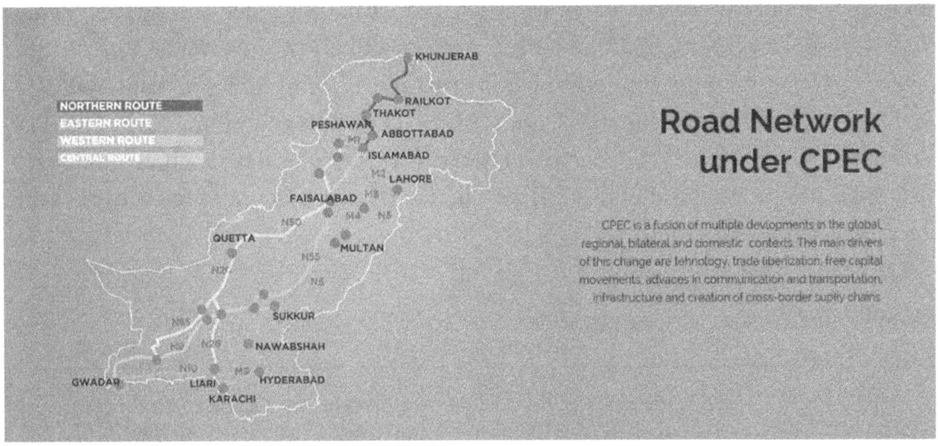

There is a total of twenty-four projects under road construction as shown in table (3) the list of completed projects with the estimated cost. However, five projects are under construction, eight projects are in pipeline, and the remaining five projects are part of a long-term plan for CPEC development.

Table 3. Completed CPEC's Road Project

#	Project Name	Length (KM)	Estimated Cost (US $ Million)
1	KKH Phase II (Hevelian - Thakot Section)	120	1,315
2	Peshawar-Karachi Motorway (Multan-Sukkur Section)	392	2,889
3	Orange Line Metro Train – Lahore	27	1626
4	Cross Border Optical Fiber Cable (Khunjrab - Rawalpindi)	820	44
5	Pilot Project of Digital Terrestrial Multimedia Broadcast (DTMB)		4
6	Hakla - D.I Khan Motorway	297	611

Railway Network

Pakistan's economy needs better logistics infrastructure since its independence. However, the development of the CPEC, project will allow the Gwadar port to gain access to western China through the construction of a rail network. This will link Gwadar, Pakistan with Xinjiang, China, Millions of tons of commodities could be moved quickly and easily, which will generate billions of dollars annually and boost economic progress (Jamil et al., 2019). The list of projects under railway network are shown in table 4.

Table 4. CPEC- Railway Network

#	Project Name	Length (KM)	Estimated Cost (US $ Million)
1	Havelian – Kashi	1,059	40
2	Reconstruction of ML-1 Karachi-Peshawar	1600	-
4	Re-construction of Quetta-Taftan	633	44
5	Quetta to Kotla ML-2	560	4
6	Gwadar – Jacobabad & Quetta	1,328	4.5

The expansion of the M-1 railway is the top priority of CPEC project. The M-1 network which is commonly known as the main-line-one (ML-1), will connect Peshawar to Karachi and will be upgraded or repaired under the development CPEC project. Likewise, this project will also involve the extension and upgrading of ML-2 and ML-3 as shown in figure (7). Furthermore, a 4,693-meter-long railway network connecting Gwadar with Xinjiang also part of CPEC, that would be completed by 2030 (Khan et al., 2019).

Figure 7. Railway network of CPEC (Ministry of Planning, Development, and Reform, 2022)

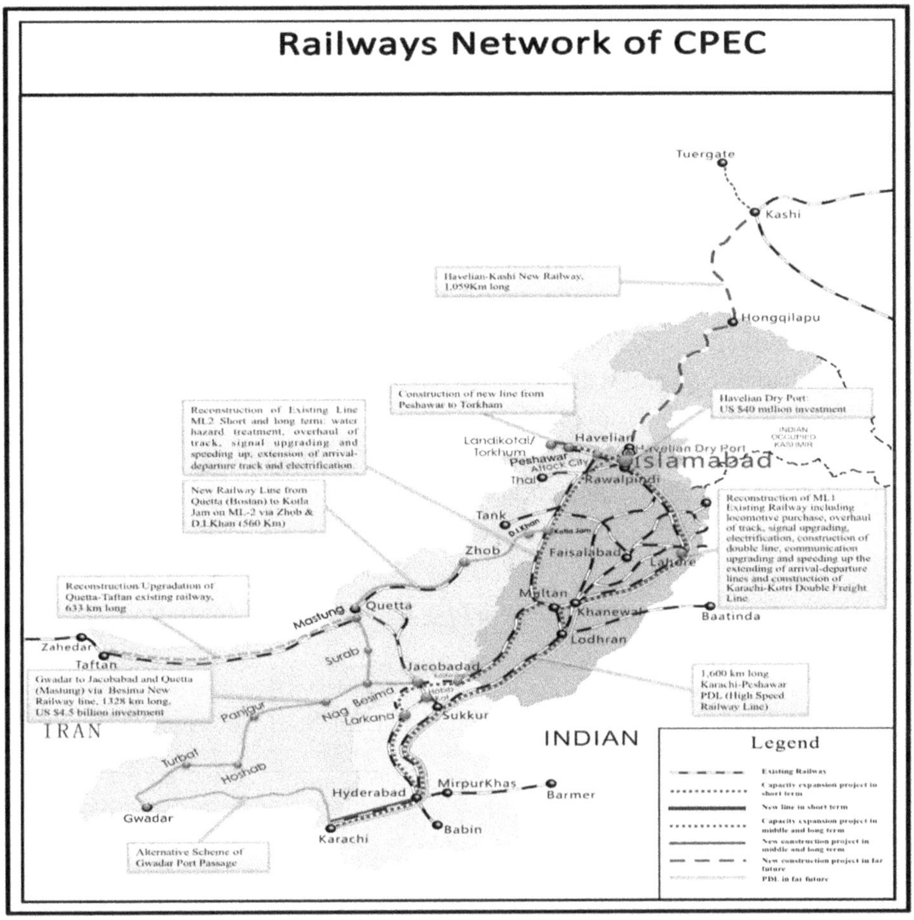

Seaport

The development of CPEC provides a realistic path to enhance Pakistan's maritime infrastructure by connecting Gwadar port with Kashgar, China (Naz & Ali, 2018). Geographically, the Gwadar port is located adjacent to Oman and Gulf coast and is strategically important and considered a trade hub, because it is the major route for oil tankers traveling to western countries and Japan from the Gulf countries (Jamil et al., 2019). This will allow Pakistan to generate a revenue of millions of dollars through cargo handling and shipping fees (Mehar, 2017). Initially, US $198 million has been invested by Beijing-based financial institutions during the first stage of the development of a deep-sea port (Jamil et al., 2019). The purpose of China's investment in the Gwadar port (Shah Afridi et al., 2016) as well as the development of road & railway networks, and the construction of pipelines (Iqbal, 2017) is to fulfill the country's rapidly growing energy requirements by importing oil directly from Middle Eastern countries to Xinjiang, China via short and safe transit route (Alam et al., 2019).

Airport

There are many distinct projects included in the CPEC's grand plan for the region i.e. alongside other transportation hubs like roads, railways, and ports, the construction of Gwadar International Airport is also the part of CPEC Plan (Mehar, 2017). It has a runway size of (1,512 x 23m) which is larger than the runway size of the newly built Islamabad airport and will be able to handle modern giant aircraft operations such as Boeing 737 & 747, double-decker, and A-300 Airbus, etc. The government of Pakistan has designated land in Gwadar for the construction of a new international airport which is located in Gurandani, 26km away from Gwadar (Ministry of Planning, Development, and Reform, 2022).

Table 5. New Gwadar Airport (Ministry of Planning, Development, and Reform, 2022)

#	Project Name	Length (Acres)	Estimated Cost (US $ Million)
1	New Gwadar International Airport	4,300	230

Pipeline

The main purpose of the construction of pipeline network is to facilitate the movement of crude oil and liquefied natural gas (LNG) from countries in the Middle East and Iran to the Xinjiang province of China via Gwadar, Pakistan (Kong, 2015) and lower transportation costs and safer delivery due to its proximity to Gulf oil routes (Alam et al., 2019). Pak-Arab Refinery Limited (Parco) intends to build a refinery in the region of Baluchistan with a capacity to refine 2,50,000 barrels per day. Likewise, through the construction of a pipeline, refined and purified crude oil will be transported to Western China via the shortest transit route with a total distance of 3,600 km. Furthermore, Chinese companies also expressed their interest in setting-up plants in Gwadar, Pakistan. Additionally, Iran has also indicated an interest in the construction of a crude oil refinery in Gwadar, Baluchistan, with a throughput of barrels 400,000 per day. This will help both countries Pakistan and

China to fulfill their energy needs (Menhas et al., 2022). The following section presents the traditional transportation routes of oil transportation from targeted countries to China.

CHINA'S IMPORT OF OIL

China's energy demands have increased over the past few years due to the country's growing economy, and this trend is likely to continue in the future (Sheu & Kundu, 2018). The table 6, shows China's import of oil from Saudi Arabia, Iraq, Angola, Oman, Kuwait, and the United Arab Emirates (OEC, 2022). These are the top six countries that account for more than fifty percent of the country's energy needs.

Table 6. China's Import of Oil (OEC, 2022)

	2016	2017	2018	2019	2020
Saudi Arabia	14.4	13.3	13.3	17.3	16.4
Iraq	9.87	8.97	10.1	10.3	11.3
Angola	14	13.9	12.1	10.4	8.07
Oman	10.3	8.05	7.79	7.11	7.53
Kuwait	4.47	4.6	5.34	4.67	5.26
UAE	3.58	2.7	3	1.94	5.72

The following figure (8) illustrates the contribution of listed countries in fulfilling China's more than fifty percent energy needs. It shows that on average between (2016-2020), 14.94 percent of Saudis contributions, 10.108 percent of Iraq contribution, 11.694 percent of Angola contribution, 8.156 of Oman's contribution, 4.868 of Kuwait's contribution and 3.38 percent contributions of UAE in fulfilling China's need of oil petroleum annually (OEC, 2022).

Figure 8. China's Import of Crude Petroleum from 2016-2020 (OEC, 2022)

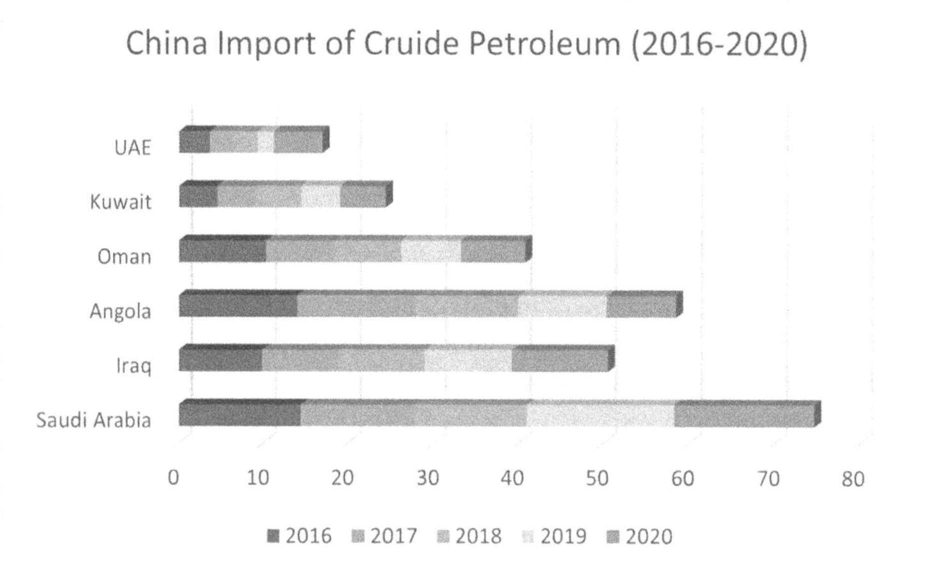

The figure (9) demonstrates China's investments in the import of oil from Saudi Arabia which is around US $118.9 billion, US $79.88 billion from Iraq, US $90.2 billion from Angola, US $62.4 billion from Oman, US $38.79 billion from Kuwait, and US $25.75 billion from the United Arab Emirates. It indicates that in the year 2016-2020 China invested around US$ 415 billion in the import of oil from the listed countries (OEC, 2022).

Figure 9. China's Investment in Crude Petroleum (OEC, 2022)

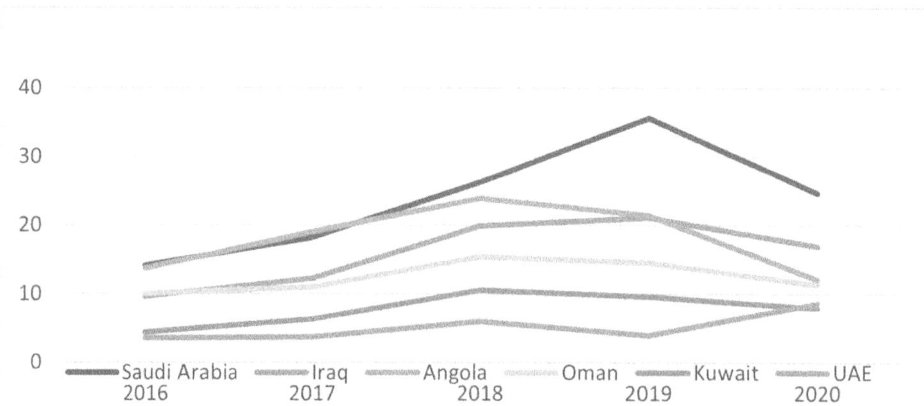

TRADITIONAL ROUTES OF OIL TRADE

This section presents the existing transportation routes of crude petroleum from targeted ports in Saudi Arabia, Iraq, Angola, Oman, Kuwait, and the United Arab Emirates to Shanghai Port, China. Shanghai is the world's largest port since 2010, when it surpassed Singapore's Port. Therefore, Shanghai port, China has been taken as a destination port for this research study. Furthermore, it represents the distance, cost, and travel time of crude petroleum shipment from targeted ports of listed countries to Shanghai, China.

Current Distance Between Origin and Destination Ports

Table 7. Distance Between Ports

Origin Port	Country	Destination Port	Country	Distance in NM	Distance in Kilometer (Km)
Jeddah, Islamic	Saudi Arabia	Shanghai	China	7341	7341 x1.852= 13,595
Basrah	Iraq			7139	7139 x1.852= 13,221
Estrela Oil Field	Angola			11093	11093 x1.852= 20,544
Salalah	Oman			6270	6270 x1.852= 11,612
Shuwaikh	Kuwait			7094	7094 x1.852= 13,138
Fateh Oil Terminal	UAE			6613	6613 x1.852= 12,247

The table (7) depicts the total distance of existing routes from Jeddah Islamic Port, Saudi Arabia, Basrah Port, Iraq, Estrela Oil Field, Angola, Salalah Port, Oman, Shuwaikh Port, Kuwait, Fateh Oil Terminal, UAE to Shanghai, China. The sea distance of current routes has been taken from online software (sea-distances.org). The sea distance is converted from nautical miles to kilometers by multiplying it by 1.852.

Transit Time

The table (8) illustrates the total transit time of existing routes from Jeddah Islamic Port, Saudi Arabia, Basrah Port, Iraq, Estrela Oil Field, Angola, Salalah Port, Oman, Shuwaikh Port, Kuwait, Fateh Oil Terminal, UAE to Shanghai, China. The transit time is converted from hours to days by dividing it by 24. The cargo ship's travel time is calculated using online software (sea-distances.org) with an average speed of 10 knots.

Table 8. Transit Time

Origin Port	Country	Destination Port	Country	Time in Hours	Time in Days
Jeddah, Islamic	Saudi Arabia	Shanghai	China	744	744/24 = 31
Basrah	Iraq			720	720/24 = 30
Estrela Oil Field	Angola			1104	1104/24 =46
Salalah	Oman			624	624/24 = 26
Shuwaikh	Kuwait			720	720/24 = 30
Fateh Oil Terminal	UAE			672	672/24 = 28

Shipping Cost

The table (9) presents the estimated cost of oil transportation via traditional routes from targeted countries to China. The cost of a very large crude container (VLCC) is estimated at US $ 20,250 per day for sea travel. However, the cost of miscellaneous expenses such as insurance, tolls, loading/ off-loading, and port expenses are varying from country to country, and port to port is not added in this study. The shipping cost of different freight forwarders varies due to route differences; therefore, the average cost is used to determine the shipping cost for all routes. The shipping cost of sea freight is taken from Hellenic shipping. These prices are valid for one month and were obtained in July 2022. The total estimated cost is calculated by multiplying travel days with the VLCC cost per day.

Table 9. Shipping Cost

Origin Port	Country	Destination Port	Country	Travel Days	Estimated Cost
Jeddah, Islamic	Saudi Arabia	Shanghai	China	31	US $ 627750
Basrah	Iraq			30	US $ 607500
Estrela Oil Field	Angola			46	US $ 931500
Salalah	Oman			26	US $ 526500
Shuwaikh	Kuwait			30	US $ 607500
Fateh Oil Terminal	UAE			28	US $ 567000

CPEC ROUTES OF OIL TRADE

This section presents the CPEC routes of crude petroleum from target ports in Saudi Arabia, Iraq, Angola, Oman, Kuwait, and the United Arab Emirates to Shanghai Port, China. Moreover, it also shows the distance, cost, and travel time of crude petroleum shipment from targeted ports to Gwadar, Pakistan, and then Xinjiang, China.

Distance from Target Ports to Gwadar

The table (10) illustrates the total distance of CPEC routes from Jeddah Islamic Port, Saudi Arabia, Basrah Port, Iraq, Estrela Oil Field, Angola, Salalah Port, Oman, Shuwaikh Port, Kuwait, Fateh Oil Terminal, UAE to Gwadar, Pakistan. Moreover, the Oil pipeline from Gwadar port to Kashgar, China adds 3,600 km more in the total distance. The sea distance of current routes has been taken from online software (sea-distances.org). The sea distance is converted from nautical miles to kilometers by multiplying it by 1.852. The total distance has been calculated by adding both the maritime route and pipeline route distance.

Table 10. Distance between Gwadar Port

Origin Port	Country	Destination Port	Country	Distance in Nm	Distance in Kilometer (Km)	CPEC Pipeline Km	Total Distance in Km
Jeddah, Islamic	Saudi Arabia	Gwadar	Pakistan	2127	2127 x1.852= 3,939	3600	7539
Basrah	Iraq	Gwadar	Pakistan	986	986 x1.852= 1,826	3600	5426
Estrela Oil Field	Angola	Gwadar	Pakistan	6985	6985 x1.852= 12,936	3600	16536
Salalah	Oman	Gwadar	Pakistan	755	755 x1.852= 1,398	3600	4998
Shuwaikh	Kuwait	Gwadar	Pakistan	942	942 x1.852= 1,745	3600	5345
Fateh Oil Terminal	UAE	Gwadar	Pakistan	621	461 x1.852= 854	3600	4454

Transit Time via CPEC Routes

The table (11) Shows the total transit time of oil shipment via CPEC routes from Jeddah Islamic Port, Saudi Arabia, Basrah Port, Iraq, Estrela Oil Field, Angola, Salalah Port, Oman, Shuwaikh Port, Kuwait, Fateh Oil Terminal, UAE to Gwadar, Pakistan. Furthermore, two more days will be required to ship crude oil via pipeline with a transmission rate of one million b/d from Gwadar, Pakistan to Kashgar, China (Bhutta, 2018). The total transit time is calculated by adding both the maritime and pipeline routes. Likewise, the transit time is converted from hours to days by dividing it by 24. The cargo ship's travel time is calculated using online software (sea-distances.org) with an average speed of 10 knots.

Table 11. Transit Time Via CPEC

Origin Port	Country	Destination Port	Country	Time in Hours	Time in Days	Pipeline	Total Transit Time in Days
Jeddah, Islamic	Saudi Arabia	Gwadar	Pakistan	216	216/24 = 9	2	11
Basrah	Iraq			96	96/24 = 4	2	6
Estrela Oil Field	Angola			696	696/24 = 29	2	31
Salalah	Oman			72	72/24 = 3	2	5
Shuwaikh	Kuwait			96	96/24 = 4	2	6
Fateh Oil Terminal	UAE			48	48/24 = 2	2	4

Shipping Cost via CPEC

The table (12) demonstrates the total estimated cost of oil transportation via CPEC routes from targeted countries to Gwadar, Pakistan, and then China. Moreover, the additional cost of oil shipment from Gwadar to Kashgar via pipeline is not added in the total cost as it's a one-time investment with an estimated cost of USD 10 billion (Bhutta, 2018). However, the cost of total expenses such as security charges, pumping, and maintenance charges of the pipeline couldn't be identified at this stage but it is estimated as on average USD 5000 per day for this research study. The cost of a very large crude container (VLCC) is estimated at US $ 20,250 per day for sea travel except other expenses such as insurance, tolls, loading/ off-loading, port expenses are varying from country to country and port to port is not added in this study. The shipping cost of different freight forwarders varies due to route differences; therefore, the average cost is used to determine the shipping cost for all routes. The shipping cost of sea freight is taken from Hellenic shipping. These prices are valid for one month and were obtained in July 2022. The total estimated cost is calculated by multiplying ship travel days with VLCC cost per day and pipeline travel days with an estimated average cost.

Table 12. Shipping Cost via CPEC Routes

Origin Port	Country	Destination Port	Country	Ship Travel Days	VLCC Cost P/d	Total Cost of Ship Travelling	Pipeline Travel Days	Avg. Cost P/d	Total Estimated Cost
Jeddah, Islamic	Saudi Arabia	Gwadar	Pakistan	9	20,250	US $ 182250	2	USD 5,000	USD 192250
Basrah	Iraq			4	20,250	US $ 81000	2	USD 5,000	USD 91000
Estrela Oil Field	Angola			29	20,250	US $ 587250	2	USD 5,000	USD 687250
Salalah	Oman			3	20,250	US $ 60750	2	USD 5,000	USD 70750
Shuwaikh	Kuwait			4	20,250	US $ 81000	2	USD 5,000	USD 91000
Fateh Oil Terminal	UAE			2	20,250	US $ 40500	2	USD 5,000	USD 50500

RESULTS

This section demonstrates the comparison of both routes (current routes and CPEC routes) in terms of distance, time, and cost. The results indicate a significant difference with respect to distance, shipping time, and cost from origin ports to China via Gwadar port, Pakistan.

Distance Comparison

The following table 13, demonstrates the distance difference between origin ports to China and origin ports to China via Gwadar port. The results have been calculated by subtracting the new CPEC routes from old routes. The comparison section illustrates the distance difference in kilometers and the difference in percentages. It indicates that the distance will reduce by 45 percent from Jeddah Islamic Port to China via new routes and 59 percent from Basrah port, 20 percent from Estrela Oil Field, 57 percent by Salalah port, 59 percent by Shuwaikh port, and 64 percent from Fateh Oil Terminal to China via Gwadar port.

Table 13. Distance Comparison

Port Origin and Country		Destination Port Shanghai		Destination Port Gwadar			Comparisons	
Port	**Country**	**Distance in nm**	**Distance in Km**	**Distance in nm**	**Distance in Km**	**Total Distance in Km**	**Difference in Km's**	**Difference in Percentage**
Jeddah, Islamic	Saudi Arabia	7341	13,595	2127	3,939	7539	6,056	45
Basrah	Iraq	7139	13,221	986	1,826	5426	7,795	59
Estrela Oil Field	Angola	11093	20,544	6985	12,936	16536	4,008	20
Salalah	Oman	6270	11,612	755	1,398	4998	6,614	57
Shuwaikh	Kuwait	7094	13,138	942	1,745	5345	7,793	59
Fateh Oil Terminal	UAE	6613	12,247	461	854	4454	7,793	64

Shipping Time Comparison

The following table 14, reveals the difference in shipping time from origin ports to China and origin ports to China via Gwadar port. The total shipping time in the day's section presents the total time of ship traveling and pipeline traveling. The results have been calculated by subtracting the new CPEC routes from old routes. The comparison section demonstrates the time difference in days and the difference in percentages. It demonstrates that the ship travelling will reduce by 65 percent from Jeddah Islamic Port to China via new routes and 80 percent from Basrah port, 33 percent from Estrela Oil Field, 81 percent by Salalah port, 80 percent by Shuwaikh port, and 86 percent accordingly from Fateh Oil Terminal to China via Gwadar port.

Table 14. Shipping Time Difference

Port Origin and Country		Destination Port Shanghai		Destination Port Gwadar			Comparisons	
Port	**Country**	**Time in Hours**	**Shipping Time in Days**	**Time in Hours**	**Shipping Time in Days**	**Total Shipping Time in Days**	**Difference in Days**	**Difference in Percentage**
Jeddah, Islamic	Saudi Arabia	744	31	216	9	11	20	65
Basrah	Iraq	720	30	96	4	6	24	80
Estrela Oil Field	Angola	1104	46	696	29	31	15	33
Salalah	Oman	624	26	72	3	5	21	81
Shuwaikh	Kuwait	720	30	96	4	6	24	80
Fateh Oil Terminal	UAE	672	28	48	2	4	24	86

Cost Comparison

The following table 14, presents the difference in cost from origin ports to China and origin ports to China via Gwadar port. The total estimated cost section presents the total cost of a ship traveling and the average cost of pipeline traveling. The results have been calculated by subtracting the new CPEC routes from old routes. The comparison section determines the cost difference in USD and the difference in percentages. It shows that the shipping cost will reduce by 69 percent from Jeddah Islamic Port to China via new routes and 85 percent from Basrah port, 26 percent from Estrela Oil Field, 87 percent by Salalah port, 85 percent by Shuwaikh port, and 91 percent accordingly from Fateh Oil Terminal to China via Gwadar port.

Table 15. Cost Comparison

Port Origin and Country		Destination Port Shanghai	Destination Port Gwadar			Comparisons	
Port	**Country**	**Estimated Cost in USD**	**Cost of Ship Travelling in USD**	**Avg Cost of Pipeline/ Day**	**Total Estimated Cost in USD**	**Cost Difference in USD**	**Difference in Percentage**
Jeddah, Islamic	Saudi Arabia	627750	182250	5,000	192250	435500	69
Basrah	Iraq	607500	81000	5,000	91000	516500	85
Estrela Oil Field	Angola	931500	587250	5,000	687250	244250	26
Salalah	Oman	526500	60750	5,000	70750	455750	87
Shuwaikh	Kuwait	607500	81000	5,000	91000	516500	85
Fateh Oil Terminal	UAE	567000	40500	5,000	50500	516500	91

PESTLE ANALYSIS OF CPEC

The PESTLE analysis is performed in this research study by focusing on the factors that government officials, planners and builders need to consider for long-term sustainability of this project (Capobianco et al., 2021). PESTLE analysis is used to classify challenges with respect to "political, economic, social, technological, legal, and environmental" (Sarjito, 2020).

Figure 10. PESTLE Analysis (Sarjito, 2020)

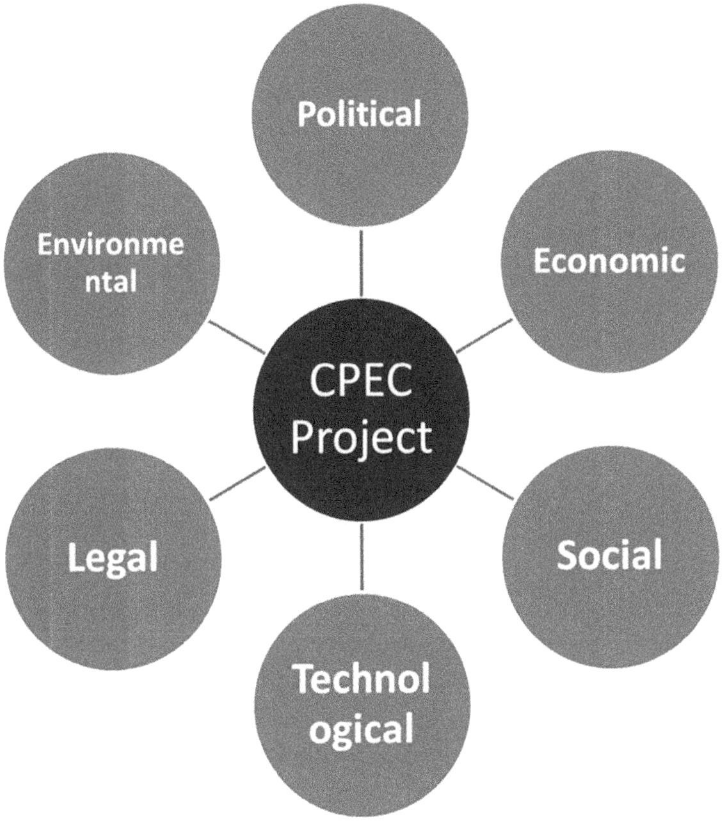

Political

Political factors are the activities associated with government policy and regulatory processes that have the potential to influence things. Political changes in Pakistan are anticipated to have an impact on China's $62 billion investment in Pakistan's CPEC. The recent change of Pakistan's prime minister and the flood in Pakistan raise some doubts about the future of the CPEC. However, China's spokesperson assured that the recent political shifts within Pakistan would have no consequence on this joint venture.

Economic

The China-Pakistan Economic Corridor (CPEC) will provide an amazing opportunity to enhance the economic and safety condition of Pakistan. The economic position of Pakistan would be improved in the region and its business situation will change with the development of a massive project. Furthermore, the construction of CPEC will promote Pakistan's economic growth by reducing energy-related issues and improving its infrastructure through the development of a transportation network.

Social

CPEC is a fantastic chance for Pakistan to enhance its strategic and economic position, with social advantages. The expansion of the CPEC would be beneficial for Pakistan across all economic and social aspects. The improvement of trade routes and diplomatic ties between Pakistan and its neighboring countries is the only way in which the progress of CPEC would benefit the country economically and socially. Likewise, the development of CPEC represents a golden chance to overcome their mutual fear of war. In addition, the construction of road and rail infrastructure from China's Kashgar to Pakistan's Gwadar is a significant source of change in the region.

Technological

The initial emphasis of this project is the development of two primary components of CPEC, such as infrastructure development with the aim to improve Pakistan's transportation system through the construction of motorways as well as a national railway network and secondly, the advancement of the energy industry to alleviate Pakistan's electrical issues. After the completion of these two components, the government intends to implement an advanced technological system across the entire project. China will assist the corporate and public sectors in educating Pakistani youths in a range of critical fields, including artificial intelligence, automation, biotechnology, machine learning, and renewable energy, etc.

Legal

China and its financial institutions have legally invested $62 billion across multiple sectors in Pakistan. This initiative is officially recognized as representing the different provinces of Pakistan i.e. Gwadar, Baluchistan, Gilgit–Baltistan, Khyber Pakhtunkhwa (KPK), and Sindh are the key development areas of the CPEC. There would be a number of legal issues that could arise during the expansion of this project however they could be resolved in a proper manner. In addition, the mechanism, which can be legislative or judicial, as well as an arbitration system between the disputing parties, will be introduced for the expansion of this massive project.

Environmental

The construction of New special trade zones and industries will have an impact on the environment, however the government is working to mitigate such effects by introducing new measures and implementing regulations that promote a green and sustainable environment. The construction of railway and highway networks inside the country would assist in the reduction of harmful gases such as carbon dioxide (CO_2) from the transportation sector due to short transit routes. Furthermore, the CPEC project is an eco-friendly project due to its proximity to other nations via short and safe transit routes.

CONCLUSION

The construction of the China-Pakistan Economic Corridor (CPEC) is beneficial for both nations i.e. Pakistan and China, nevertheless, the results indicate that China will gain the most rewards from it. The analysis of route distances demonstrates that China will gain a significant reduction in cost and delivery time that will further promote a sustainable environment. The results present the comparison of both routes i.e. traditional routes and new CPEC routes of crude petroleum. Currently, the routes being used for the transportation of crude petroleum are very long and time taking in contrast, the new CPEC routes are very short and safe. It demonstrates that the total cost will reduce by USD 2.68 million per shipment and the delivery time will reduce by 20 days from Jeddah Islamic Port, Saudi Arabia, 24 days from Basrah Port, Iraq, 15 days from Estrela Oil Field, Angola, 21 days from Salalah Port, Oman, 24 days from Shuwaikh Port, Kuwait, and 24 days from Fateh Oil Terminal, United Arab Emirates to China via Gwadar Port. Furthermore, the Gwadar port also provides direct access to the Arabian Sea, connecting China with countries in Africa and the Middle East via short and secure transportation routes resulting in saving billion dollars annually on transportation costs. The CPEC project is in the development stage therefore, it is difficult to get specific transit route, schedule, and cost information at the moment however, ports that have been taken in this research study are the main ports of oil transportation.

REFERENCES

Abdel Warith, K., Kandil, A., Haddock, J., & Shaaban, K. (2019). A new framework for addressing high-level decisions related to sustainable transportation development. *International Journal of Sustainable Transportation, 14*(11), 843–859. doi:10.1080/15568318.2019.1639861

Ahmad, R., & Mi, H. (2017). China-Pakistan Economic Corridor and Its Social Implication on Pakistan: How Will CPEC Boost Pakistan's Infrastructures and Overcome the Challenges? *Arts and Social Sciences Journal, 8*(2). Advance online publication. doi:10.4172/2151-6200.1000265

Alam, G., Al-Amin, A., Forhad, A., & Mubarak, M. (2020). Does the private university sector exploit sustainable residential life in the name of supporting the fourth industrial revolution? *Technological Forecasting and Social Change, 159*, 120200. doi:10.1016/j.techfore.2020.120200

Alam, K., Li, X., & Baig, S. (2019). Impact of Transport Cost and Travel Time on Trade under China-Pakistan Economic Corridor (CPEC). *Journal of Advanced Transportation, 2019*, 1–16. doi:10.1155/2019/7178507

Anwar, S., Khan, M., & Sarwar, A. (2017). Minhas Majeed Khan, et al. (eds.). China-Pakistan Economic Corridor—A Game Changer. Islamabad, Pakistan: Institute of Strategic Studies Islamabad (ISSI). 2016. iii+164 Pages. Pak Rupees 500.00 (Hardback). The Pakistan Development Review, 56(1), 79-82. doi:10.30541/v56i1pp.79-82

Bhutta, Z. (2018). From Gwadar-Kashgar: Crude oil pipeline requires $10 billion investment. *The Express Tribune*. Retrieved 29 August 2022, from https://tribune.com.pk/story/1712888/gwadar-kashgar-crude-oil-pipeline-requires-10-billion-investment

Capobianco, N., Basile, V., Loia, F., & Vona, R. (2021). Toward a Sustainable Decommissioning of Offshore Platforms in the Oil and Gas Industry: A PESTLE Analysis. *Sustainability, 13*(11), 6266. doi:10.3390u13116266

Chowdhary, M. (2015). China's Billion-Dollar Gateway To The Subcontinent: Pakistan May Be Opening A Door It Cannot Close. *Forbes*, 1–3.

Coyne, H. (2020). When Kyoto Failed, Paris Stepped Up: How the Paris Agreement Changed Global Climate Negotiations. *Global Affairs Review, 1*(1). Advance online publication. doi:10.51330/gar.0020116

CPIC Global. (2022). *China-Pakistan Economic Corridor: CPEC Projects & Progress*. CPIC Global. Retrieved 18 August 2022, from https://www.cpicglobal.com/pakistan-overview/cpec/

ESCAP. (2017). China's "One Belt, One Road" Initiative: An ESCAP Report. *Population and Development Review*, *43*(3), 583–587. doi:10.1111/padr.12089

Garceau, T., Atkinson-Palombo, C., Garrick, N., Outlaw, J., McCahill, C., & Ahangari, H. (2013). Evaluating selected costs of automobile-oriented transportation systems from a sustainability perspective. *Research In Transportation Business & Management*, *7*, 43–53. doi:10.1016/j.rtbm.2013.02.002

Hong, P. (2016). Jointly Building the 'Belt and Road' towards the Sustainable Development Goals. SSRN *Electronic Journal*. doi:10.2139/ssrn.2812893

Hosain, M., & Hossain, M. (2019). *One Belt One Road initiative: A Revolution on Regional and Global Development*. Academic Press.

Ibrahim, H. (2017). *China-Pakistan Economic Corridor (Part-1)*. https://www.jukuko.com/china-pakistan-economic-corridor-part-1/

Iqbal, K. (2017). *Significance and Security of CPEC: A Pakistani Perspective*. Retrieved 1 September 2022, from https://www.ciis.org.cn/english/ESEARCHPROJECTS/Articles/202007/t20200715_3600.html

Jamil, S., Malik, M., & Shah, S. (2019). *China-Pakistan economic cooperation: Trade, investment, energy, infrastructure and Gwadar Port*. doi:10.31703/ger.2019(IV-II).05

Joshi, M. (2017). The Eco-Politics of CPEC and India. SSRN *Electronic Journal*. doi:10.2139/ssrn.2982942

Khadim, Z., Batool, I., & Bilal Lodhi, M. (2021). China–Pakistan Economic Corridor, Logistics Developments and Economic Growth in Pakistan. *Logistics*, *5*(2), 35. doi:10.3390/logistics5020035

Khan, S., & Liu, G. (2018). The China–Pakistan Economic Corridor (CPEC): Challenges and prospects. *Area Development And Policy*, *4*(4), 466–473. doi:10.1080/23792949.2018.1534549

Khan, Z., Changgang, G., & Afzaal, M. (2019). China-Pakistan Economic Corridor at the Cross Intersection of China, Central Asia and South Asia: Opportunities for Regional Economic Growth. *Chinese Economy*, *53*(2), 200–215. doi:10.1080/10971475.2019.1688005

Kong, L. (2015). The Belt and Road Initiative and China's Foreign Policy Toward Its Territorial and Boundary Disputes. *China Quarterly Of International Strategic Studies, 01*(02), 325–345. doi:10.1142/S2377740015500165

Li, K., Jin, M., Qi, G., Shi, W., & Ng, A. (2017). Logistics as a driving force for development under the Belt and Road Initiative – the Chinese model for developing countries. *Transport Reviews, 38*(4), 457–478. doi:10.1080/01441647.2017.1365276

Litman, T. (2007). Developing Indicators for Comprehensive and Sustainable Transport Planning. *Transportation Research Record: Journal of the Transportation Research Board, 2017*(1), 10–15. doi:10.3141/2017-02

Mahapatra, S., & Ratha, K. (2016). The 21st Conference of the Parties Climate Summit in Paris: A Slippery Slope. *Journal of International Development, 28*(6), 991–996. doi:10.1002/jid.3221

Maizland, L. (2021). *China's Fight Against Climate Change and Environmental Degradation*. Council on Foreign Relations. Retrieved 18 August 2022, from https://www.cfr.org/backgrounder/china-climate-change-policies-environmental-degradation

Mehar, A. (2017). Infrastructure development, CPEC and FDI in Pakistan: Is there any connection? *Transnational Corporations Review, 9*(3), 232–241. doi:10.1080/19186444.2017.1362857

Menhas, R., Mahmood, S., Tanchangya, P., Safdar, M., & Hussain, S. (2022). *Sustainable Development under Belt and Road Initiative: A Case Study of China-Pakistan Economic Corridor's Socio-Economic Impact on Pakistan*. Academic Press.

Ministry of Planning. Pakistan. (2022). *Projects Under CPEC | China-Pakistan Economic Corridor (CPEC) Authority Official Website*. Retrieved 24 August 2022, from https://cpec.gov.pk/energy

Ministry of Planning, Development and Reform. (2017). *Long Term Plan for China-Pakistan Economic Corridor (2017-2030)*. Retrieved 1 September 2022, from https://www.pc.gov.pk/uploads/cpec/CPEC-LTP.pdf

Mubarik, M., Devadason, E., & Govindaraju, C. (2020). Human capital and export performance of small and medium enterprises in Pakistan. *International Journal of Social Economics, 47*(5), 643–662. doi:10.1108/IJSE-03-2019-0198

Mubarik, M., Kazmi, S., & Zaman, S. (2021). Application of gray DEMATEL-ANP in green-strategic sourcing. *Technology in Society, 64*, 101524. doi:10.1016/j.techsoc.2020.101524

Mubarik, M., Naghavi, N., & Mubarak, M. (2019). Impact of Supplier Relational Capital on Supply Chain Performance in Pakistani Textile Industry. *Asian Economic And Financial Review*, *9*(3), 318–328. doi:10.18488/journal.aefr.2019.93.318.328

Naz, A., & Ali, F. (2018). Gwadar Port: As an Economic hub for Maritime Trade in the World Corridor (CPEC). *Journal Of Business And Social Review In Emerging Economies*, *4*(1), 7–16. doi:10.26710/jbsee.v4i1.352

OEC. (2022). *Where does import from? (2016, 2017, 2018, 2019, 2020)*. OEC - The Observatory of Economic Complexity. Retrieved 25 August 2022, from https://oec.world/en/visualize/tree_map/hs92/import/chn/all/52709/2016.2017.2018.2019.2020/.

Oswald Beiler, M. (2012). Measuring Sustainable Transportation: Incorporating Social Sustainability Indicators into Transportation Rating Systems. *The International Journal Of Environmental Sustainability*, *8*(1), 101–114. doi:10.18848/2325-1077/CGP/v08i01/55038

Parton, K. (2013). Economic, Social and Environmental Sustainability of the Murray-Darling Basin. *The International Journal of Environmental, Cultural, Economic, and Social Sustainability Annual Review*, *8*(1), 29–43. doi:10.18848/1832-2077/CGP/v08/55141

Reza, S., Mubarik, M., Naghavi, N., & Rub Nawaz, R. (2020). Relationship marketing and third-party logistics: Evidence from hotel industry. *Journal Of Hospitality And Tourism Insights*, *3*(3), 371–393. doi:10.1108/JHTI-07-2019-0095

Rizvi, H. (2015). The China-Pakistan Economic Corridor: Regional Cooperation and Socio-Economic Development. *Strategic Studies*, 1-17.

Sarjito, A. (2020). PESTLE Analysis of Production Management Landing Platform Dock Warship PT PAL Indonesia (Persero) For National Defense. *Advances In Social Sciences Research Journal*, *7*(11), 368–386. doi:10.14738/assrj.711.9329

Shah, A. (2016). Building a Sustainable 'Belt and Road'. *Journal of International Relations and Sustainable Development, 7.*

Shah, Z. (2015) China-Pakistan economic corridor and its importance. Preston University.

Shah Afridi, H., Bibi, S., & Muhammad, B. (2016). The economic viability of gwadar port: An economic hub for maritime trade. *Global Political Review*, *1*(1), 19–31. doi:10.31703/gpr.2016(I-I).03

Shahin, A., & Jaferi, F. (2015). The shortest route for transportation in supply chain by minimum spanning tree. *International Journal Of Logistics Systems And Management, 22*(1), 43. doi:10.1504/IJLSM.2015.070893

Sheu, J., & Kundu, T. (2018). Forecasting time-varying logistics distribution flows in the One Belt-One Road strategic context. *Transportation Research Part E, Logistics and Transportation Review, 117*, 5–22. doi:10.1016/j.tre.2017.03.003

Surahio, M., Gu, S., Mahesar, H., & Soomro, M. (2022). China–Pakistan Economic Corridor: Macro Environmental Factors and Security Challenges. *SAGE Open, 12*(1), 215824402210798. doi:10.1177/21582440221079821

United Nations. (2021). Sustainable Transport. *Sustainable Development.*

Zalengera, C., Blanchard, R., Eames, P., Juma, A., Chitawo, M., & Gondwe, K. (2014). Overview of the Malawi energy situation and A PESTLE analysis for sustainable development of renewable energy. *Renewable & Sustainable Energy Reviews, 38*, 335–347. doi:10.1016/j.rser.2014.05.050

Zhang, Y., & Zhang, H. (2016). "One Belt One Road" Strategy and the Sustainable Development of Asia: The Case of Afghanistan and DPRK. *Destech Transactions on Economics and Management*. doi:10.12783/dtem/icem2016/4051

Zhang, Z. (2011). China's energy security, the Malacca dilemma and responses. *Energy Policy, 39*(12), 7612–7615. doi:10.1016/j.enpol.2011.09.033

Zheng, J., Garrick, N., Atkinson-Palombo, C., McCahill, C., & Marshall, W. (2013). Guidelines on developing performance metrics for evaluating transportation sustainability. *Research In Transportation Business &Amp. Management, 7*, 4–13. doi:10.1016/j.rtbm.2013.02.001

APPENDIX

a) Saudi to Shanghai, China

Figure 11. Jeddah Islamic Port to Shanghai

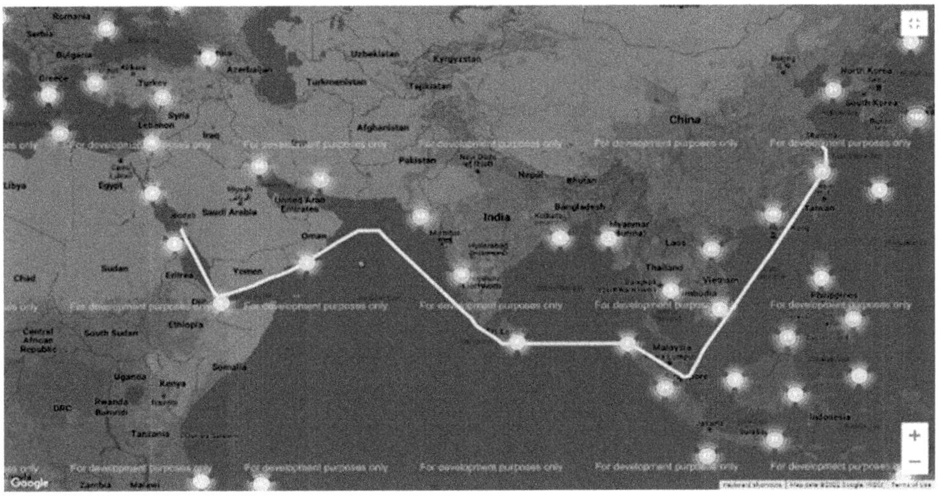

Figure 12. Jeddah Islamic Port to Gwadar Port

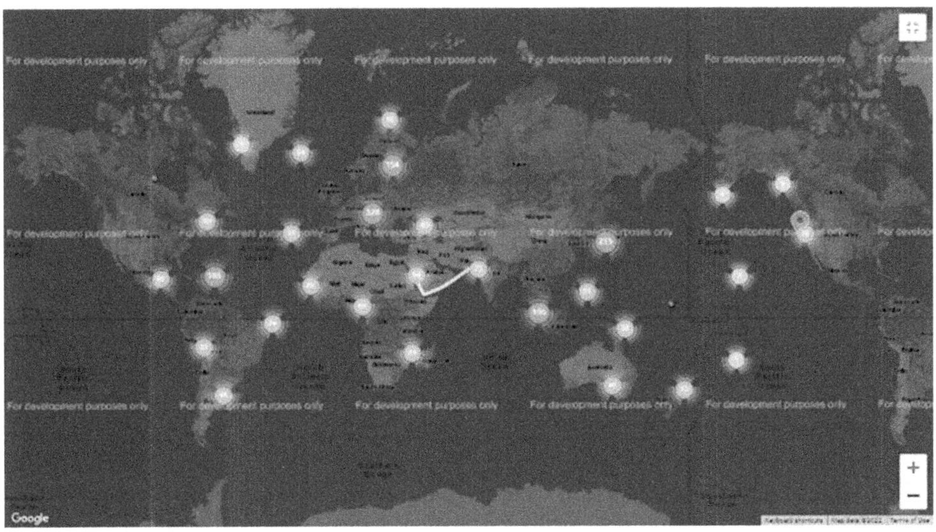

b) Oman to Shanghai, China

Figure 13. Basrah, Oman to Shanghai Port, China

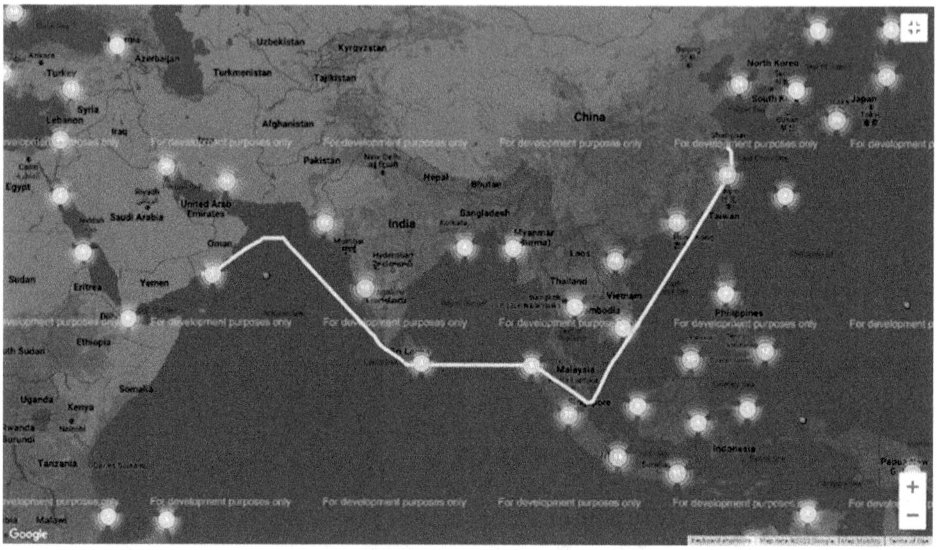

Figure 14. Basra, Oman to Gwadar Port

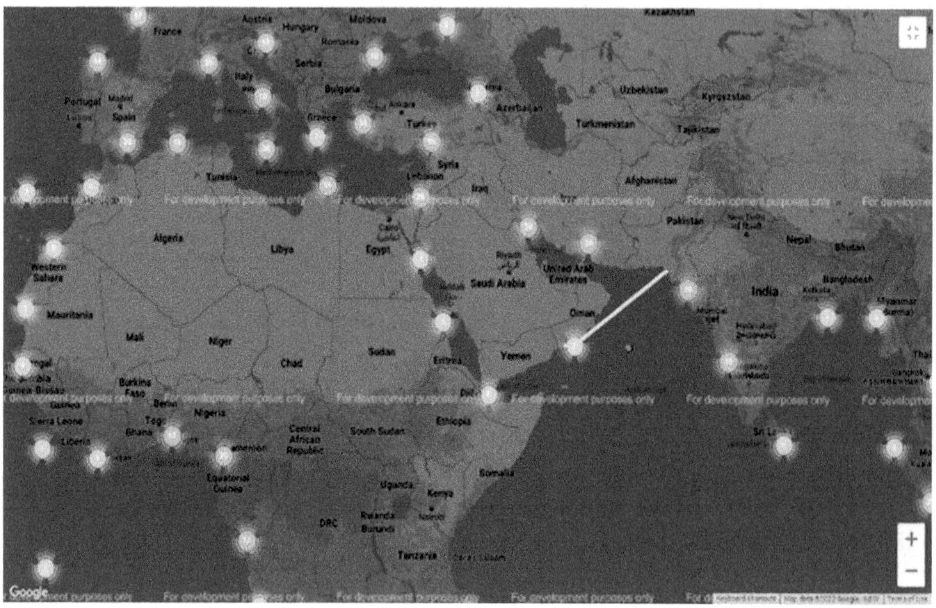

c) UAE to Shanghai, China

Figure 15. UAE to Shanghai, China

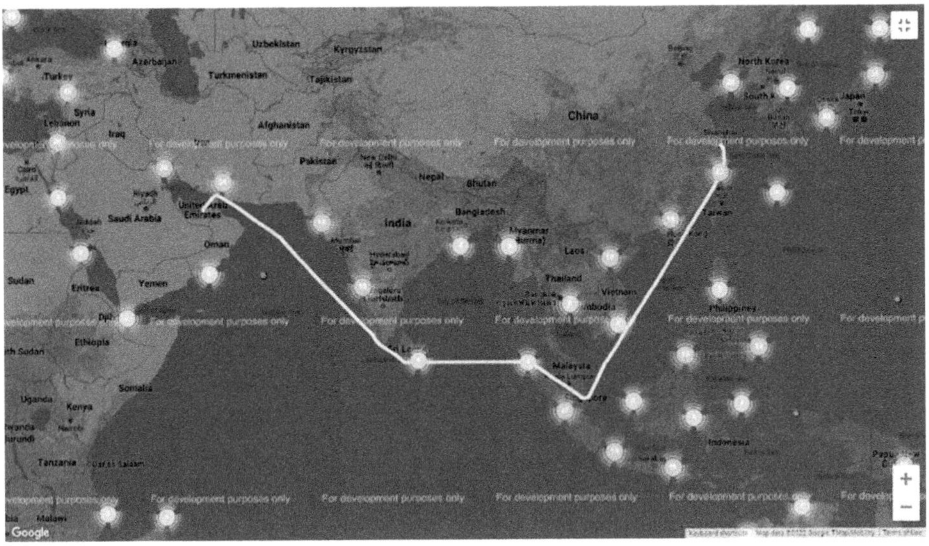

Figure 16. UAE to Gwadar Port

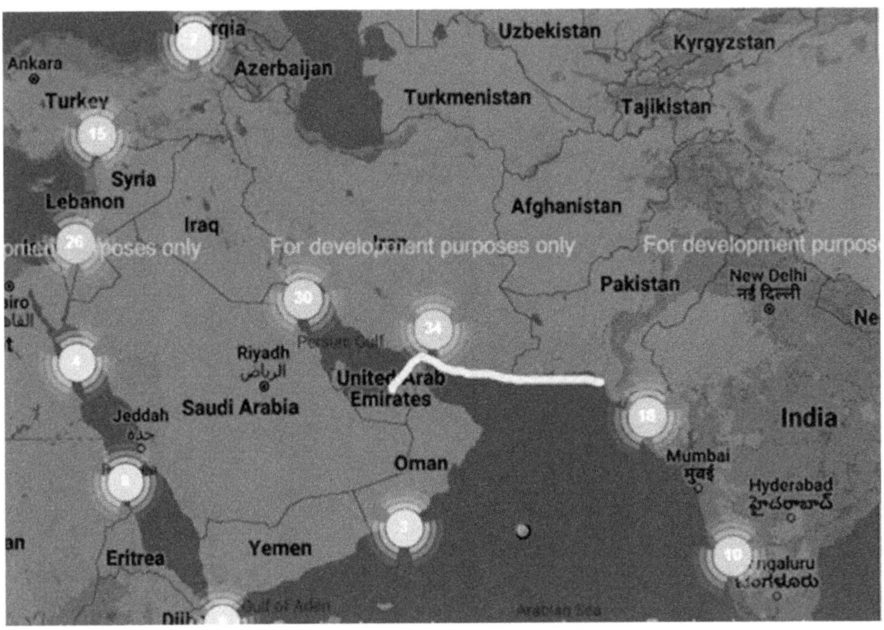

d) Iraq to shanghai

Figure 17 . Iraq to Shanghai

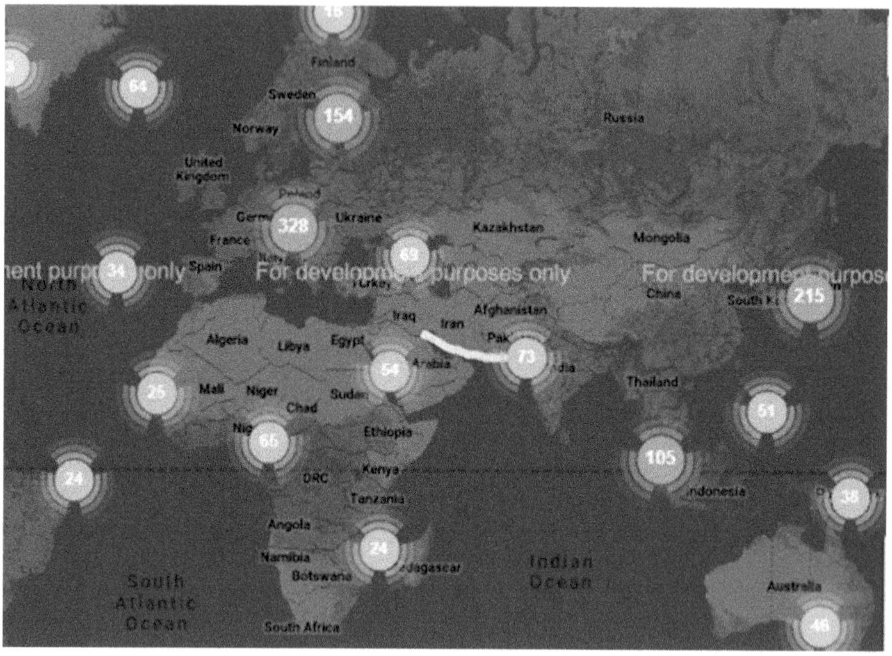

Figure 18. Iraq to Gwadar

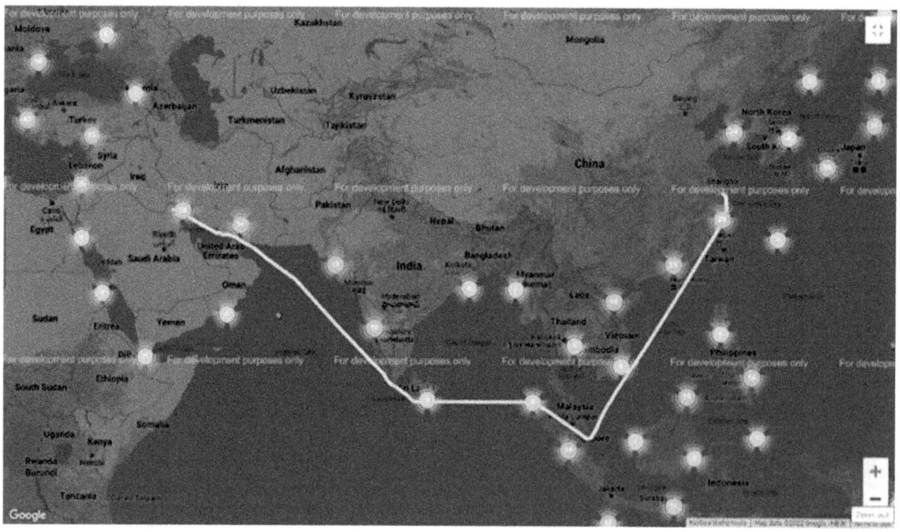

e) Angola to shanghai

Figure 19. Angola to Shanghai

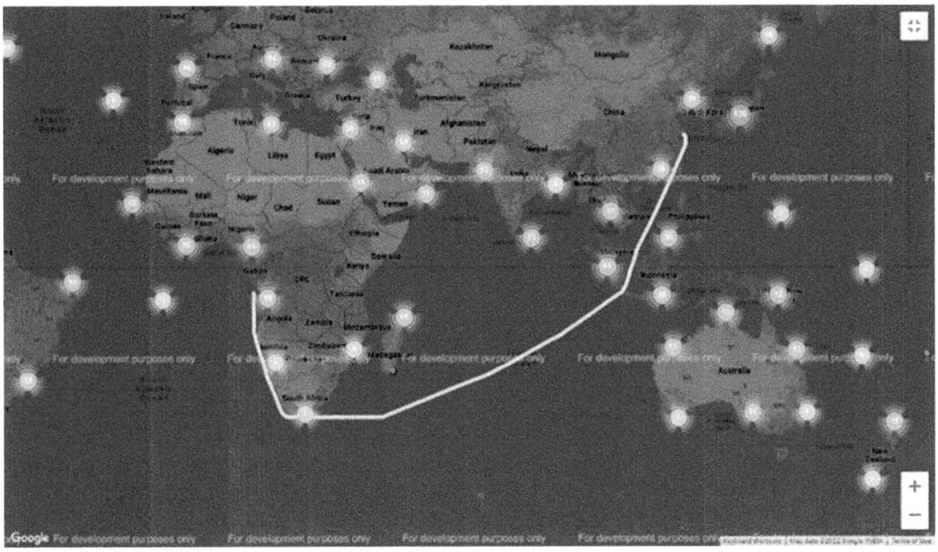

f) Kuwait to Shanghai

Figure 20 Angola to Gwadar

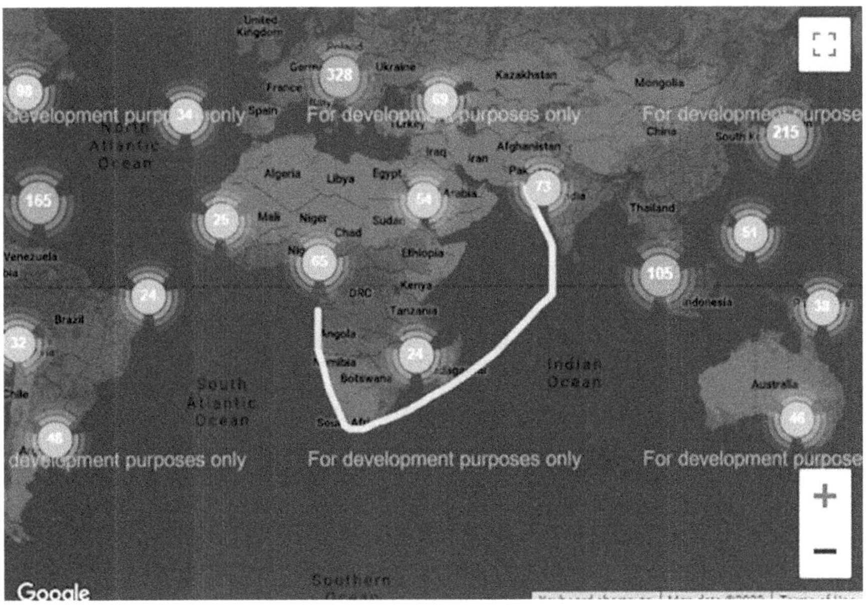

Figure 21. Kuwait to Shanghai

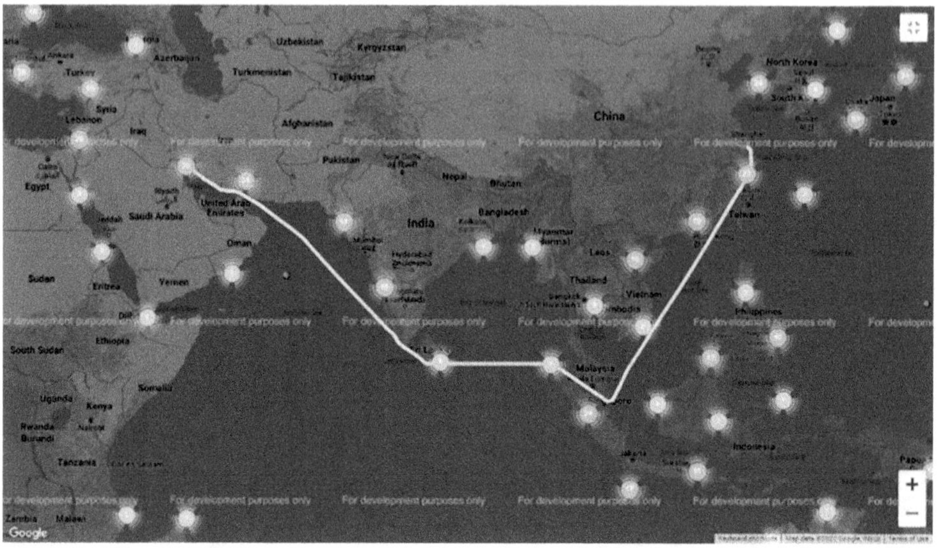

Figure 22. Kuwait to Gwadar

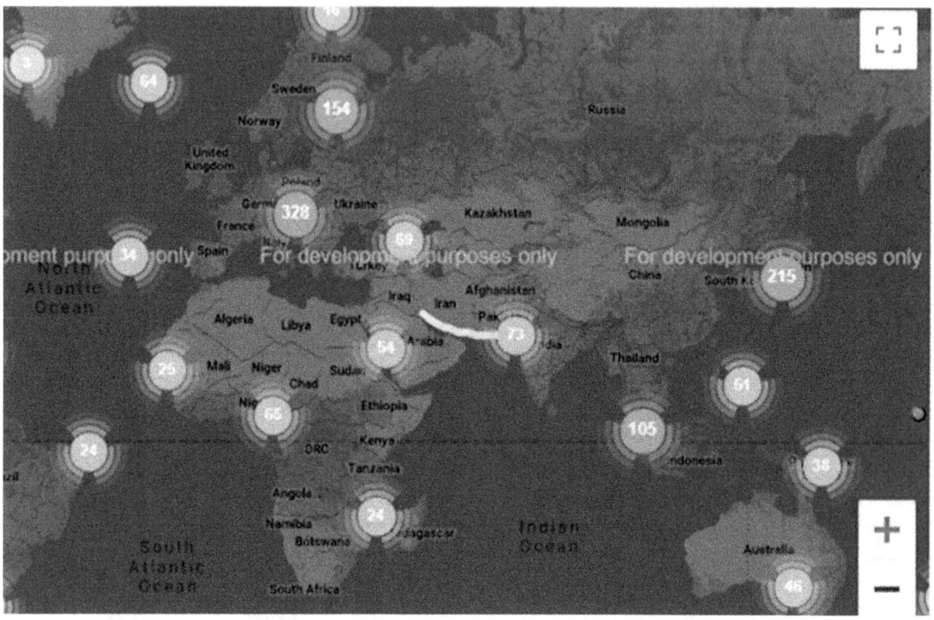

Compilation of References

Ab Malik, M., Omar, E., & Maon, S. (2020). Humanitarian Logistics: A Disaster Relief Operations Framework During Pandemic Covid-19 in Achieving Healthy Communities. *Advances in Business Research International Journal*, *6*(2), 101. doi:10.24191/abrij.v6i2.11114

Abbad, H. (2014). La gestion mutualisée des approvisionnements: Mythe ou réalités? *Logistique & Management*, *22*(2), 41–50. doi:10.1080/12507970.2014.11517051

Abdel Warith, K., Kandil, A., Haddock, J., & Shaaban, K. (2019). A new framework for addressing high-level decisions related to sustainable transportation development. *International Journal of Sustainable Transportation*, *14*(11), 843–859. doi:10.1080/15568318.2019.1639861

Abugabah, A., Nizamuddin, N., & Abuqabbeh, A. (2020). A review of challenges and barriers implementing RFID technology in the Healthcare sector. *Procedia Computer Science*, *170*, 1003–1010. doi:10.1016/j.procs.2020.03.094

Accenture. (2016). *Blockchain Technology: How Banks are Building a Real-Time Global Payment Network*. https://www.accenture.com/_acnmedia/pdf-35/accenture-blockchain-how-banksbuilding-real-time-global-payment-network.pdf

Adams, C., Buck, R., Herzberg, G., Mandel, J., & Mueller, C. (2020). *We are harnessing the power of simplicity in a complex consumer-product environment*. McKinsey.com.

Adams. C., Alldredge. K., Mueller. C., & Whitmore. J. (2020). *Simpler is (sometimes) better: Managing complexity in consumer goods*. McKinsey.com.

Adams, R., Jeanrenaud, S., Bessant, J., Denyer, D., & Overy, P. (2016). Sustainability oriented innovation: A systematic review. *International Journal of Management Reviews*, *18*(2), 180–205. doi:10.1111/ijmr.12068

Aday, S., & Aday, M. S. (2020). Impact of COVID-19 on the food supply chain. *Food Quality and Safety*, *4*(4), 167–180. doi:10.1093/fqsafe/fyaa024

ADEME. (2007). *Calcul des facteurs d'émissions et sources bibliographiques utilisées, Méthode bilan carbone*. Agence de l'Environnement, Mission Interministérielle et de la Maîtrise de l'Energie.

ADEME. (2014). *Documentation des facteurs d'émissions de la base carbone*. Agence de l'Environnement, Mission Interministérielle et de la Maîtrise de l'Energie.

Agan, Y., Acar, M. F., & Borodin, A. (2013). Drivers of environmental processes and their impact on performance: A study of Turkish SMEs. *Journal of Cleaner Production, 51*, 23–33. doi:10.1016/j.jclepro.2012.12.043

Agrawal, P., & Narain, R. (2018). Digital supply chain management: An Overview. *IOP Conference Series. Materials Science and Engineering, 455*(1).

Ahmad, R., & Mi, H. (2017). China-Pakistan Economic Corridor and Its Social Implication on Pakistan: How Will CPEC Boost Pakistan's Infrastructures and Overcome the Challenges? *Arts and Social Sciences Journal, 8*(2). Advance online publication. doi:10.4172/2151-6200.1000265

Ahmad, S., Abdullah, A., & Talib, F. (2020). Lean-green performance management in Indian SMEs: A novel perspective using the best-worst method approach. *Benchmarking, 28*(2), 737–765. doi:10.1108/BIJ-05-2020-0255

Akbari, V., & Shiri, D. (2022). An online optimization approach for post-disaster relief distribution with online blocked edges. *Computers & Operations Research, 137*, 105533. doi:10.1016/j.cor.2021.105533

Akenroye, T. O. (2012). Factors Influencing Innovation in Healthcare: A conceptual synthesis. *The Innovation Journal, 17*(2).

Alam, G., Al-Amin, A., Forhad, A., & Mubarak, M. (2020). Does the private university sector exploit sustainable residential life in the name of supporting the fourth industrial revolution? *Technological Forecasting and Social Change, 159*, 120200. doi:10.1016/j.techfore.2020.120200

Alam, K., Li, X., & Baig, S. (2019). Impact of Transport Cost and Travel Time on Trade under China-Pakistan Economic Corridor (CPEC). *Journal of Advanced Transportation, 2019*, 1–16. doi:10.1155/2019/7178507

Alexander, D. (2002). *Principles of emergency planning and management.* Terra Publishing.

Ali, I., & Aboelmaged, M. G. S. (2021). Implementation of supply chain 4.0 in the food and beverage industry: Perceived drivers and barriers. *International Journal of Productivity and Performance Management.*

Ali, I., Arslan, A., Khan, Z., & Tarba, S. Y. (2021). The role of Industry 4.0 technologies in mitigating supply chain disruption: Empirical evidence from the Australian food processing industry. *IEEE Transactions on Engineering Management.*

Ali, I., & Gölgeci, I. (2020). Managing climate risks through social capital in agrifood supply chains. *Supply Chain Management.*

Alkahtani, M., Omair, M., Khalid, Q. S., Hussain, G., Ahmad, I., & Pruncu, C. (2021). A COVID-19 Supply Chain Management Strategy Based on Variable Production under Uncertain Environment Conditions. *International Journal of Environmental Research and Public Health, 18*(4), 1662. doi:10.3390/ijerph18041662 PMID:33572380

Al-Mudimigh, A., Zairi, M., & Ahmed, A.M.M., (2004). Extending the concept of the supply chain: the effective management of value chains. *Int. J. Prod. Econ., 87*, 309-320.

Altay, N., & Green, W. III. (2006). OR/MS research in disaster operations management. *European Journal of Operational Research, 175*(1), 475–493. doi:10.1016/j.ejor.2005.05.016

Altay, N., & Ramirez, A. (2010). Impact of disasters on firms in different sectors: Implications for supply chains. *The Journal of Supply Chain Management, 46*(4), 59–80. doi:10.1111/j.1745-493X.2010.03206.x

Amrina, U., Hidayatno, A., & Zagloel, T. Y. M. (2021). Mapping challenges in developing sustainable small and medium industries: Integrating Lean and green principles. *Journal of Industrial Engineering and Management, 14*(2), 311–328. doi:10.3926/jiem.3401

Anparasan, A. A., & Lejeune, M. A. (2018). Data laboratory for supply chain response models during epidemic outbreaks. *Annals of Operations Research, 270*(1), 53–64. doi:10.100710479-017-2462-y

Antràs, P. (2020). *Conceptual Aspects of Global Value Chains*. Discussion Paper. No. DP14191. London: Centre for Economic Policy Research.

Anwar, S., Khan, M., & Sarwar, A. (2017). Minhas Majeed Khan, et al. (eds.). China-Pakistan Economic Corridor—A Game Changer. Islamabad, Pakistan: Institute of Strategic Studies Islamabad (ISSI). 2016. iii+164 Pages. Pak Rupees 500.00 (Hardback). The Pakistan Development Review, 56(1), 79-82. doi:10.30541/v56i1pp.79-82

Arivazhagan, D. (2020). The Role Of Technology In Supply Chain Management. *International Journal of Scientific & Technology Research, 9*, 2. www.ijstr.org

Aste, T., Tasca, P., & Di Matteo, T. (2017). Blockchain Technologies: The Foreseeable Impact on Society and Industry. *Computer, 50*(9), 18–28. doi:10.1109/MC.2017.3571064

Aviv-Reuven, S., & Rosenfeld, A. (2020). *Publication Patterns' Changes due to the COVID-19 Pandemic: A longitudinal and short-term scientometric analysis*. arXiv preprint arXiv:2010.02594.

Awan, M.A., & Ali, Y. (2022). Risk Assessment in Supply Chain Networks of China–Pakistan Economic Corridor (CPEC). *Chin. Polit. Sci. Rev.* doi:10.1007/s41111-021-00199-w

Azmeh, S., & Nadvi, K., (2014). Asian firms and the restructuring of global value chains. *Int. Bus. Rev., 23*(4), 708-717.

Azzone, G., & Noci, G. (1998). Seeing ecology and "green" innovations as a source of change. *Journal of Organizational Change Management, 11*(2), 94–111. doi:10.1108/09534819810212106

Baah, C., Opoku-Agyeman, D., Acquah, I. S. K., Issau, K., & Abdoulaye, F. A. M. (2020). Understanding the influence of environmental production practices on firm performance: A proactive versus reactive approach. *Journal of Manufacturing Technology Management, 32*(2), 266–289. doi:10.1108/JMTM-05-2020-0195

Baidoo, J. (2017). Humanitarian Logistics - An Exposition of the Challenges to Rapid Response in Disaster Relief Operations in Ghana. *Texila International Journal of Management, 3*(2), 252–259. doi:10.21522/TIJMG.2015.03.02.Art024

Balamir, M. (2022). The "disaster cycle" (DC) and actors in disaster management. *International Journal of Disaster Resilience in the Built Environment*. Advance online publication. doi:10.1108/IJDRBE-01-2022-0008

Balcik, B., Beamon, B. M., & Smilowitz, K. (2008). Last mile distribution in humanitarian relief. *Journal of Intelligent Transport Systems, 12*(2), 51–63. doi:10.1080/15472450802023329

Balcik, B., Beamon, B., Krejci, C., Muramatsu, K., & Ramirez, M. (2010). Coordination in humanitarian relief chains: Practices, challenges and opportunities. *International Journal of Production Economics, 126*(1), 22–34. doi:10.1016/j.ijpe.2009.09.008

Baldwin, R., & Lopez-Gonzalez, J., (2015). Supply-chain trade: a portrait of global patterns and several testable hypotheses. *World Econ., 38*(11), 1682-1721.

Ballard, G. (2001). Cycle time reduction in home building. *Proceedings of the 9th Annual Conference of the International Group for Lean Construction, 6*(8).

Ballou, R. H. (2006). *The evolution and future of logistics and supply chain management.* SciELO Brasil.

Banga, R. (2014). Linking into Global Value Chains Is Not Sufficient: Do You Export Domestic Value-Added Contents? *Journal of Economic Integration, 29*(2), 267–297. doi:10.11130/jei.2014.29.2.267

Barrientos, S., Gereffifi, G., & Rossi, A., (2011). Economic and social upgrading in global production networks: a new paradigm for a changing world. *Int. Labour Rev., 150*(3-4), 319-340.

Bashir, R., Gaur, B., & Salil, A. (2021). Logistics and IoT Based Survival Strategies to Facilitate Supply Chain Engineering during Pandemic. *Proceedings of 2nd IEEE International Conference on Computational Intelligence and Knowledge Economy, ICCIKE 2021*, 1–7. 10.1109/ICCIKE51210.2021.9410682

Basu, R., & Wright, J. N. (2012). *Quality beyond six sigma*. Routledge. doi:10.4324/9780080515502

Bechtold, J., Kern, A., Lauenstein, C., & Bernhofer, L. (2014). *Industry 4.0-The Capgemini Consulting View*. Capgemnini Consulting.

Belhadi, A., Kamble, S., Jabbour, C. J. C., Gunasekaran, A., Ndubisi, N. O., & Venkatesh, M. (2021). Manufacturing and service supply chain resilience to the COVID-19 outbreak: Lessons learned from the automobile and airline industries. *Technological Forecasting and Social Change, 163*, 120447. doi:10.1016/j.techfore.2020.120447 PMID:33518818

Belhadi, A., Sha'ri, Y. B. M., Touriki, F. E., & El Fezazi, S. (2018). Lean production in SMEs: Literature review and reflection on future challenges. *Journal of Industrial and Production Engineering, 35*(6), 368–382. doi:10.1080/21681015.2018.1508081

Belhadi, A., Touriki, F. E., & El Fezazi, S. (2018). Benefits of adopting lean production on green performance of SMEs: A case study. *Production Planning and Control*, *29*(11), 873–894. doi:10.1080/09537287.2018.1490971

Bellgran, M., & Säfsten, E. K. (2009). *Production development: design and operation of production systems* (Vol. 2). Springer Science & Business Media.

Bengtsson-Palme, J. (2017). Antibiotic resistance in the food supply chain: Where can sequencing and metagenomics aid risk assessment? *Current Opinion in Food Science*, *14*, 66–71. doi:10.1016/j.cofs.2017.01.010

Berg, C., Davidson, S., & Potts, J. (2019). Blockchain Technology as Economic Infrastructure: Revisiting the Electronic Markets Hypothesis. *Front. Blockchain*, *2*(22), 1–6. doi:10.3389/fbloc.2019.00022

Bergmiller, G. G., & McCright, P. R. (2009). Are lean and green programs synergistic. *Proceedings of the 2009 Industrial Engineering Research Conference*.

Berkoune, D., Renaud, J., Rekik, M., & Ruiz, A. (2012). Transportation in disaster response operations. *Socio-Economic Planning Sciences*, *46*(1), 23–32. doi:10.1016/j.seps.2011.05.002

Bernard, A. B., Jensen, J. B., Redding, S. J., & Schott, P. K. (2007). Firms in International Trade. *The Journal of Economic Perspectives*, *21*(3), 105–130. doi:10.1257/jep.21.3.105

Bernardes, E. S. (2010). The effect of supply management on aspects of social capital and the impact on performance: A social network perspective. *The Journal of Supply Chain Management*, *46*(1), 45–55. doi:10.1111/j.1745-493X.2009.03185.x

Bhatia, M. S., & Gangwani, K. K. (2020). Green supply chain management: Scientometric review and analysis of empirical research. *Journal of Cleaner Production*, 124722.

Bhutta, Z. (2018). From Gwadar-Kashgar: Crude oil pipeline requires $10 billion investment. *The Express Tribune*. Retrieved 29 August 2022, from https://tribune.com.pk/story/1712888/gwadar-kashgar-crude-oil-pipeline-requires-10-billion-investment

Bıçakcıoğlu-Peynirci, N., & Tanyeri, M. (2020). Stakeholder and resource-based antecedents and performance outcomes of green export business strategy: Insights from an emerging economy. *International Journal of Emerging Markets*.

Blomsma, F., & Brennan, G. (2017). The Emergence of Circular Economy: A New Framing Around Prolonging Resource Productivity. *Journal of Industrial Ecology*, *21*(3), 603–614. doi:10.1111/jiec.12603

Böckel, A., Nuzum, A. K., & Weissbrod, I. (2021). Blockchain for the Circular Economy: Analysis of the Research-Practice Gap. In Sustainable Production and Consumption (Vol. 25, pp. 525–539). Elsevier B.V. doi:10.1016/j.spc.2020.12.006

Boiral, O., Baron, C., & Gunnlaugson, O. (2014). Environmental leadership and consciousness development: A case study among Canadian SMEs. *Journal of Business Ethics*, *123*(3), 363–383. doi:10.100710551-013-1845-5

Bradt, D. (2009). Evidence-Based Decision-Making (Part II): Applications in Disaster Relief Operations. *Prehospital and Disaster Medicine*, *24*(6), 479–492. doi:10.1017/S1049023X0000738X PMID:20301064

Brown, B., Sikes, J., & Willmott, P. (2013). Bullish on digital: McKinsey global survey results. *The McKinsey Quarterly*, *12*, 1–8.

Bruzzone, A., & Longo, F. (2014). An application methodology for logistics and transportation scenarios analysis and comparison within the retail supply chain. *European Journal of Industrial Engineering*, *8*(1), 112–142. doi:10.1504/EJIE.2014.059352

Brynjolfsson, E., & McAfee, A. (2014). *The second machine age: Work, progress, and prosperity in a time of brilliant technologies*. WW Norton & Company.

Buckley, P.J. (2011). International integration and coordination in the global factory. *Manage. Int. Rev.*, *51*, 269-283.

Buckley, P.J., & Ghauri, P.N. (2004). Globalisation, economic geography and the strategy of multinational enterprises. *J. Int. Bus. Stud.*, *35*(2), 81-98.

Buckley, P.J., & Strange, R. (2015). The governance of the global factory: Location and control of world economic activity. *Acad. Manage. Perspect.*, *29*(2), 237-249.

Büyüközkan, G., & Göçer, F. (2018). Digital Supply Chain: Literature review and a proposed framework for future research. *Computers in Industry*, *97*, 157–177. doi:10.1016/j.compind.2018.02.010

Caldera, H., Desha, C., & Dawes, L. (2019). Evaluating the enablers and barriers for successful implementation of sustainable business practice in 'lean' SMEs. *Journal of Cleaner Production*, *218*, 575–590. doi:10.1016/j.jclepro.2019.01.239

CapGemini. (2016). *The current and future state of digital supply chain transformation*. GT Nexus.

Capobianco, N., Basile, V., Loia, F., & Vona, R. (2021). Toward a Sustainable Decommissioning of Offshore Platforms in the Oil and Gas Industry: A PESTLE Analysis. *Sustainability*, *13*(11), 6266. doi:10.3390u13116266

Carey, N., & Klayman, B. (n.d.). *May is crunch time for US auto suppliers amid coronavirus shutdown*. Reuters.

Carson, B., Romanelli, G., Walsh, P., & Zhumaev, A. (2018). *Blockchain beyond the hype: What is the strategic business value*. McKinsey Company. https://www.mckinsey.com/business-functions/mckinsey-digital /our-insights/blockchain-beyond-the-hype-what-is-the-strateg ic-businessvalue

Carter, N. (2008). *Disaster Management A Disaster Manager's Handbook* (2nd ed.). Asian Development Bank.

Castañeda-Navarrete, J., Hauge, J., & López-Gómez, C. (2020). COVID-19's impacts on global value chains, as seen in the apparel industry. *Development Policy Review, 39*(6), 953–970. Advance online publication. doi:10.1111/dpr.12539

Centobelli, P., Cerchione, R., & Singh, R. (2019). The impact of leanness and innovativeness on environmental and financial performance: Insights from Indian SMEs. *International Journal of Production Economics, 212*(3), 111–124.

Ch'ng, P.-C., Cheah, J., & Amran, A. (2021). Eco-innovation practices and sustainable business performance: The moderating effect of market turbulence in the Malaysian technology industry. *Journal of Cleaner Production, 283*, 124556. doi:10.1016/j.jclepro.2020.124556

Chakraborty, I., & Maity, P. (2020). COVID-19 outbreak: Migration, effects on society, global environment and prevention. *The Science of the Total Environment, 728*, 138882. doi:10.1016/j.scitotenv.2020.138882 PMID:32335410

Chari, F., Ngcamu, B., & Novukela, C. (2020). Supply chain risks in humanitarian relief operations: A case of Cyclone Idai relief efforts in Zimbabwe. *Journal Of Humanitarian Logistics And Supply Chain Management, 11*(1), 29–45. doi:10.1108/JHLSCM-12-2019-0080

Charles, A., Lauras, M., & Van Wassenhove, L. (2010). A model to define and assess the agility of supply chains: Building on humanitarian experience. *International Journal of Physical Distribution & Logistics Management, 40*(8/9), 722–741. doi:10.1108/09600031011079355

Chen, Y., Li, J., & Zhang, J. (2022). Digitalisation, data-driven dynamic capabilities and responsible innovation: An empirical study of SMEs in China. *Asia Pacific Journal of Management*, 1–41. doi:10.100710490-022-09845-6

Cherrafi, A., Garza-Reyes, J. A., Kumar, V., Mishra, N., Ghobadian, A., & Elfezazi, S. (2018). Lean, green practices and process innovation: A model for green supply chain performance. *International Journal of Production Economics, 206*, 79–92. doi:10.1016/j.ijpe.2018.09.031

Choi, D., & Hwang, T. (2015). The impact of green supply chain management practices on firm performance: The role of collaborative capability. *Operations Management Research, 8*(3), 69–83. doi:10.100712063-015-0100-x

Choi, T. Y., Dooley, K. J., & Rungtusanatham, M. (2001). Supply networks and complex adaptive systems: Control versus emergence. *Journal of Operations Management, 19*(3), 351–366. doi:10.1016/S0272-6963(00)00068-1

Choi, T. Y., Shao, B. B. M., & Shi, Z. (2015). Hidden suppliers can make or break your operations. *Harvard Business Review.*

Chopra, S. (2013). *Supply chain management* (5th ed.). Pearson.

Chowdhary, M. (2015). China's Billion-Dollar Gateway To The Subcontinent: Pakistan May Be Opening A Door It Cannot Close. *Forbes*, 1–3.

Chowdhury, P., Paul, S. K., Kaisar, S., & Moktadir, M. A. (2021). COVID-19 pandemic related supply chain studies: A systematic review. *Transportation Research Part E, Logistics and Transportation Review*, *148*, 102271. doi:10.1016/j.tre.2021.102271 PMID:33613082

Chowell, G., & Mizumoto, K. (2020). The COVID-19 pandemic in the USA: What might we expect? *Lancet*, *395*(10230), 1093–1094. doi:10.1016/S0140-6736(20)30743-1 PMID:32247381

Christopher, M. (2005). *Logistics and Supply Chain Management: Creating Value-added Networks*. Pearson Education.

Christopher, M. (2000). The agile supply chain: Competing in volatile markets. *Industrial Marketing Management*, *29*(1), 37–44. doi:10.1016/S0019-8501(99)00110-8

Christopher, M., & Tatham, P. (2011). *Humanitarian logistics* (1st ed.). Kogan.

Cobo, M. J., López-Herrera, A. G., Herrera-Viedma, E., & Herrera, F. (2011). Science mapping software tools: Review, analysis, and cooperative study among tools. *Journal of the American Society for Information Science and Technology*, *62*(7), 1382–1402. doi:10.1002/asi.21525

Colavizza, G., Costas, R., Traag, V. A., Van Eck, N. J., Van Leeuwen, T., & Waltman, L. (2021). A scientometric overview of CORD-19. *PLoS One*, *16*(1), e0244839. doi:10.1371/journal.pone.0244839 PMID:33411846

Cowger, G. (2016). All-out lean half measures get less than half results. *Mechanical Engineering (New York, N.Y.)*, *138*(1), 30–35. doi:10.1115/1.2016-Jan-1

Cox, A. (1999). Power, value and supply chain management. *Supply Chain Manage. Int. J.*, *4*(4), 167-175.

Coyne, H. (2020). When Kyoto Failed, Paris Stepped Up: How the Paris Agreement Changed Global Climate Negotiations. *Global Affairs Review*, *1*(1). Advance online publication. doi:10.51330/gar.0020116

CPIC Global. (2022). *China-Pakistan Economic Corridor: CPEC Projects & Progress*. CPIC Global. Retrieved 18 August 2022, from https://www.cpicglobal.com/pakistan-overview/cpec/

CRAIG (International Reference Centre for the Life Cycle of Products Processes and Services). (2015). *Circular Economy: a Critical Literature Review of Concepts*. Author.

Crosby, M., Nachiappan, P., Verma, S., & Kalyanaraman, V. (2016). Blockchain Technology: Beyond Bitcoin. *Applied Innovation Review*, *2*, 6–19.

Cukier, K., & Mayer-Schoenberger, V. (2013). The rise of big data: How it is changing the way we think about the world. *Foreign Affairs*, *92*, 28.

da Silva, A. F., Marins, F. A. S., Dias, E. X., & Ushizima, C. A. (2021). Improving manufacturing cycle efficiency through new multiple criteria data envelopment analysis models: An application in green and lean manufacturing processes. *Production Planning and Control, 32*(2), 104–120. doi:10.1080/09537287.2020.1713413

Darko, A., & Chan, A. P. (2016). Critical analysis of green building research trend in construction journals. *Habitat International, 57*, 53–63. doi:10.1016/j.habitatint.2016.07.001

Darko, A., Chan, A. P., Adabre, M. A., Edwards, D. J., Hosseini, M. R., & Ameyaw, E. E. (2020). Artificial intelligence in the AEC industry: Scientometric analysis and visualization of research activities. *Automation in Construction, 112*, 103081. doi:10.1016/j.autcon.2020.103081

Darko, A., Chan, A. P., Huo, X., & Owusu-Manu, D.-G. (2019). A scientometric analysis and visualization of global green building research. *Building and Environment, 149*, 501–511. doi:10.1016/j.buildenv.2018.12.059

Das, B. (2022). *A prolonged drought destroyed Indus Valley Civilisation, new study says*. nature.com. doi:10.1038/nindia.2018.61

Davarpanah, M., & Aslekia, S. (2008). A scientometric analysis of international LIS journals: Productivity and characteristics. *Scientometrics, 77*(1), 21–39. doi:10.100711192-007-1803-z

De Aguiar, E. J., Faiçal, B. S., Krishnamachari, B., & Ueyama, J. (2020). A survey of blockchain-based strategies for healthcare. *ACM Computing Surveys, 53*(2), 1–27. doi:10.1145/3376915

de Bolle, M., & Zettelmeyer, J. (2019). *Measuring the Rice of Economic Nationalism*. PIIE Working Paper. No. 19–15. Washington, DC: Peterson Institute for International Economics.

De Marchi, V.D., Maria, E.D., & Micelli, S. (2013). Environmental strategies, upgrading and competitive advantage in global value chains. *Bus. Strategy Environ., 22*(1), 62-72.

De Smet, H., Schreurs, B., & Leysen, J. (2015). The Response Phase of the Disaster Management Life Cycle Revisited Within the Context of "Disasters Out of the Box". *Journal of Homeland Security and Emergency Management, 12*(2). Advance online publication. doi:10.1515/jhsem-2015-0005

De Sousa Jabbour, A. B. L., Jabbour, C. J. C., Godinho Filho, M., & Roubaud, D. (2018). Industry 4.0 and the circular economy: A proposed research agenda and original roadmap for sustainable operations. *Annals of Operations Research, 270*(1-2), 273–286. doi:10.100710479-018-2772-8

Del Brìo, J. A., & Junquera, B. (2003). A review of the literature on environmental innovation management in SMEs: Implications for public policies. *Technovation, 23*(12), 939–948. doi:10.1016/S0166-4972(02)00036-6

del Giudice, M., Chierici, R., Mazzucchelli, A., & Fiano, F. (2020). Supply chain management in the era of circular economy: The moderating effect of big data. *International Journal of Logistics Management, 32*(2), 337–356. doi:10.1108/IJLM-03-2020-0119

Deloitte. (2016). Industry 4.0 enables the digital transformation of supply chains. Deloitte University Press.

Dettmer, H. W. (1992). *Goldratt's theory of constraints*. ASQ Quality Press.

Di Domenico, C., Ouzrout, Y., Savinno, M. M., & Bouras, B. (2007). Supply chain management analysis: a simulation approach of the value chain operations reference model (VCOR). In Advances in Production Management Systems. Springer.

Dües, C. M., Tan, K. H., & Lim, M. (2013). Green as the new Lean: How to use Lean practices as a catalyst to greening your supply chain. *Journal of Cleaner Production*, *V40*, 93–100. doi:10.1016/j.jclepro.2011.12.023

Duong, L. N. K., & Chong, J. (2020). Supply chain collaboration in the presence of disruptions: A literature review. *International Journal of Production Research*, *58*(11), 3488–3507. doi:10.1080/00207543.2020.1712491

Conhecimento, R. I. (2020). *Coronavirus COVID-19 Global Cases by the Center for Systems Science and Engineering*. CSSE.

Edward, S. (2019). The Policy Environment for Blockchain Innovation and Adoption. In *2019 OECD Global Blockchain Policy Forum Summary Report*. OECD.

El Baz, J., & Ruel, S. (2020). Can supply chain risk management practices mitigate the disruption impacts on supply chains' resilience and robustness? Evidence from an empirical survey in a COVID-19 outbreak era. *International Journal of Production Economics*, 107972.

El Bouazzaoui, Y., Abou Elala, M., Kébé, S., & Mimouni, F. (2020). Environmental impact assessment in the case of pooling Moroccan hydrocarbon supply chain resources. *Computer Science 2020 5th International Conference on Logistics Operations Management (GOL).*

Ellegaard, O., & Wallin, J. A. (2015). The bibliometric analysis of scholarly production: How great is the impact? *Scientometrics*, *105*(3), 1809–1831.

Elliott. R., Thomas. C., & Muhammad. K. (2019). *Supply chain resilience report 2019*. Business Continuity Institute.

EMAF (Ellen MacArthur Foundation). (2012). Towards the Circular Economy. FICF and McKinsey.

Emdat.be. (2022). *emdat_db*. Available at: https://www.emdat.be/emdat_db/

Emiliani, M. L. (2006). Origins of lean management in America: The role of Connecticut businesses. *Journal of Management History*, *12*(2), 167–184. doi:10.1108/13552520610654069

Ertem, M., İşbilir, M., & Şahin Arslan, A. (2017). Review of intermodal freight transportation in humanitarian logistics. *European Transport Research Review*, *9*(1), 10. doi:10.100712544-017-0226-z

ESCAP. (2017). China's "One Belt, One Road" Initiative: An ESCAP Report. *Population and Development Review*, *43*(3), 583–587. doi:10.1111/padr.12089

Escudero, L., Garín, M., Monge, J., & Unzueta, A. (2018). On preparedness resource allocation planning for natural disaster relief under endogenous uncertainty with time-consistent risk-averse management. *Computers & Operations Research*, *98*, 84–102. doi:10.1016/j.cor.2018.05.010

Explainer. (2013). *What have scientists learned from the Chelyabinsk meteor?* RadioFreeEurope/ RadioLiberty. Retrieved from https://www.rferl.org/a/explainer-meteor-russia/25161323.htm l

Fahimnia, B., Pournader, M., Siemsen, E., Bendoly, E., & Wang, C. (2019). Behavioral operations and supply chain management–a review and literature mapping. *Decision Sciences*, *50*(6), 1127–1183.

Farahani, P. (2015). *Digital Supply Chain Management 2020 Vision.* https://www.researchgate.net/publication/301350882

Felipe. J. (2012). Product complexity and economic development. *Structural Change and Economic Dynamics, 23*(1), 36-68.

Feng, Y., Zhu, Q., & Lai, K.-H. (2017). Corporate social responsibility for supply chain management: A literature review and bibliometric analysis. *Journal of Cleaner Production*, *158*, 296–307.

Fisher, M. L. (1997). What is the right supply chain for your product? *Harvard Business Review*, *75*, 105–117.

Fitzgerald, J., Cook, A., DeMarinis, T., & Smetana, K. (2018). *Utilizing virtual reality to drive supply chain innovation.* Deloitte Development LLC.

Florida, R. (1996). Lean and green: The move to environmentally conscious manufacturing. *California Management Review*, *39*(1), 80–105. doi:10.2307/41165877

Fornell, C., & Larcker, D. F. (1981). Evaluating structural equation models with unobservable variables and measurement error11. *JMR, Journal of Marketing Research*, *18*(1), 39–50. doi:10.1177/002224378101800104

Frankel, J. A. (1997). *Regional Trading Blocs in the World Economic System.* Peterson Institute for International Economics.

Friedman, N., & Ormiston, J. (2022). Blockchain as a sustainability-oriented innovation?: Opportunities for and resistance to Blockchain technology as a driver of sustainability in global food supply chains. *Technological Forecasting and Social Change*, *175*, 121403. doi:10.1016/j.techfore.2021.121403

Frohlich, M. T., & Westbrook, R. (2001). Arcs of integration: An international study of supply chain strategies. *Journal of Operations Management*, *19*(2), 185–200. doi:10.1016/S0272-6963(00)00055-3

Fullerton, R. R., & Wempe, W. F. (2009). Lean manufacturing, non-financial performance measures, and financial performance. *International Journal of Operations & Production Management*, *29*(3), 214–240. doi:10.1108/01443570910938970

Gallie, W. B. (1956). Essentially contested concepts. *Proceedings of the Aristotelian Society, 55*(1), 167–198. doi:10.1093/aristotelian/56.1.167

Gangwar, H., Date, H., & Raoot, A. D. (2014). Review on IT Adoption: Insights from Recent Technologies. *Journal of Enterprise Information Management, 27*(4), 488–502. doi:10.1108/JEIM-08-2012-0047

Garay-Rondero, C. L., Martinez-Flores, J. L., Smith, N. R., Caballero Morales, S. O., & Aldrette-Malacara, A. (2020). Digital supply chain model in Industry 4.0. *Journal of Manufacturing Technology Management, 31*(5), 887–933. doi:10.1108/JMTM-08-2018-0280

Garceau, T., Atkinson-Palombo, C., Garrick, N., Outlaw, J., McCahill, C., & Ahangari, H. (2013). Evaluating selected costs of automobile-oriented transportation systems from a sustainability perspective. *Research In Transportation Business & Management, 7*, 43–53. doi:10.1016/j.rtbm.2013.02.002

Garcia-Buendia, N., Moyano-Fuentes, J., Maqueira-Marín, J. M., & Cobo, M. (2020). 22 Years of Lean Supply Chain Management: A science mapping-based bibliometric analysis. *International Journal of Production Research*, 1–21.

Garnett, J., & Moore, M. (2010). Enhancing Disaster Recovery: Lessons from Exemplary International Disaster Management Practices. *Journal of Homeland Security and Emergency Management, 7*(1). Advance online publication. doi:10.2202/1547-7355.1711

Gatto, A., Drago, C., & Ruggeri, M. (2022). On the Frontline—A bibliometric Study on Sustainability, Development, Coronaviruses, and COVID-19. *Environmental Science and Pollution Research International*, 1–17.

Gavidia, J. (2017). A model for enterprise resource planning in emergency humanitarian logistics. *Journal of Humanitarian Logistics and Supply Chain Management, 7*(3), 246–265. doi:10.1108/JHLSCM-02-2017-0004

Geissbauer, R., Weissbarth, R., & Wetzstein, J. (2016). Procurement 4.0: are you ready for the digital revolution. PwC.

Geissdoerfer, M., Savaget, P., Bocken, M. N. P., & Hultink, E. J. (2017). The Circular Economy – a new sustainability paradigm? *Journal of Cleaner Production, 143*, 757–768. doi:10.1016/j.jclepro.2016.12.048

General Motors. (2018). *Our management approach to supply chain.* gmsustainability.com/manage/supply.html.

George, K. G, Ramaswamy, S., & Ramsey, L. (2014). Next-shoring: A CEO's guide. *McKinsey Quarterly.*

Gereffifi, G., & Fernandez-Stark, K. (2011). *Global Value Chain Analysis: A Primer. Center on Globalization, Governance & Competitiveness (CGGC).* Duke University.

Gereffi, G., Pananond, P., & Pedersen, T. (2022). Resilience Decoded: The Role of Firms, Global Value Chains, and the State in COVID-19 Medical Supplies. *California Management Review*, (2), 46–70. Advance online publication. doi:10.1177/00081256211069420

Ghisellini, P., Cialani, C., & Ulgiati, S. (2016). A review on circular economy: the expected transition to a balanced interplay of environmental and economic systems. *J. Clean. Prod., 114*, 11–32. Available at: https://www.sciencedirect.com/science/article/pii/S0959652615012287

Giannakis, M., Spanaki, K., & Dubey, R. (2019). A cloud-based supply chain management system: Effects on supply chain responsiveness. *Journal of Enterprise Information Management, 32*(4), 585–607. doi:10.1108/JEIM-05-2018-0106

Giuseppina, T., & Michele, S. (2018). Re-shoring and Resilience in Italy During and After the Crisis. *American Journal of Industrial and Business Management., 8*(05), 1172–1196. doi:10.4236/ajibm.2018.85081

Goering, K., Kelly, R., & Mellors, N. (2018). The next horizon for industrial manufacturing: Adopting disruptive digital technologies in making and delivering. *McKinsey Quarterly*.

Golan, M. S., Jernegan, L. H., & Linkov, I. (2020). Trends and applications of resilience analytics in supply chain modeling: Systematic literature review in the context of the COVID-19 pandemic. *Environment Systems & Decisions, 40*, 222–243.

Goldsby, T. J., Zinn, W., Closs, D. J., Daugherty, P. J., Stock, J. R., Fawcett, S. E., & Waller, M. (2019). Reflections on 40 years of the journal of business logistics: From the editors. *Journal of Business Logistics, 40*(1), 4–29. doi:10.1111/jbl.12208

Golinelli, D., Nuzzolese, A. G., Boetto, E., Rallo, F., Greco, M., Toscano, F., & Fantini, M. P. (2020). *The impact of early scientific literature in response to COVID-19: a scientometric perspective*. MedRxiv.

Government of Pakistan (GoP). (2011). *Pakistan: Flood Impact Assessment*. Available at: http://www.finance.gov.pk/survey/chapter_11/Special%20Section_2.pdf

Govindan, K., Kannan, D., & Shankar, M. (2015). Evaluation of green manufacturing practices using a hybrid MCDM model combining DANP with PROMETHEE. *International Journal of Production Research, 53*(21), 6344–6371. doi:10.1080/00207543.2014.898865

Gunasekaran, A., Papadopoulos, T., Dubey, R., Wamba, S. F., Childe, S. J., Hazen, B., & Akter, S. (2017). Big data and predictive analytics for supply chain and organizational performance. *Journal of Business Research, 70*, 308–317. doi:10.1016/j.jbusres.2016.08.004

Gupta, M., Digalwar, A., Gupta, A., & Goyal, A. (2022). Integrating Theory of Constraints, Lean and Six Sigma: A framework development and its application. *Production Planning and Control*, 1–24. doi:10.1080/09537287.2022.2071351

Gürlek, M., & Tuna, M. (2018). Reinforcing competitive advantage through green organizational culture and green innovation. *Service Industries Journal, 38*(7-8), 467–491. doi:10.1080/02642069.2017.1402889

Haddow, G. D., Bullock, J. A., & Coppola, D. P. (2008). Introduction to emergency management. In *Butterworth-Heinemann homeland security series*. Elsevier Inc.

Haddow, J. A. B. (2004). *Introduction to Emergency Management*. ButterworthHeinemann.

Haghani, M., & Bliemer, M. C. (2020). Covid-19 pandemic and the unprecedented mobilisation of scholarly efforts prompted by a health crisis: Scientometric comparisons across SARS, MERS and 2019-nCov literature. *Scientometrics, 125*(3), 2695–2726.

Haghani, M., Bliemer, M. C., Goerlandt, F., & Li, J. (2020). The scientific literature on Coronaviruses, COVID-19 and its associated safety-related research dimensions: A scientometric analysis and scoping review. *Safety Science, 129*, 104806.

Hanifan, G., Sharma, A., & Newberry, C. (2014). *The digital supply network: a new paradigm for the supply chain management.* Accenture Global Management Consulting.

Hashim, M., Nazam, M., Zia-ur-Rehman, M., Abrar, M., Baig, S., Nazim, M., & Hussain, Z. (2022). Modeling Supply Chain Sustainability-Related Risks and Vulnerability: Insights from the Textile Sector of Pakistan. *AUTEX Research Journal, 22*(1), 123–134. doi:10.2478/aut-2021-0008

Hayes, A. F. (2013). *Introduction to mediation, moderation, and conditional process analysis: Methodology in the Social Sciences*. Academic Press.

Hayes, A. F. (2018). *Introduction to mediation, moderation, and conditional process analysis: A regression-based approach* (Vol. 2). Guilford Publications.

He, F., & Zhuang, J. (2016). Balancing pre-disaster preparedness and post-disaster relief. *European Journal of Operational Research, 252*(1), 246–256. doi:10.1016/j.ejor.2015.12.048

Heijmans & Nguyen. (2020, Nov. 15). Asia Pacific Nations Sign Biggest Regional Trade Deal. *Bloomberg*.

He, K., Zhang, J., & Zeng, Y. (2019). Knowledge domain and emerging trends of agricultural waste management in the field of social science: A scientometric review. *The Science of the Total Environment, 670*, 236–244.

Hendricks, B. K., & Singhal, R. V. (2003). *An empirical analysis of the effect of supply chain disruption on long-run stock price performance and equity risk of the firm*. Academic Press.

Herrera-Franco, G., Montalván-Burbano, N., Carrión-Mero, P., Jaya-Montalvo, M., & Gurumendi-Noriega, M. (2021). Worldwide Research on Geoparks through Bibliometric Analysis. *Sustainability, 13*(3), 1175.

Heyes, G., Sharmina, M., Mendoza, J. M. F., Schmid, A. J., & Azapagic, A. (2018). Developing and Implementing Circular Economy Business Models in Service –Oriented Technology Companies. *Journal of Cleaner Production, 177*, 621–632. doi:10.1016/j.jclepro.2017.12.168

Hickman, J., Hassel, D., Joumard, R., Samaras, Z., & Sorenson, S. (1999). *Methodology for Calculating Transport Emissions and Energy Consumption (Report for the Project MEET).* Transport Research Laboratory.

Hines, T. (2014). *Supply chain strategies: Demand-driven and customer-focused.* Routledge.

Ho, D., Kumar, A., & Shiwakoti, N. (2019). A literature review of supply chain collaboration mechanisms and their impact on performance. *Engineering Management Journal, 31*(1), 47–68. doi:10.1080/10429247.2019.1565625

Hoekstra, A., & Wiedmann, T. (2014). Humanity's unsustainable environmental footprint. *Science, 344*(6188), 1114–1117. doi:10.1126cience.1248365 PMID:24904155

Hong, P. (2016). Jointly Building the 'Belt and Road' towards the Sustainable Development Goals. SSRN *Electronic Journal.* doi:10.2139/ssrn.2812893

Hosain, M., & Hossain, M. (2019). *One Belt One Road initiative: A Revolution on Regional and Global Development.* Academic Press.

Hosseini, M. R., Maghrebi, M., Akbarnezhad, A., Martek, I., & Arashpour, M. (2018). Analysis of citation networks in building information modeling research. *Journal of Construction Engineering and Management, 144*(8), 04018064.

Hosseini, M., & Gordijn, B. (2020). A review of the literature on ethical issues related to scientific authorship. *Accountability in Research, 27*(5), 284–324.

Hosseini, S., & Ivanov, D. (2020). Bayesian networks for supply chain risk, resilience and ripple effect analysis: A literature review. *Expert Systems with Applications, 161*, 113649.

Hou, Y., Iqbal, W., Muhammad Shaikh, G., Iqbal, N., Ahmad Solangi, Y., & Fatima, A. (2019). Measuring energy efficiency and environmental performance: A case of South Asia. *Processes (Basel, Switzerland), 7*(6), 325. doi:10.3390/pr7060325

Huang, C.-C., Wang, Y.-M., Wu, T.-W., & Wang, P.-A. (2013). An empirical analysis of the antecedents and performance consequences of using the moodle platform. *International Journal of Information and Education Technology, 3*(2), 217–221. doi:10.7763/IJIET.2013.V3.267

Huang, C.-F. (2019). Evaluation of system reliability for a stochastic delivery-flow distribution network with inventory. *Annals of Operations Research, 277*(1), 33–45.

Hudecheck, M., Sirén, C., Grichnik, D., & Wincent, J. (2020). How companies can respond to the Coronavirus. *MIT Sloan Management Review.*

Huff, A. G., Beyeler, W. E., Kelley, N. S., & McNitt, J. A. (2015). How resilient is the United States' food system to pandemics? *Journal of Environmental Studies and Sciences, 5*(3), 337–347.

Hung, M. (2017). Leading the iot, Gartner insights on how to lead in a connected world. *Gartner Research*, *1*, 1–5.

Hussain, G., Nazir, M. S., Rashid, M. A., & Sattar, M. A. (2022). From supply chain resilience to supply chain disruption orientation: The moderating role of supply chain complexity. *Journal of Enterprise Information Management*. Advance online publication. doi:10.1108/JEIM-12-2020-0558

Hwang, W.-S., & Kim, H.-S. (2022). Does the adoption of emerging technologies improve technical efficiency? Evidence from Korean manufacturing SMEs. *Small Business Economics*, *59*(2), 627–643. doi:10.100711187-021-00554-w

Iansiti, M., & Lakhani, K. R. (2017). The truth about blockchain. *Harvard Business Review*, 1–11.

IBM. (2016). *Leading the Pack in Blockchain Banking*. https://www.ibm.com/downloads/cas/PA8V4RMX

Ibrahim, H. (2017). *China-Pakistan Economic Corridor (Part-1)*. https://www.jukuko.com/china-pakistan-economic-corridor-part-1/

Inman, R. A., & Green, K. W. (2018). Lean and green combine to impact environmental and operational performance. *International Journal of Production Research*, *56*(14), 4802–4818. doi:10.1080/00207543.2018.1447705

IP Specialist. (2022). *How Blockchain Technology Works*. Medium.

Iqbal, K. (2017). *Significance and Security of CPEC: A Pakistani Perspective*. Retrieved 1 September 2022, from https://www.ciis.org.cn/english/ESEARCHPROJECTS/Articles/202007/t20200715_3600.html

Iqbal, M., Ahmad, N., Waqas, M., & Abrar, M. (2021). COVID-19 pandemic and construction industry: Impacts, emerging construction safety practices, and proposed crisis management. *Brazilian Journal of Operations & Production Management*, *18*(2), 1–17.

Iqbal, M., Ma, J., Ahmad, N., Ullah, Z., & Hassan, A. (2022). Energy-Efficient supply chains in construction industry: An analysis of critical success factors using ISM-MICMAC approach. *International Journal of Green Energy*, 1–19.

Iqbal, M., Ma, J., Ullah, Z., Ahmad, N., Ibrahim, M., Waqas, M., & Ahmad, M. (2022). Identifying Lockdown Relaxation Strategies and Policy Implications to Fight against COVID-19: Medical Experts Perspective from Pakistan. *Social Work in Public Health*, 1–22.

Islam, M. S., Karia, N., Taib, F. M., Ara, H., & Moeinzadeh, S. (2021). Ethico-religious green supply chain management (GSCM): Embedding Islamic ethics' codes for improving environmental concerns. *Journal of Islamic Accounting and Business Research*.

Ito, J., Narula, N., & Ali, R. (2017). *The Blockchain Will do to the Financial System what the internet did to Media*. https://hbr.org/2017/03/the-blockchain-will-do-to-banks-and-law-firms-whatthe-internet-did-to-media

Ivanov, D. (2020). Predicting the impacts of epidemic outbreaks on global supply chains: A simulation-based analysis on the coronavirus outbreak (COVID-19/SARS-CoV-2) case. *Transportation Research Part E, Logistics and Transportation Review*, *136*, 101922.

Ivanov, D., & Dolgui, A. (2020). Viability of intertwined supply networks: Extending the supply chain resilience angles towards survivability. A position paper motivated by COVID-19 outbreak. *International Journal of Production Research*, *58*(10), 2904–2915.

Ivanov, D., & Dolgui, A. (2021). A digital supply chain twin for managing the disruption risks and resilience in the era of Industry 4.0. *Production Planning and Control*, *32*(9), 775–788. doi:10.1080/09537287.2020.1768450

Jamil, S., Malik, M., & Shah, S. (2019). *China-Pakistan economic cooperation: Trade, investment, energy, infrastructure and Gwadar Port*. doi:10.31703/ger.2019(IV-II).05

Jesse, N. (2018). Organizational evolution - how digital disruption enforces organizational agility. *IFAC-PapersOnLine*, *51*(30), 486–491. doi:10.1016/j.ifacol.2018.11.310

Joshi, M. (2017). The Eco-Politics of CPEC and India. SSRN *Electronic Journal*. doi:10.2139/ssrn.2982942

Jun, Z. (2015). Collaboration evaluation of supply logistics based on supply-hub. *2015 Seventh International Conference on Measuring Technology and Mechatronics Automation*, 279-284. 10.1109/ICMTMA.2015.74

Juzwishin, D. (2017). *Health System Procurement and Supply Management: Managing the Life Cycle of Technology for Maximum Value: What's New, What Stays, and What Must Go*. Academic Press.

Kagan, D., Moran-Gilad, J., & Fire, M. (2020). Scientometric trends for coronaviruses and other emerging viral infections. *GigaScience, 9*(8), giaa085.

Kalbassi, R. (2015). Lean and Green Parallel Implementation Impact on Outcomes of Supply Chain in Canadian Aerospace Industry. Concordia University.

Kelly, J. (2019). Craig Wright Has In No Way Been Officially "Recognised" As Satoshi Nakamoto. *Financial Times*. https://ftalphaville.ft.com/2019/05/22/1558547272000/Craig-Wright-has-in-noway-been-officially--recognised--as-Satoshi-Nakamoto/

Kelly, S. (2020). *Oil price crashes into negative territory for the first time in history amid pandemic*. Reuters.

Kelly, S., & Baertlein, L. (2020). *Beer may lose its fizz as CO2 supplies go flat during a pandemic*. Reuters.

Kengpol, A., Tuammee, S., & Tuominen, M. (2014). The development of a framework for route selection in multimodal transportation. *International Journal of Logistics Management*, *25*(3), 581–610. doi:10.1108/IJLM-05-2013-0064

Khadim, Z., Batool, I., & Bilal Lodhi, M. (2021). China–Pakistan Economic Corridor, Logistics Developments and Economic Growth in Pakistan. *Logistics*, *5*(2), 35. doi:10.3390/logistics5020035

Khan, M., Hussain, M., Gunasekaran, A., Ajmal, M. M., & Helo, P. T. (2018). Motivators of social sustainability in healthcare supply chains in the UAE—Stakeholder perspective. *Sustainable Production and Consumption*, *14*, 95–104. doi:10.1016/j.spc.2018.01.006

Khan, S. A. R., Zhang, Y., Anees, M., Golpîra, H., Lahmar, A., & Qianli, D. (2018). Green supply chain management, economic growth and environment: A GMM based evidence. *Journal of Cleaner Production*, *185*, 588–599. doi:10.1016/j.jclepro.2018.02.226

Khan, S., & Liu, G. (2018). The China–Pakistan Economic Corridor (CPEC): Challenges and prospects. *Area Development And Policy*, *4*(4), 466–473. doi:10.1080/23792949.2018.1534549

Khan, Z., Changgang, G., & Afzaal, M. (2019). China-Pakistan Economic Corridor at the Cross Intersection of China, Central Asia and South Asia: Opportunities for Regional Economic Growth. *Chinese Economy*, *53*(2), 200–215. doi:10.1080/10971475.2019.1688005

Killmeyer, J., & Holdowsky, J. (2019). From siloed to distributed. Blockchain enables the digital supply network. *Deloitte Insights*. https://www2.deloitte.com/us/en/insights/topics/understanding-blockchain-potential/digital-supply-network-blockchain-adoption.html

King, A. A., & Lenox, M. J. (2001). Lean and green? An empirical examination of the relationship between lean production and environmental performance. *Production and Operations Management*, *10*(3), 244–256.

Kleinberg, J. M. (1999). Hubs, authorities, and communities. *ACM Computing Surveys*, *31*(4es), 5.

Koengkan, M., Fuinhas, J. A., Kazemzadeh, E., Osmani, F., Alavijeh, N. K., Auza, A., & Teixeira, M. (2022). Measuring the economic efficiency performance in Latin American and Caribbean countries: An empirical evidence from stochastic production frontier and data envelopment analysis. *Inter Economics*, *169*, 43–54. doi:10.1016/j.inteco.2021.11.004

Kong, L. (2015). The Belt and Road Initiative and China's Foreign Policy Toward Its Territorial and Boundary Disputes. *China Quarterly Of International Strategic Studies*, *01*(02), 325–345. doi:10.1142/S2377740015500165

Koopman, R., Wang, Z., & Wei, S. (2008). *How Much of Chinese Exports Is Really Made in China? Assessing Domestic Value-Added When Processing Trade Is Pervasive*. NBER Working Paper. No. 14109. Cambridge, MA: National Bureau of Economic Research.

Korhonen, J., Nuur, C., Feldmann, A., & Birkie, S. E. (2018). Circular Economy as an Essentially Contested Concept. *Journal of Cleaner Production*, *175*, 544–552. doi:10.1016/j.jclepro.2017.12.111

Kovács, G., & Spens, K. (2007). Humanitarian logistics in disaster relief operations. *International Journal of Physical Distribution & Logistics Management*, *37*(2), 99–114. doi:10.1108/09600030710734820

Krafcik, J. F. (1988). Triumph of the lean production system. *MIT Sloan Management Review*, *30*(1), 41.

Kumar, S., & Chandra, C. (2010). Supply chain disruption by avian flu pandemic for US companies: A case study. *Transportation Journal*, *49*(4), 61–73.

L'Hermitte, C., Bowles, M., Tatham, P., & Brooks, B. (2015). An integrated approach to agility in humanitarian logistics. *Journal of Humanitarian Logistics and Supply Chain Management*, *5*(2), 209–233. doi:10.1108/JHLSCM-04-2014-0016

L'Hermitte, C., Tatham, P., & Bowles, M. (2014). Classifying logistics-relevant disasters: Conceptual model and empirical illustration. *Journal of Humanitarian Logistics and Supply Chain Management*, *4*(2), 155–178. doi:10.1108/JHLSCM-07-2013-0025

La Londe, B. J., Grabner, J. R., & Robeson, J. F. (1976). Integrated Distribution Systems: a Management Perspective. In P. M. Van Buytenen, M. G. Christopher, & G. S. C. Wills (Eds.), *Business Logistics* (pp. 3–19). Springer US. doi:10.1007/978-1-4613-4379-0_1

Laengle, S., Lobos, V., Merigó, J. M., Herrera-Viedma, E., Cobo, M. J., & De Baets, B. (2021). Forty years of fuzzy sets and systems: A bibliometric analysis. *Fuzzy Sets and Systems*, *402*, 155–183.

Lan, W., & Hou, X. (2022). *How Physical Activity Affects The Health Of College Students During Covid-19 Pandemic-Based On Citespace Analysis.* Paper presented at the 2022 3rd Asia Sport Science Conference (ASSC).

Lazarevic, D., & Valve, H. (2017). Narrating expectations for the circular economy: Towards a common and contested European transition. *Energy Research & Social Science*, *31*, 60–69. doi:10.1016/j.erss.2017.05.006

Lee, D. H. (2013). *The role of Triple-A in green supply chain management practices and organizational performance.* University of Nebraska - Lincoln. Retrieved from https://digitalcommons.unl.edu/dissertations/AAI3558860

Lee, H. W., & Zbinden, M. (2003). *Marrying logistics and technology for effective relief.* Forced.

Lee, K. H., & Kim, J. W. (2011). Integrating suppliers into green product innovation development: An empirical case study in the semiconductor industry. *Business Strategy and the Environment*, *20*(8), 527–538. doi:10.1002/bse.714

Lee, S. M., Kim, S. T., & Choi, D. (2012). Green supply chain management and organizational performance. *Industrial Management & Data Systems*, *112*(8), 1148–1180. doi:10.1108/02635571211264609

Leitner, R., Meizer, F., Prochazka, M., & Sihn, V. (2011). Structural concepts for horizontal cooperation to increase efficiency in logistics. *CIRP Journal of Manufacturing Science and Technology*, *4*(3), 332–337. doi:10.1016/j.cirpj.2011.01.009

Le, T. T., Vo, X. V., & Venkatesh, V. (2022). Role of green innovation and supply chain management in driving sustainable corporate performance. *Journal of Cleaner Production*, *374*, 133875. doi:10.1016/j.jclepro.2022.133875

Li, K., Jin, M., Qi, G., Shi, W., & Ng, A. (2017). Logistics as a driving force for development under the Belt and Road Initiative – the Chinese model for developing countries. *Transport Reviews*, *38*(4), 457–478. doi:10.1080/01441647.2017.1365276

Li, L., & Tang, S. (2008). An Artificial Emergency-Logistics-Planning System for Severe Disasters. *IEEE Intelligent Systems*, *23*(4), 86–88. doi:10.1109/MIS.2008.56

Linton, T., & Vakil, B. (2020). Coronavirus is proving we need more resilient supply chains. *Harvard Business Review*.

Litman, T. (2007). Developing Indicators for Comprehensive and Sustainable Transport Planning. *Transportation Research Record: Journal of the Transportation Research Board*, *2017*(1), 10–15. doi:10.3141/2017-02

Liu, H., Liu, Y., Wang, Y., & Pan, C. (2019). Hot topics and emerging trends in tourism forecasting research: A scientometric review. *Tourism Economics*, *25*(3), 448–468.

Li, Y., Xu, Z., Wang, X., & Wang, X. (2020). A bibliometric analysis on deep learning during 2007–2019. *International Journal of Machine Learning and Cybernetics*, *11*(12), 2807–2826.

Lockamy, A. III. (2014). Assessing disaster risks in supply chains. *Industrial Management & Data Systems*.

Luthra, S., Garg, D., & Haleem, A. (2014). Green supply chain management: Implementation and performance–a literature review and some issues. *Journal of Advances in Management Research*, *11*(1), 20–46. doi:10.1108/JAMR-07-2012-0027

Mackelprang, A. W., & Nair, A. (2010). Relationship between just-in-time manufacturing practices and performance: A meta-analytic investigation. *Journal of Operations Management*, *28*(4), 283–302. doi:10.1016/j.jom.2009.10.002

Maghfiroh, M., & Hanaoka, S. (2020). Multi-modal relief distribution model for disaster response operations. *Progress In Disaster Science*, *6*, 100095. doi:10.1016/j.pdisas.2020.100095

Maghsoudi, A., & Moshtari, M. (2020). Challenges in disaster relief operations: Evidence from the 2017 Kermanshah earthquake. *Journal Of Humanitarian Logistics And Supply Chain Management*, *11*(1), 107–134. doi:10.1108/JHLSCM-08-2019-0054

Mahapatra, S., & Ratha, K. (2016). The 21st Conference of the Parties Climate Summit in Paris: A Slippery Slope. *Journal of International Development*, *28*(6), 991–996. doi:10.1002/jid.3221

Mahutga, M. C. (2011). When do value chains go global? A theory of the spatialization of global value chains. *Global Networks, 12*(1), 1–21. doi:10.1111/j.1471-0374.2011.00322.x

Maizland, L. (2021). *China's Fight Against Climate Change and Environmental Degradation.* Council on Foreign Relations. Retrieved 18 August 2022, from https://www.cfr.org/backgrounder/china-climate-change-policies-environmental-degradation

Majeed, A. A., & Rupasinghe, T. D. (2017). Internet of things (IoT) embedded future supply chains for industry 4.0: An assessment from ERP-based fashion apparel and footwear industry. *International Journal of Supply Chain Management, 6*(1), 25–40.

Makris, D., Hansen, Z. N. L., & Khan, O. (2019). Adapting to supply chain 4.0: An explorative study of multinational companies. *Supply Chain Forum: An International Journal.*

Manuel Maqueira, J., Moyano-Fuentes, J., & Bruque, S. (2019). Drivers and consequences of innovative technology assimilation in the supply chain: Cloud computing and supply chain integration. *International Journal of Production Research, 57*(7), 2083–2103.

Manzoor, F., Wei, L., Nurunnabi, M., & Abdul Subhan, Q. (2019). Role of SME in poverty alleviation in SAARC region via panel data analysis. *Sustainability, 11*(22), 6480. doi:10.3390u11226480

Marbouh, D., Abbasi, T., Maasmi, F., Omar, I. A., Debe, M. S., Salah, K., Jayaraman, R., & Ellahham, S. (2020). Blockchain for COVID-19: Review, Opportunities, and a Trusted Tracking System. *Arabian Journal for Science and Engineering, 45*(12).

Marodin, G. A., & Saurin, T. A. (2013). Implementing lean production systems: Research areas and opportunities for future studies. *International Journal of Production Research, 51*(22), 6663–6680. doi:10.1080/00207543.2013.826831

Martínez-Jurado, P. J., Moyano-Fuentes, J., & Gómez, P. J. (2013). HR management during lean production adoption. *Management Decision, 51*(4), 742–760. doi:10.1108/00251741311326545

Martínez-López, F. J., Merigó, J. M., Valenzuela-Fernández, L., & Nicolás, C. (2018). Fifty years of the European Journal of Marketing: A bibliometric analysis. *European Journal of Marketing.*

Massaro, M., Dal Mas, F., Chiappetta Jabbour, C. J., & Bagnoli, C. (2020). Crypto-economy and new sustainable business models: Reflections and projections using a case study analysis. *Corporate Social Responsibility and Environmental Management, 27*(5), 2150–2160.

Mathur, A., Mittal, M., & Dangayach, G. S. (2012). Improving productivity in Indian SMEs. *Production Planning and Control, 23*(10-11), 754–768. doi:10.1080/09537287.2011.642150

Mazingo, C., Peptides, T., Petrov, A., & Schröck, G. (2014). *Introducing a holistic approach to stress testing.* McKinsey.com.

McIsaac, J., Brulle, J., Burg, J., Tarnacki, G., Sullivan, C., & Wassel, R. (2019). Blockchain Technology for Disaster and Refugee Relief Operations. *Prehospital and Disaster Medicine, 34*(s1), s106–s106. doi:10.1017/S1049023X1900222X

McMaster, M., Nettleton, C., Tom, C., Xu, B., Cao, C., & Qiao, P. (2020). Risk management: Rethinking fashion supply chain management for multinational corporations in light of the COVID-19 outbreak. *Journal of Risk and Financial Management, 13*(8), 173.

Mehar, A. (2017). Infrastructure development, CPEC and FDI in Pakistan: Is there any connection? *Transnational Corporations Review, 9*(3), 232–241. doi:10.1080/19186444.2017.1362857

Menhas, R., Mahmood, S., Tanchangya, P., Safdar, M., & Hussain, S. (2022). *Sustainable Development under Belt and Road Initiative: A Case Study of China-Pakistan Economic Corridor's Socio-Economic Impact on Pakistan*. Academic Press.

Mentis, A. (2017). *Understanding Australian small to medium businesses*. Retrieved from https://business.nab.com.au/wp-content/uploads/2017/06/J002580_MTM-Whitepaper-IPSOS-FINAL_C1-2.pdf

Merlino, M., & Sproge, I. (2017). The Augmented Supply Chain. *Procedia Engineering, 178*, 308–318. doi:10.1016/j.proeng.2017.01.053

Mihelcic, J. R., Crittenden, J. C., Small, M. J., Shonnard, D. R., Hokanson, D. R., Zhang, Q., Chen, H., Sorby, S. A., James, V. U., Sutherland, J. W., & Schnoor, J. L. (2003). Sustainability science and engineering: The emergence of a new Meta Discipline. *Environmental Science & Technology, 37*, 5314–5324.

Ministry of Planning, Development and Reform. (2017). *Long Term Plan for China-Pakistan Economic Corridor (2017-2030)*. Retrieved 1 September 2022, from https://www.pc.gov.pk/uploads/cpec/CPEC-LTP.pdf

Ministry of Planning. Pakistan. (2022). *Projects Under CPEC | China-Pakistan Economic Corridor (CPEC) Authority Official Website*. Retrieved 24 August 2022, from https://cpec.gov.pk/energy

Mittal, V. K., & Sangwan, K. S. (2014). Prioritizing barriers to green manufacturing: Environmental, social and economic perspectives. *Procedia CIRP, 17*, 559–564. doi:10.1016/j.procir.2014.01.075

Mohan, U., Viswanadham, N., & Trikha, P. (2009). Impact of Avian Influenza in the Indian poultry industry: A supply chain risk perspective. *International Journal of Logistics Systems and Management, 5*(1-2), 89–105.

Mohd Suki, N. (2017). Green products usage: Structural relationships on customer satisfaction and loyalty. *International Journal of Sustainable Development and World Ecology, 24*(1), 88–95. doi:10.1080/13504509.2016.1169563

Mohd, S., Fathi, M., Harun, A., & Omar Chong, N. (2018). Key issues in the management of the humanitarian aid distribution process during and post-disaster in Malaysia. *Planning Malaysia Journal, 16*(5). Advance online publication. doi:10.21837/pmjournal.v16.i5.425

Mohsin, M., Abbas, Q., Zhang, J., Ikram, M., & Iqbal, N. (2019). Integrated effect of energy consumption, economic development, and population growth on CO2 based environmental degradation: A case of transport sector. *Environmental Science and Pollution Research International, 26*(32), 32824–32835. doi:10.100711356-019-06372-8 PMID:31502046

Montoya-Torres, J. R., Muñoz-Villamizar, A., & Vega-Mejía, C. A. (2016). On the impact of collaborative strategies for goods delivery in city logistics. *Production Planning and Control, 27*(6), 443–455. doi:10.1080/09537287.2016.1147092

Montzka, S., Dlugokencky, E., & Butler, J. (2011). Non-CO2 greenhouse gases and climate change. *Nature, 476*(7358), 43–50. doi:10.1038/nature10322 PMID:21814274

Moutaoukil, A., Derrouiche, R., & Neubert, G. (2013). *Modélisation d'une stratégie de mutualisation logistique en intégrant les objectifs de Développement Durable pour des PME agroalimentaires*. In 13e Congrès International de Génie Industriel (CIGI' 13), la rochelle, France.

Mrabti, N., Hamani, N., & Delahoche, L. (2018). Mutualisation logistique, approche par simulation. In 12ème Conférence Internationale de Modélisation, Optimisation et SIMulation, MOSIM 2018, Toulouse, France.

Mrabti, N., Hamani, N., & Delahoche, L. (2019). Vers un modèle de simulation de la mutualisation logistique 4.0. *Logistique & Management*, 1-15.

Mrabti, N., Hamani, N., & Delahoche, L. (2022). A sustainable collaborative approach to the distribution network design problem with CO2 emissions allocation. *International Journal of Shipping and Transport Logistics, 14*(1-2), 114–140. doi:10.1504/IJSTL.2022.120676

Mubarik, M., Devadason, E., & Govindaraju, C. (2020). Human capital and export performance of small and medium enterprises in Pakistan. *International Journal of Social Economics, 47*(5), 643–662. doi:10.1108/IJSE-03-2019-0198

Mubarik, M., Kazmi, S., & Zaman, S. (2021). Application of gray DEMATEL-ANP in green-strategic sourcing. *Technology in Society, 64*, 101524. doi:10.1016/j.techsoc.2020.101524

Mubarik, M., Naghavi, N., & Mubarak, M. (2019). Impact of Supplier Relational Capital on Supply Chain Performance in Pakistani Textile Industry. *Asian Economic And Financial Review, 9*(3), 318–328. doi:10.18488/journal.aefr.2019.93.318.328

Murray, A., Skene, K., & Haynes, K. (2017). The Circular Economy: An Interdisciplinary Exploration of the Concept and Application in a Global Context. *Journal of Business Ethics, 140*(3), 369–380.

Mussomeli, A., Neier, M., Takayama, B., Sniderman, B., & Holdowsky, J. (2019). Building a cognitive digital supply network. *Deloitte Insights*. https://www2.deloitte.com/us/en/insights/focus/industry-4-0/digital-supply-networks-cognitive-automation.html

Narwane, V. S., Raut, R. D., Gardas, B. B., Narkhede, B. E., & Awasthi, A. (2022). Examining smart manufacturing challenges in the context of micro, small and medium enterprises. *International Journal of Computer Integrated Manufacturing*, 1–18. doi:10.1080/0951192X.2022.2078508

Nasiri, M., Ukko, J., Saunila, M., & Rantala, T. (2020). Managing the digital supply chain: The role of smart technologies. *Technovation, 96-97*, 96–97. doi:10.1016/j.technovation.2020.102121

Naustdalslid, J., (2017). Circular economy in China e the environmental dimension of the harmonious society. *Int. J. Sustain. Dev. World Ecol., 21*(4), 303-313.

Nayak, G., & Dhaigude, A. S. (2019). A conceptual model of sustainable supply chain management in small and medium enterprises using blockchain technology. *Cogent Economics and Finance, 7*(1), 1667184. Advance online publication. doi:10.1080/23322039.2019.1667184

Naylor, J. B., Naim, M. M., & Berry, D. (1999). Leagility: Integrating the lean and agile manufacturing paradigms in the total supply chain. *International Journal of Production Economics, 62*(1-2), 107–118. doi:10.1016/S0925-5273(98)00223-0

Naz, A., & Ali, F. (2018). Gwadar Port: As an Economic hub for Maritime Trade in the World Corridor (CPEC). *Journal Of Business And Social Review In Emerging Economies, 4*(1), 7–16. doi:10.26710/jbsee.v4i1.352

Negi, S. (2022). Humanitarian logistics challenges in disaster relief operations: A humanitarian organisations' perspective. *Journal of Transport and Supply Chain Management, 16*. Advance online publication. doi:10.4102/jtscm.v16i0.691

Negrão, L. L. L., Godinho Filho, M., & Marodin, G. (2017). Lean practices and their effect on performance: A literature review. *Production Planning and Control, 28*(1), 33–56.

Nelan, M., Wachtendorf, T., & Penta, S. (2018). Agility in Disaster Relief: A Social Construction Approach. *Risk, Hazards &Amp. Crisis In Public Policy, 9*(2), 132–150. doi:10.1002/rhc3.12135

News European Parliament. (2022). *Circular economy: the importance of reusingreusing products and materials | News | European Parliament*. Europa. EU.

Nikbakhsh, E., & Zanjirani Farahani, R. (2011). *Humanitarian Logistics Planning in Disaster Relief Operations*. Logistics Operations and Management. doi:10.1016/B978-0-12-385202-1.00015-3

Noruzi, A., Gholampour, B., Gholampour, S., Jafari, S., Farshid, R., Stanek, A., & Saboury, A. A. (2022). Current and Future Perspectives on the COVID-19 Vaccine: A Scientometric Review. *Journal of Clinical Medicine, 11*(3), 750.

Novitasari, M., Wijaya, A. L., Agustin, N. M., Gunardi, A., & Dana, L. P. (2022). Corporate social responsibility and firm performance: Green supply chain management as a mediating variable. *Corporate Social Responsibility and Environmental Management*, csr.2353. doi:10.1002/csr.2353

OEC. (2022). *Where does import from? (2016, 2017, 2018, 2019, 2020)*. OEC - The Observatory of Economic Complexity. Retrieved 25 August 2022, from https://oec.world/en/visualize/tree_map/hs92/import/chn/all/52709/2016.2017.2018.2019.2020/.

Ohno, T. (1988). *Toyota production system: beyond large-scale production* (Vol. 3). CRC Press.

Ohno, T., & Bodek, N. (2019). *Toyota production system: beyond large-scale production*. Productivity Press. doi:10.4324/9780429273018

Oke, A., & Gopalakrishnan, M. (2009). Managing disruptions in supply chains: A case study of a retail supply chain. *International Journal of Production Economics*, *118*(1), 168–174.

Okolie, C. C., & Ogundeji, A. A. (2022). Effect of COVID-19 on agricultural production and food security: A scientometric analysis. *Humanities and Social Sciences Communications*, *9*(1), 1–13.

Okorie, O., Salonitis, K., Charnley, F., Moreno, M., Turner, C., & Tiwari, A. (2018). Digitisation and the Circular Economy: A Review of Current Research and Future Trends. *Energies*, *11*(11), 3009.

Omar, I. A., Jayaraman, R., Debe, M. S., Salah, K., Yaqoob, I., & Omar, M. (2021). Automating Procurement Contracts in the Healthcare Supply Chain Using Blockchain Smart Contracts. *IEEE Access: Practical Innovations, Open Solutions*, *9*, 37397–37409. doi:10.1109/ACCESS.2021.3062471

Oswald Beiler, M. (2012). Measuring Sustainable Transportation: Incorporating Social Sustainability Indicators into Transportation Rating Systems. *The International Journal Of Environmental Sustainability*, *8*(1), 101–114. doi:10.18848/2325-1077/CGP/v08i01/55038

Ouhader, H., & El Kyal, M. (2017). The impact of horizontal collaboration on CO2 emissions due to road transportation. *Proceedings of the International Conference on Industrial Engineering and Operations Management*, 11-13.

Ozdemir, D., Sharma, M., Dhir, A., & Daim, T. (2022). Supply chain resilience during the COVID-19 pandemic. *Technology in Society*, *68*, 101847.

Pal, B., Sarkar, A., & Sarkar, B. (2023). Optimal decisions in a dual-channel competitive green supply chain management under promotional effort. *Expert Systems with Applications*, *211*, 118315.

Pangboonyanon, V., & Kalasin, K. (2018). The impact of within-industry diversification on firm performance: Empirical evidence from emerging ASEAN SMEs. *International Journal of Emerging Markets*.

Pang, X. (2022). *COVID-19 in Genomics: A Bibliometric Analysis*. Authorea Preprints.

Panizzolo, R., Garengo, P., Sharma, M. K., & Gore, A. (2012). Lean manufacturing in developing countries: Evidence from Indian SMEs. *Production Planning and Control*, *23*(10-11), 769–788. doi:10.1080/09537287.2011.642155

Pan, S., Ballot, E., & Fontane, F. (2013). The reduction of greenhouse gas emissions from freight transport by pooling supply chains. *International Journal of Production Economics*, *143*(1), 86–94. doi:10.1016/j.ijpe.2010.10.023

Pan, S., Ballot, E., Fontane, F., & Hakimi, D. (2014). Environmental and economic issues arising from the pooling of SMEs' supply chains: Case study of the food industry in western France. *Flexible Services and Manufacturing Journal*, *26*(1-2), 92–118. doi:10.100710696-012-9162-3

Parton, K. (2013). Economic, Social and Environmental Sustainability of the Murray-Darling Basin. *The International Journal of Environmental, Cultural, Economic, and Social Sustainability Annual Review*, *8*(1), 29–43. doi:10.18848/1832-2077/CGP/v08/55141

Parvez, M., Hazelton, J., & Guthrie, J. (2019). *Greenhouse gas emissions disclosure by cities: the expectation gap. Sustainability Accounting, Management and Policy Journal.*

Patil, S. (2020). *A scientometric analysis of global COVID-19 research based on dimensions database.* Available at SSRN 3631795.

Paton, E. (2020). Our situation is apocalyptic: Bangladesh garment workers face ruin. *New York Times.*

Pedraza Martinez, A., Stapleton, O., & Van Wassenhove, L. (2010). Field Vehicle Fleet Management in Humanitarian Operations: A Case-Based Approach. SSRN *Electronic Journal.* doi:10.2139/ssrn.1437544

Pendell, D. L., Leatherman, J. C., Schroeder, T. C., & Alward, G. S. (2007). The economic impacts of a foot-and-mouth disease outbreak: a regional analysis. *Journal of Agricultural and Applied Economics, 39*, 19-33.

Penthin, S., & Dillman, R. (2015). *Digital SCM.* Available at: www. BearingPoint. com

Peterman, R. (2017). *What Is Project Management?* https://project-management.com/what-is-project-management/

Pettit, T. J., Fiksel, J., & Croxton, K. L. (2010). Ensuring Supply Chain Resilience: Development of a Conceptual Framework. *Journal of Business Logistics*, *31*(1), 1–21. https://doi.org/10.1002/j.2158-1592.2010.tb00125.x

Pfefferbaum, B., & North, C. S. (2020). Mental health and the Covid-19 pandemic. *The New England Journal of Medicine*, *383*(6), 510–512.

Polvora, ´. A., Nascimento, S., Lourenço, J. S., & Scapolo, F. (2020). Blockchain for industrial transformations: A forward-looking approach with multi-stakeholder engagement for policy advice. *Technological Forecasting and Social Change, 157*, 120091.

Preindl, R., Nikolopoulos, K., & Litsiou, K. (2020). Transformation strategies for the supply chain: The impact of industry 4.0 and digital transformation. *Supply Chain Forum: An International Journal.*

Primo, M. A., DuBois, F. L., de Oliveira, M. L., Amaro, E. S. M., & Moser, D. D. (2021). Lean manufacturing implementation in time of crisis: The case of Estaleiro Atlântico Sul. *Production Planning and Control*, *32*(8), 623–640. doi:10.1080/09537287.2020.1747655

Pyun, J., & Rha, J. S. (2021). Review of research on digital supply chain management using network text analysis. In Sustainability (Switzerland) (Vol. 13, Issue 17). MDPI. doi:10.3390u13179929

Qarahasanlou, A. N., Barabadi, A., & Ayele, Y. Z. (2018). Production performance analysis during operation phase: A case study. *Proceedings of the Institution of Mechanical Engineers. Part O, Journal of Risk and Reliability*, *232*(6), 559–575. doi:10.1177/1748006X17744383

Queiroz, M. M., Ivanov, D., Dolgui, A., & Wamba, S. F. (2020). Impacts of epidemic outbreaks on supply chains: Mapping a research agenda amid the COVID-19 pandemic through a structured literature review. *Annals of Operations Research*, 1–38.

Rabta, B., Wankmüller, C., & Reiner, G. (2018). A drone fleet model for last-mile distribution in disaster relief operations. *International Journal of Disaster Risk Reduction*, *28*, 107–112. doi:10.1016/j.ijdrr.2018.02.020

Raj, S., & Sharma, A. (2014). Supply chain management in the cloud. *Accenture Global Management Consulting*, 1-12.

Raj, A., Mukherjee, A. A., de Sousa Jabbour, A. B. L., & Srivastava, S. K. (2022). Supply chain management during and post-COVID-19 pandemic: Mitigation strategies and practical lessons learned. *Journal of Business Research*, *142*, 1125–1139.

Ramayah, T., Mohamad, O., Omar, A., Marimuthu, M., & Leen, J. Y. A. (2013). Green manufacturing practices and performance among SMEs: evidence from a developing nation. In *Green Technologies and Business Practices: An IT Approach* (Vol. 2, pp. 208–225). IGI Global. doi:10.4018/978-1-4666-1972-2.ch013

Ramos-Rodríguez, A. R., & Ruíz-Navarro, J. (2004). Changes in the intellectual structure of strategic management research: A bibliometric study of the Strategic Management Journal, 1980–2000. *Strategic Management Journal*, *25*(10), 981–1004.

Rana, I., Asim, M., Aslam, A., & Jamshed, A. (2021). Disaster management cycle and its application for flood risk reduction in urban areas of Pakistan. *Urban Climate*, *38*, 100893. doi:10.1016/j.uclim.2021.100893

Ranganathan, C., & Balasubramani, R. (2014). Scientometric profile of research activities on green energy: An Indian perspective. *International Journal of Research in Applied Natural and Social Sciences*, *2*(1), 23–30.

Rashid, A., Asif, F., Krajnik, P., & Nicolescu, C. M. (2013). Resource Conservative Manufacturing: An essential change in business and technology paradigm for sustainable manufacturing. *Journal of Cleaner Production*, *57*, 166–177.

Ratten, V. (2015). Cloud computing technology innovation advances: A set of research propositions. *International Journal of Cloud Applications and Computing*, *5*(1), 69–76. doi:10.4018/ijcac.2015010106

ReliefWeb. (2005). *The Kashmir earthquake of October 8, 2005: Impacts in Pakistan - Pakistan*. Available at: https://reliefweb.int/report/pakistan/kashmir-earthquake-october-8-2005-impacts-pakistan

Reliefweb.int. (2018). *Natural catastrophes and man-made disasters in 2017: a year of record- breaking losses*. Available at: https://reliefweb.int/sites/reliefweb.int/files/resources/sigma1_2018_en.pdf

Reza, S., Mubarik, M., Naghavi, N., & Rub Nawaz, R. (2020). Relationship marketing and third-party logistics: Evidence from hotel industry. *Journal Of Hospitality And Tourism Insights*, *3*(3), 371–393. doi:10.1108/JHTI-07-2019-0095

Richard, P. J., Devinney, T. M., Yip, G. S., & Johnson, G. (2009). Measuring organizational performance: Towards methodological best practice. *Journal of Management*, *35*(3), 718–804. doi:10.1177/0149206308330560

Ritchie, H., & Roser, M. (2022). *Natural Disasters Empirical View*. Our World in Data. Available at: https://ourworldindata.org/natural-disasters

Rizvi, H. (2015). The China-Pakistan Economic Corridor: Regional Cooperation and Socio-Economic Development. *Strategic Studies*, 1-17.

Roscoe, S., Subramanian, N., Jabbour, C. J., & Chong, T. (2019). Green human resource management and the enablers of green organisational culture: Enhancing a firm's environmental performance for sustainable development. *Business Strategy and the Environment*, *28*(5), 737–749. doi:10.1002/bse.2277

Rouse, M. (2016). *Digital supply chain, Search manufacturing*. http://searchmanufacturingerp. TechTarget. com/definition n/ digital-supply-chain? vgnextfmt= print

Roy, P., Albores, P., & Brewster, C. (2014). *Logistical framework for last mile relief distribution in humanitarian supply chains: Considerations from the field*. Scholar Bank. Available at: http://dr.lib.sjp.ac.lk/bitstream/handle/123456789/1598/Applicability%20of%20Last%20Mile%20Humanitarian%20Logistics%20Optimization%20for%20Natural%20Flood%20Disasters%20A%20Systematic%20Review.pdf?sequence=1&isAllowed=y

Ruiz-Rosero, J., Ramirez-Gonzalez, G., Williams, J. M., Liu, H., Khanna, R., & Pisharody, G. (2017). Internet of things: A scientometric review. *Symmetry*, *9*(12), 301.

Saberi, S., Kouhizadeh, M., Sarkis, J., & Shen, L. (2018). Blockchain technology and its relationships to sustainable supply chain management. *International Journal of Production Research*, *57*, 2117–2135.

Sahoo, S., & Pandey, S. (2020). Evaluating research performance of Coronavirus and Covid-19 pandemic using scientometric indicators. *Online Information Review*.

Sangwan, K. S. (2011). Quantitative and qualitative benefits of green manufacturing: an empirical study of Indian small and medium enterprises. In *Glocalized Solutions for Sustainability in Manufacturing* (Vol. 2, pp. 371–376). Springer. doi:10.1007/978-3-642-19692-8_64

Sankaran, K. (2019). Carbon emission and plastic pollution: How circular economy, blockchain, and artificial intelligence support energy transition? *Journal of Innovation Management*, *7*(4), 7–13. doi:10.24840/2183-0606_007.004_0002

Santos, H., Lannelongue, G., & Gonzalez-Benito, J. (2019). Integrating green practices into operational performance: Evidence from Brazilian manufacturers. *Sustainability*, *11*(10), 2956. doi:10.3390u11102956

Sarjana, S., Khayati, N., Warini, L., & Wiyati, P. (2020). The Importance of Transportation Management in Optimizing Supply Chain Management at Industrial Estate. *Jurnal Transportasi Multimoda*, *18*(1). Advance online publication. doi:10.25104/mtm.v18i1.1643

Sarjito, A. (2020). PESTLE Analysis of Production Management Landing Platform Dock Warship PT PAL Indonesia (Persero) For National Defense. *Advances In Social Sciences Research Journal*, *7*(11), 368–386. doi:10.14738/assrj.711.9329

Sarkis, J. (2020). Supply chain sustainability: Learning from the COVID-19 pandemic. *International Journal of Operations & Production Management*.

Saryatmo, M. A., & Sukhotu, V. (2021). The influence of the digital supply chain on operational performance: A study of the food and beverage industry in Indonesia. *Sustainability (Switzerland)*, *13*(9), 5109. Advance online publication. doi:10.3390u13095109

Sawik, T. (2022). Stochastic optimization of supply chain resilience under ripple effect: A COVID-19 pandemic related study. *Omega*, *109*, 102596.

Scholten, K., Sharkey Scott, P., & Fynes, B. (2014). Mitigation processes – antecedents for building supply chain resilience. *Supply Chain Management*, *19*(2), 211–228. doi:10.1108/SCM-06-2013-0191

Schonberger, R. J. (2008). *World class manufacturing*. Simon and Schuster.

Schrauf, S., & Berttram, P. (2016). Industry 4.0: How digitization makes the supply chain more efficient, agile, and customer-focused. *Strateg. & Technology*, 1-32.

Scuotto, V., Caputo, F., Villasalero, M., & del Giudice, M. (2017). A multiple buyer–supplier relationship in the context of SMEs' digital supply chain management. *Production Planning and Control*, *28*(16), 1378–1388. doi:10.1080/09537287.2017.1375149

Seth, I. (2022). *An overview of Destruction in Pompeii*. RTF. Retrieved 9 August 2022, from https://www.re-thinkingthefuture.com/city-and-architecture/a4900-an-overview-of-destruction-in-pompeii/

Shah Afridi, H., Bibi, S., & Muhammad, B. (2016). The economic viability of gwadar port: An economic hub for maritime trade. *Global Political Review*, *1*(1), 19–31. doi:10.31703/gpr.2016(I-I).03

Shah, A. (2016). Building a Sustainable 'Belt and Road'. *Journal of International Relations and Sustainable Development, 7*.

Shah, Z. (2015) China-Pakistan economic corridor and its importance. Preston University.

Shahin, A., & Jaferi, F. (2015). The shortest route for transportation in supply chain by minimum spanning tree. *International Journal Of Logistics Systems And Management, 22*(1), 43. doi:10.1504/IJLSM.2015.070893

Shao, B. B. M., Shi, Z., Choi, T. Y., & Chae, S. (2018). A data-analytics approach to identifying hidden critical suppliers in supply networks: Development of nexus supplier index. *Decision Support Systems, 114*, 37–48. doi:10.1016/j.dss.2018.08.008

Sharma, V. (2018). Demand-Driven Forecasting in the Supply Chain. *The Cloud-Based Demand-Driven Supply Chain*, 1-41.

Sheffi, Y. (2016). The power of resilience: how the best companies manage the unexpected. *Choice Reviews Online, 53*(7). doi:10.5860/choice.195121

Sheng, M., Zhou, J., Song, B., & Wang, E. (2022). *Knowledge Domain and Emerging Trends in Internet-based diagnosis and treatment services: A Scientometric Review Based on CiteSpace V Analysis*. Academic Press.

Sheu, J., & Kundu, T. (2018). Forecasting time-varying logistics distribution flows in the One Belt-One Road strategic context. *Transportation Research Part E, Logistics and Transportation Review, 117*, 5–22. doi:10.1016/j.tre.2017.03.003

Shingala, M. C., & Rajyaguru, A. (2015). Comparison of post hoc tests for unequal variance. *International Journal of New Technologies in Science and Engineering, 2*, 22–33.

Shingo, S., & Dillon, A. P. (1989). *A study of the Toyota production system: From an Industrial Engineering Viewpoint*. CRC Press.

Shingo, S., & Dillon, A. P. (2019). *A revolution in manufacturing: the SMED system*. Routledge. doi:10.4324/9781315136479

Shukor, A. A. A., Newaz, M. S., Rahman, M. K., & Taha, A. Z. (2020). Supply chain integration and its impact on supply chain agility and organizational flexibility in manufacturing firms. *International Journal of Emerging Markets*.

Simchi-Levi, D., Schmidt, W., & Wei, Y. (2014). From superstorms to factory fires: Managing unpredictable supply chain disruptions. *Harvard Business Review*.

Singanayagam, A., Patel, M., Charlett, A., Bernal, J. L., Saliba, V., Ellis, J., ... Gopal, R. (2020). Duration of infectiousness and correlation with RT-PCR cycle threshold values in cases of COVID-19, England, January to May 2020. *Eurosurveillance, 25*(32), 2001483.

Singh, M. P., Chakraborty, A., & Roy, M. (2017). *Developing an Extended Theory of Planned Behavior Model to Explore Circular Economy Readiness in Manufacturing MSMEs, India. Resources, Conservation and Recycling*. Available at https://www.sciencedirect.com/science/article/pii/S0921344917301945

Singh, S. K., Chen, J., Del Giudice, M., & El-Kassar, A.-N. (2019). Environmental ethics, environmental performance, and competitive advantage: Role of environmental training. *Technological Forecasting and Social Change*, *146*, 203–211. doi:10.1016/j.techfore.2019.05.032

Sinha, A., Bernardes, E., Calderon, R., & Wuest, T. (2021). *Digital supply networks*. McGraw Hill-Ascent Audio.

Sinha, P., Kumar, S., & Chandra, C. (2023). Strategies for ensuring required service level for COVID-19 herd immunity in Indian vaccine supply chain. *European Journal of Operational Research*, *304*(1), 339–352.

SMEDA. (2018). Retrieved from https://smeda.org/

Sombultawee, K., Lenuwat, P., Aleenajitpong, N., & Boon-itt, S. (2022). COVID-19 and Supply Chain Management: A Review with Bibliometric. *Sustainability*, *14*(6), 3538.

Spieske, A., Gebhardt, M., Kopyto, M., & Birkel, H. (2022). Improving resilience of the healthcare supply chain in a pandemic: Evidence from Europe during the COVID-19 crisis. *Journal of Purchasing and Supply Management*, 100748.

Stabell, C.B., & Fjeldstad, Ø.D. (1998). Configuring value for competitive advantage: on chains, shops, and networks. *Strateg. Manage. J.*, 413-437.

Stock, J. R. (2013). Supply chain management: A look back, a look ahead. *Supply Chain Quarterly*, *2*, 22–26.

Subramanian, A., & Kessler, M. (2013). *The Hyperglobalization of Trade and Its Future*. Working Paper Series No. 13-6. Washington, DC: Peterson Institute for International Economics.

Sugandini, D., Susilowati, C., Siswanti, Y., & Syafri, W. (2020). Green supply management and green marketing strategy on green purchase intention: SMEs cases. *Journal of Industrial Engineering and Management*, *13*(1), 79–92. doi:10.3926/jiem.2795

Su, H.-N., & Lee, P.-C. (2010). Mapping knowledge structure by keyword co-occurrence: A first look at journal papers in Technology Foresight. *Scientometrics*, *85*(1), 65–79.

Sulaiman, C., & Abdul-Rahim, A. S. (2018). Population growth and CO2 emission in Nigeria: A recursive ARDL approach. *SAGE Open*, *8*(2). doi:10.1177/2158244018765916

Supriadi, B., Astuti, W., & Firdiansyah, A. (2017). Green product and its impact on customer satisfaction. *IOSR Journal of Business and Management*, *19*(8), 1.

Surahio, M., Gu, S., Mahesar, H., & Soomro, M. (2022). China–Pakistan Economic Corridor: Macro Environmental Factors and Security Challenges. *SAGE Open*, *12*(1), 215824402210798. doi:10.1177/21582440221079821

Suri, R., & Burke, J. (2020). *Quick response manufacturing: A companywide approach to reducing lead times*. Productivity Press.

Taieb, N. H., Mellouli, R., & Affes, H. (2014). Impact of means and resources pooling on supply-chain management: Case of large distribution. *2014 International Conference on Advanced Logistics and Transport (ICALT)*, 160-166. 10.1109/ICAdLT.2014.6864111

Tan, C. L., Zailani, S. H. M., Tan, S. C., & Shaharudin, M. R. (2016). The impact of green supply chain management practices on firm competitiveness. *International Journal of Business Innovation and Research*, *11*(4), 539–558. doi:10.1504/IJBIR.2016.079507

Tandon, A., Dhir, A., Islam, N., & Mantymaki, M. (2020). Blockchain in healthcare: A systematic literature review, synthesizing framework and future research agenda. *Computers in Industry*, 1–22.

Teuteberg, A. J. F. (2015). Integrating cloud computing in supply chain processes: A comprehensive literature review. *Journal of Enterprise Information Management*, *28*(6), 872–904. doi:10.1108/JEIM-08-2014-0085

The Economist Newspaper Limited. (2015). The trust machine. *The Economist*. https://www.economist.com/leaders/2015/10/31/the-trust-machi
ne

Thomas, A. (2004). *International Aid and Trade Review: Evaluating Humanitarian Logistics*. Available at: https://fritzinstitute.org/PDFs/InTheNews/2004/AidandTrade_0
104.pdf

Titievskaia, J., Kononenko, V., Navarra, C., Stamegna, C., & Zumer, K. (2020). *Slowing Down or Changing Track? Understanding the Dynamics of "Slowbalisation."* European Parliamentary Research Service.

Todo, Y., Nakajima, K., & Matous, P. (2015). How do supply chain networks affect the resilience of firms to natural disasters? Evidence from the Great East Japan Earthquake. *Journal of Regional Science*, *55*(2).

Tomasini, R., & Van Wassenhove, L. N. (2009). *Humanitarian Logistics*. Palgrave Macmillan. doi:10.1057/9780230233485

Tranfield, D., Denyer, D., & Smart, P. (2003). Towards a methodology for developing evidence-informed management knowledge by means of systematic review. *British Journal of Management*, *14*(3), 207–222.

Udara Willhelm Abeydeera, L. H., Wadu Mesthrige, J., & Samarasinghalage, T. I. (2019). Global research on carbon emissions: A scientometric review. *Sustainability*, *11*(14), 3972.

Ülkü, M. A. (2012). Dare to care: Shipment consolidation reduces not only costs, but also environmental damage. *International Journal of Production Economics*, *139*(2), 438–446. doi:10.1016/j.ijpe.2011.09.015

United Nations. (2021). Sustainable Transport. *Sustainable Development*.

Van Bavel, J. J., Baicker, K., Boggio, P. S., Capraro, V., Cichocka, A., Cikara, M., ... Druckman, J. N. (2020). Using social and behavioural science to support COVID-19 pandemic response. *Nature Human Behaviour*, *4*(5), 460–471.

van Hoek, R., Gibson, B., & Johnson, M. (2020). Talent Management For a Post-COVID-19 Supply Chain—The Critical Role for Managers. *Journal of Business Logistics*.

Van Wassenhove, L. (2006). Humanitarian aid logistics: Supply chain management in high gear. *The Journal of the Operational Research Society*, *57*(5), 475–489. doi:10.1057/palgrave.jors.2602125

Van Wassenhove, L., & Pedraza Martinez, A. (2010). Using OR to adapt supply chain management best practices to humanitarian logistics. *International Transactions in Operational Research*, *19*(1-2), 307–322. doi:10.1111/j.1475-3995.2010.00792.x

Verrier, B., Rose, B., Caillaud, E., & Remita, H. (2014). Combining organizational performance with sustainable development issues: The Lean and Green project benchmarking repository. *Journal of Cleaner Production*, *85*, 83–93. doi:10.1016/j.jclepro.2013.12.023

Vuong, Q. H., La, V. P., Nguyen, H. K. T., Ho, M. T., Vuong, T. T., & Ho, M. T. (2021). Identifying the moral–practical gaps in corporate social responsibility missions of Vietnamese firms: An event-based analysis of sustainability feasibility. *Corporate Social Responsibility and Environmental Management*, *28*(1), 30–41. doi:10.1002/csr.2029

Walker, C. R., & Guest, R. H. (1952). *The man on the assembly line*. Academic Press.

Wang, F., Lai, X., & Shi, N. (2011). A multi-objective optimization for green supply chain network design. *Decision Support Systems*, *51*(2), 262–269. doi:10.1016/j.dss.2010.11.020

Wang, M., Liu, P., Gu, Z., Cheng, H., & Li, X. (2019). A scientometric review of resource recycling industry. *International Journal of Environmental Research and Public Health*, *16*(23), 4654.

Wang, Y. (2016). What are the biggest obstacles to growth of SMEs in developing countries?– An empirical evidence from an enterprise survey. *Borsa Istanbul Review*, *16*(3), 167–176. doi:10.1016/j.bir.2016.06.001

Who.int. (2011). *Pakistan floods 2010 Early recovery plan for the health sector*. Available at: https://www.who.int/hac/crises/pak/pakistan_early_recovery_plan_12february2011.pdf

Wickramasinghe, G., & Wickramasinghe, V. (2017). Implementation of lean production practices and manufacturing performance. *Journal of Manufacturing Technology Management*, *28*(4), 531–550. doi:10.1108/JMTM-08-2016-0112

Womack, J. P., Jones, D. T., & Roos, D. (1990). *The machine that changed the world*. Rawson Associates.

Womack, J. P., Jones, D. T., & Roos, D. (2007). *The machine that changed the world: The story of lean production—Toyota's secret weapon in the global car wars that is now revolutionizing world industry*. Simon and Schuster.

World Bank. (2005). *Pakistan 2005 Earthquake Preliminary Damage and Needs Assessment.* Available at: http://siteresources.worldbank.org/PAKISTANEXTN/Resources/Publications-and-Reports/Damage-Assessment-Main.pdf

World Trade Organization. (2020). *Trade shows signs of rebound from COVID- 19, recovery still uncertain.* https://www.wto.org/engli sh/news_e/pres20_e/pr862_e.htm

Wu, Y., Cegielski, C. G., Hazen, B. T., & Hall, D. J. (2013). Cloud computing in support of supply chain information system infrastructure: Understanding when to go to the cloud. *The Journal of Supply Chain Management*, *49*(3), 25–41. doi:10.1111/j.1745-493x.2012.03287.x

Xu, J. (2014). *Managing digital enterprise: ten essential topics*. Springer. doi:10.2991/978-94-6239-094-2

Xu, M., David, J. M., & Kim, S. H. (2018). The fourth industrial revolution: Opportunities and challenges. *International Journal of Financial Research*, *9*(2), 90–95. doi:10.5430/ijfr.v9n2p90

Yadav, G., Luthra, S., Huisingh, D., Mangla, S. K., Narkhede, B. E., & Liu, Y. (2020). Development of a lean manufacturing framework to enhance its adoption within manufacturing companies in developing economies. *Journal of Cleaner Production*, *245*, 118726. doi:10.1016/j.jclepro.2019.118726

Yalcin, H., Shi, W., & Rahman, Z. (2020). A review and scientometric analysis of supply chain management (SCM). *Operations and Supply Chain Management: An International Journal*, *13*(2), 123–133.

Yang, M. G. M., Hong, P., & Modi, S. B. (2011). Impact of lean manufacturing and environmental management on business performance: An empirical study of manufacturing firms. *International Journal of Production Economics*, *129*(2), 251–261. doi:10.1016/j.ijpe.2010.10.017

Yan, M. R., Chien, K. M., & Yang, T. N. (2016). Green component procurement collaboration for improving supply chain management in the high technology industries: A case study from the systems perspective. *Sustainability (Switzerland)*, *8*(2), 105. Advance online publication. doi:10.3390u8020105

Yong, J. Y., Yusliza, M.-Y., Jabbour, C. J. C., & Ahmad, N. H. (2019). Exploratory cases on the interplay between green human resource management and advanced green manufacturing in light of the Ability-Motivation-Opportunity theory. *Journal of Management Development*, *39*(1), 31–49. doi:10.1108/JMD-12-2018-0355

Yudi, F., & Wei Lin, H. (2017). Impacts of energy management practices on energy efficiency and carbon emissions reduction: A survey of malaysian manufacturing firms. *Resources, Conservation and Recycling*, *126*, 62–73. doi:10.1016/j.resconrec.2017.07.023

Yue, X., Wang, H., Jin, D., Li, M., & Jiang, W. (2016). Healthcare data gateways: Found healthcare intelligence on blockchain with novel privacy risk control. *Journal of Medical Systems*, *40*(10), 1–8.

Yu, K. D. S., & Aviso, K. B. (2020). Modelling the economic impact and ripple effects of disease outbreaks. *Process Integration and Optimization for Sustainability*, *4*(2), 183–186.

Yusuf, Y. Y., Gunasekaran, A., Adeleye, E. O., & Sivayoganathan, K. (2004). Agile supply chain capabilities: Determinants of competitive objectives. *European Journal of Operational Research*, *159*(2), 379–392. doi:10.1016/j.ejor.2003.08.022

Zalengera, C., Blanchard, R., Eames, P., Juma, A., Chitawo, M., & Gondwe, K. (2014). Overview of the Malawi energy situation and A PESTLE analysis for sustainable development of renewable energy. *Renewable & Sustainable Energy Reviews*, *38*, 335–347. doi:10.1016/j.rser.2014.05.050

Zhai, Z., Shan, M., Darko, A., & Le, Y. (2020). Visualizing the Knowledge Domain of Project Governance: A Scientometric Review. *Advances in Civil Engineering*, 2020.

Zhang, Y., & Zhang, H. (2016). "One Belt One Road" Strategy and the Sustainable Development of Asia: The Case of Afghanistan and DPRK. *Destech Transactions on Economics and Management*. doi:10.12783/dtem/icem2016/4051

Zhang, S., Wang, Z., Chang, R., Wang, H., Xu, C., Yu, X., ... Cai, Y. (2020). COVID-19 containment: China provides important lessons for global response. *Frontiers of Medicine*, 1–5.

Zhang, X., & Yousaf, H. A. U. (2020). Green supply chain coordination considering government intervention, green investment, and customer green preferences in the petroleum industry. *Journal of Cleaner Production*, *246*, 118984. doi:10.1016/j.jclepro.2019.118984

Zhang, Z. (2011). China's energy security, the Malacca dilemma and responses. *Energy Policy*, *39*(12), 7612–7615. doi:10.1016/j.enpol.2011.09.033

Zhao, L., Tang, Z.-y., & Zou, X. (2019). Mapping the knowledge domain of smart-city research: A bibliometric and scientometric analysis. *Sustainability*, *11*(23), 6648.

Zhao, X. (2017). A scientometric review of global BIM research: Analysis and visualization. *Automation in Construction*, *80*, 37–47.

Zheng, J., Garrick, N., Atkinson-Palombo, C., McCahill, C., & Marshall, W. (2013). Guidelines on developing performance metrics for evaluating transportation sustainability. *Research In Transportation Business &Amp. Management*, *7*, 4–13. doi:10.1016/j.rtbm.2013.02.001

About the Contributors

Muhammad Waqas is an Assistant professor of Logistics and supply chain management at Ghazi University, Dera Ghazi Khan, Pakistan. Dr Waqas received his PhD in Logistics and Supply Chain Management from Chang'an University, Shaanxi, China, in 2019. After completing my PhD. Dr Waqas worked as a postdoctoral fellow at the Xi'an Jiatong University, Shaanxi, China, from December 2019 to December 2021, and as an Assistant Professor at School Economic and Finance, X'ian Jiaotong University, Shaanxi, China 2021. Dr Waqas has over three years of industry and academic experience in supply chain and logistics. He has attended several international conferences. Dr Waqas has published more than 17 research articles in a well-known journal indexed in SSCI, SCI, ESCI, ABS & ABDC. His current research includes sustainable development, green innovation, green brand image and brownfield redevelopment.

Syed Abdul Rehman Khan is a professor of Supply Chain and Logistics Management. Dr. Khan achieved his CSCP—Certified Supply Chain Professional certificate from the U.S.A. and completed his postdoctoral fellowship from Tsinghua University. Prof. Khan has attended several international conferences and has been invited as a keynote speaker in different countries. He has published 100+ scientific research papers in different well-renowned international journals and conferences. Also, Dr. Khan has achieved several research projects and scientific innovation awards.

* * *

Muhammad Junaid Ahsan is doing a Ph.D. in Business and Management studies from the Department of Economics and Management at the University of Pisa, Italy. His research interests are sustainability, leadership, CSR, and organization management.

Abdessalem Jerbi was born in Sfax, Tunisia in 1975. He graduated from the National School of Engineering of Sfax, Tunisia, in 1999. In 2004, he received his

Master's degree in Mechanical Engineering from the National School of Engineering of Sfax, Tunisia. In 2010, he got his Ph.D. in Mechanical Engineering from the National School of Engineering of Sfax, Tunisia. He is an assistant professor in the Department of quality management at the Higher Institute of Industrial Management at the University of Sfax, Tunisia. Dr. Abdessalem Jerbi developed his research in the design and management of flexible manufacturing systems. His research areas include flexible manufacturing systems, supply chain management, optimization methodologies, discrete event simulation, scheduling rules, and experimental design.

Haifa Jribi was born in Sfax, Tunisia in 1996. She graduated from The Faculty of Economic Sciences and Management of Sfax, Tunisia, in 2018. In 2021, she received his Master's degree in modeling, optimization, and decision from the Faculty of Economic Sciences and Management of Sfax, Tunisia. Actually, she is preparing for a Ph.D. in Management Informatics at the Higher Institute of Management of Tunis, Tunisia. Her research area includes the management of pooled supply chain: the key role of the logistics service provider (LSP).

Muzammil Khurshid is serving as Assistant Professor in Department of Banking and Finance at University of the Punjab, Gujranwala Campus. He has received Ph.D degree in Business Administration from Dokuz Eylul University, Izmir, Turkey.

Sajid Nazir, CSCA, MCIPS, DGLP, Sr. Lecturer, Logistics and Supply Chain Management, has completed his Master's in Supply Chain Management from Coventry University Main Campus; United Kingdom in 2018. Moreover, along with his MSc. SCM Sajid Nazir has joined the Coventry University Global Leadership Program and hold a Diploma in Global Leadership from UK as well. As a part of global leader program, he has been to different countries for presentations and leadership trainings. He has completed his Bachelors' in Business Administration from Iqra University. Before Joining IoBM, Sajid has worked in corporate sector on national as well as on international level such as Banking, Aviation, Pharmaceutical and other service industries as a supply chain professional. He also has done the research analysis on the impact of China Pakistan Economic Corridor (CPEC) on transit routes from China to overseas markets.

Wasim ul Rehman is an Assistant Professor of Business Administration. He holds a Ph.D. degree in Business Administration from The Superior University Lahore, Pakistan. His areas of research are intellectual capital initiative in knowledge economies, strategic management, strategic human resource and marketing, corporate and behavioural finance.

Ayesha Saeed is a Research Scholar and PhD student of Logistics Engineering at Southwest Jiaotong University, Chengdu, China. He received his Master in Project Management from Bahria University, Islamabad, Pakistan, in 2017. Cost reductions, green logistics, deep learning, and intermodal and multimodal freight transportation are among his primary research interests. He has several years of experience in several industrial sectors in Pakistan, including research and development, quality assurance, supply chain, and project management.

Rizwan Shoukat is a Research Scholar and PhD student of Logistics Engineering at Southwest Jiaotong University, Chengdu, China. He received his MS in Total Quality Management from the University of the Punjab, Pakistan, in 2017 and Mechanical Engineering in 2007. Cost reductions, green logistics, deep learning, and intermodal and multimodal freight transportation are among his primary research interests. He has 12 years of experience in several industrial sectors in Pakistan, including production and operations, research and development, quality assurance, supply chain, and total productive maintenance. He has published 7 academic papers, six of which were retrieved by SCI.

Cui Ying, tutor of master's degree, is an expert of the master's degree evaluation committee of the Ministry of education and the academic dean of the Accounting School of Yunnan Business University. Presided over and completed the western project of the National Social Science Fund, the Provincial Academy and school cooperation project, and the key projects of Yunnan Academy of Educational Sciences. As a senior visiting scholar, he went to Kyoto University in Japan, the University of Western Australia in Australia, Lingnan University in South Korea, and Gripp University in India to study; Published 11 books such as advanced financial accounting; Published more than 40 academic papers.

Zhang Yu is affiliated with Chang'an University, China. Her research interest is reverse logistics, end-of-life vehicles, recycling techniques, and green practices in the corporate sector. She has published 25 research papers in different international journals and conferences. Also, she is an author of three books related to supply chain and business management.

R.M. Ammar Zahud is currently affiliated with Yunnan Technology and Business University, China. He has 15 years of academic and industry experience including 4 years post Ph.D. He earned his post doctorate from Xi'an Jiaotong University, China, and a doctoral degree from the Izmir University of Economics, Turkey. He is also an Associate member of the Pakistan Institute of Public Finance Accountants (PIPFA). His current research focused on International Accounting and Finance, International Financial Reporting Standards (IFRS) adoption issues, Capital markets, ESG (Environment, Social, Governance), Regional Trade Agreements, and Corporate Governances issues in emerging markets. His research work has appeared in many internationally recognized journals, and he also participated in a number of national & international conferences and workshops across the world.

Index

www.ingramcontent.com/pod-product-compliance
Lightning Source LLC
LaVergne TN
LVHW081335300926
849161LV00008B/1978